Youth Crime in America

 A Modern Synthesis

ROY LOTZ

John Jay College of Criminal Justice

PEARSON

Prentice
Hall

Upper Saddle River, New Jersey 07458

Library of Congress Cataloging-in-Publication Data

Lotz, Roy
 Youth crime in America : a modern synthesis / by Roy Lotz.
   p. cm.
Includes bibliographical references and index.
 ISBN 0-13-026184-X
 1. Juvenile delinquency--United States. I. Title.
 HV9104.L675 2005
 364.36'0973--dc22

 2004005035

Executive Editor: Frank Mortimer, Jr.
Associate Editor: Sarah Holle
Production Editor: Linda Duarte, Pine Tree Composition, Inc.
Production Liaison: Barbara Marttine Cappuccio
Director of Manufacturing and Production: Bruce Johnson
Managing Editor: Mary Carnis
Manufacturing Buyer: Cathleen Petersen
Creative Director: Cheryl Asherman
Cover Design Coordinator: Miguel Ortiz
Cover Designer: Carey Davies
Cover Image: Michael Wong, Getty Images Inc.—Stone/Allstock
Editorial Assistant: Barbara Rosenburg
Marketing Manager: Tim Peyton
Formatting and Interior Design: Pine Tree Composition, Inc.
Printing/Binding: Phoenix Book Tech Park

Pearson Education LTD.
Pearson Education Singapore, Pte. Ltd
Pearson Education, Canada, Ltd
Pearson Education–Japan
Pearson Education Australia PTY, Limited
Pearson Education North Asia Ltd
Pearson Educaçion de Mexico, S.A. de C.V.
Pearson Education Malaysia, Pte. Ltd

10 9 8 7 6 5 4 3 2 1
ISBN 0-13-026184-X

Contents

Preface

Thomas Carlyle long ago described economics as the dismal science. There is some question about what he had in mind when he used this unflattering term. One line of argument is that the dour Scot was accusing the field of being boring, confusing, and contradictory, its paragraphs bogged down in "on the one hand, on the other hand" kinds of statements. Economics does not stand alone in this respect. For instance, there have been times when crime and delinquency texts, too, relied on these techniques, which students find puzzling and off-putting.

Here I try to (1) avoid opaque writing and (2) engage students in a lively conversation about youth crime, its nature, causes, and attempts at control. The focus is on newer theories and prevention methods, not the dated ones that would be rejected by most sociologists and psychologists. Some of the newer approaches may be controversial, but academics who are worth their salt do not shy away from controversy. New ideas, be they absorbing or disturbing, fascinate readers—they help to keep the mind alive.

How do Americans typically acquire their views about crime and delinquency? In most cases, it's not from textbooks, because that would mean they had to make the trek to some perhaps far-off university's bookstore. Instead, as a rule, they rely on sources closer to home and easier to access: the many crime stories appearing in the newspaper or on television news programs. Unfortunately, these reports are usually lean on information and barren of analysis. Rules of objectivity force reporters to isolate crimes and treat each as a sample of one; the rules virtually forbid generalizing to the wider picture. Reading about someone being mugged in a subway, we don't know whether this means that subways are becoming more dangerous or less. News reporters hug the shoreline; that is, they take great pains to present small details and rudimentary facts while paying scant attention to the larger picture.

On the other hand, weekly magazines go far beyond these narrow particulars, far beyond perfunctory findings by the police. They delve into wider issues, look at the crime picture in general, and do not hesitate to make sweeping conclusions. In the mid-1990s, they focused on crimes committed by young people, arguing that their rates of violence were rapidly rising at that time and promised to get far worse in the next few years.

The views developed by writers in these mass market magazines were more than mere exercises; they influenced America's thinking and policy regarding youth crime. They reinforced public attitudes and opinion about the danger posed by out-of-control youth. They also pushed political officeholders and office seekers into drumming up support for harsher treatment of underage offenders. Soon, political rhetoric poured forth about the need for more punishment, longer sentences, tougher courts, less lenience, and less talk of rehabilitation.

If Americans derive much of their information about crime and delinquency from the media (such as the newsmagazines), how valid are the claims these media make—should they be taken as gospel or with a grain of salt? Criminologists have developed several ways of producing data bearing on the basic questions: official data, self-report data, and victimization surveys. These data tell us, for instance, how old most offenders are, whether they are male or female, what their race or ethnicity is, where the offenses are most likely to occur, and (in some research) why the offenders committed the offenses. These findings can then be used to test the many claims made by the news media or politicians or criminological theories. Eventually, if the claims are overstated or the theories are misguided, this will be revealed.

Because our interest lies in the crimes committed by adolescents, a specific domain, we need to spend some time investigating the larger terrain of adolescence to determine what is known about that particular stage of growth. Most of this territory has been staked out by psychologists, but a few biological and sociological factors have also been studied. Biological factors have been thought important because adolescence begins with a series of sometimes dramatic biological changes in height, weight, musculature, and secondary sexual characteristics. Early theorists said this period was inevitably a time of storm and stress, even of temporary psychosis. More recent work has focused on the impact of pubertal timing to find out if early maturation leads to psychological problems and deviant behavior. Sociologists began to examine the adolescent subculture to determine if the rise of peer influence and the declining impact of parents created problems of a different sort for teens.

Criminologists take great delight in devising answers to the question: Why do they do it (why do people commit crime)? At first, centuries ago, religious people explained criminal behavior by referring to the supernatural; later, philosophers created the classical school, which focused on free will and the rational pursuit of pleasure and avoidance of pain. After that, the early positivists (especially Lombroso) introduced the notion of biological forces acting on people to push or pull them toward criminal activity. Much of that literature is now of only antiquarian interest.

More important in the modern world is the work of evolutionary psychologists, who have pointed out how Darwin's theory of evolution applies to the everyday behavior of men and women in the present day. To be sure, most of this work does not focus on crime, but a small subsection does, including the contributions of Daly and Wilson on homicide and Thornhill and Palmer on rape. This provocative work may never become part of mainstream criminology, but a student of human behavior needs, at the very least, to be familiar with it.

Like evolutionary psychology, behavioral genetics offers another challenge to the view that human beings are a blank slate that society writes its cultural instructions on. But in this case, the challenge comes in the form of quantitative findings, not some new theory. Behavioral geneticists study personality, IQ, and sometimes even criminality, always with the same purpose in mind: to divide the influences on these into environmental and genetic. In recent years, they have devised a new method for doing so: They study twins (identical and fraternal) who were separated at birth and raised apart.

The sociological theories of crime and delinquency burst into prominence with the rise of the University of Chicago and its department of sociology. Shaw and McKay were more empiricists than theorists, but they emphasized the group nature of delinquency, the importance of neighborhood conditions, and crime as a tradition one generation passed to the next. Next, Edwin Sutherland theorized that crime was learned in interaction within intimate groups, as people taught each other attitudes toward crime and techniques of offending. The attitudes that were learned by the pupils were then taken to heart and acted out.

At the same time that Sutherland was polishing his differential association theory, Robert Merton was creating his strain/anomie approach, which stressed American culture's worship of wealth and the social structure's obstacles to achieving it through legitimate channels such as education, a steady job, and saving money. For some people, this contradiction led to innovation, that is, pursuing wealth through moneymaking crimes. Like Sutherland's theory, Merton's became immensely popular with students, who embraced it despite the fact that the most pertinent evidence cast grave doubts over it.

Albert Cohen drew from both Sutherland and Merton in his theory of status frustration. He argued that many lower-class parents failed to prepare their sons to live up to middle-class norms and values such as achievement, individual responsibility, good manners, and respect for property. Once these boys entered school, they were evaluated by the teachers and other students. Boys who failed to live up to the middle-class norms were looked down upon. These boys then got together and formed an adolescent subculture, which featured exactly the opposite of the culture's rules. That is, lack of achievement, bad manners, contempt for others' property, and so on.

Cloward and Ohlin also tried to combine some elements of both strain and Chicago School theories. They carried on the notion of adolescent subculture introduced by Cohen but said there were three, not one. The criminal subculture emerged in communities that were organized; that is, there were successful adult criminals who passed on their know-how to the younger generation. In disorganized slums, there were no successful criminals or opportunities to make much money (legally or illegally), so boys were frustrated and turned to violence to vent their feelings and gain a measure of respect.

Travis Hirschi in 1969 wrote *Causes of Delinquency,* which challenged both differential association and strain theories. This was the beginning of strain theory's fall from grace, although later theorists would try to revive it. Hirschi also introduced his version of social control theory, a viewpoint that said people would naturally gravitate toward crime and delinquency if it weren't for obstacles such as attachment (to family, school, and peers), commitment to conventional lines of action, involvement in conventional activities, and belief in the moral validity of conventional norms. This kind of thinking went against the grain in the late 1960s, for labeling and radical theories were riding high at the time. But eventually it caught on, because the data seemed to support it.

Aside from social control theory, sociological theories have given more attention to peers than to family members (this is especially true of differential association). On the other hand, psychologists have sometimes made the family their focus. Diana Baumrind identified three parenting styles that she said had different impacts on children. The authoritative style led to mature, well-behaved youngsters. The authoritarian style cowed them into obedience for the most part but stunted their imagination, learning, and social development. Permissive parenting led to all kinds of deviance, because parents failed to exert the necessary controls over their offspring.

Judith Rich Harris originally accepted this orthodox view but later came to question it. She argued that correlations from developmental psychology are ambiguous; they could be due to parent effects, genetic effects, or children effects on parents. She says doubts about parent effects are raised by several findings:

1. Children without siblings bear the full brunt of parental influence, yet they seem no different than children with siblings.
2. Children who start day care almost immediately seem no different than children who spent their first three years at home with parents.
3. Children of immigrants end up speaking English without a foreign accent, even if they continue to speak their parents' language at home.

In the school arena, many reports and parents have expressed dismay with our current educational system; they suspect that teachers are making only feeble efforts to teach, and students are committed to avoiding learning if at all possible. There are some indications that disorder prevails in urban public schools, and that students are disengaged. Many theories have been proposed to account for students' failure to thrive academically and to behave appropriately in school. Copperman attributes this to the loss of teacher authority, Greenberg blames it on teachers' being too authoritarian, labeling theorists lay the responsibility on tracking, Hirschi says it starts with low IQ and disliking school, whereas a more recent view says some students are naturally sensation seekers.

The contribution of peers to youth crime has long been a staple of sociological criminology. Shaw and McKay contributed to this line of thought by emphasizing that children early on began by playing together; eventually, their innocent pastime grew into something more risky and serious. Males in particular were drawn to these kinds of collective activities. Girls were less apt to join delinquent gangs and more likely to drop out of such groups once they grew older, got married, or had children.

In many cases, children in their early years at school are rejected by their peers if they act in a particularly aggressive manner. This kind of behavior does not simply appear out of the blue, but constitutes a continuing pattern learned or at least reinforced by family life in the years before the child attends school. Once the child has been rejected at school by most of his prosocial fellow students, he turns to other aggressive/rejected mates for companionship. They then become more aggressive than they were, as each boy encourages the others to engage in increasingly outrageous feats of deviance and rebellion (according to Thomas Dishion).

In the juvenile justice system, the three main elements are the police, courts, and corrections. The police were never designed to deal with problems of youth, which were traditionally viewed as relatively minor if not insignificant. The macho image of the police encouraged them to focus on more serious, more dangerous, older offenders, whose capture and arrest brought the officer praise and respect from his fellow officers for a difficult job well done. Arresting a youngster might bring instead a few snickers or derisive laughter.

The police are generally looked on favorably by the public as a whole. Despite this, they are often regarded with disdain by younger people and by African Americans. The negative attitudes are more evident among individuals who are delinquent and have frequent police encounters. Sociologists have shown special interest in juvenile demeanor and the police response during their encounters. Black and Reiss found that complainants play an important role; what they want done with the suspect, police usually do.

There has been a punitive trend in recent decades in America, as more and more people call for a crackdown on serious violent juvenile offenders. Where this pressure has been felt the most is in the courts. Increasingly, legislatures have been insisting that serious offenses be tried in the criminal courts, which are widely assumed to be more retributive than the juvenile courts, which are regarded as excessively lenient and devoted to rehabilitation.

The punitive trend has spread to the next phase of the juvenile justice system: corrections. Lawmakers have expressed enthusiasm for panaceas, such as scared straight and boot camps, and more and longer sentences to more secure institutions. Legislatures have not shown nearly as much interest in programs of prevention, perhaps because so little is known about them. Nevertheless, among the hundreds of prevention programs mounted in recent years, some have proven to be quite successful. Chapter 12 covers these in detail.

Acknowledgments

We'd like to thank the reviewers: Steven Burkett, Washington State University; Brenda Foster, Elmhurst College; Norman White, University of Missouri; Derek Mason, Utah State University; L. Edward Day, The Pennsylvania State University, Altoona College; and Craig Hemmens, Boise State University.

CHAPTER 1

Making Youth Crime into a Social Issue

Moral Panic

Like a long-dormant volcano that explodes without warning, the issue of youth crime erupted suddenly following years of quietude. What caused such an outburst—what forces were strong enough to thrust youth crime onto the national agenda? Perhaps, if you had to guess, you might say that criminologists were the main power source (and, in fact, a couple of them did apply some of the pressure). But most of the impetus came from elsewhere, namely, *the press, the public, and politicians.*

First, newspapers and television in the 1990s gave lavish time and space to a rash of violent and sensational crimes. Magazines then exaggerated their significance, citing them as evidence of a **plague** or **epidemic.** Readers swayed by the coverage feared they were witnessing the rise of a generation bent on belligerence. Politicians, given a window of opportunity, exploited the public's anxiety: Thundering from their bully pulpits, they declared America should (1) stop **coddling** juvenile offenders, (2) send the culprits to adult courts, and (3) throw the book at them.

The media, public, and politicians, convinced that legions of dangerous youths posed a serious threat, decided to do something about it: Flexing their collective biceps, they created a *moral panic.* Like other panics, it followed the classic pattern.

1. People become worried about a category or group and its behavior. Evidence of such concern appears in public opinion polls, media commentary, and legislation.

1

2. Members of the group or category get portrayed as an enemy, their behavior is described as menacing, and hostility is directed at them; the popular press paints them as deviant and disreputable.

3. A feeling develops, then spreads throughout society, that the threat is serious and the group responsible for it is dangerous.

4. In the fervor of the moment, experts exaggerate the threat, cite disturbing statistics, and overstate the harm caused.

5. Moral panics are volatile, short lived, erupt suddenly, and then recede. Because the fever pitch cannot be sustained, concern then shifts to other issues.[1]

The 1990s uproar over defiant youngsters represented a reversal of the way Americans traditionally regarded teens. Adults in earlier decades, seemingly more tenderhearted and restrained, usually regarded the young as innocent, vulnerable, and frivolous. In the placid 1950s, for example, they thought boys spent their free time on baseball or souped-up cars, and they assumed girls were wrapped up in Elvis Presley, circle pins, or cashmere sweaters. Adults in those days generally maintained a compassionate view; they did not accuse adolescents of posing a threat to society. That kind of notion was too far-fetched for anyone to entertain.

This Norman Rockwell portrait of youth—as naïve, freckle-faced innocents living in sleepy little cornbelt towns—hung on awhile but eventually vanished, replaced by the stereotype of apathetic Generation-X slackers. Later on, in the 1990s, youths were portrayed as sullen, smoldering with resentment, and **predatory.** Television news, movies, and reality programming helped spread these ideas. But they weren't alone: Other media also did their part to discredit teens, by deploring their grisly crimes against vulnerable members of the community. This chapter will first

In the 1950s, kids were widely regarded as innocent and immature, and the TV show "Leave it to Beaver" reinforced such a view. (*AP/Wide World Photos*)

detail the way one of those "other media," the mass-market magazines, depicted youth in the mid-1990s. Afterwards, it will show how political candidates and ordinary citizens reacted to these issues.

Images of Youth and Crime in Magazines

Unlike the more popular media (newspapers and TV news), magazines appear only weekly or monthly and assume that readers already know a story's basic facts: the who, what, when, and where. This gives them the luxury of concentrating on the *why*. With increased depth and analysis, plus a distinct point of view, magazine articles offer readers a broader and more entertaining picture of events, not some dry, abbreviated summary dwelling on the most mundane facts of a single incident.

Crime discussions in the magazines have an array of possibilities to choose from. They could target the political side of the story, the economic factors, moral questions, psychological elements, criminal peers' and associates' influence, the availability of guns, the extent of drug markets, the rise of street gangs, overly lenient courts, prison conditions and policies, and so on. But between 1993 and 1997, they tended to concentrate on one element above all others: offenses by a particular *age category*—the young. During the mid-1990s, articles beamed their spotlight on adolescents.

The eleven claims that follow are not mine. Instead, they are statements frequently expressed by mass-market magazines between 1993 and 1997. Although they are plausible, you should regard them with a skeptical eye instead of assuming they're true. After all eleven have been presented, a few will be chosen for testing. (There is not room in one-third of a chapter to evaluate all of them.) Then we will see if the pertinent data tend to support them or to cast doubt on them.

Claim 1. *From the mid-1980s to the mid-1990s, while the crime rate was falling among adults, it soared out of control among 14- to 17-year-olds.*

Magazine writers said that although the number of teenagers shrank during this ten-year period, they compensated for this population decline with a burst of violence. According to the press, young males, not content with their fair share of violent crime, committed a staggering amount: adolescents between 14 and 17 replaced 18- to 24-year-olds as the most crime-prone, most violent group; and between 1985 and 1994, their murder rate practically tripled. Reporters described America as caught in the grip of an ***epidemic*** *of youth crime.* They claimed that crime rates were skyrocketing and identified youth violence as "society's most urgent problem."[2]

Claim 2. *Juveniles committed more violent crimes during the late 1980s and early 1990s than at any other time in recorded history.*

Commentators branded this generation "Public Enemy #1" and claimed that no previous generation could match it for the sheer boldness, nastiness, and prevalence of crime. Articles recited tales of youths' gunning people down, either intentionally or accidentally, at new and grotesque rates. According to media pundits, each generation of young criminals exceeded its predecessor in the extent of violence and ruthlessness. Every twenty years, they proclaimed, the incidence of violent crime committed by persons under 18 rises steeply, indeed threefold.[3] This specter of menacing youth was presented as though it were a brute fact. If there were any contrary findings or alternative interpretations to be found, these authors gave readers no hint of them.

> Claim 3. *Writers said that (a) young black males are grossly overrepresented in crime and violence, and (b) this would increase in the years to come.*

On this issue, magazine essayists did not mince words. More than a few of their comments seemed to carry **racist** overtones. Ruffling feathers and wounding sensitivities did not deter them, as the following quotations reveal. According to veteran political scientist James Q. Wilson: "The rate at which young males, ages fourteen to seventeen, kill people has gone up significantly for whites and incredibly for blacks." The pugnacious conservative and passionate advocate John J. DiIulio, Jr., added: "As many as half of these juvenile super-predators could be young black males." "At just above 1 percent of the population, black males in this age group [14 to 24] now makes up 17 percent of the victims of homicide and over 30 percent of the perpetrators," noted James Alan Fox. Media mogul Mortimer Zuckerman argued that "It is easy to see why the symbol of criminality has become the young black male," while David Rubinstein chimed in with "There is a growing recognition of the embeddedness of crime in the culture of the black underclass."[4] These columnists failed to mention the various adversities many African Americans struggle with, such as poverty, substandard housing, family problems, segregation, police prejudice, discrimination, lack of jobs, or substandard schools. Instead, they seemed to imply that somehow *race itself* (a biological term often bandied about by nonbiologists who have only the most superficial idea of what it is) were to blame, as if crime derived from one's skin tone.

> Claim 4. *Violent crime, according to several commentators, has turned inner cities into virtual war zones.*

Articles portrayed the **inner city** as a place where armies of mercenaries were locked in a war of attrition. For instance, they insisted that "America does not have a crime problem; inner-city America does" (John J. DiIulio, Jr.). Conservative moralist William Bennett said, "Our modern tangle of pathologies is concentrated in urban centers and inner cities." According to *Time's* Richard Lacayo, "Much of that increase [in violent crime] reflects the daily shooting spree in the nation's inner cities" and "It's in the inner cities where an interlocking universe of guns, gangs and the drug trade has made mayhem a career path for kids." Another writer alleged that "Many inner-city youngsters go to more funerals than movies." Sometimes the comments lapsed into **ethnocentrism,** as when *U.S. News and World Report* said,

"Parts of America's inner cities have become as foreign to many Americans as Sarajevo or Chechnya." These caustic remarks exoticize the ghetto: By zeroing in on the excesses, they tarnish and stigmatize entire neighborhoods.[5]

Claim 5. *The thriving trade in illegal drugs, writers said, is instrumental in raising the level of violence.*

Liberal and conservative journalists agreed with many criminologists on this issue. Crack cocaine became popular in American cities in the mid- to late 1980s. Along with the crack vials came drug distribution rings, composed mostly of juveniles, who joined for the ready cash and who could count on receiving shorter sentences (than adults) if caught and convicted. These youths carried ample drugs or sums of money, making them subject to robbery. Their response was to arm themselves, which led to a rash of gun purchases by dealers, their associates, plus competitors, neighbors, and other teenagers in the area. After a while, fighting erupted over drug territories, exacting a heavy toll in bloodshed.[6]

Claim 6. *The youthful generation of the 1990s, judging by their audacious conduct, apparently had no respect for human life.*

Magazines said juveniles with a gun were quick to pull the trigger, often for no reason that anyone could discern. Once Americans enter adolescence, it was claimed, they tend to become **sociopaths** (i.e., persons with an antisocial personality who are criminal and aggressive).[7]

Even more shocking than the sheer volume of violent juvenile crime is the brutality of the crime committed for trivial motives: a pair of sneakers, a jacket, a real or imagined insult, a momentary cheap thrill. . . . The crimes are senseless, the motives banal, and the perpetrators all so young.[8]

This implies that people walking along the city streets face the prospect of being randomly gunned down by malignant youths with casual attitudes toward killing. According to commentators, young offenders caught by the cops aren't stung by the faintest twinge of shame. Instead, amoral and incapable of empathy, they display the unremorseful faces of sullen and **feral beings** (which is to say, wild animals or savages).[9] Here the articles are implicitly reviving a notion developed a century ago by Cesare Lombroso (who argued that criminals were **atavistic,** meaning that they were throwbacks to an earlier stage of evolution).

Claim 7. *Juvenile crime and violence are caused mainly by the proliferation of broken homes (or single-parent families).*

With the possible exception of *USA Today* employees, journalists are not trained to search for good news. Instead, they are always on the lookout for possible award-winning stories about the seamy side, of humans at their worst. Reporters notify readers of breaking news. Columnists soon follow up such news with explanations and blame placing. Many commentators' knee-jerk reaction to youth crime is to blame it on "family breakdown." From 1993 to 1997, articles singled out illegitimacy as the most vivid symbol of a declining moral climate. Families, they said, are disintegrating, as separations, divorces, and annulments mount rapidly. Seventy percent of the juvenile offenders who are locked up in institutions, they said, come from broken homes. Moreover, they insisted, single-parent homes are acutely "**dysfunctional**"—a buzzword of uncertain meaning. In these settings, the stories asserted, abuse, neglect, and drug use are rife, while violence spills forth virtually every day. This is why elementary schools are filled with kids who pack guns instead of lunches. Any area having a majority of single-parent families, according to the columnists, will be saddled with a high rate of violence, because of the many youths who are essentially devoid of socialization.[10]

> Claim 8. *The juvenile justice system is hopelessly outmoded. Because its philosophy calls for "coddling" youths, it cannot cope with the new, more violent generation.*

The juvenile justice system was originally designed for more innocent and corrigible children, whose antics never exceeded scrawling graffiti or swiping hubcaps. But, according to the writers, the juvenile court in the mid-1990s had to deal with twin specters it couldn't handle: family disintegration and hordes of young predators. Columnists rebuked idealistic judges for gullibly believing that there's no such thing as a bad boy, and they called the juvenile court a revolving door, which set offenders free as soon as they enter the system, letting them commit crimes with impunity. Hence, many of these youths go on to amass long rap sheets before they finally commit a truly grisly crime, and only then do they face their first stint behind bars. Infuriated by indulgent judges, media alarmists clamored for a new, get-tough approach: lock up all youths who commit violent acts and don't let them out via the back door (such as parole).[11]

> Claim 9. *Youngsters used to be seized by fear at the prospect of prison, but by the 1990s, kids in some communities viewed incarceration as merely a **rite of passage**.*

Prison has become an important institution in the inner cities of America, magazine essays contended, shaping the culture and wielding more influence than traditional institutions such as schools and churches. They said that in the inner city, one's father was probably behind bars, along with one's brothers and cousins, perhaps. All of them had experienced the pains of imprisonment, according to the articles; this was an integral part of growing up. But by becoming so normal a part of life, it lost its power to devastate. "Harsh treatment, rather than scaring youths straight, may have the opposite effect, by making matters worse and engendering bitterness, leading youths to take pride in criminal exploits."[12] Once back on the street, guys did not find it embarrassing to be ex-cons—quite the contrary, it was a mark of distinction, which they would flaunt. Prison taught inmates new ways of thinking, acting, dressing, and carrying themselves, which spread to the neighborhood, where youngsters picked up the mores of maximum security. Prison became as socially acceptable as a sleep-away camp, according to the magazines.[13] It did not discourage youths from engaging in crime. One writer, for instance, dismissed the idea of deterrence out of hand:

> Neither the electric chair, the snake-infested swamp, the five-foot hickory club, the tiny stifling cell without TV, nor even the mortification of wearing stripes in public was ever once considered at the moment a violent crime was perpetrated.[14]

Claim 10. *The size of the juvenile population, which decreased for several years, is about to experience a large increase.*

Periodicals announced that although the number of youths aged 14 to 17 was small in 1993 (in some quarters it was identified as the "birth dearth" or "baby bust" generation), a resurgence was just around the corner. The number of people in this age range would grow 23 percent over the next dozen years (that is, by 2005). These children of aging baby boomers would soon be entering the high-risk years for crime.[15] Some authors added that between 1993 and 2005, *African Americans* aged 14 to 17 would increase even more dramatically, their number soaring 50 percent.[16]

Claim 11. *This **demographic time bomb** will inevitably produce an unprecedented wave of youthful violence.*

In the near future, pundits warned, America would confront a ticking time bomb. Data for this argument were provided courtesy of criminologist/statistician James Alan Fox, who foretold a future bloodbath of teenage violence, with 5,000 young killers each year, which he said would make 1995 (then regarded as a horrific year in terms of homicide rates) look like the good old days. James Q. Wilson predicted that we would be inundated by 30,000 more muggers, killers, and thieves, as half a million more males entered the 14 to 17 age range. Not to be outdemagogued, John DiIulio estimated that there would be 270,000 new **superpredators,** whose arrival would bring the number of annual homicides up to 35 or 40 thousand. Magazine articles anticipated a meteoric rise in crime, one they said would be dominated by black youths.

> "The code of the street is to kill or be killed," says John Perkins. . . . "I think we're seeing the first signs of a bomb that's ready to blow. We're seeing a whole generation of young people reacting to two decades of neglect, poverty, and the scourge of the dysfunctional family. The only values they aspire to are survival, power, and greed. . . . We're talking about kids who no longer have hope."[17]

Evaluating the Claims

These were the assertions that magazines made over and over during the mid-1990s. How much credence should we give such statements? Are they accurate versions of what was going on in America at the time and later? Or were they mostly hot air, inflammatory rhetoric, and polemics? Many readers probably accepted them as factual. This is understandable. After all, the reports were bolstered by many statistics and statements made by well-known and self-proclaimed experts. (Plus, it is true, there was in fact a period of years leading up to 1994 in which the number of youth arrests for murder did rise substantially.) Moreover, the articles were published in respectable outlets. *Atlantic Monthly, U.S. News and World Report,* and *Time* are not to be sneered at; nobody would confuse them with the **tabloids** or scandal sheets found at supermarket checkout counters. They exude respectability, which adds gravity to the eleven statements. These are reasons why readers might accept the stories as valid reports. But maybe they should have been more skeptical. Over the years, the press has been known to exaggerate, as shown in Exhibit 1-1.

Some of the eleven claims made by the magazines and cited earlier cannot be subjected to testing. DiIulio defines moral poverty as growing up in the company of deviant adults and in "chaotic, dysfunctional, fatherless, Godless, and jobless settings where drug abuse and child abuse are twins and self-respecting young men literally aspire to get away with murder."[19] This kind of florid oratory does not actually set forth a hypothesis. It defines, moralizes, and condemns, but makes no claims whose validity can be tested by social science research.

Other statements, however, can be empirically evaluated—for instance, the claim that a 23 percent increase in the youth population ages 14 to 17 would lead to an explosive growth in crime and violence by youth in the coming years. Observers did not have to wait until 2005 to test that hypothesis, because *almost half of the projected 23 percent growth in population had already taken place by 1997* (14- to 17-year-olds increased 11 percent, from 13.9 million to 15.4 million, between 1993 and 1997). Therefore, any crime wave that was going to emerge should have arrived before the new millennium. According to FBI Uniform Crime Reports, the anticipated explosion in the number of crimes never materialized. Instead, between 1993 and 1997, murders actually *declined* 26 percent. Moreover, forcible rapes dropped by 9 percent, robberies slumped by 24.5 percent, and aggravated assault fell by 10 percent. Rather than surge out of control as predicted, crime rates sank to levels not seen since the 1960s.

What about levels of criminality among *young people?* Did these rise? Actually, fewer persons under the age of 18 were arrested in 1997 than in 1993. The number of youngsters arrested for murder plunged 39 percent. For forcible rape, the number of youths arrested fell 16 percent; robbery arrests of youngsters went down 2 percent; aggravated assault arrests of youths dropped 5 percent; and young people arrested for weapons carrying or possession fell 23 percent. **Alarmists** in the press insisted it was only a matter of time before violent crime by youngsters would erupt. But almost as soon as they made their prognostications, the rate plummeted. The slope in crime rates that had been going up for several years abruptly reversed course, plunging as quickly as it had risen. Perhaps no one could have foreseen it. Like individuals who bought stocks at the end of the bull run on Wall Street, those who climbed aboard the crime bandwagon just *assumed* youth violence was headed

EXHIBIT 1-1 Yellow Journalism's Approach to Crime

Historically, the American news media have overstated the seriousness of problems by dwelling on the more extreme incidents. **Yellow journalism** in the Hearst-Pulitzer era, for instance, was notorious for such excesses. The eccentric Joseph Pulitzer bought the *New York World* and shrewdly transformed it into a high-circulation newspaper within three years. He did so by tailoring the paper to the city's working class, slighting foreign and political news, expanding coverage of crime and tragedy, and introducing provocative headlines. Impressed by Pulitzer's accomplishment, William Randolph Hearst soon followed suit. He purchased the *New York Journal* and made murder, scandal, adultery, and disaster the paper's prime topics. "When peace brooded over the city and nobody was being robbed or murdered, he would come down to the office with despondency written on his face."[18] Murders so invigorated him that he would dance around the page proofs. Pulitzer and Hearst are not merely historical oddities—despite their fondness for hyperbole, they influenced subsequent generations of journalists by setting the standards. All journalists in America now take it for granted that the most important *news values* are conflict (wars, riots, killings), novelty (the exceptional and atypical), prominence (celebrated, notorious or highly placed figures), and disaster (destruction and catastrophe). They're taught this in journalism school and on the job.

News media back in the days of Hearst and Pulitzer (70 to 100 years ago) did not report every event or a "representative" sample of them, nor do they now. For one thing, that would be impossible. Instead, they select about 10 percent of the news items available to them and usually shine their beacon at the spicier, seamier, more dangerous, unusual, or frightening incidents and leave the mundane and repetitive events for sociologists to mull over. News media relentlessly batter readers and viewers with conflict, excitement, and bad news, no matter how atypical they may be. Hence, the many stories of youth crime in newspapers, magazines, and television today *could be* a reflection merely of the media's predilection for conflict and drama.

upward for years to come. But the bull market in crime turned bearish, and the pundits proved not to be prescient.

Some of them said crime would spike upward, especially among African-American youths. This prediction proved to be no more accurate than the hypothesis about crime in general. Black youths *did not* go on a violent rampage. On the contrary, from 1993 to 1997, arrests of African Americans aged 14 to 17 headed downward, and not by just a smidgen. The number of homicide arrests of black youths plummeted by more than half, their arrests for rape skidded by 30 percent, while their robbery arrests dropped more than 40 percent. These jaw-dropping losses were unexpected, and no one has been able to offer a convincing explanation for them.

Journalists who claimed that the population of black youngsters aged 14 to 17 would rise by 50 percent between 1993 and 2005 were also off the mark. The census figure for 1993 was 2.167 million black youths aged 14 to 17, and at that time the Census Bureau projected there would be 2.667 million such youths in 2005, which meant an increase of only 26 percent—in essence, then, only half of commentators' figure of 50 percent. The official figure was not some secret zealously guarded by a few demographers. It was available to anyone who consulted the *Statistical Abstract of the U.S.* or other census publications available in research libraries. Or visited the local bookstore and picked up an almanac. No one needed to hazard a guess.

What about DiIulio's claim that there would be 270,000 new superpredators repeatedly committing especially vicious crimes? This implied that *6 percent of all children under 18 in the year 2005 would be superpredators.* Doubts began to surface when it was realized that this would have to include infants, two-year-olds, four-year-olds, six-year-olds, and so forth. Kindergartners and toddlers, however, are not hardened felons with lengthy rap sheets. They don't make frequent court appearances and clog judges' calendars. Of those under 18 who get arrested, nearly all are adolescents, *not children.* Among adolescents, 6 percent are **chronic offenders,** but chronic offenders usually aren't *violent* offenders. *Less than 1 percent* of 13- to 17-year-olds are arrested for repeatedly committing *especially violent or vicious crimes.* Even if a *full* 1 percent of 13- to 17-year-olds in 2005 were to become superpredators, that would still yield fewer than 27,000, which is only one-tenth of what DiIulio predicted.

The hypothesis that there will be hordes of murderous youth plaguing the nation can also be tested another way, by examining the youths who are sent to institutions by the juvenile court. If there are thousands upon thousands of juvenile predators on a murderous rampage, this should be reflected in the kinds of youngsters who are given residential placements by the court. That is, a large proportion of youths put away in institutions should be there *for the crime of homicide.* Nearly all juveniles accused of homicide are, in fact, formally processed in court, and a majority of those found guilty are locked away. Nevertheless, those arrested for homicide do not make up a very substantial proportion of juvenile inmates—only about 1 percent. Of the twenty offenses cited in one study, homicide ranked almost last (19th) in the *number* of offenders the court sent there. In fact, there were thirty times as many youths sent to institutions for obstruction of justice![20]

Is the juvenile court outmoded, incapable of handling the present generation? One way to test this is to compare two sets of youths: those sent to juvenile court and those tried in adult court. This has been done with juveniles in Florida, where large numbers of delinquents are waived to criminal court for trial. The results do not substantiate the pundits' predictions. Instead of being chastened or scared straight by the experience, juveniles dealt with by the adult court later commit *more offenses,* and they do so *sooner* after discharge from corrections than a matched sample of youths handled in juvenile court. Research conducted in New York and New

Jersey also found that criminal courts fail to have the beneficial effect that hard-liners promised.[21] This is important, for it suggests that the drop in juvenile crime since 1993 is *not* due to youths being sent to criminal courts.

Next, consider the single-parent family; blaming *it* for youth crime seems to have become almost a national pastime. Publications offer claims like the following: 72 percent of America's adolescent murderers, 70 percent of long-term prison inmates, and 60 percent of rapists come from fatherless homes. By themselves, these statements do not provide firm evidence that broken homes *cause* rape, murder, or other crimes. First of all, these kinds of data are examples of what some statistics teachers used to label "**Dear Abby tables**": this means that the tables are both (a) incomplete (some of the cells are empty, they do not contain a percentage or frequency) *and* (b) the figures that are provided are percentaged in the wrong direction for making causal statements. When percentaged in the correct direction, each column of *the independent variable* (broken home, intact home) *should add up to 100 percent*. In "Dear Abby" tables, only one column adds up to 100 percent, and that is a column of *the dependent variable* (Table 1-1).

Furthermore, having no father living at home is *itself* one of the factors that leads police to arrest some adolescents and courts to convict and cart them off to reform school. Officials just *assume* that a single mother cannot control her child. To avoid these justice-system biases and methodological problems, researchers should *begin with* a sample of children from the *general population*. Once such a sample has been drawn, researchers can *compare* children from *two-parent* households with those from *one-parent* families (family structure is the independent variable) to see which category then becomes more involved in delinquency or crime (the dependent variable). They should use self-report studies rather than official data because police and courts have a well-established prejudice against father-absent youths. Then the results *might* look like the hypothetical figures in Table 1-2.

People repeatedly claim that broken homes are the primary cause of delinquency. But this is not a matter to be decided based on mere opinion or argument. Instead, we can turn to the pertinent research. Studies examining the proposed link between broken homes and delinquency are so numerous that criminologists have done **meta-analyses;** that is, they've combined the many previous research studies and summarized the results by using a single type of statistic. Summarizing 68 books and articles on the topic published in recent years, Marvin Free concluded that the literature fails to show a relationship between broken homes and *serious crimes,* that

TABLE 1-1   Example of a Table That's Incomplete and Percentaged in the Wrong Direction

	Institutionalized	*Not Institutionalized*
Broken Home	72%	—
Intact Home	28%	—
Total	100%	—

TABLE 1-2   Hypothetical Example of a Complete Table That's Percentaged in the Right Direction

	Broken Home	Intact Home
Chronic Delinquent	7%	5%
Moderately Delinquent	53%	50%
Nondelinquent	40%	45%
Total	100%	100%

is, violence or theft. (On the other hand, he did find a relationship between broken homes and *status offenses,* such as smoking, truancy, breaking curfew, incorrigibility, and the like.)[22]

Another meta-analysis, by Wells and Rankin (1991), covered 50 studies, some of them published as far back as 1926;[23] they arrived at the same conclusion that Free had: The relationship is very weak. In addition, they noted that methodologically stronger research studies (those employing large probability samples with more reliable measures of the key variables, for instance) yielded very modest correlations between broken homes and delinquency. On the other hand, small, unreliable, clinical studies, relying on self-selected populations of patients, produced high correlations. Thus, strong findings may be suspect, because they come from studies that fail to meet the most basic standards of research.

When critics and commentators lament the decline of the American family, one of the examples they cite is the rising divorce rate. The best measure of this is the refined divorce rate, which is the number of divorces in a particular year per 1,000 married women aged 15 and over. This figure rose rapidly twice, right after World War II and during the 1970s. It reached a peak of 22.8 in 1979, and since that year has been headed slightly downward. Divorces are not on the rise and haven't been for decades. This fact, though ignored by virtually all the commentators, could have been verified by consulting any textbook on the family.

Public Opinion About Crime

As noted, magazines described youth violence as soaring or skyrocketing. Although the media are commonly accused of having a liberal bias and being dominated by elites,[24] their opinions on crime reveal a more conservative, get-tough ideology. This hard line also crops up in most newspaper op-ed pages.[25] Does the American public agree with the commentators that crime is surging out of control, that the younger generation is at fault, and that the obvious solution is to inflict more severe punishment?

Not many Americans subscribe to elite publications such as the *Atlantic Monthly* or *The Public Interest,* nor do many of them peruse essays in *Vital Speeches of the Day* or even news items in *U.S. News & World Report.* Typically, the message of elite and other magazines about youth crime reaches a limited number of people. Hence, most citizens are not directly influenced by this message. Nevertheless, many Americans apparently see eye to eye with it. Perhaps this is because they *do* often read local newspapers and watch television, where they are bombarded with stories containing graphic violence, some of it by offenders whose youth is prominently cited. Celebrated cases can stimulate people's imagination and lead them to believe that a few examples are typical—that youth crime is rampant.[26] Some stories in the news thus may influence public views of crime rates, crime seriousness, and appropriate sentencing.[27]

In the mid-1990s, crime and violence attracted massive attention. In 1993, for example, news about Polly Klaas, Nancy Kerrigan, and the Long Island commuter train massacre dominated the airwaves as did the trials of Reginald Denny and the Menendez brothers. Over half the stories on youth on local television news in California dealt with violence, and two-thirds of the stories on violence dealt with youth. One startling sign of the times: O. J. Simpson's case is said to have drawn more media coverage than the entire Vietnam War. (Of course, the rise and spread of cable television explains much of that finding.)[28] On the other hand, officially measured *crime rates* were headed in the opposite direction (i.e., downward). This allows us to test which of them influenced public perceptions more, the media presentations or the actual crime statistics?

It appears (based on several sources) that Americans as a rule were more influenced by the media; in fact, few of them had any knowledge at all of what the official data showed. Consider, for instance, the results when people were asked by the Gallup Poll what they believed was the most important problem facing the country. During the 1980s, scarcely anyone (only 2 to 4 percent) cited crime as the most important problem. From early 1994 to early 1998 (when crime rates fell but crime in the media grew to unprecedented heights), thirteen polls asked what was the most important problem confronting the nation, and on twelve of these polls, more people cited crime than the economy, health care, the deficit, or drugs.[29]

Polls in the *Los Angeles Times* and elsewhere show that people normally say that the media, especially television, serve as their main source of information about crime and justice.[30] Because their experience as victims is limited or nonexistent, most people turn to newspapers and television for the facts about crime and justice. They may also be influenced by their own general belief systems; that is, those who hold socially conservative or fundamentalist religious beliefs tend to think crime is on the rise, to blame crime on the character of the offender, and to favor punitive responses to crime and deviance by juveniles.[31]

Nowadays, when ordinary adults talk about *adolescents*, they are more apt to complain about youths' moral defects than to extol their virtues. Discussions may include youngsters' use of drugs and alcohol, having sex, being greedy, committing crimes, or being reckless, risk-taking, rebellious, rude, undisciplined, impulsive, and selfish.[32] It is not unusual for adults to rely on a handful of sensational cases to paint an entire generation with the same brush. Readers and viewers who have been exposed to news media that are driven by catastrophe (and this is definitely true of American media) are likely to accept this depiction as a true description of crime. Scapegoating the young for crime and deviance is almost never considered prejudice. Although Americans may refer to racism and, occasionally, sexism, ageism is not a word commonly mentioned. Most people think accusing teenagers of committing the bulk of crime and violence is just *common sense*.[33]

Academic studies rarely examine attitudes and public opinion about adolescents. There are no sociological theories of adult attitudes toward youth that researchers could test. In public opinion polls, too, this topic receives only a modest amount of coverage. If survey researchers are reluctant to delve into the subject, that does not mean that American adults have no attitudes about it. Social scientists with an urge to eavesdrop, to listen to conversations over the backyard fence or around the office water cooler, might get an earful on the topic of teens.

In a sense, researcher Theodore Sasson has done just this kind of snooping. He did not conceal microphones or tap anyone's phone lines. But he did create twenty discussion groups of adults in various neighborhoods and ask them to talk about crime and its causes. Most participants, he found, spoke of what Sasson called "social breakdown." They blamed the high crime rates in the United States on parents' failure to supervise their offspring. Respondents argued that youths would naturally gravitate to drugs and crime unless parents and others monitored them carefully and instilled traditional values, moral standards, and discipline. As one of them (Janice) said,

> It's church, schools, home, no one's doing their job. That's why it is. It used to be that—church used to play a big part in the family. Your family did. Your friends. If you were out here acting up, you didn't want anybody to know it. Now you brag about it because you're not taught any values at home. And if you are not taught—if it doesn't start at home, the street's got you.[34]

According to other studies, adults believe that youngsters in modern America are lacking in proper socialization. The polling organization *Public Agenda* conducted a large telephone survey and convened **focus groups** to explore adult attitudes toward youths. The responses were far more critical than experts had anticipated, perhaps because so little research of this kind had been done previously. Respondents dwelt largely on what they considered teenagers' antisocial demeanor and deviant behavior. When asked what came to their minds when they thought about American adolescents, two-thirds of the sample emphasized negative traits such as rudeness, irresponsibility, and wildness. A mere one out of every eight people questioned spoke about more flattering traits (e.g., smart or helpful). Most instead said that youths have not learned honesty, respect, or responsibility. Focus groups, too, handed out more brickbats than compliments. Only a handful said that teens treat people with respect and are friendly toward their neighbors.[35]

Public Agenda survey researchers found that most adults are quick to blame parents for the failings of their sons and daughters. Half of them believe that mothers and fathers do not use enough discipline. More than half of them contend that parents get divorced too readily; they think parents should forego personal fulfillment, learn to put up with their spouse's flaws, and stay together for the children's sake. Two out of three claim that people give birth before they are prepared to take on this awesome responsibility. Few respondents in the study had a good word to say about parents. Scarcely any of them deemed parents "good role models." Parents were just as critical of them as nonparents were.

Pollsters Hart and Teeter asked a 1999 sample of people to examine and rank a list of fourteen problems facing America. Respondents said the most important one was parents' not paying enough attention to what's going on in their children's lives—83 percent called it a very serious problem.[36] The high rate of divorce and the breakup of families were chosen as the fourth most serious problem. Families thus lead the way as the institution most involved in determining the social welfare of the nation—at least in the minds of this sample. This is not a new discovery; parent blaming goes back for centuries.

In the *Public Agenda* study, schooling also came in for its share of the blame, with respondents suggesting that primary and secondary school educators have forsaken their traditional mission of developing integrity, respect, and responsibility in youngsters. Judging from these findings, adults apparently want teachers to place at least as much emphasis on traditional morality as on academics. Although respondents felt parents and schools were to blame for the younger generation's forays into crime, they also believed some other factors were at fault (Table 1-3).[37]

In September of 1994, Gallup asked Americans what percent of violent crime is committed by people under the age of 18. The response, according the Uniform Crime Reports, should have been about 13 percent. But very few respondents chose a number close to that figure. Most of them instead settled on considerably higher numbers, typically *three to four times* the official percentage.[38] Perhaps this should not come as a great surprise, in view of what people now read in the news. After all, 90 percent of the newspaper stories written about youth crime involves crimes of violence.[39]

Although youngsters are commonly described as being exceptionally prone to violence, they are not the only group in America to have been categorized this way. How do people regard teenagers compared with the other devalued groups? In December 1993, a Gallup Poll gave respondents nine categories or groups to evaluate: Asian Americans, blacks, Hispanics, homeless, immigrants, male teenagers in general, male teenagers in your neighborhood, police, and whites. People in the sample were asked (for each group), Does it commit more, less, or the same level of crime as other people in America? The results were skewed: 58 percent said male teens in general (MTIG) commit more crime than average, whereas only 6 percent said MTIG commit less crime than average.[40] No other group came close to these

TABLE 1-3 What Americans Think Is to Blame for Crime by Young People

Kids seeing too much violence on TV	69%
Not learning honesty, respect, responsibility	61%
Welfare encourages single-parent families	58%
Kids suffer because of parents' economics	44%

damning figures. Teenage males thus stand alone, at least in the public mind, when it comes to committing crime.

Because the public assumes that crime is dominated by youngsters, one might ask whether it also thinks the young should be severely punished. There is anecdotal evidence that it does indeed. Some years ago, American teenager Michael Fay was about to receive a rattan cane beating, the kind of whipping that lacerates the skin, sprays lots of blood, and creates painful welts. This expected punishment was in response to Michael's spray-painting graffiti on some cars in Singapore. Although some observers expected Americans to cringe at such harshness and to rise en masse to protest the brutality, few people rallied to his defense. Rather than express outrage at the upcoming savage beating, many Americans applauded Singapore's hard-nosed approach. Moreover, in a *Newsweek* poll, a majority of adults said they favored using canes in the United States for people who were convicted of assault, robbery, drug dealing, or gang fighting.[41]

Unlike most people, sociologists and psychologists tend to oppose harsh sentencing for criminal offenses. When social scientists conduct research on juvenile and criminal justice policy, they often hope to uncover evidence that other people share their view, that the public, too, has a soft heart and favors treatment of juveniles instead of punitive policies.[42] Researchers have found that the general public is not so punitive when it is given a variety of sentence options to choose from, when it is given more specific details about cases and offenders, and when it is given real cases to deal with.[43] Nevertheless, there is clear evidence that Americans as a rule have a penchant for punishment. Public attitudes apparently hardened during the early to mid-1990s.[44]

1. Support for rehabilitation has dropped in recent decades and support for punishment has increased[45]
2. Eighty-eight percent feel juvenile court sentences are too lenient[46]
3. Respondents think that children under 16 should be subject to curfew[47]
4. Texans are almost unanimous in calling juvenile crime a serious problem, and one-fourth are in favor of death sentences for 11-year-olds[48]

Studies often find that the public wants safety first (putting offenders in custodial institutions). Once that is assured, *then* they are willing to consider various modes of treatment, such as training, education, and counseling.[49]

In a 1993 article, Ira Schwartz and his colleagues asked how delinquents should be handled by the courts. Respondents were questioned about offenders who committed a serious property offense, a drug offense, or a violent offense, and whether the youths should be tried in adult court and sentenced to adult prisons. Here we will consider the responses given by African Americans and whites (with controls for education, fear of crime, gender, parental status, and work status). Table 1-4 shows the percentages of respondents who agreed or strongly agreed with the stated position. Except for putting property offenders in prison, Americans generally favored getting tough with young offenders (Exhibit 1-2).

TABLE 1-4   What Americans Say Should Be Done with Young Offenders

	Afr Amer	White
Try property offenders in adult court[50]	51%	50%
Try drug offenders in adult court	58%	63%
Try violent offenders in adult court	65%	68%
Put property offenders in adult prison	17%	15%
Put drug offenders in adult prisons	34%	29%
Put violent offenders in adult prisons	42%	40%

Some commentators claim that Americans are very astute about crime and that the public's views should determine criminal justice policy. This stance, however, does not stand up well under analysis. Actually, more people believe in astrology than evolution. Less than 40 percent of Americans can even identify the three branches of the federal government. In addition, the average American thinks the number of jobless is four times higher than it actually is. Nearly one in four believes the current unemployment rate tops 25 percent. Americans believe prices are rising four times faster than they actually are.[62] The public exaggerates the punitiveness of police, the lenience of judges, the luxury of prison life, the seriousness of crime, the rate of homicide, the rise in crime, the victimization rates of women and the elderly, the role of juveniles in violent crime, the amount of violence in schools, and the dangerousness of neighborhoods other than their own.[63] When asked what should be done with offenders, people often imagine someone at the extreme end of the spectrum, say Ted Bundy or John Wayne Gacy.[64]

Upon being shown that crime rates have gone down, some individuals simply scoff, contending that the data have been fudged (as in this passage from a crime novel).

> This city was dangerous. . . . Never mind the reassuring bulletins from the Mayor's office. Ask the Mayor to take an unescorted two A.M. stroll through any of the city's barren moonscapes and then interview him in his hospital bed the next morning to ask him about lower crime rates and improved police patrols. Or just watch the first ten minutes of the eleven o'clock news every night and you'll learn in the wink of an eye exactly what the people of this city were capable of doing.[65]

Such cynicism often passes for worldly wisdom whereas optimism is derided as naiveté. People see or hear many vivid reports of violent crimes; there are no stories of residences or businesses where crime has not occurred—that is not dramatic, not considered news. So it does not appear in the media and does not register in our consciousness.

EXHIBIT 1-2   Public Opinion Regarding the Death Penalty

The ultimate in punishment severity is the death penalty, which is imposed on children only by the United States, Congo, Iran, Nigeria, Pakistan, and Saudi Arabia.[51] Between 1988 and 2000, the United States executed more juvenile offenders than the other countries combined. For years, the American public recoiled at the thought of executing minors. Young people were considered innocent and immature, and such a punishment struck most people as excessive. But by the mid-1990s, public opinion had undergone a noticeable hardening regarding capital punishment in general and for youths specifically. For example, in 1957 few of the adults surveyed by Gallup considered the death penalty appropriate for an individual under age 18 convicted of murder—only 11 percent. By 1994, however, what had once been considered unthinkable came to be seen by many people as acceptable. Sixty percent of adults in America gave their approval to executing teenagers for murder. This stunning change was a clear sign of the new punitiveness toward youth.[52]

Why do people favor capital punishment? Some criminologists originally argued in favor of a *rational model,* that citizens endorsed capital punishment because they were afraid of crime, perceived crime rates to be increasing, and believed punishment functioned as a deterrent.[53] But research has not provided much backing for this line of argument. Studies show that people who have been victimized, who fear for their own safety *are no more likely than others to support capital punishment.*[54]

A second viewpoint contends that traditional values are more important factors. The argument goes like this: If law-abiding citizens have to suffer privations in the name of conventional morality, then they will want criminals to suffer for flouting such moral values. If criminals are *not* going to suffer for their deviant acts, it means that law-abiding citizens have deprived themselves needlessly, or worse, meaninglessly. And that leaves the law-abiding citizens feeling frustrated by the criminal justice system and angry at the offenders who get away with their misdeeds.

Research has provided some support for this notion that capital punishment backers hold traditional values and are infuriated by law violators. The best predictors of pro-death-penalty sentiment were *favoring* solitary confinement for disobedient inmates and *opposition to* (1) providing inmates with room, light, heat and ventilation; (2) giving them weekend leaves to visit relatives or search for employment; and (3) letting them complain to the courts about prison conditions.[55] These represent traditional morality, social conservatism, and hostility toward offenders—not fear, victimization, deterrence, or belief that the crime problem is serious and crime rates are rising.[56] Other research has found support for the death penalty to be particularly high among those who are irrational, emotional, dogmatic, authoritarian, prejudiced, and fundamentalists.[57]

In addition, there is the possibility that punitive attitudes (including support for the death penalty) spring from a misunderstanding of how the criminal and juvenile justice systems operate. That such misunderstanding exists is evident from some recent studies. Vandiver and Giacopassi found that about half of a sample of college students thought that a quarter-million murders are committed each year in the United States, and 15 percent estimated the figure to be at least a million a year.[58] The actual figure is less than 20,000. Lotke found the number of murders by juveniles was also wildly overestimated by university students.[59] If collegians are so far off in their estimates, then presumably the rest of the citizenry is also badly misinformed. Moreover, the less that people know about the criminal justice system, the more punitive they are.[60] Plus, the fewer years of education people have, the more punitive they tend to be.[61]

Politics and Proposed Punishments

Since 1964, when Barry Goldwater made law and order a hot-button issue, Republicans have turned to crime when elections loomed. The national Democrats, after a series of crushing defeats in presidential elections (McGovern, Carter in 1980, Mondale, and Dukakis), finally saw the light and adopted the same tactics.

"Get-tough-on-crime policies are so popular that it is politically difficult for an elected official to oppose them. . . ."[66]

"Clanging prison bars, flashing police lights and shackled criminals are showing up more and more on TV this fall, as campaign ads focus on the election's most powerful theme."[67]

"In election years like this one, politicians vie to outdo one another on who can talk toughest on crime. . . . Bad ideas are hawked to the public based on panic, distortion, and exaggeration."[68]

"Politicians can always get the majority of Americans riled up about crime, and there is virtually no constituency that opposes reducing crime."[69]

For some candidates, tough talk on crime is merely campaign oratory but others take it seriously and go on to enact laws, including truth in sentencing, good faith exclusionary rule exceptions, and mandatory minimums. Congress and state legislatures began getting tougher, and this has had several results. The first is that prisons began bulging at the seams with inmates.

There was a time in history when the prison population remained relatively constant for about half a century. In fact, a 1973 criminology article said this was akin to a law of nature and would hold true for the foreseeable future.[70] That future, however, turned out to be as insubstantial as a hologram. Prison population size quickly changed, leaving the authors red-faced. The 200,000 in state and federal pens grew to approximately 1.2 million in 1997, rising sixfold in 25 years and showed no signs of slowing until 1999 (long after crime rates had receded).

Inevitably, this put intense pressure on the prison system, which relied on some buildings that had been constructed as long ago as the 1800s. To relieve the pressure, construction began to boom, and a new prison was built every week from 1985 to 1995. During that decade, the inmate population doubled, and the number of inmates incarcerated because of drug offenses increased by a factor of six. In Texas, politicians committed their state to building 48 prisons in two years.

The United States has a rate of imprisonment that is about 600 per 100,000 people. By itself, this figure means little. We can understand it better by comparing it with rates of imprisonment found in other countries in the modern world (Table 1-5).

Several explanations could be given for the sudden rise in prisoners, including the simplest one—rising crime rates. Crime may indeed have fueled the growth during the 1970s, but other factors took over from 1980 onward. Findings show that after 1980, the bulk of the increase in inmates was due to (1) a higher percentage of arrestees being sent to prison and (2) people in prison serving longer terms.[72] Legislatures took away some of the judges' discretion and forced them to send more people to prison and give them longer sentences.

Conservative legislators defended these policies by referring to a paper written by Justice Department economist Edwin Zedlewski.[73] His analysis, relying on data published by the Rand Corporation, said that by sending a single offender to prison, the justice system prevents hundreds of crimes and saves taxpayers over $400,000. The Rand Corporation disavowed their report, but congressional conservatives were not impressed by this—they continued to cite Zedlewski's work as gospel.

Legislators during the 1990s called for more punitive sanctions against juveniles as well as adults, and the predictable result was overcrowding in correctional institutions. *(Frank Pedrick/The Image Works)*

TABLE 1-5   Rates of Imprisonment in Various Countries[71]

Austria	85
Belgium	75
Denmark	65
England & Wales	100
France	95
Germany	85
Ireland	55
Italy	85
Japan	37
Netherlands	65
Norway	55
Spain	105
Sweden	65
Switzerland	80
United States	600

It did not take long for the law-and-order frenzy to catch up with youthful of-fenders. They, too, attracted the political spotlight and got swept up in the punitive movement. Several developments helped make this possible. Here, only one of them will be mentioned. Robert Martinson and some of his colleagues were hired by New York State to survey the literature on the rehabilitation of juvenile offend-ers. At first the state suppressed their report (because of the embarrassing findings), but eventually Martinson published a summary of it in *The Public Interest,* a jour-nal of conservative opinion.[74] The Martinson Report found no reason to be opti-mistic about rehabilitation programs. Education, vocational training, individual counseling, group counseling, **milieu therapy** (transforming the entire environ-ment into a therapeutic atmosphere)—all of these proved ineffective; they failed to prevent *recidivism* (i.e., offenders being rearrested after being released from insti-tutions). Martinson concluded that rehabilitation programs had proven to be fail-ures and that the time had come for corrections policy makers to shift their attention to some other goal, such as deterrence.

Officials in many states took this suggestion seriously. Their faith in rehabilita-tion shaken, criminal justice policy elites turned their attention to other justifica-tions for punishment:

1. General deterrence. Punishing X puts fear in the hearts of others. They see what happened to him, so they choose not to commit the crime he committed.
2. Special deterrence. Punishing X puts fear in his heart. He does not want the same punishment again, so he elects not to commit that offense again.

3. Incapacitation. While X is locked behind bars he cannot commit offenses against people on the outside.
4. Retribution. Punishing X makes him pay for the sins he has committed. For reasons of morality or justice, he deserves to suffer for his past misdeeds.

Later, Martinson had second thoughts about his original conclusion. And with good reason. When Mark Lipsey analyzed more than 400 studies of interventions with juvenile offenders, he found that some kinds of treatment reduced recidivism from 20 to 40 percent.[75] But conservative politicians in the states had already made up their minds, and by the 1990s they were also firmly in control of crime policy at the national level.

With young people and violence closely linked in the national consciousness, conservative politicians in all 50 states played the crime game, and led by Florida's Bill McCollum, Congress tried to do the same. Because getting tough on juveniles was in vogue, legislators advocated the following message—for a serious crime, there must be serious time. They decided that age should no longer be a **mitigating factor**—the courts should treat young and old alike.

This means being tried in criminal court instead of juvenile court.

The age at which youths can be sent to criminal court must be lowered from 18 to 14 (and in some cases 13).

Juveniles can be kept in facilities where they will have regular contact with adult prisoners.

Waiving kids to criminal court is a decision that should be taken out of the hands of judges and given to prosecutors.

Records of juvenile offenses should be made available to schools, colleges and others.

Trials should be open to the general public.

Judges should be allowed to consider the offender's entire record during sentencing.

The offender should not be released from incarceration just because he or she has reached the age of 18.

States must agree to graduated sanctions: juveniles committing any offense (no matter how minor) should be punished or perform community service or restitution.

A federal task force should be set up to apprehend youths.

There should be a mandatory minimum sentence for juveniles who use firearms in a crime.

Under the proposed legislation, states would have to adhere to these rules if they wished to get federal funds.[76]

Congress considered each of these legislative proposals. According to them, adolescents are not immature or impulsive kids who will soon grow out of their youthful deviance. The assumption was that the die is cast, and these kids are on their way to becoming mature career criminals and therefore must be held "accountable." Candidates no longer talked about rehabilitation or prevention or reintegration of youths into society. Instead, they enthusiastically endorsed funneling juveniles into adult courts and locking them up as long as possible.[77]

Legislators gave little attention to research. They advocated boot camps because they believed discipline would straighten out recalcitrant youths. Maybe this thinking was based on wistful memories of years spent in the army.[78] Washington, in its fever to incarcerate middle schoolers, failed to consider studies that evaluated such programs (and found them ineffective). Politicians also passed *waiver laws*, which automatically sent juvenile offenders to adult court for certain types of crime. Here again, they paid scant attention to the consequences: embittered inmates, sexual victimization, staff beatings, and high suicide rates. Among legislators, symbolism counted heavily; reality could be ignored.

> Once again the real crime is partisan one-upmanship. The House already has enacted a Draconian bill that would force states to treat more kids, and younger ones, as lost-cause criminals—and thus pretty much assure that they would turn into adult versions of just that. The real idea is to recapture for Republicans the sole ownership of law-and-order issues that they so enjoyed until sly Bill Clinton came along and snatched a piece of the action with overwrought anti-crime legislation of his own.[79]

Conclusion

Social issues and social problems are usually **social constructions**: matters of collective definition, not objective conditions. Conditions in the real world are seldom so compelling that they automatically dominate public consciousness. People make claims, seek recognition from influential officials, attribute responsibility, and propose remedies. Often they seek champions of their point of view, including supposed experts who can supply analysis and telling statistics. In America, youth crime became a social problem, especially in the mid-1990s, whereas other conditions (such as unequal distribution of wealth and the destruction of the Brazilian rain forest) failed to make it onto the public agenda. Facts must be shaped and the arts of publicity employed.

In ordinary periods, youth crimes, like inactive volcanoes, garner little attention. Just as years go by without smoke, steam, tremors, or lava from volcanoes, there are long periods in which youth crime is ignored. Those are the times when people are complacent or their attention swings to other issues (war, terrorism, Wall Street, the cost of health care). Sometimes, though, there's a burst of media attention, the general populace gets aroused, and politicians swoop in with promises of swift action to combat the threat. Commentators tell us that

> we need to eliminate the presumption that juvenile criminals are misguided youths who just need a little bit of straightening out to make everything right. They are hardened, vicious, predatory criminals, and they simply need to be locked up and kept away from law-abiding members of society. . . . They should be kept in prison as long as it takes to protect society.[80]

In extraordinary times, the stage is set for a moral panic, and it may be incited by well-publicized, frightening cases. When the issue of youth crime was riding high, there were tales of carjackings, hate crimes, drive-by shootings, and shootings at school. Incidents that were out of the ordinary got transformed into representative examples of youths out of control. Plus there were new numbers produced to dramatize the extent of youth crime. These data were carefully selected by "experts" and reiterated by commentators. They wanted to frighten the public. In the end they succeeded, even more than they wished. Youths became marginalized, and the crime scare got out of hand.

Key Terms

Plague:	a sudden, destructive outbreak
Epidemic:	an outbreak of disease that spreads rapidly
Coddling:	pampering, treating like a baby
Moral panic:	public fears fanned by media scare tactics
Predatory:	victimizing others for one's own gain
Racist:	being prejudiced or discriminatory against people of another race
Inner cities:	central parts of cities where minorities and low-income residents are concentrated
Ethnocentrism:	believing that one's own group is superior to other groups
Sociopaths:	people who have a personality disorder featuring aggression and antisocial behavior
Feral beings:	wild animals or savages
Atavistic:	having a trait that is a reversion to an earlier stage of evolution
Dysfunctional homes:	impaired families that fail to raise children properly
Rite of passage:	an event symbolizing moving to another stage (such as from adolescence to adulthood)
Demographic time bomb:	a large group of people is about to enter an age when their tendency to commit crime and wreak havoc on society reaches its peak
Tabloids:	small-format papers that condense the news and focus on the vivid and sensational
Yellow journalism:	an exaggeration of the news that dwells on the most extreme instances of behavior
News values:	criteria used by editors when deciding which stories to emphasize and which ones to downplay or ignore
Alarmists:	those who proclaim that crime rates are rapidly rising at the moment and are higher than ever before

Superpredators:	those who repeatedly commit especially violent and vicious offenses
Chronic offenders:	those who commit many offenses; repeat offenders
"Dear Abby" tables:	tables that are incomplete and percentaged in the wrong direction for causal interpretations
Meta-analyses:	reports that combine many previous studies to reveal how strongly two variables are related (using a common measure of association)
Status offenses:	behaviors that are not illegal if engaged in by adults but are illegal if juveniles commit them
Focus group:	a sample of people chosen from the larger population and asked by researchers to have an open discussion of a selected topic
Milieu therapy:	a setting in which all the workers are expected to contribute to the rehabilitation of the individual (not just the therapists)
Mitigating factor:	a factor that makes the offense less serious or the offender less blameworthy
Social construction:	problems are made to seem worse than they really are by the mass media, ideology, hysteria, political power, and so on

End Notes

[1] Erich Goode and Nachman Ben-Yehuda, *Moral Panics* (Cambridge, MA: Blackwell, 1994); Kenneth Thompson, *Moral Panics* (London: Routledge, 1998); James C. Howell, *Preventing and Reducing Juvenile Delinquency* (Thousand Oaks, CA: Sage, 2003); Patricia M. Torbet and Linda Szymanski, *State Legislative Responses to Violent Juvenile Crime: 1996–1997 Update* (Washington: Office of Juvenile Justice and Delinquency Prevention, 1998).

[2] Rita Kramer, "Taking Off the Kid Gloves," *City Journal, 4*, no. 2 (Spring 1994), pp. 48–53; Richard Zoglin, "Now for the Bad News," *Time* (January 15, 1996), pp. 52–3; James Alan Fox, "The Calm Before the Juvenile Crime Storm," *Population Today, 24*, no. 9 (September 1996), pp. 4–5; John J. DiIulio, Jr., "My Black Crime Problem, and Ours," *City Journal, 6*, no. 2 (Spring 1996), pp. 14–28; Dave Shiflett, "Crime in the South," *Oxford American* (Spring 1996), pp. 136–7; Paul J. McNulty, "Natural Born Killers?" *Policy Review,* no. 71 (Winter 1995), pp. 84–7.

[3] John J. DiIulio, Jr., "Crime in America: It's Going to Get Worse," *Reader's Digest* (August 1995), pp. 55–60; Don Sundquist, "Con," *Congressional Digest, 79*, nos. 8–9 (August 1996), pp. 197, 199, 201; Marc Smirnoff, "In Praise of Prisons," *Oxford American* (Spring 1996), pp. 6–7; Glenn Loury, "The Impossible Dilemma," *New Republic* (January 1, 1996), pp. 21–5.

[4]James Q. Wilson, "What to Do About Crime," *Commentary* (September 1994), p. 26; John J. DiIulio, Jr., "My Black Crime Problem, and Ours," p. 14; James Alan Fox, "The Calm Before the Juvenile Crime Storm," p. 4; Mortimer B. Zuckerman, "What to Do About Crime," *U.S. News and World Report* (November 8, 1993), p. 99; David Rubinstein, "Cut Cultural Root of Rising Crime," *Insight on the News* (August 8, 1994), pp. 18–20.

[5]John J. DiIulio, Jr., "The Question of Black Crime," *The Public Interest* (Fall 1994), p. 3; William J. Bennett, *Commentary* (November 1995), p. 29; Richard Lacayo, "Lock 'em Up," *Time* (February 7, 1994), p. 52; Richard Lacayo, "When Kids Go Bad," *Time* (September 19, 1994), p. 61; Craig Sautter, "Standing Up to Violence," *Phi Delta Kappan, 76*, no. 5 (January 1995), p. K3; Scott Minerbrook, "Lives Without Father," *U.S. News and World Report* (February 27, 1995), p. 50; Loic J. D. Wacquant, "Three Pernicious Premises in the Study of the American Ghetto," *International Journal of Urban and Regional Research, 21*, no. 2 (June 1997), pp. 341–53.

[6]Thomas Toch, Ted Gest, and Monika Guttman, "Violence in Schools," *U.S. News and World Report* (November 8, 1993), pp. 30–7; Ted Gest and Dorian Friedman, "The New Crime Wave," *U.S. News and World Report* (August 29, 1994), pp. 26–8; Ted Gest and Victoria Pope, "Crime Time Bomb," *U.S. News and World Report* (March 25, 1996), pp. 28–36; Scott Minerbrook, "A New Generation of Stone Killers," *U.S. News and World Report* (January 17, 1994), pp. 33–7; Alfred Blumstein, "Youth Violence, Guns, and the Illicit Drug Industry," *Journal of Criminal Law and Criminology, 86,* no. 1 (Fall 1995), pp. 10–36; Alfred Blumstein and Richard Rosenfeld, "Explaining Recent Trends in U.S. Homicide Rates," *Journal of Criminal Law and Criminology, 88,* no. 4 (Summer 1998), pp. 1175–216.

[7]Thomas Toch, Ted Gest, and Monika Guttman, "Violence in Schools"; Tom Morganthau, "The Lull Before the Storm," *Newsweek* (December 4, 1995), pp. 40–2; Jon D. Hull, "A Boy and His Gun," *Time* (August 2, 1993), pp. 20–7; Glenn Loury, "The Impossible Dilemma"; David T. Lykken, *The Antisocial Personalities* (Hillsdale, NJ: Erlbaum, 1995).

[8]James Wootton and Robert O. Heck, "How State and Local Officials Can Combat Violent Juvenile Crime," *http://www.heritage.org* (October 28, 1996), p. 4

[9]James Alan Fox, "Pro," *Congressional Digest* (August 1996), pp. 206, 208, 210, 212; Richard Zoglin, "Now for the Bad News"; James Q. Wilson, "What to Do About Crime."

[10]Mortimer B. Zuckerman, "What to Do About Crime"; Rita Kramer, "Taking Off the Kid Gloves"; Patrick Fagan, "The Real Root Cause of Violent Crime," *Vital Speeches of the Day* (December 15, 1995), pp. 157–8; John J. DiIulio, Jr., "How to Deal with the Youth Crime Wave," *Weekly Standard* (September 16, 1996), pp. 30–2; Andrew Peyton Thomas, "The South Must Save the Union," *Oxford American* (Spring 1996), pp. 27–30; Ed Rubenstein, "The Economics of Crime," *Vital Speeches of the Day* (October 15, 1995), pp. 19–21; Paul J. McNulty, "Natural Born Killers?"; James Alan Fox and Glenn Pierce, "American Killers are Getting Younger," *USA Today* (January 1994), pp. 24–6.

[11]Richard Lacayo, "When Kids Go Bad"; Rita Kramer, "Taking Off the Kid Gloves"; Eugene H. Methvin, "We Must Get Tough with Killer Kids," *Reader's Digest* (June 1993), pp. 103–7; Don Sundquist, "Con"; Paul J. McNulty, "Natural Born Killers?"

[12]Laureen D'Ambra, "A Legal Response to Juvenile Crime," *Roger Williams University Law Review, 2* (Spring 1997), p. 296; Ted Conover, *Newjack* (New York: Random House, 2000), pp. 19–20.

[13]Mortimer B. Zuckerman, "What to Do About Crime"; Jill Smolowe, ". . . And Throw Away the Key," *Time* (February 7, 1994), pp. 54–9; Barbara Kantrowitz, "Wild in the Streets," *Newsweek* (August 2, 1993), pp. 40–7; Adam Walinsky, "The Crisis of Public Order," *Atlantic* (July 1995), pp. 39–54.

[14]Hal Crowther, "Unsafe at Any Speed," *Oxford American* (Spring 1996), pp. 16–7.

[15]Ted Gest and Dorian Friedman, "The New Crime Wave"; Ted Gest and Victoria Pope, "Crime Time Bomb"; James Alan Fox, "The Calm Before the Juvenile Crime Storm"; James Alan Fox, "Pro"; James Q. Wilson, "What to Do About Crime."

[16]Dave Shiflett, "Crime in the South"; Glenn Loury, "The Impossible Dilemma."

[17]Ted Gest and Dorian Friedman, "The New Crime Wave"; Ted Gest and Victoria Pope, "Crime Time Bomb"; Mortimer B. Zuckerman, "Scary Kids Around the Corner," *U.S. News and World Report* (December 4, 1995), p. 96; Richard Zoglin, "Now for the Bad News"; John J. DiIulio, Jr., "Crime in America"; James Q. Wilson, "What to Do About Crime"; Adam Walinsky, "The Crisis of Public Order"; Brian Bird, "Reclaiming the Urban War Zones," *Christianity Today* (January 15, 1990), p. 17; Peter Brimelow, "The Wild Ones," *Forbes* (February 24, 1997), pp. 46–8; Cheryl Russell, "True Crime," *American Demographics, 17* (August 1995), pp. 22–6.

[18]James Ford, *Forty-Odd Years in the Literary Shop* (New York: Dutton, 1921), p. 260.

[19]Quoted in James Traub, "The Criminals of Tomorrow," *The New Yorker* (November 4, 1996), p. 53.

[20]Howard N. Snyder and Melissa Sickmund, *Juvenile Offenders and Victims* (Washington: National Center for Juvenile Justice, September 1999); James C. Howell, *Preventing and Reducing Juvenile Delinquency.*

[21]Donna M. Bishop, Charles E. Frazier, Lonn Lanza-Kaduce, and Lawrence Winner, "The Transfer of Juveniles to Criminal Court," *Crime and Delinquency, 42,* no. 2 (April 1996), pp. 171–91; Jeffrey Fagan, "The Comparative Advantage of Juvenile Versus Criminal Court Sanctions on Recidivism Among Adolescent Felony Offenders," *Law and Policy, 18,* no. 1 (January 1996), pp. 77–114; James C. Howell, *Preventing and Reducing Juvenile Delinquency.*

[22]Marvin D. Free, Jr., "Clarifying the Relationship Between the Broken Home and Juvenile Delinquency," *Deviant Behavior, 12,* no. 2 (April 1991), pp. 109–67.

[23]L. Edward Wells and Joseph H. Rankin, "Families and Delinquency," *Social Problems, 38,* no. 1 (February 1991), pp. 71–90.

[24]Robert Lichter, Stanley Rothman, and Linda Lichter, *The Media Elite* (Bethesda, MD: Adler and Adler, 1986); Bernard Goldberg, *Bias* (Washington: Regnery, 2001); Ann Coulter, *Slander* (New York: Crown, 2002).

[25]Roy Edward Lotz, *Crime and the American Press* (New York: Praeger, 1991).

[26]Kathleen Daly, "Celebrated Crime Cases and the Public's Imagination," *Australian and New Zealand Journal of Criminology,* Special supplementary issue (1995), pp. 6–22.

[27]Julian V. Roberts and Anthony N. Doob, "News Media Influences on Public Views of Sentencing," *Law and Human Behavior, 14,* no. 5 (October 1990), pp. 451–68.

[28]Lori Dorfman, Katie Woodruff, and Vivian Chavez, "Youth and Violence on Local Television News in California," *American Journal of Public Health, 87,* no. 8 (August 1997), pp. 1311–16; Elizabeth Gleick, "Did He or Didn't He?" *Time* (February 6, 1995), pp. 56–9.

[29]"Gallup Short Subjects," *Gallup Poll Monthly,* no. 391 (April 1998), pp. 22–45.

[30]James Turpin, "How Much Does the Public Know?" *Corrections Today, 61,* no. 3 (June 1999), p. 16.

[31]Harold G. Grasmick and Anne L. McGill, "Religion, Attribution Style, and Punitiveness Toward Juvenile Offenders," *Criminology, 32,* no. 1 (February 1994), pp. 23–46.

[32]Christy M. Buchanan and Grayson N. Holmbeck, "Measuring Beliefs About Adolescent Personality and Behavior," *Journal of Youth and Adolescence, 27,* no. 5 (October 1998), pp. 607–27.

[33]Charles R. Acland, *Youth, Murder, Spectacle* (Boulder, CO: Westview, 1995).

[34]Theodore Sasson, *Crime Talk: How Citizens Construct a Social Problem* (Hawthorne, NY: Aldine de Gruyter, 1995), p. 64.

[35]Steve Farkas and Jean Johnson, *Kids These Days: What Americans Really Think About the Next Generation* (New York: Public Agenda, 1997).

[36]Charlie Cook, "Behind the Sudden Surge of Pessimism," *National Journal* (July 10, 1999), pp. 2038–9.

[37]Steve Farkas and Jean Johnson, *Kids These Days: What Americans Really Think About the Next Generation,* p. 40.

[38]David W. Moore, "Majority Advocate Death for Teenage Killers," *Gallup Poll Monthly,* no. 348 (September 1994), pp. 2–6.

[39]Jane B. Sprott, "Understanding Public Views of Youth Crime and the Youth Justice System," *Canadian Journal of Criminology, 38,* no. 3 (July 1996), pp. 271–90.

[40]"Racial Overtones Evident in Americans' Attitudes About Crime," *Gallup Poll Monthly,* no. 339 (December 1993), pp. 37–42.

[41]Michael Elliott, "Crime and Punishment," *Newsweek* (April 18, 1994), pp. 18–22.

[42]Brandon K. Applegate, Francis T. Cullen, Michael G. Turner, and Jody L. Sundt, "Assessing Public Support for Three-Strikes-and-You're-Out Laws," *Crime and Delinquency, 42,* no. 4 (October 1996), pp. 517–34; Vincent Schiraldi and Mark Soler, "The Will of the People?" *Crime and Delinquency, 44,* no. 4 (October 1998), pp. 590–601.

[43]Julian V. Roberts and Loretta J. Stalans, *Public Opinion and Criminal Justice* (Boulder, CO: Westview, 2000).

[44]Phoebe C. Ellsworth and Samuel R. Gross, "Hardening of Attitudes," *Journal of Social Issues, 50,* no. 2 (Summer 1994), pp. 19–52.

[45]Jody L. Sundt, Francis T. Cullen, Brandon K. Applegate, and Michael G. Turner, "The Tenacity of the Rehabilitative Ideal Revisited," *Criminal Justice and Behavior, 25,* no. 4 (December 1998), pp. 426–42; George Pettinico, "Crime and Punishment," *Public Perspective, 5,* no. 6 (September 1994), pp. 29–32.

[46]Jane B. Sprott, "Understanding Public Opposition to a Separate Youth Justice System," *Crime and Delinquency, 44,* no. 3 (July 1998), pp. 399–411.

[47]Stephen W. Baron and Timothy F. Hartnagel, "'Lock 'em Up:' Attitudes Toward Punishing Juvenile Offenders," *Canadian Journal of Criminology, 38,* no. 2 (April 1996), pp. 191–212.

[48]John W. Gonzalez, "Many in Poll Want Stiffer Laws on Juvenile Criminals," *Houston Chronicle,* June 21, 1998, p. 1.

[49]Christopher A. Innes, "Recent Public Opinion in the United States Toward Punishment and Corrections," *Prison Journal, 73,* no. 2 (June 1993), pp. 220–36.

[50]Ira M. Schwartz, Shenyang Guo, and John J. Kerbs, "The Impact of Demographic Variables on Public Opinion Regarding Juvenile Justice," *Crime and Delinquency, 38,* no. 1 (January 1993), pp. 22–3.

[51]Sara Rimer and Raymond Bonner, "Young and Condemned," *New York Times,* August 22, 2000, p. A1; Peter Elikann, *Superpredators* (New York: Insight Books, 1999).

[52]David W. Moore, "Majority Advocate Death for Teenage Killers."

[53]Charles W. Thomas and Samuel C. Foster, "A Sociological Perspective on Public Support for Capital Punishment," *American Journal of Orthopsychiatry, 45,* no. 4 (July 1975), pp. 641–57.

[54]Ezzat A. Fattah, "Perceptions About Violence, Concern About Crime, Fear of Victimization, and Attitudes Toward the Death Penalty," *Canadian Journal of Criminology, 21,* no. 1 (January 1979), pp. 22–38; James Alan Fox, Michael Radelet, and Julie L. Bonsteel, "Death-Penalty Opinion in the Post-Furman Years," *New York University Review of Law and Social Change, 18,* no. 2 (1991), pp. 499–528; Joseph H. Rankin, "Changing Attitudes Toward Capital Punishment," *Social Forces, 58,* no. 1 (September 1979), pp. 194–211; Arthur L. Stinchcombe, Rebecca Adams, Carol A. Heimer, Kim Lane Scheppele, Tom W. Smith, and D. Garth Taylor, *Crime and Punishment* (San Francisco: Jossey-Bass, 1980); Tom R. Tyler and Renee Webber, "Support for the Death Penalty," *Law and Society Review, 17,* no. 1 (February 1982), pp. 21–45.

[55]Roy Lotz and Robert M. Regoli, "Public Support for the Death Penalty," *Criminal Justice Review, 5,* no. 1 (Spring 1980), pp. 55–66.

[56]Samuel R. Gross, "American Public Opinion on the Death Penalty—It's Getting Personal," *Cornell Law Review, 83* (September 1998), pp. 1448–69.

[57]Tom R. Tyler and Robert J. Boeckmann, "Three Strikes and You're Out, but Why?" *Law and Society Review, 31,* no. 2 (June 1997), pp. 237–65; Marian J. Borg, "The Southern Subculture of Punitiveness?" *Journal of Research in Crime and Delinquency, 34,* no. 1 (February 1997), pp. 25–45; Steven E. Barkan and Steven F. Cohn, "Racial Prejudice and Support for the Death Penalty by Whites," *Journal of Research in Crime and Delinquency, 31,* no. 2 (May 1994), pp. 202–9; M. Shelley Curtis, "Attitudes Toward the Death Penalty as it Relates to Political Party Affiliation, Religious Belief, and Faith in

People," *Free Inquiry in Creative Sociology, 19,* no. 2 (November 1991), pp. 205–12; Robert M. Bohm, *The Death Penalty in America* (Cincinnati: Anderson, 1991); John A. Arthur, "Racial Attitudes and Opinions About Capital Punishment," *International Journal of Comparative and Applied Criminal Justice, 22,* no. 1 (Spring 1998), pp. 131–44.

[58]Margaret Vandiver and David Giacopassi, "One Million and Counting," *Journal of Criminal Justice Education, 8,* no. 2 (Fall 1997), pp. 135–43.

[59]Eric R. Lotke, "Youth Homicide: Keeping Perspective on How Many Kill," *Valparaiso University Law Review, 31* (Spring 1997), pp. 395–418.

[60]Ronald W. Fagan, Sources of Pro-Criminal Justice System Sentiment. Unpublished Ph.D. dissertation, Washington State University (1978).

[61]Richard C. McCorkle, "Punish and Rehabilitate?" *Crime and Delinquency, 39,* no. 2 (April 1993), pp. 240–52.

[62]Malcolm Potts and Roger Short, *Ever Since Adam and Eve* (New York: Cambridge University Press, 1999); Richard Morin and John M. Berry, "A Nation that Poor-Mouths Its Good Times," *Washington Post,* October 13, 1996, p. A1; Michael J. Mazarr, "The Pessimism Syndrome," *Washington Quarterly* (Summer 1998), p. 94; James Turpin, "Knowledge of the Juvenile Justice System," *Corrections Today, 61,* no. 3 (June 1999), p. 17.

[63]Julian V. Roberts and Loretta J. Stalans, *Public Opinion and Criminal Justice.*

[64]Ezzat A. Fattah, "Public Opposition to Prison Alternatives and Community Corrections," *Canadian Journal of Criminology, 24,* no. 4 (October 1982), pp. 371–85; Sharon Begley, "The Roots of Evil," *Newsweek* (May 21, 2001), pp. 30–5.

[65]Ed McBain, *The Big Bad City* (New York: Simon and Schuster, 1999), pp. 31–2.

[66]Corina Eckl, "Playing Hardball with Criminals," *State Legislatures, 20,* no. 9 (September 1994), p. 14.

[67]Leslie Phillips, "Crime Pays—as a Political Issue," *USA Today* (October 10, 1994), p. 11A.

[68]Christopher Johns, "Politics of Crime in 2000," *Arizona Republic* (July 3, 1994), p. C1.

[69]John Irwin, James Austin, and Chris Baird, "Fanning the Flames of Fear," *Crime and Delinquency, 44,* no. 1 (January 1998), p. 32.

[70]Alfred Blumstein and Jacqueline Cohen, "A Theory of the Stability of Punishment," *Journal of Criminal Law and Criminology, 64,* no. 2 (June 1973), pp. 198–207.

[71]Marc Mauer, *The Race to Incarcerate* (New York: The New Press, 1999), pp., 21–2.

[72]Alfred Blumstein and Allen J. Beck, "Population Growth in U.S. Prisons, 1980–1996," in Michael Tonry and Joan Petersilia, eds., *Prisons* (Chicago: University of Chicago Press, 1999), pp. 17–61.

[73]Edwin W. Zedlewski, *Making Confinement Decisions* (Washington: National Institute of Justice, July 1987).

[74]Robert Martinson, "What Works?—Questions and Answers About Prison Reform," *The Public Interest* (Spring 1974), pp. 22–54.

[75]Mark W. Lipsey, "Juvenile Delinquency Treatment," in Thomas D. Cook, ed., *Meta Analysis for Explanation* (New York: Russell Sage, 1992), pp. 83–127.

[76]Michael Tonry, "Rethinking Unthinkable Punishment Policies in America," *UCLA Law Review, 46,* no. 6 (August 1999), pp. 1751–91; Greg Krikorian, "Juvenile Justice Systems—A Success Story Under Fire," *Los Angeles Times,* July 7, 1999, p. A1; Fox Butterfield, "With Juvenile Courts in Chaos, Some Propose Scrapping Them," *New York Times,* July 21, 1997, p. A1; Craig Hemmens, Eric J. Fritsch, and Tory J. Caeti, "The Rhetoric of Juvenile Justice Reform," *Quinnipiac Law Review, 18* (1999), pp. 661–685; Barry C. Feld, "Race and the Crackdown on Youth Crime," *Minnesota Law Review, 84,* no. 2 (December 1999), pp. 327–95; Joseph F. Yeckel, "Violent Juvenile Offenders: Rethinking Federal Intervention in Juvenile Justice," *Washington University Journal of Urban and Contemporary Law, 51* (Winter 1997), pp. 331–62; James C. Howell, *Preventing and Reducing Juvenile Delinquency.*

[77]Elizabeth S. Scott and Thomas Grisso, "The Evolution of Adolescence," *Journal of Criminal Law and Criminology," 88,* no. 1 (Fall 1997), pp. 137–89.

[78]Russell K. Van Vleet, "The Attack on Juvenile Justice," *Annals of the American Academy of Political and Social Science,* no. 564 (July 1999), pp. 203–14; Wendy Kaminer, "Federal Offense," *Atlantic* (June 1994), p. 114.

[79]Tom Teepen, "Justice Would be Served if Juvenile Crime Bill Were to Die," *Atlanta Journal and Constitution,* May 31, 1998, p. 3E.

[80]Richard K. Willard, "There is No Alternative to Building More Prisons," *The American Enterprise* (May/June 1995), pp. 46–8.

Recommended Readings

James C. Howell, *Preventing and Reducing Juvenile Delinquency* (Thousand Oaks, CA: Sage, 2003).

Gary W. Potter and Victor E. Kappeler, *Constructing Crime* (Prospect Heights, IL: Waveland Press, 1998), especially the article by Vincent Sacco.

Richard C. McCorkle and Terance D. Miethe, *Panic* (Upper Saddle River, NJ: Prentice Hall, 2002).

Roy Edward Lotz, *Crime and the American Press* (New York: Praeger, 1991).

Theodore Sasson, *Crime Talk: How Citizens Construct a Social Problem* (Hawthorne, NY: Aldine de Gruyter, 1995).

Timothy J. Flanagan and Dennis R. Longmire, eds., *Americans View Crime and Justice* (Thousand Oaks, CA: Sage, 1996).

Ray Surette, *Media, Crime, and Criminal Justice,* 2nd ed. (Belmont, CA: West/Wadsworth, 1998).

Doris A. Graber, *Crime News and the Public* (New York: Praeger, 1980).

CHAPTER 2

Official Data, Self-Reports, and Victim Surveys

On occasion, a crime story can be so riveting it makes readers identify with the victim or fear they'll be next.[1] Before the crime's grisly details are burned into our long-term memory, though, maybe we should step back a moment and reflect on some basic facts about the craft of journalism. News organizations don't print everything (far from it); when it comes to crime, for instance, they are very selective about which incidents to cover. Completely ignoring the minor, prosaic larceny, they reserve their biggest headlines for vicious cases that fit melodramatic stereotypes, such as a fearsome, unprovoked predator attacking a weak, defenseless victim (Exhibit 2-1). Moreover, there are millions of people who sail through life unscathed, that is, without once being raped, robbed, assaulted, or murdered. Their ordinary lives go unmentioned because journalists are preoccupied with bad news. In their profession, good news is not considered news at all; instead, to their way of thinking, it is a contradiction in terms.

Geared to entertainment and voyeurism, commercial news offers a slice of Americana laden with slaughter and scandals. Readers interested in a more accurate picture of the world in general and crime specifically would be wise to turn elsewhere, such as

1. Respected sociology journals (*American Sociological Review, American Journal of Sociology,* and *Social Forces*)
2. Research journals in criminology (*Criminology, Journal of Research in Crime and Delinquency,* and *Journal of Quantitative Criminology*)

3. Textbooks or readers (i.e., books containing a collection of articles) devoted to the study of crime and delinquency)[4]
4. Summary reports by the Department of Justice that contain graphs, tables of statistics, and accompanying discussion
5. College courses taught by reputable scholars who have spent decades studying the area

---

EXHIBIT 2-1   Example of How Crimes are Covered in Newspapers

Crimes the media dwell on are not typical of crimes in general. This can be illustrated by describing a particular case. Several years ago an Atlanta man was victimized. Here are some of the basic facts as described by reporters in the local paper.

1. Because Charles Conrad, 55, a former sales manager, suffered from multiple sclerosis, he had to use either a walker or wheelchair to get around.
2. One day, three youngsters sneaked into his home, tied him up, and tortured him for more than 24 hours.
3. After hitting him in the head with a sawed-off shotgun, they demanded his money and bank account numbers.
4. The offenders, using seven knives and a barbecue fork, stabbed him 40 times in the back and neck, then poured salt in his wounds to see if he was still alive.
5. Mr. Conrad asked for the shotgun, so he could kill himself and bring a merciful end to his suffering.
6. Finally, the youths hit him in the back with a brass eagle and he bled to death.
7. The offenders then left the home, taking his wheelchair-equipped van, a stereo, VCR, camcorder, and shotgun.[2]

This incident, like most media reports of criminal incidents, emphasizes the exceptional. Despite what stories on television and in print imply, *most crimes are not violent, and only a small fraction of violent crimes are murders.* Unlike the unfortunate Mr. Conrad, most robbery victims are not murdered, and very few murder victims are tortured. Not many murder victims are as old as Mr. Conrad was. Rarely are they middle-class and minding their own business. Finally, most of the people who commit murder are *not* youngsters under 18. *Newsweek* could have soothed its largely middle-class, middle-aged readers by noting that the chances of this crime happening to *them* were virtually nil. Instead, it warned that this was "not an isolated incident" and suggested that teenagers as a generation are bent on murder and mayhem.[3]

Official Data

Because most criminologists are social scientists, they rely on social science data. There are many ways to categorize such data, including primary versus secondary. **Primary data** are those that (1) you analyze and (2) are taken from a study that you designed with your own research purposes in mind. **Secondary data** are taken from *someone else's study*, which was designed for that person's purposes, not yours. The advantage of primary data is obvious: they are tailor-made for answering questions that are central to your interests. All the items are intended to shed light on your intellectual concerns.

Typically, the lone scholar does not have a large grant and instead has to make do with a modest sample and a one-shot cross-sectional study. A large research organization, on the other hand, can produce a massive data set, because it has the funds, personnel, time, experience, and expertise. Hence, it will generate data that scholars around the nation could access and analyze. The user would first want to find out if the study included questions or variables that fit his or her research interests. These might include, for example, criminal or deviant behavior, plus other variables such as sex, age, class, attitudes, and beliefs.

When it comes to the basic facts about the nature and incidence of crime, financially strapped lone scholars do not supply the data. Instead, these come from a secondary source known as **official data** (i.e., administrative statistics generated by officials who work in the juvenile justice or criminal justice system). The resulting statistics are a by-product of officials' record-keeping in police departments, courts, or correctional agencies. The most frequently mentioned data on deviant youth are the Uniform Crime Reports (UCR) of the Federal Bureau of Investigation (FBI) and Juvenile Court Statistics of the Office of Juvenile Justice and Delinquency Prevention.

Of the two, the FBI data are cited much more often. They are police statistics and include primarily (1) crimes known to the police and (2) arrests made by the police in cities and towns around the country. These data have been forwarded to Washington, D.C., where they're compiled and published once a year. The annual FBI report does not reveal what happens to the arrested individuals later—that is, whether they are sent to juvenile or criminal court and whether they end up in an institution.

The category "crimes known to the police" includes a large number of criminal incidents but not a *complete* listing of them. Inevitably, it underestimates the number of crimes committed, because several stages must be passed through before a crime gets recorded as known to the police.

1. A crime must take place (of course).
2. Someone, typically the victim, must witness it.
3. The witness must call the police and notify them of the incident.
4. The precinct must send out a patrol car to investigate.
5. Patrol officers must agree that the act constitutes a real crime.
6. They must be willing to write it down.
7. This information must be compiled, passed on, and accepted as valid by the FBI.

If this process is interrupted anywhere along the line, the incident does not become part of "crimes known to the police." Perhaps there was no witness, or the witness failed to call the police (because the property would not be recovered, the crime was unsuccessful or the harm was negligible, or it was considered a private matter). Maybe police were called but never showed up, or they arrived at the scene but decided not to call the incident a crime. Attrition occurs, and as a result the recorded number of crimes is lower than the true number. This gap between the true number of crimes and the recorded number is known as *the* **dark figure of crime.**[5]

$$\text{True Number} - \text{Recorded Number} = \text{Dark Figure of Crime}$$

This figure can only be estimated because the true number is unknown. The dark figure is especially large for nonserious crimes, attempts, and **"victimless crimes"** (drug use, prostitution, drunkenness, disorderly conduct, and gambling), which are often known only to the participants, who don't want the police to discover what they're up to.

When tallying the number of crimes known to the police, the FBI emphasizes a select few called the *Crime Index.* This well-known index includes

1. Murder and nonnegligent manslaughter: willful killing of one human by another
2. Forcible rape: carnal knowledge of a female by force and against her will (includes attempts)
3. Robbery: taking something of value from someone by force or threat of force (includes attempts)
4. Aggravated assault: unlawful attack on someone in order to inflict severe bodily injury, usually by using a weapon (includes attempts)
5. Burglary: unlawful entry of a structure to commit a felony or theft
6. Larceny-theft: unlawfully taking property from another via shoplifting, pocket-picking, purse-snatching, or from motor vehicles (no force or fraud)
7. Motor vehicle theft: the vehicles that are stolen may be cars, trucks, buses, motorcycles, motor scooters, or snowmobiles (includes joyriding)
8. Arson: willful or malicious burning of a house, public building, motor vehicle, aircraft, or personal property

Tradition endows these items with greater significance than they deserve. When social scientists construct an index, all items in it must reflect *the same concept.* Unfortunately, the Crime Index items tap two distinctly different concepts: (A) very serious crimes that occur comparatively rarely, such as murder, rape, and robbery and (B) much less serious crimes that occur quite often, such as larceny and burglary. (Aggravated assault and motor vehicle theft are difficult to classify, whereas arson is usually counted by fire departments, who have a habit of not relaying the information to the police.)[6]

Many Americans assume that Index offenses are brutal and appalling. In fact, some are *not serious,* and these nonserious crimes are the most common.

Larceny-theft, typically shoplifting, makes up *60 percent* of all the index crimes recorded. Burglary adds another *20 percent.* This leaves little room in the index (only 20 percent) for *all the other offenses.* At the serious end of the spectrum, murder makes up only *one-tenth of 1 percent* of the total number of index crimes each year, and forcible rape also constitutes less than 1 percent. Including the terms "murder" and "rape" gives the Index the *appearance* of high seriousness and provides ammunition for political bluster, but these two crimes are so rare (compared to the others) that they carry little actual weight. They have virtually no effect on whether the total number of Index offenses rises or falls from year to year.

Using the Crime Index to describe the nature and extent of crime invites distortion and confusion. Therefore, researchers would be better off turning to the FBI's *entire list of crimes* (that is, Index crimes plus the many nonindex crimes). Or they could examine only one kind of crime at a time (say, burglary). A researcher might decide to use the violent crime index (murder, rape, robbery, aggravated assault) to reflect serious crime, but even this has drawbacks, because the number of murders and rapes is swamped by the far more common aggravated assaults and robberies.

Besides crimes known to police, the FBI also publishes the number of arrests made and characteristics of persons arrested. These data let criminologists peer into research questions they find compelling. The UCR identifies arrested persons by their age, sex, and race, and location (i.e., where the arrest occurred: city,

---

EXHIBIT 2-2   Purpose and Politics of the Uniform Crime Reports

Back in 1929, the International Association of Chiefs of Police (IACP) hoped that by creating the new UCR system it would bring order and consistency into crime statistics and discourage overblown rhetoric about crime waves. Up to that time, newspaper reporters and other people made exaggerated claims about crime, which tended to undermine the public's faith in government. Once the UCR was established, however, FBI director J. Edgar Hoover took full advantage of it. He had a penchant for scare tactics and liked to claim that crime was on a rampage and threatened every man, woman, and child. These ploys defeated the IACP's purpose, which was to create an objective reporting system.

The UCR system was designed to answer, above all else, one simple question: To what extent is crime rising or falling? But this proved to be a daunting task. Over the decades, police have become more competent, better educated, better trained, less corrupt; departments now keep far better records than they once did; computers have been introduced to the force; citizens now are more likely to have telephones and they are more willing to report crimes. The result is that *recorded* crime rates have increased over the years regardless of what has been happening to the *true* crime rate. Thus it is misleading to contrast today's crime rates with those of 1950, 1960, or 1970, when data collection was more haphazard.

suburban county, or rural county). Arrest data are provided for nonindex crimes as well, including other assaults, fraud, stolen property, weapons carrying, prostitution, drug abuse violations, drunkenness, disorderly conduct, and offenses against family and children.

With these statistics, researchers can explore many relationships, including the link between age and crime. Most Americans believe that crime is dominated by adolescents, and that adults have too much sense and civility to rob an Exxon station or steal a new Escalade. Some age groups do indeed account for more than their share of arrests, whereas others are less apt to offend. The very old and the very young commit a small fraction of the total number of offenses: senior citizens (people over 65) and preteens (people under 13) make up over 30 percent of the population but only two percent of the arrests.

On the other hand, 13- to 39-year-olds (with less than 40 percent of the population) are responsible for 82 percent of the arrests. Their **arrest rates** are considerably higher than their share of the population, as demonstrated by the figures in Table 2-1.

Although teenagers account for more than their share of arrests, they are not the only age group to do so. The media may neglect to mention it but "twenty-" and "thirty-somethings" also engage in more offenses than their relative population size warrants. Although the figures cited in Table 2-1 refer to age clusters of three or five years, it is possible to make finer distinctions, such as arrest rates for each year of age. These rates appear in Table 2-2 and are computed using a base of 10,000. The arrest rate is the number of arrests per 10,000 people of each age for the year in question. This is calculated by first dividing the number of arrests (for people that age) by the number of people that age in the United States. The resulting figure is multiplied by 10,000.

$$\text{Arrest rate} = 10,000 \times \frac{\text{Number of persons arrested}}{\text{Number of persons in the population}}$$

In Table 2-2, the first rate of arrest is for all FBI crimes (except curfew/loitering and running away), whereas the second arrest rate involves only the most serious crimes,

TABLE 2-1   Under-40 Age Distribution of the Population and of Persons Arrested

	U.S. population	Persons arrested[7]
Under 13	18.3%	1.7%
13 to 15	4.3	8.0
16 to 18	4.3	13.9
19 to 21	4.1	12.4
22 to 24	3.8	9.3
25 to 29	7.0	13.7
30 to 34	7.7	12.9
35 to 39	8.5	11.6

TABLE 2-2   Arrest Rates by Age for All Crimes and for the Most Serious Crimes

Age	Arrest rates: All crimes	Arrest rates: Most serious[8]
13–14	507	25
15	815	42
16	1039	55
17	1156	59
18	1406	68
19	1293	60
20	1178	54
21	1086	55
22	1010	50
23	965	49
24	899	46

namely, murder, forcible rape, robbery, and aggravated assault. (Most discussions of age and crime use the Crime Index, which is numerically dominated by larceny-thefts and burglaries, the two crimes in which youths are most overrepresented. Hence, *any study of age and crime* will be hopelessly biased if it relies on the Index.)

The press, public, and politicians typically believe that crime reaches its highest point during the juvenile years (i.e., *before the age of 18*). Renowned criminologists Travis Hirschi and Michael Gottfredson go so far as to argue that crime is dominated by youths in *all societies and all eras.*[9] But in Table 2-2, when all crimes are examined, the highest arrest rates occur among *adults,* specifically those aged 18, 19, and 20. Rather than being highest, 17-year-olds are only fourth in overall arrest rates. Persons aged 16 are further back, in sixth place. Indeed, *seven of the nine years with the highest total arrest rates are adult ages* (namely, the years 18 through 24). And a 13- or 14-year-old is only *half* as likely as a 22-year-old to get arrested.

These are arrest data. Do the results change markedly when we switch from arrests to clearances? Clearances are a better reflection of the proportion of crime committed by youngsters, because they count offenses, not offenders. (In *arrest data,* juveniles are overcounted as offenders because they tend to commit crimes together, that is, as part of a group). Data from 1999, like other years, show that juveniles account for a much lower percentage of clearances than of arrests: 35 percent of the motor vehicle theft arrests but only 19 percent of the clearances, 33 percent of burglary arrests but only 19 percent of the clearances, 25 percent of robbery arrests but only 15 percent of the clearances, 31 percent of larceny arrests but only 23 percent of the clearances.[10] Hence, clearance rates indicate that juvenile crime is rarer than is usually assumed.

The FBI is in the process of developing a new system for reporting crime and arrest statistics known as the National Incident-Based Reporting System (NIBRS).

This will include a large set of incident attributes for each crime. Using these data from several states, Howard Snyder discovered that

> expressed in terms of the odds of increased risk of arrest, and controlling for other incident characteristics, these data find that juvenile robbery offenders are 32% more likely to be arrested than are adult robbery offenders. . . . [It] appears that law enforcement agencies and the public treat all juvenile robberies as serious and make an arrest whenever possible. . . .[11]

Snyder has demonstrated that even clearances overstate the proportion of crimes that are committed by juveniles. One reason is that juveniles are less sophisticated, more likely to talk to other kids about their acts, and thus easier for the police to catch.

These findings on age and crime have implications for sanctions. You may recall (from Chapter 1) that alarmists often reproach the juvenile court, saying it fails to deter youngsters from a life of crime. They argue that juveniles take advantage of the court's excessive lenience, committing many more offenses than they would if it were strict. Only when they become eligible for criminal court, at age 18 in most states, do individuals curb their criminal tendencies; at that time, they do so in order to avoid severe punishment. If this conventional argument were valid, arrest rates would decline sharply between 17 and 18 (as they try to avoid tough sentences meted out by adult courts). But, in fact, instead of a decline between ages 17 and 18, arrests keep climbing and actually *reach their peak* at ages 18 and 19.

Thus far, we have been discussing *all crime*. Commentators who contend that *serious, violent crime* is the only crime that matters, however, may dismiss these findings—regarding arrests for all crimes—as immaterial. They may argue that juveniles have the highest arrest rates when it comes to the *serious offenses* such as murder, rape, robbery, and aggravated assault. Is this argument valid? Arrest rates for these offenses appear in the right-hand column of Table 2-2. Contrary to the commentators, adults aged 18 and 19 have the highest rates of arrest. This time, juveniles aged 17 finish third, and 16-year-olds are tied for fourth. Seven of the nine highest rates again involve adults aged 18 to 24. Once again, youths who are 13 and 14 have an arrest rate only half that of 22-year-olds. Hence, serious crime, like crime in general, is largely the province of adults.

Arrest data also permit criminologists to inspect other basic issues, for instance, differences between males and females. When it comes to arrests of people under age 18, as shown in Table 2-3, sex differences are substantial. This table includes (1) the offenses that produce a large number of arrests, plus (2) two of the most serious crimes, murder and rape.

From these findings, several conclusions can be drawn. First, males are overrepresented in juvenile arrests. This is true for every offense in the table except for the status offense of running away. Status offenses are ones that juveniles can be arrested for, but adults cannot. Theorists once predicted that when women become more liberated, they would closely approximate males in the number of violent crimes (according to Freda Adler) or property crimes (according to Rita James Simon). But these authors appear to have overstated their case. There is no sign

Table 2-3   The Percent Female of 1999 Arrestees Under Age 18[12]

1. Running away	59
2. Larceny-theft	36
3. Liquor laws	31
4. Other assaults	30
5. Curfew	30
6. Disorderly conduct	28
7. Aggravated assault	22
8. Drunkenness	20
9. DUI	17
10. Motor vehicle theft	16
11. Drug violations	14
12. Stolen property	13
13. Vandalism	12
14. Burglary	11
15. Weapons	9
16. Robbery	9
17. Murder	8
18. Forcible rape	2

Arrests remain dominated by males, but the number of females who have become gang members has risen over the years. (© *Scott Houston/Corbis. All rights reserved.*)

that juvenile or adult females are catching up to males in the number of arrests. Females accounted for 23 percent of juvenile arrests in 1997, which is the same percentage as in 1992.[13]

Second, the offenses where females are furthest behind males are the most serious offenses (i.e., murder, robbery, and of course, forcible rape). Where female arrests are closer to males, the offenses are mild and mundane: running away, curfew, larceny, and liquor laws. According to research conducted in Dunedin, New Zealand, boys suffer more **neurological** abnormalities than girls, perform worse on neurological tests at age 13, and do not read as well as girls; these risk factors explain much of the difference in male and female delinquency. In addition, boys are more hyperactive than girls and have more delinquent peers and weaker attachment to peers in general than girls have. Sex differences in early temperament and hyperactivity explain more than a third of the sex differences in deviance. Differences in peer relationships explain one-fourth of the sex differences in antisocial behavior.[14]

Data on race and crime are, in a sense, the opposite of those on gender and crime. *According to official data,* whereas females commit fewer and less-serious crimes than males, blacks commit more of them and more serious ones than whites.

Because African Americans make up only 15 percent of the youthful population, most of the arrest percentages in this table are quite high. Why this should be the case is unknown, though various explanations have been offered. One of them

TABLE 2-4   Percent of 1999 Arrestees Under Age 18 Who Were Black[15]

1. Robbery	54
2. Murder	49
3. Motor vehicle theft	39
4. Stolen property	38
5. Aggravated assault	35
6. Forcible rape	34.5
7. Other assaults	32
8. Disorderly conduct	31
9. Weapons	30
10. Drug violations	29
11. Larceny-theft	26
12. Curfew	25
13. Burglary	24.5
14. Running away	18
15. Vandalism	15.5
16. Drunkenness	8
17. DUI	5
18. Liquor laws	5

attributes the higher crime rates to social conditions in African Americans' daily lives. That is, blacks are much more likely than whites to reside in underclass neighborhoods with concentrated poverty and other problems (e.g., discrimination) that few whites ever have to contend with, and these conditions contribute significantly to criminality. Robert Sampson is among those who argue that blacks are more exposed to criminogenic structural conditions. He says that

1. Race and poverty tend to be confounded.
2. Even whites who are poor rarely live in urban poverty zones; poor blacks, however, often do.
3. Most poor blacks live in areas with high rates of family disruption, whereas poor whites, even those from broken homes, usually live in neighborhoods in which there is considerable family stability.
4. There is not a single city over 100,000 in which blacks live in ecological equality with whites (that is, the proportion living in poverty and the proportion of single-parent families).

Accordingly, racial differences in poverty and family disruption are so strong that the "worst" urban contexts in which whites reside are considerably better off than the average context of black communities.[16]

This is a **structural argument,** that is, it's based on how communities or ecological zones affect crime rates. In general, structuralists such as Sampson focus on the way crime is linked to poverty and disorganization. They say that very disadvantaged neighborhoods have high crime rates, whether they are white communities or black ones. This is because disadvantaged neighborhoods are isolated from mainstream society and conventional role models, and they lack formal and informal mechanisms of social control. At issue is *not race itself* but living in a dangerous and disadvantaged area.[17]

A second point of view emphasizes the impact of police culture and practices. Are police actions, particularly arrests, influenced by the police officer's beliefs about blacks? Some social scientists think so. According to Wordes and Bynum, *juvenile officers* believe that black youths are overrepresented in court referrals for various reasons: (1) single-parent homes and lack of supervision, (2) neighborhoods high in poverty and unemployment, (3) problems with drugs or grades, (4) officers biased and neighbors more likely to report black youths, and (5) black youths commit more, and more serious, offenses. *Patrol officers* believe more black youths are arrested because they act suspicious or are out of place, are not supervised or controlled by parents, or have a hostile attitude toward the police.[18]

Because, as structuralists point out, race is closely associated with social class, this leads to the next question: Is crime largely dominated by the lower class? Are people from the lower class much more likely to get arrested than others? The Uniform Crime Reports do not provide an answer to such questions because they do not include data on the arrestee's income, education, or occupational status.

Occasionally, though, researchers have used arrest data in a particular city to examine the link between crime and *neighborhood* social class. In Philadelphia, for instance, Wolfgang, Figlio, and Sellin found that boys living in lower-class census areas had more police contacts than boys from elsewhere. Almost half (45 percent) of the former had at least one contact; only about one-fourth (27 percent) of boys from other areas had any.[19] Studies generally find that areas of concentrated poverty have much higher arrest rates for serious and violent crime.

Self-Report Studies of Youth

In the early years of criminology in America, scholars had only official data to work with, usually those produced by the police. Criminologists may have had some misgivings about these data, but in the absence of an alternative there was little they could do. Prospects brightened when **self-reports** were introduced. These **surveys** (that is, interviews or questionnaires) asked members of the general population, usually high school or junior high students, whether they had committed various criminal or deviant acts. It was quickly discovered that they had indeed— far more often than police records showed. After some preliminary work in the 1940s, self-reports entered the mainstream in the 1950s, thanks to a series of articles by James Short and Ivan Nye.[20]

These sociologists sampled white high school youth from small towns and rural areas in the Pacific Northwest and the Midwest. Kids answered anonymous questionnaires about their own deviant behavior. Rather than inquire about serious offenses like robbery or aggravated assault, Short and Nye elected to focus on minor mischief: drinking beer, taking little things worth less than two dollars, and going hunting or fishing without a license. Youths could say that they had never done these, done them only once or twice, several times, or very often. From their original list of 21 items, Short and Nye developed a scale of nine offenses (Exhibit 2–3).

In the 1950s, crime and delinquency theories assumed social class and illegal behavior were closely connected. Tittle and Meier said, "It is no overstatement that the relationship between social class and criminal behavior is one of the most important and perennial issues in the sociology of crime,"[22] a pronouncement that no one has contradicted. Theorists felt confident in saying criminality is a predominantly male, urban, lower-class behavior.[23] Some evidence seemed to support this: most youths sent to juvenile court and reform school were from poor families, and poverty-stricken neighborhoods had the highest rates of crimes, arrests, and court appearances. So criminologists in the first half of the twentieth century were convinced that most delinquents and gang members were lower class.

Short and Nye's self-report studies, however, disputed this and instead said that lower-, middle-, and upper-strata youths were equally likely to break the law. Therefore, the authors concluded that *social class and delinquency were not related.* This came as thunderbolt, striking the most fundamental axiom in criminology. Although many criminologists dismissed the findings as a fluke or an aberration, others were intrigued by the findings and chose to do their own studies. The second wave of

---

Exhibit 2-3   The Short and Nye Delinquency Scale[21]

Have you

1. Driven a car without a driver's license or permit?
2. Taken little things (worth less than $2) that did not belong to you?
3. Bought or drank beer, wine, or liquor?
4. Purposely damaged or destroyed public or private property that did not belong to you?
5. Skipped school without a legitimate excuse?
6. Had sex relations with a person of the opposite sex?
7. Defied your parents' authority to their face?
8. Run away from home?
9. Taken things of medium value (between $2 and $50)?

---

self-report studies produced results that were the same as Short and Nye's: they found class and delinquency to be unrelated.[24]

In subsequent years, when critics examined such findings more closely, they discovered a series of flaws in the methods. First of all, critics said, delinquency *theories* refer to *large cities,* such as Chicago, Los Angeles, New York, and Philadelphia, in which lower-class individuals tend to live in the slums, where they are isolated from members of other social classes. Thus it struck the critics as bizarre that anyone would elect to investigate the class-delinquency relationship by scouring the hinterland. Geography aside, in the 1950s, small towns and rural areas were worlds apart culturally from big-city slums. How was studying kids from rustic locales like Andy Griffith's *Mayberry RFD* going to provide insight into the gang members living amidst urban blight? This question has never been satisfactorily answered. (Why Short and Nye tested urban theories on rural youth remains a mystery. Perhaps, they originally chose their sample for its convenience and just never expected that they would be testing any theory.)

Critics also took self-reports studies to task for failing to grasp what delinquency theorists meant when they spoke of *social class.* Self-reports ask about the father's *occupation* (because youngsters are usually not privy to other measures of social class, such as parents' income and education), then researchers rank them by level of *prestige.* But *theorists* emphasized *economic deprivation,* not occupational prestige. To measure deprivation would require using indicators such as living below the poverty line, living in a high-poverty neighborhood, living in a housing project, being jobless, on welfare, homeless, on food stamps, receiving rent subsidies, or getting subsidized school lunches. Historically, self-report studies have not used any of these measures.

Surveys also asked about *status offenses* (acts for which only juveniles can be arrested, such as drinking, smoking, having sex, curfew violations, running away, truancy, and incorrigibility) *and peccadilloes* (trivial matters, such as stealing things worth less than two dollars and hunting or fishing without a license). How quaint these seem—unlike the crimes committed on today's mean streets of Camden, New Jersey, Compton, California, Gary, Indiana, or East St. Louis, Illinois. The bucolic villages Short and Nye selected had no Bloods or Crips, no Lords or Latin Kings, no gangs of any kind. Because rural kids in the 1950s did not engage in serious crimes, self-report researchers felt they had no choice but to focus on the most trifling of misdemeanors.

Self-report studies have traditionally suffered from other problems in addition to their dubious measures of social class, their rural samples, and their insignificant offenses. Critics also faulted them for stressing **prevalence** rather than **incidence.** This means that self-reports asked youngsters *if* they had committed the offenses in the past year or over a lifetime (prevalence is the percent of respondents who said yes they had). Researchers would have been better off asking about incidence: exactly *how many times* they had committed each offense (options such as "several times" or "very often" are much too vague and subjective). It is important to distinguish between youths who have committed an offense once or twice and those who have done it a hundred times.

Eventually, of course, some scholars took great pains to avoid the mistakes made by Short and Nye; in this vein, Delbert Elliott and his colleagues deserve special mention. They generated a large sample, including youngsters from big cities (as well as smaller areas) across the nation. They constructed a much-improved measure

Dismal new slums have been created as some smaller cities collapsed in the post-industrial era. One of these is Camden, NJ, across the river from Philadelphia, PA. *(George Goodwin.)*

of crime, including 47 offenses, some of them quite serious. They asked each youth how often he or she committed each particular act. This way they could calculate the mean number of times that youths in each social class committed crimes.

In their National Youth Study (NYS), Elliott and Ageton found a substantial relationship between social class and *predatory crimes against persons* (robbery and various kinds of assault). According to initial results, working-class youths committed these acts 2.5 times as often as middle-class youngsters, and lower-class kids committed them 3.5 times as often as the middle-class teens. *Predatory crimes against property* (vandalism, burglary, auto theft, larceny, stolen goods, fraud, joyriding) also were more commonly engaged in by the lower class. Later, however, more complete findings from the NYS suggested that the impact of social class was minimal.[25]

Although Elliott and Ageton overcame many problems plaguing early self-report studies, one thorny issue eluded them: how to measure social class. Years later, this problem was solved by Margaret Farnworth and her colleagues at SUNY Albany. First of all, they oversampled youths in the dangerous parts of a high-crime city (Rochester, New York). Then, instead of relying on parents' occupational prestige or education level, they stressed economic deprivation (what delinquency theorists originally had in mind when they discussed social class). Specifically, the Farnworth article measured poverty, unemployment, welfare receipt, and underclass membership. In addition, they examined the crime–class relationship longitudinally; that is, they followed the same sample of youngsters for several years.

When they examined the relationship between class at time one and crime a few years later, they found that there was indeed a connection. The F-ratios, which are used to measure whether differences are statistically significant, are presented in Table 2-5. Those with an asterisk are significant (at the .01 level).

The relationship between class and crime thus appears to depend on *the way class and crime are measured.* When measured by parents' education and occupation, social class has a weak relationship with criminality. When crime is measured by mostly theft or status offenses, the relationship continues to be weak. Only when class is measured by *economic deprivation* (especially being on welfare) *and the offenses are serious or official data are used, does the relationship between class and crime become strong.* These represent important discoveries, for they indicate that some measures of social class do indeed correlate with some measures of crime.

TABLE 2-5   F-Ratios for Relationships Between Social Class and Delinquency[26]

	General Deling.	Common Deling.	Street Crimes	Official Deling.
Poverty	.58	2.11	.93	7.19*
Unemployment	.51	1.21	9.30*	8.32*
Welfare	7.34*	.27	15.22*	32.78*
Underclass	.36	.48	7.10*	16.72*

Unfortunately, the authors did not interpret the findings. They offered no explanation of why welfare receipt strongly predicts criminality. If Farnworth et al. had nothing to say about the connection between welfare receipt and youth crime, they were not alone. Other criminologists, too, were silent regarding this relationship. Perhaps it was too sensitive an issue for liberal social scientists to confront. After all, if they discussed the link between welfare and delinquency, this might be used by politicians to further stigmatize recipients, get rid of welfare programs, or cut back on them drastically. When liberals (including criminologists) held back, conservatives leaped into the fray. They did not worry about offending single mothers, residents of inner cities, or minorities (Exhibit 2–4).

Although Farnworth's findings represent a leap forward compared to the flawed self-reports of the 1950s, this was only one study. It is possible that conclusions would have been quite different if researchers had picked another city. Or the Farnworth results may be anomalous in some other respect as yet unknown. Therefore, criminologists need to conduct other studies using similar techniques to see if such results emerge again. If they do, this would help resuscitate social class as an

---

EXHIBIT 2-4   Conservatives' Take on Poverty and Welfare

In 1980, when Ronald Reagan swept into office on a conservative platform, he slashed antipoverty programs and research. Those experts who remained in the upper levels of the administration were forced to hew to the conservative ideology, which was forcefully expressed in the new think tanks on the right: the Heritage Foundation, the American Enterprise Institute, and the Manhattan Institute. Even liberal analysts, such as Bane and Ellwood of the Kennedy School of Government (Harvard), moved to the right, identifying family breakup as a cause of poverty. According to this line of argument, single motherhood increased the chances that children would experience poverty, welfare dependency, school dropout, and low achievement. What did this leave out? Many traditional concerns of liberals: such as economic stagnation, high unemployment, increasing inequality, and declining blue-collar work opportunities.

Even before the Reagan revolution, journalists were focusing on the underclass. They used this term to refer to the undeserving poor. In common parlance, it came to mean sexually promiscuous, drug-addicted, jobless, inner-city, black criminals. Poverty became less central to the concept, whereas deviance became more central. When Daniel Moynihan wrote about the black family, liberal social scientists criticized him unmercifully. This led other liberals and moderates to shy away from discussing black families, poverty, and welfare. Conservatives then stepped into the breach and dominated the discussion, from the 1970s onward. Charles Murray, in his book *Losing Ground* lumped the poor and deviant into one pathological subculture.[27]

important variable in the study of youth crime. As of now, the class-delinquency relationship remains uncertain, clouded by lingering doubts.

We have seen that class and crime can be investigated using self-report studies; the same holds true for race and crime. *Self-reports* do not find the race–crime relationship to be as strong as arrest data indicate. In the National Youth Survey, for instance, Elliott found that there was a 3 to 2 difference. That is, among equal-sized samples of black and white males, for every two violent offenses by white males there were three by black males. (Elliott said that *official data,* i.e., arrest rates, show a much more pronounced difference, 4 to 1 rather than 3 to 2.) Are the self-report data on race and crime valid? There is much uncertainty and controversy surrounding this issue. Some researchers suggest that self-report data are suspect in this comparison because the black youths may be less willing to admit some of their offenses. Others dispute this.[28] It may be that both are right. Official data are right in showing that black youths are more prone to commit serious offenses. Self-reports are right in showing that there are no differences in the likelihood of committing minor offenses.

In addition to studying social class and race, self-reports also reveal how common the various deviant, delinquent, and criminal activities are. They show that the *least serious* acts are the ones engaged in *most often* (these include smoking, drinking, marijuana use, drunkenness, truancy, defying parents). The most serious offenses (armed robbery, grand theft, aggravated assault) are committed rarely. This has important implications for those theories that say delinquency produces substantial profits. Actually, research shows that delinquents mostly spend their time smoking, drinking, using pot, and truanting, none of which brings in any money; on the contrary, the first three of these activities actually *cost* money, hence they are more attractive to kids with cash to spend (generally, those in the middle class).

The greatest value of self-reports is that, unlike Uniform Crime Report data, they provide extensive personal data on individuals. The criminologist can ask many questions and then, in the analysis, discover which of these variables are good predictors of crime or delinquency. The results then can be used to *test existing causal theories of crime and delinquency* or to *create new ones*. This is something that the UCR aggregate data cannot do so well.

The social control theory of Travis Hirschi is a prime example of how self-reports can be used to construct a new theory. Nevertheless, most of the well-known theories, emerged in the years before self-reports became popular. Once the number of self-report studies mounted, critics used the findings to attack the weaknesses of these theories. Later on, self-reports seem to have had an inhibiting effect on criminologists; given the wealth of data available to prove them wrong, criminologists have not constructed many new theories lately.

Victimization Surveys

In the 1964 Presidential campaign, Barry Goldwater may have lost by a large margin but he did inject a new issue into presidential politics: crime and lawlessness. His opponent, President Johnson, had no effective way to counter Goldwater's claims, so after the election he appointed a commission and fobbed the issue off on them. The commission criticized the Uniform Crime Reports and proposed a new method of studying crime, one that would focus on victims. Not content just to issue a recommendation, it asked several criminologists to conduct their own surveys on victimization. These were carried out, and the results showed that only about half of the victimizations that took place were ever reported to police.

In later years, the task of studying victimization was handed over to the Census Bureau and the Bureau of Justice Statistics. The intent was to make the National Crime Victimization Survey (NCVS) comparable to the UCR: both would be nationwide, focusing on crime index offenses, with the same format used each year, and the results would be published annually. J. Edgar Hoover tried to scuttle the **victimization surveys,** and he might have succeeded, but the Republican White House in 1972 expected that the UCR would show a rising crime rate. Richard Nixon figured it would be in his interest to have another set of data, one that contradicted the UCR's claim of an upward trend.

These victim surveys, however, have proved to be an expensive undertaking, requiring samples of about 50,000 households with 100,000 persons in them. (To save money, most respondents are now questioned over the phone instead of in person.) Furthermore, the NCVS no longer includes crimes against organizations or businesses, nor does it count homicides (there is no victim to question) or the great majority of nonindex offenses (some of which are consensual). It does collect details about each victimization: the extent of injuries or losses, how much the victim resisted, why the crime was or was not reported to police, plus the age, sex, race, ethnicity, marital status, income level, and education of the victim.[29]

Thus the victim survey has become a great source of data for victimologists (those few criminologists who are interested primarily in the victims of crime). It could also serve as a check on the official UCR data and their interpretation. When the Attorney General or the FBI director declares that a crime wave is sweeping the country, people could turn to the NCVS to see if it supports such a claim. If it does not agree with the claim, then the official data might need to be scrutinized for flaws. In fact, however, the FBI data receive much more media attention (most of it uncritical) than the victimization data, so the UCR claims about crime rising are not questioned nearly as much as they could be.

Originally, proponents expressed confidence in the victimization surveys. Some criminologists even thought that these would *supplant* the Uniform Crime Reports as a measure of crime trends. They assumed that victims would remember each incident in vivid detail and would readily convey all the particulars to researchers. But it turns out that some people *forget* that they have been victims of theft or violence. They may have been upset at the time of the incident, but later on, as they recovered from it, they regained their composure and let the event slip out of their memory. As months go by, people remember less and less. Victimologists call this *memory decay.*

Most criminologists do not focus on changing crime rates, nor do they specialize in victimology, interesting though it may be. Instead, they prefer to delve into the nature of *crimes and criminals.* How much information about these can they glean from victimization surveys? Not a lot. Victim surveys have little to say about the offenders. Sometimes, the offender's sex and race are known. But even if the victim got a good look at the culprit (and that rarely happens in property crimes), it would be impossible to determine the offender's exact age, education, income level, or place of residence.

On the other hand, victim surveys do provide useful data about who's likely to be victimized. According to most such surveys,

1. Young people have a higher risk than older persons have.
2. Males get victimized more frequently than females do.
3. African Americans experience victimization at a higher rate than whites do.
4. People living in large cities have more crimes committed against them than people living in the suburbs or rural areas.

If victims and offenders are very similar and share the same characteristics, then victimization *indirectly* gives a criminologist some hints about who the *offenders* are. Consider for instance what Michael Hindelang was able to do with some of the early victimization data (Exhibit 2–5).

EXHIBIT 2-5   Hindelang and the Lifestyle Theory of Victimization

In order to account for some of the basic findings of victim research, Hindelang and his colleagues constructed a lifestyle theory of victimization. According to their analysis,

1. The more time a person spends on the street or in parks and other public spaces (especially at night), the greater the chance of being raped or robbed.
2. Time spent in public spaces depends on a person's lifestyle, that is, how one distributes one's time among the common roles and routine activities (such as leisure and work) of everyday life.
3. Social interaction tends to take place between individuals who have the same characteristics (e.g., young single males in the city) and lifestyle.
4. An individual who resembles the people who are most apt to be offenders is more likely to be victimized. Rape, robbery, assault, and larceny are more often committed by male, urban, young, lower SES, unemployed, unmarried school dropouts. Spending time with them increases one's chances of becoming a victim.
5. The amount of time spent with non–family members varies by lifestyle and demographic variables. Young children and senior citizens, for instance, tend to stay home with their parents or spouse.

6. The more time spent with non–family members, the greater the chance of victimization. Nearly all robberies and personal larcenies, for instance, are committed by strangers.

7. Lifestyle affects the ability to insulate oneself from the offender population to some extent. For example, people with higher incomes can move out of high-crime areas, use private transportation, and purchase elaborate security systems.

8. Some lifestyles make an individual a more convenient, more desirable, easier target to take advantage of or subdue. For example: being in a public place not far from the offender's home, being a prostitute or looking to buy drugs (and hence unwilling to go to the police to file a complaint), or being outdoors and alone at night.[30]

The ideas of Hindelang et al. were latched onto years later by Cohen and Felson, who used them to create the routine activity approach. James Q. Wilson, the conservative commentator, had asked why the liberal programs of Lyndon Johnson's War on Poverty and other programs of the Great Society failed to reduce crime, why violence and theft rates soared instead of plummeting during an era of rising prosperity.[31] Cohen and Felson said the answer could be found in **routine activities,** the everyday acts people engage in that make them more susceptible to victimization. In times of economic prosperity, people buy new houses, luxury cars and SUVs, boats, airplanes, and a wealth of gadgets for their homes. Then they spend hours each day away from home, venturing out into the public to eat, drink, work, or play; sometimes they spend weeks away on luxurious vacations to Bali or Bermuda. All this time away from home makes the house more vulnerable to burglary and the individuals who are away from it more likely to be robbed or assaulted. This is how Cohen and Felson explain crime rates climbing during times of economic prosperity. Unfortunately for this line of argument, the crime rates tumbled for nine years in a row during the 1990s, when prosperity was on the rise. Even in the Bronx, economic opportunities increased, and this did not bring a big boost in the rate of crime. Quite the contrary. In the 41st precinct, for instance, (an area made famous by the 1981 movie *Fort Apache*), between the 1970s and 2001, the population increased but the number of homicides, burglaries, and robberies *dropped by 95 percent.* Routine activities theory has a hard time accounting for that.[32]

In victimization surveys, respondents reveal that they have suffered many non-serious offenses—far more than are enumerated in the Uniform Crime Reports (even though the victim surveys mostly ask about the same kinds of crime as the UCR). This result has led some experts to question the validity of the UCR. But it has also alerted them to some problems in the NCVS. When asked by interviewers, college-educated respondents are three times as likely as those with only an elementary education to say they have been assault victims; similar results have emerged in victim surveys in Europe. Also, whites report higher rates of being assaulted than blacks. These findings are not very plausible; hence, victim surveys too must be regarded with a healthy degree of skepticism.

Doing Causal Research

If you wanted to conduct your own research project, what steps would you take? First of all, you'd start with a topic you find compelling, one worth spending months investigating. If you are a sociologist, you can direct your attention toward almost anything. There is a sociology of art, a sociology of death and dying, a sociology of deviance, of education, of knowledge, of family, of mass communication, of the military, of organizations, of religion, of science, of social movements, and of work. Not to mention comparative, economic, feminist, historical, medical, rural, political, and urban sociology. Or criminology, demography, human ecology, minority group relations, social psychology, and social stratification.

Let us say that you decide to explore the impact of sensation seeking on youthful deviance. First, you need to define what you mean by these concepts, then measure them by selecting specific indicators of them. While searching the professional literature, you discover that sensation seeking has four dimensions:

1. Thrill and adventure seeking, such as liking scuba diving, mountain climbing, and surfing
2. Experience seeking, such as trying new foods and exploring new cities without any particular agenda
3. Boredom susceptibility, which means disliking routines and things one has done or seen previously
4. Disinhibition, which means liking exciting things such as wild parties, sexy movie scenes, and dating physically exciting people[33]

Examining these, you decide that the fourth one will predict youthful deviance better than the first two. So you will be certain to include some measures of disinhibition. You may include the other dimensions, too (in case you were wrong or want some comparisons).

There are many indicators of youthful deviance, some more likely than others to be related to sensation seeking. Robert Agnew found that youthful assaults and vandalism are usually motivated by revenge or retaliation, alcohol and marijuana are usually motivated by social pressure, and running away is motivated by pain avoidance. On the other hand, thrills and curiosity were the most common motives for theft, auto theft, illegal entry, and hard drug use.[34] In your research, you will want to give sensation seeking a *chance* to have an impact on deviance, so you'll be sure to include items on theft, auto theft, illegal entry, and hard drug use. Other acts, such as violence and vandalism, should be asked about, too, although you don't expect them to be as strongly linked to sensation seeking.

In selecting a sample, you will want it to be large enough for you to compare different *subsamples*. For instance, ideally, you would prefer each subsample to contain at least 100 respondents. That would usually be easy to achieve in the case of whites, males, females, students, and people above the poverty line. But it may be more difficult to build a sample containing at least 100 each of categories such as blacks, Hispanics, Asians, dropouts, and the impoverished. So, perhaps your overall sample should ideally be between one and two thousand. (Realistically, given money and time constraints you face, you probably won't be able to achieve this.)

If you use a questionnaire, you need to create questions that are well written and pertinent to your research problem. They should also be varied in their format, so that the respondent does not become bored. You need to avoid items that are unclear, double-barreled, have a **social desirability** bias, or deal with issues that the respondents don't know or care about. Consider a few examples of what to *avoid*.

Unclear: *How many crimes have you committed?* (This question is defective, because it does not specify which crimes or what time period.)

Double-barreled: *Do you think that ancient history is too boring and more high schools should offer courses on poverty, hate crimes, and hunger?* (This item is flawed, because it forces people to give one answer to several questions.)

Social desirability: *Are you very intelligent?* (Wanting to present themselves in a good light, people tend to say yes to this, whether it's true or not.)

Do not know about: *How many hours a week do your children watch violent programs on TV?* (Because people do not keep detailed records of such matters, their answers are likely to be nothing more than guesses.)

Once the questionnaire has been drawn up, pretested, revised, and administered to a sample, the answers must be coded (numbers assigned to each answer) so that all the responses to the questions can be read by the computer. Then you may run correlations between the **independent** (causal) and **dependent** (effect) **variables** that are of most interest to you, conduct tests of significance, and interpret the results. In the analysis stage, it is important that you not *build in* a relationship. That is, you *should not have any item that measures **both** your independent variable* (sensation seeking) *and your dependent variable* (youthful deviance).

Suppose you find that sensation seeking is very strongly related to youthful deviance. Next you must deal with the question of causal order: Which comes first, the deviance or the sensation seeking? In *experiments,* if they are conducted properly, causal order is not a problem. The experimental group is exposed to the experimental condition (e.g., electric shock after smiling) and the control group is not, then the experimenter sees how they respond. In social research, *longitudinal studies* help us to solve the problem of causal order by measuring the group several times over a period of years, to see if change in the independent variable precedes change in the dependent variable. On the other hand, in a *cross-sectional study* people are surveyed only one time, so causal order may be much harder to establish. In your study, though, this may not be such a problem. Luckily for you, there are some indications that sensation seeking may be heritable to a substantial degree.[35] It is therefore not likely to be caused by deviant behavior that takes place during adolescence.

The next step is to consider the possibility that the relationship is **spurious.** This means that your two variables (sensation seeking and youth deviance) are related to each other only because both of them are *caused by some (unknown) third variable.* If there is such a variable, you probably don't know what it is, so you can only guess, by considering the most plausible candidates. In this case, the candidates might be age and gender. So you test these possibilities. You compare the male subsample with the female subsample. Is the relationship between sensation seeking and youth still strong both in the male group and the female group? If so, the relationship is not spurious due to gender. Then compare the subsamples of different age groups to see if the relationship between your two variables still holds for each subsample. If so, the relationship is not spurious due to age.

Having taken all these steps, are you sure that sensation seeking causes youth crime? Have you proved it to be true? No. Any day, someone might come along with better data or a more sophisticated way of looking at your own data and show that you made a mistake or that things are more complicated than you thought. In social research, *no **theory** or **hypothesis** can be proved to be correct.* The most that can be said of a hypothesis is that so far the relevant data that we have seem to be compatible with it. We never achieve closure in the social sciences. We must always be open to new discoveries. (Those deeply committed to some ideology make good arguers but bad methodologists; they wear blinders, rejecting new findings that contradict their politicized views.)

Finally, it may be worthwhile to consider how *not* to do research. What would be the worst way to design a study? First, choose the worst sample. This would be a sample of one person. Then have the interviewer be completely biased, someone tainted by partisanship. Then interview someone who is unlikely to be truthful in the answers he or she gives. Criminals locked up in prison are the best candidates, especially those with an antisocial personality disorder. These individuals blame others for their problems (e.g., the police, defense attorney, prosecutor, or judge), cheat without compunction, and lie with aplomb. They are not tried for perjury even when they are found guilty and it is clear that they have lied under oath.[36] The worst research design imaginable would involve accepting everything the inmate said, never checking out his statements to see if they are valid. Then, as a last step, use this method (retrospective, sample of one) to make causal statements about what leads a person to get into a pattern of behavior. Incredible as it may seem, there are researchers who take this approach, even today.

Conclusion

We have covered considerable ground in these first two chapters, but one issue keeps resurfacing: the relation between age and crime. Hirschi and Gottfredson claim that the age–crime relationship is a brute fact, a law of nature that holds true across all social and cultural conditions. They contend that young people commit a great deal of crime, but as they grow older their criminality rapidly diminishes (for reasons that remain a mystery). As evidence, Hirschi and Gottfredson cite three graphs: criminal offenders in England and Wales in the 1840s, male criminals at first conviction in England in 1908, and persons arrested in the United States in 1977.[37] *But the three graphs cited do not show* that arrests or convictions peak at the same age, *nor do any of them peak before the age of 18* (the juvenile years).

Now consider another study, this time of Oakland, California, in 1900. Here, once again, police did not arrest a particularly large number of teenagers. The highest rate of arrests (74 per 1000) occurred among people in their thirties, followed by people in their twenties (60 per 1000), people aged 40 or more (53 per 1000), *and then kids aged 15 to 19* (47 per 1000). No matter which kind of crime was involved, in Oakland between 1872 and 1910, the age when people usually got arrested was 27 to 39—long after their teens.[38]

If we turn to arrests for the entire United States nowadays, the age at which crime peaks depends on which crime is considered. A few peak quite early: arson, vandalism, motor vehicle theft, burglary, larceny-theft, and robbery. Other offenses peak late: prostitution, driving under the influence, drunkenness, fraud, forgery, aggravated assault, and other assault. Steffensmeier and his colleagues contend that in contrast to adults, youngsters are rewarded for engaging in offenses such as burglary, vandalism, and robbery.

> These crimes tend to be committed in peer groups and to be relatively unsophisticated in that the perpetrators rely more on physical strength, mobility, and daring than on skills and contacts. For most juveniles, they are also "low-yield" offenses that, like the drug and alcohol offense categories, provide "thrills" and peer acceptance as much as or more than real financial gain.[39]

He notes that young offenders want to obtain valued goods, demonstrate loyalty, pursue revenge, or just get their kicks out of mischief and hell-raising. Some parts of his description do indeed fit the findings. (1) Youthful offenders are much more likely to engage in crimes of mischief or destruction (arson and vandalism). (2) They are also much more likely to commit crude, high-risk, perhaps low-yield property crimes (motor vehicle theft, burglary, larceny-theft, and robbery). On the other hand, drug and alcohol offenses result in arrests of older people much more than adolescents.[40] Thus even legendary criminologists (Hirschi, Gottfredson, and Steffensmeier) may overstate the case. Their word processor runs away with them. They weave beautiful theories, then some researcher comes along and destroys them with a couple of ugly little facts. You may find this cruel and unusual punishment, but the fact is that the only way criminology can progress is by eliminating theories that are deeply flawed.

Key Terms

Primary data:	data that have been produced and analyzed by the same person or group
Secondary data:	data produced by one person or organization but now analyzed by someone else

Official data:	data produced by government officials for bureaucratic purposes, not designed for use by social scientists
Dark figure of crime:	the gap between the recorded number of crimes and the true number
Victimless crimes:	offenses in which both parties consent to the activity and don't want it reported to the police
Arrest rate:	the number of persons arrested per 10,000 people in the population
Neurological:	having to do with the brain and nervous system and related disorders
Structural argument:	argument that minorities commit more crimes because of the social and economic conditions they experience in their neighborhoods
Surveys:	interviews or questionnaires
Prevalence:	the percentage of people who have committed a particular (deviant) act
Incidence:	how often people have committed a particular (deviant) act
Self-reports:	surveys of the general population (about what acts they have engaged in)
Victim surveys:	surveys of the general population about what acts have been committed against them or their property
Memory decay:	as months pass, people remember less and less about the offenses committed against them
Routine activities:	everyday activities people engage in that may increase or decrease their chances of being victimized
Social desirability:	choosing an answer to a question that makes you look good, even though it is not true
Independent variable:	the variable being treated as a possible cause (such as age, race, or gender)
Dependent variable:	the variable being treated as the effect (such as being sentenced in juvenile or criminal court)
Longitudinal studies:	repeated studies of the same sample of people over a period of several years
Cross-sectional studies:	studies of a sample of people at only one point in time
Spurious:	two variables are related to each other, but it is because there is a third variable that causes both of them
Hypothesis:	a prediction about how two or more variables are connected to each other
Theory:	a series of hypotheses that form a coherent explanation

End Notes

[1]Linda Heath, "Impact of Newspaper Crime Reports on Fear of Crime," *Journal of Personality and Social Psychology, 47*, no. 2 (August 1984), pp. 263–76.

[2]Richard Greer and Graig Guthey, "Teens Accused of Killing Disabled Man Tortured Victim, Suspect Tells Police," *Atlanta Journal and Constitution*, July 21, 1993, p. B3; Richard Greer, "Dunwoody Horror," *Atlanta Journal and Constitution* (July 22, 1993), p. A1.

[3]Barbara Kantrowitz, "Wild in the Streets," *Newsweek* (August 2, 1993), p. 42.

[4]For example, Frank R. Scarpitti and Amie L. Nielsen, eds., *Crime and Criminals* (Los Angeles: Roxbury, 1999); or Joseph F. Sheley, ed., *Criminology*, 3rd ed. (Belmont, CA: Wadsworth, 1999).

[5]Albert D. Biderman and Albert J. Reiss, Jr., "On Exploring the 'Dark Figure' of Crime," *Annals of the American Academy of Political and Social Science*, no. 374 (November 1967), pp. 1–15; Marianne W. Zawitz, Patsy A. Klaus, Ronet Bachman, Lisa D. Bastian, Marshall M. Deberry, Michael R. Rand, and Bruce M. Taylor, *Highlights From 20 Years of Survey Crime Victims* (Washington: Bureau of Justice Statistics, 1993); President's Commission on Law Enforcement and the Administration of Justice, *Crime in a Free Society* (Belmont, CA: Dickenson, 1968).

[6]*Crime in the United States, 1997* (Washington: Federal Bureau of Investigation, 1998).

[7]Kathleen Maguire and Ann L. Pastore, *Sourcebook of Criminal Justice Statistics 1997* (Washington: Bureau of Justice Statistics, 1998), p. 327

[8]*Crime in the United States, 1997.*

[9]Travis Hirschi and Michael Gottfredson, "Age and the Explanation of Crime," *American Journal of Sociology, 89*, no. 3 (November 1983), pp. 552–84.

[10]Howard N. Snyder, "Juvenile Arrests, 1999," *OJJDP Juvenile Justice Bulletin*, December 2000, p. 2; James C. Howell, *Preventing and Reducing Juvenile Delinquency* (Thousand Oaks, CA: Sage, 2003).

[11]Howard N. Snyder, "The Over-Representation of Juvenile Crime Proportions in Robbery Clearance Statistics," *Journal of Quantitative Criminology, 15*, no. 2 (June 1999), pp. 157, 159; Howard N. Snyder, "Juvenile Arrests, 1997," *OJJDP Juvenile Justice Bulletin* (January 1999); for a discussion of NIBRS, see Clayton J. Mosher, Terance D. Miethe, and Dretha M. Phillips, *The Mismeasure of Crime* (Thousand Oaks, CA: Sage, 2002).

[12]*Crime in the United States, 1999* (Washington: Federal Bureau of Investigation, 2000).

[13]Freda Adler, *Sisters in Crime* (New York: McGraw-Hill, 1975); Rita James Simon, *Women and Crime* (Lexington, MA: Lexington Books, 1975); Howard N. Snyder and Melissa Sickmund, *Juvenile Offenders and Victims: A National Report* (Washington: U.S. Department of Justice, 1995); *Juvenile Offenders and Victims: 1999 National Report* (Washington: U.S. Department of Justice, 1999).

[14]Terrie E. Moffitt, Avshalom Caspi, Michael Rutter, and Phil A. Silva, *Sex Differences in Antisocial Behavior* (New York: Cambridge University Press, 2001).

[15]*Crime in the United States, 1999.*

[16]Robert J. Sampson and Janet L. Lauritsen, "Racial and Ethnic Disparities in Crime and Criminal Justice in the United States," in Michael Tonry, ed., *Ethnicity, Crime, and Immigration* (Chicago: University of Chicago Press, 1997), pp. 311–74.

[17]Carolyn Wolpert, "Considering Race and Crime," *American Criminal Law Review, 36*, no. 2 (Spring 1999), pp. 265–89; Lauren J. Krivo and Ruth D. Peterson, "Extremely Disadvantaged Neighborhoods and Urban Crime," *Social Forces, 75*, no. 2 (December 1996), pp. 619–48.

[18]Madeline Wordes and Timothy S. Bynum, "Policing Juveniles: Is There Bias Against Youths of Color?" in Kimberly Kempf Leonard, Carl E. Pope, and William Feyerherm, eds., *Minorities in Juvenile Justice* (Thousand Oaks, CA: Sage, 1995), pp. 47–65.

[19]Marvin E. Wolfgang, Robert M. Figlio, and Thorsten Sellin, *Delinquency in a Birth Cohort* (Chicago: University of Chicago Press, 1972).

[20]James F. Short, Jr. and F. Ivan Nye, "Extent of Unrecorded Juvenile Delinquency," *Journal of Criminal Law and Criminology, 49*, no. 4 (November–December 1958), pp. 296–302; James F. Short, Jr. and F. Ivan Nye, "Reported Behavior as a Criterion of Deviant Behavior," *Social Problems, 5*, no. 3 (Winter 1957–58), pp. 207–13; F. Ivan Nye, James F. Short, Jr., and Virgil Olson, "Socio-Economic Status and Delinquent Behavior," *American Journal of Sociology, 22*, no. 3 (June 1957), pp. 326–32.

[21]F. Ivan Nye and James F. Short, Jr., "Scaling Delinquent Behavior," *American Sociological Review, 22*, no. 3 (June 1957), pp. 328.

[22]Charles R. Tittle and Robert F. Meier, "Specifying the SES/Delinquency Relationship," *Criminology, 28*, no. 2 (May 1990), p. 271.

[23]Albert K. Cohen, *Delinquent Boys* (New York: Free Press, 1955); Richard A. Cloward and Lloyd E. Ohlin, *Delinquency and Opportunity* (New York: Free Press, 1960); Walter B. Miller, "Lower-Class Culture as a Generating Milieu of Gang Delinquency," *Journal of Social Issues, 14*, no. 3 (Summer 1958), pp. 5–19.

[24]Ronald L. Akers, "Socio-Economic Status and Delinquent Behavior," *Journal of Research in Crime and Delinquency, 1*, no. 1 (January 1964), pp. 38–46; John P. Clark and Eugene P. Wenninger, "Socio-Economic Class and Area as Correlates of Illegal Behavior Among Juveniles," *American Sociological Review, 27*, no. 6 (December 1962), pp. 826–34; Robert A. Dentler and Lawrence J. Monroe, "Social Correlates of Early Adolescent Theft," *American Sociological Review, 26*, no. 5 (October 1961), pp. 733–43; LaMar T. Empey and Maynard L. Erickson, "Hidden Delinquency and Social Status," *Social Forces, 44*, no. 4 (June 1966), pp. 546–54; Harwin L. Voss, "Socio-Economic Status and Reported Delinquent Behavior," *Social Problems, 13*, no. 3 (Winter 1966), pp. 314–24; Jay R. Williams and Martin Gold, "From Delinquent Behavior to Official Behavior," *Social Problems, 20*, no. 2 (Fall 1972), pp. 209–29.

[25]Delbert S. Elliott and Suzanne Ageton, "Reconciling Race and Class Differences in Self-Reported and Official Estimates of Delinquency," *American Sociological Review, 45*, no. 1 (February 1980), pp. 95–110.

[26]Margaret Farnworth, Terence P. Thornberry, Marvin D. Krohn, and Alan J. Lizotte, "Measurement in the Study of Class and Delinquency," *Journal of Research in Crime and Delinquency, 31*, no. 1 (February 1994), p. 50.

[27]Mary Jo Bane and David Ellwood, "Slipping Into and Out of Poverty," *Journal of Human Resources, 21,* no. 1 (Winter 1986), pp. 1–23; Mary Jo Bane, "Household Composition and Poverty," in Sheldon H. Danziger and Daniel H. Weinberg, eds., *Fighting Poverty* (Cambridge: Harvard University Press, 1986), pp. 209–31; Herbert J. Gans, *The War Against the Poor* (New York: Basic, 1995); Ken Auletta, *The Underclass* (New York: Random House, 1982); Lee Rainwater and William L. Yancey, eds., *The Moynihan Report and the Politics of Controversy* (Cambridge: MIT Press, 1967); Charles Murray, *Losing Ground* (New York: Basic, 1984). For criticisms of the latter book, see Robert Greenstein, "Losing Faith in Losing Ground," *New Republic* (March 25, 1985), pp. 12–7; Christopher Jencks, "How Poor Are the Poor?" *New York Review of Books* (May 9, 1985), p. 41.

[28]Delbert Elliott, John Hagan, and Joan McCord, *Youth Violence: Children at Risk* (Washington: American Sociological Association, 1988); Terence P. Thornberry and Marvin D. Krohn, "The Self-Report Method for Measuring Delinquency and Crime," in David Duffee, ed., *Measurement and Analysis of Crime and Justice,* Volume four of *Criminal Justice 2000* (Washington: National Institute of Justice, 2000), pp. 38–84; Stephen Magura and Sung-Yeon Kang, "The Validity of Self-Reported Cocaine Use in Two High Risk Populations," in Lana Harrison and Arthur Hughes, eds., *The Validity of Self-Reported Drug Use* (Rockville, MD: National Institute on Drug Abuse, 1997), pp. 227–46; Marvin E. Wolfgang, Robert M. Figlio, and Thorsten Sellin, *Delinquency in a Birth Cohort;* Michael J. Hindelang, Travis Hirschi, and Joseph G. Weis, *Measuring Delinquency* (Beverly Hills, CA: Sage, 1981); Travis Hirschi, *Causes of Delinquency* (Berkeley, CA: University of California Press, 1969); David Huizinga and Delbert S. Elliott, "Reassessing the Reliability and Validity of Self-Report Delinquent Measures," *Journal of Quantitative Criminology, 2,* no. 4 (December 1986), pp. 293–327.

[29]Andrew Karmen, *Crime Victims,* 3rd ed. (Belmont, CA: Wadsworth, 1996); nowadays, the sample is larger, with 86,890 households and 159, 420 people interviewed.

[30]Michael J. Hindelang, Michael R. Gottfredson, and James Garofalo, *Victims of Personal Crime* (Cambridge, MA: Ballinger, 1978).

[31]James Q. Wilson, *Thinking About Crime* (New York: Basic Books, 1975).

[32]Lawrence E. Cohen and Marcus Felson, "Social Change and Crime Rate Trends," *American Sociological Review, 44,* no. 4 (August 1979), pp. 588–608; Gregg Easterbrook, *The Progress Paradox* (New York: Random House, 2003).

[33]Marvin Zuckerman, *Sensation Seeking* (Hillsdale, NJ: Lawrence Erlbaum, 1979).

[34]Robert Agnew, "The Origins of Delinquent Events," *Journal of Research in Crime and Delinquency, 27,* no. 3 (August 1990), pp. 267–94.

[35]Marvin Zuckerman, *Behavioral Expression and Biological Bases of Sensation Seeking* (Cambridge University Press, 1994); Judith R. Koopmans, Dorret I. Boomsma, Andrew C. Heath, Lorenz J. P. van Doornen, "A Multivariate Genetic Analysis of Sensation Seeking," *Behavior Genetics, 25,* no. 4 (July 1995), pp. 349–56.

[36]Evelin Sullivan, *The Concise Book of Lying* (New York: Farrar, Straus, and Giroux, 2001).

[37]Travis Hirschi and Michael Gottfredson, "Age and the Explanation of Crime."

[38]Lawrence M. Friedman and Robert V. Percival, *The Roots of Justice* (Chapel Hill: University of North Carolina Press, 1981). See also Russian murder rates by age of

the offenders in Veleriy V. Chervyakov, Vladimir M. Shkolnikov, William Alex Pridemore, and Martin McKee, "The Changing Nature of Murder in Russia," *Social Science and Medicine, 55,* no. 10 (November 2002), pp. 1713–24 and William Alex Pridemore, "Social Problems and Patterns of Juvenile Delinquency in Transitional Russia," *Journal of Research in Crime and Delinquency, 39,* no. 2 (May 2002), pp. 187–213, English convictions in David P. Farrington, Sandra Lambert, and Donald J. West, "Criminal Careers of Two Generations of Family Members in the Cambridge Study in Delinquent Development," *Studies on Crime and Crime Prevention, 7,* no. 1 (March 1998), pp. 85–106, and French convictions in L. Adolphe J. Quetelet, *Treatise on Man and the Development of His Faculties* (Edinburgh: Chambers, 1842).

[39]Darrell J. Steffensmeier, Emilie Andersen Allan, Miles D. Harer, and Cathy Streifel, "Age and the Distribution of Crime," *American Journal of Sociology, 94,* no. 4 (January 1989), p. 807; Darrell Steffensmeier and Cathy Streifel, "Age, Gender, and Crime Across Three Historical Periods," *Social Forces, 69,* no. 3 (March 1991), p. 872.

[40]Furthermore, self-report data show that people in their early adult years (18 to 25) are more likely than 12 to 17-year-olds to admit drinking alcohol and using marijuana, cocaine, and hallucinogens and smoking cigarettes. This is reported in Clayton J. Mosher, Terance D. Miethe, and Dretha M. Phillips, *The Mismeasure of Crime,* p. 118.

Recommended Readings

Howard N. Snyder and Melissa Sickmund, *Juvenile Offenders and Victims* (Washington: Office of Juvenile Justice and Delinquency Prevention, 1999).

Joseph F. Sheley, ed., *Criminology,* 3rd ed. (Belmont, CA: Wadsworth, 2000).

Albert D. Biderman and James P. Lynch, *Understanding Crime Incidence Statistics* (New York: Springer-Verlag, 1991).

Michael J. Hindelang, Travis Hirschi, and Joseph G. Weis, *Measuring Delinquency* (Beverly Hills, CA: Sage, 1981).

Travis Hirschi and Michael Gottfredson, "Age and the Explanation of Crime," *American Journal of Sociology, 89,* no. 3 (November 1983), pp. 552–84.

CHAPTER 3

American Adolescence Today

All cultures distinguish between the young and the old, but **adolescence** is a different matter. Some cultures have no concept of a teenager. Thus, it seems as though children in labor-intensive agrarian cultures of the past skipped adolescence and made a smooth segue to adulthood. Instead of preparing to leave home, they spent their childhood years with adults at the same tasks. Hence, agrarian societies valued large numbers of children—as virtually free labor, they were economic assets. What they needed in the way of food and clothing could be either grown or sewn. Children would grow up, stay nearby, and later on support their aging parents.

When girls' **puberty** as measured by **menarche** (i.e., first menstruation) arrived, it was late by our standards, at around 17 years of age, because nutrition was inadequate and protein was often lacking. Cultures long ago welcomed it as a sign of adulthood, and in many of the world's societies it was not long before the girl typically married and started a family. There was no socially recognized period of adolescent moratorium, no time when youths wrestled with weighty issues such as identity, nor was there a prolonged maidenhood (the years between menarche and marriage).[1]

In industrial and postindustrial societies, on the other hand, adolescence is widely acknowledged: people are convinced that it really exists. Still, there are questions about its boundaries. That is, whereas teenagers in modern societies experience multiple transitions in multiple institutions, they occur at different ages. Hence the markers for adolescence are conflicting, leading to confusion over when it begins and ends (Exhibit 3-1). In education, an individual could be said to enter adolescence when junior high begins and to exit adolescence when schooling is finally complete.

EXHIBIT 3-1   Different Conceptions of When Adolescence Begins and Ends

	When it begins	*When it ends*[2]
Biological	Onset of puberty	Becoming capable of reproduction
Emotional	Beginning of detachment from parents	Attaining separate sense of identity
Cognitive	More advanced reasoning abilities emerge	Advanced reasoning abilities consolidated
Interpersonal	Interest begins to shift from parents to peers	Capacity for intimacy with peers develops
Social	Training for adult work, family and citizen roles	Full attainment of adult status and privileges
Legal	Attain juvenile status	Attain adult status

But other transitions also lay claim to being the starting and finishing lines of this stage in life.

The question of when adolescence *ends* remains in dispute, and this uncertainty will probably continue indefinitely. On the other hand, there is a fair amount of consensus that biological puberty marks adolescence's *beginning*. Although this may seem perfectly reasonable as the beginning of adolescence, in fact, puberty is not a single, discrete event that happens at one moment. Instead, it's a series of processes, lasting four, five, or more years and encompassing a number of physical changes, some of which start very early (especially among girls in the United States). Several hormonal changes occur two or three years before major body changes are visible. Moreover, although some physical changes may be apparent to the rest of society, others aren't. Thus, outsiders do not know very much about a youngster's pubertal status and may not be able to classify the youth very accurately.

Among girls, the signs may be more obvious: breasts bud, height spurts, pubic hair appears, axillary (underarm) hair shows, the strength spurt peaks, the height spurt peaks, hips widen, menarche occurs, adult height is reached, breast growth is completed, and public hair growth is completed. For boys, some of the changes are the same, but others are different (for instance, testes and penis enlarge, facial hair begins to grow, shoulders widen, and the voice deepens).[3] In addition, for both sexes, body fat and muscle are redistributed, and changes even occur in circulation and respiration. Pubertal changes also make it possible to reproduce.

Puberty is controlled by the endocrine system, which first operates before birth. Events are controlled by the brain, the pituitary gland, and the gonads (i.e., the ovaries or testes). The pituitary gets signals from the brain and releases hormones into the blood. Such hormones regulate growth and various body functions. Signals back to the brain complete the circuit. The hypothalamus-pituitary-gonadal axis is especially critical.

Before birth, gonads develop in males and begin to secrete hormones called **androgens**. Androgens set in motion a series of events that result in the development of male internal and external sex organs, and specifically in the formation of the hypothalamus-pituitary-gonadal axis. This process results in the birth of a boy; if it does not occur, the child is a girl. After what appears to be a short burst of sex steroid activity in the first few months of life, this hormonal system then operates at a fairly low level until middle childhood.[4]

When a certain level of fat is attained (17 percent for girls), the hormonal system, which the brain had suppressed for years, starting not long after birth, swings back into action, and this brings the onset of puberty. For ballet dancers and long-distance runners, fat levels remain low longer, which delays pubertal onset. On the other hand, certain family arrangements, such as father absence, tend to hasten onset.

Storm and Stress

G. Stanley Hall, the first American to receive a Ph.D. in psychology and generally recognized as the "founder" of the study of adolescence, believed that individual lives recapitulate the evolution of the species. He claimed that infancy corresponds to the era in which humans were primitive, like animals, and the period from ages 7 to 13 parallels the stage of barbarism. Hall thought children this age were incapable of sympathy, love, morality, or reasoning. When adolescence begins, at around age 14, Hall said, it is like moving into the stage of civilization. Hormonal changes associated with puberty bring about an upheaval, a period of turbulence or storm and stress. Teens will be tormented, mercurial, and unpredictable, and because this is part of a predetermined biological timetable, parents cannot do a thing about it; they have to let the raging hormones run their course.

Hall and, later on, psychoanalytic thinkers such as Anna Freud and Peter Blos[5] believed that instinctual forces associated with puberty cause this turbulence. Teens regress psychologically, feel confused and ambivalent, rebel, and act out; the older adolescents face a serious identity crisis. These internal disturbances become most evident in their dealings with parents, which are riddled with conflict. Hall was influenced by Germany's "Sturm und Drang" (storm and stress) literature, which described youngsters as full of anxiety and angst. This standard academic view later filtered down to the general public, becoming part of the modern folk wisdom (Exhibit 3-2).

Is adolescence tempest tossed for nearly everyone going through it, a period of temporary psychosis, a time when all teenagers feel storm and stress, and go through mood swings because of their raging hormones? Does this turbulence push parents of teens to the limit of their tolerance? Psychoanalytic thinkers such as Anna Freud thought so. They insisted that a serious and prolonged identity crisis was the rule; and for a youngster to be *normal* during adolescence was itself *abnormal*. The few adolescents these clinicians encountered were ones they treated in clinics; to be sure, such patients usually had real problems, but this was not a typical group of teens. Inevitably, clinical samples are a biased sample, not reflective of youngsters

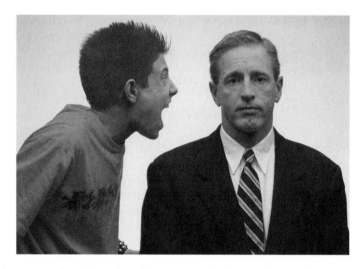

Most adolescents admit that they have a good relationship with their parents, but this should not be taken to mean that they have no conflicts. (*© John Madere/Corbis. All rights reserved.*)

in general. (This is obvious if we think of adults. Imagine how ridiculous it would seem if you said that sampling mental hospital patients is a good way to study American grownups.)

Eventually, some of the psychoanalytic hypotheses were tested using surveys of broader, nonclinical samples of adolescents, and these studies found that few teens were emotionally disturbed. Most youths instead handled daily stresses without any

---

Exhibit 3-2   Media Descriptions Paint Adolescence as Full of Turmoil

There are various tip-offs that newspapers and mass-market magazines embrace the old storm and stress view of adolescence expressed by G. Stanley Hall and the psychoanalytic school. These media describe puberty and adolescence as traumatic experiences, hormonal upheavals, periods of temporary insanity, and turbulence. When these terms are trotted out, the writer has accepted the old "disease theory" of adolescence. Even when news reports do not refer to trauma, turmoil, mood swings, and raging hormones, they imply that adolescence is abnormal and parents should be prepared for a period of unruly behavior.

Adolescence is an excruciating state of limbo between childhood and adulthood. At its worst, it is a time when model children go off the rails and seem lost forever; at best, it is a time of slamming doors, black eyeliner, loud music, and excessive phone bills.[6]

damage to their mental health. Rather than succumbing to suicidal feelings or lapsing into psychosis, they coped reasonably well. To be sure, they were not invulnerable; but most of them were fairly resilient, which is to say, they seemed to bounce back after a while from the various problems and losses they experienced.

The leaders in the movement to study a wider array of adolescents were Daniel Offer and his colleagues, who created the Offer Self-Image Questionnaire for Adolescents and administered it to more than 30,000 respondents aged 13 to 19 in a dozen countries. A majority of the teens said they were pleased most of the time, proud of their physique, believed they were strong and healthy, looked forward to a career, felt good about their parents, viewed the future with high hopes, and had no major hangups. At the very most, 20 percent were found to have mental health problems (such as feeling empty emotionally, thinking life is full of problems with no end in sight, or feeling confused most of the time).[7]

Mental health professionals who had been most strongly influenced by the ideas of Hall and Anna Freud greatly exaggerated the problem. The facts are more prosaic. The psychological disturbances that they assumed were characteristic of *most* adolescents, are not. Plus, the few youngsters who *do* have mental health problems typically experienced them prior to adolescence, in short, *as children.* The problems did not suddenly spring up with the advent of puberty. Carryover from childhood is common: life continues pretty much as was in preadolescence. Still, there are a *few adolescents here and there* with problems brought on by puberty and the reactions of other people to it. These youngsters will now be discussed in some detail.

Puberty, Timing, and Effects

The physical and biological changes that appear to herald the arrival of puberty are cause for celebration in preindustrial societies that have traditional rites of passage. In the modern world, because youngsters are eager to shed the title of children and be considered mature and adult, you might think that puberty would be embraced just as eagerly. But bodily changes are not always a sublime and blissful experience—for the youths undergoing them or for their parents watching from the sidelines. How happy or upset any particular youngster becomes may depend on *when* these changes take place.

Studies of pubertal timing refer to biological changes arriving *early, on time,* or *late*—compared to the normal timetable for youths. In general, girls begin puberty about 18 months to two years before boys do.[8] So early maturing girls are the first youngsters of all to mature. Conceivably, it could be advantageous for a boy to become taller, heavier, and stronger early than other boys his age; in many cases, he becomes more relaxed, popular, and confident—perhaps a better athlete too. But it is different for females: *for an early maturing girl, the advantages are fewer and the disadvantages greater.*

The following are some of the discoveries made by Stattin and Magnusson when they studied early maturation among girls who were growing up in Sweden.

1. A new social life opens up for the early developer but at a time when she is not experienced enough to cope with it.

2. Because girls in general mature sooner than boys, the early maturer may date boys considerably older than herself. This arouses the envy of other girls.

3. She is more likely to have sexual experiences, get pregnant, and have an abortion.

4. She is more likely to be physically conspicuous, to stand out in weight and height, which may make her self-conscious and may lead others to stigmatize her. Her female friends are likely to be early maturers too.

5. She is likely to have strained relations with her parents.

6. She tends to have less motivation in school, and she is unlikely to eventually go on to college.[9]

In studies of early maturing girls in the United States, researchers also mention sex, dating, and interpersonal relations, but they concentrate a bit more on psychological distress.

It is difficult for some early adolescents to adapt to the physical changes that are part of puberty. Once puberty is under way, physical appearance and body image become crucial elements of the person's self-image. This is the time when physical traits are scrutinized and self-consciousness is heightened. Early adolescents are more anxious about their appearance than any other aspect of themselves. Not only do physical traits affect their self-esteem, but they also influence how peers regard them.[10] American studies point out that

1. Girls are maturing earlier than in the past. Early in the nineteenth century, menarche happened at 15 or 16; now it's around 12. According to recent data, white girls show some breast development one year and African-American girls two years before modern medical textbooks indicate.[11]

2. Prior to adolescence, boys are slightly more prone to depression than girls. But between 11 and 13, depression rises steeply for girls, and by 15 they are twice as likely as boys to have had a bout of depression. This disadvantage lasts for another 35 or 40 years.[12] Male teens score higher than females on all aspects of self-concept.[13]

3. Early maturing girls weigh more than on-time and late-maturing girls. Girls going through puberty add more body fat, bigger hips, and less muscle than boys. And early maturers eventually end up shorter than their on-time and late-developing peers.[14]

4. By virtue of the added weight, early maturing girls do not fit the cultural preference for thinner, leaner, toned, taut bodies with buns of steel. In America, being fat is regarded more unfavorably than just about any other "handicap."[15]

5. Early maturing girls have an unfavorable image of their body. Though grateful for breasts, they lament their height, weight, and figure; mostly, they hate the new body fat they are carrying.[16] Body image is perhaps the most important element in self-concept during the adolescent years. Girls emphasize thinness and physical attractiveness in judging themselves and others.[17]

6. Normal girls tend to think they're overweight; often they compare themselves to "ideal" figures, superwaif fashion models displayed in magazine ads.

Ninety percent of white teenage girls are dissatisfied with their bodies, and two-thirds of those aged 13 to 18 try to lose weight.[18]

7. Girls who mature early have higher levels of depression, anxiety, eating disorders, psychiatric disorders, lower self-esteem, poorer coping skills, more suicide attempts, more substance use, and lower self-rated health and engage in more delinquency. Developing *late* helps protect against depression.[19]

Research on early maturation and "psychopathology" has concentrated on girls instead of boys and on **internalizing symptoms** (depression, anxiety, headaches, nausea) more than **externalizing symptoms** (vandalism, fights, fire setting, stealing, behavior problems at school). But there are exceptions. A few studies indicate that early maturing girls are more delinquent. The best known of these is the research by Caspi et al., which found that early maturing girls in coed schools were more delinquent at ages 13 and 15 than were their counterparts: on-time or late-maturing girls anywhere and early maturing girls at all-girl schools.

The early maturing girl in a mixed-sex school . . . is physically developed, psychologically immature, and socially vulnerable. Although the physically mature girl is more likely to be attractive to boys and to affiliate with older youths, [she may not possess] the requisite cognitive skills with which to confront situations that are likely to tax her ability to resist social pressures from peers [i.e., predatory males].[20]

For years, psychologists believed that early maturation is an advantage for boys. It means they are taller, are stronger, and have a better chance to excel in contact sports such as basketball and football and to attract girlfriends. Recently, however, researchers have begun to question these assumptions. Today, there are two positions regarding pubertal timing. The **deviance hypothesis** maintains that being off time (maturing either earlier or later than peers) causes adaptation problems: the individual is labeled deviant, odd, or different by them and subjected to a certain amount of scorn or rejection. The **stage termination hypothesis**, on the other hand, says that only early maturation creates difficulties because the child is thrust into adolescence before being ready for the transition, and therefore is not prepared to cope with the new role expectations.

Williams and Dunlop asked 14-year-old males about their pubertal status and their extent of involvement in thirty-one kinds of delinquency. They found (in keeping with the deviance hypothesis) that early and late maturers both engaged in more deviance (particularly crime and school opposition) than boys who matured on time. But Williams and Dunlop's findings are not typical. A series of other studies found that only the early developers were more likely to get involved in crime and deviance. This is in keeping with the stage termination argument. Exactly why this should be so is uncertain, though several explanations have been suggested. One of them is that (like early maturing girls) the early maturing males are more apt than their on-time peers to hang out with the older boys, and in doing so they pick up the older boys' habits, such as smoking, drinking, and vandalism.[21]

Mood Swings

Mood swings have been part of the folklore about adolescents since the days of G. Stanley Hall, who attributed them to raging hormones that were said to plague early adolescence. But this was merely speculation, because until the 1980s, evidence about adolescent hormones' activational effects was anecdotal—hormone levels of adolescents hadn't been measured yet. Hormone assay technology did not exist. Today, studying the endocrine system remains difficult. Nevertheless, the public continues to assume that hormones wreak havoc in the early teens; that's why adolescents are called emotional, impulsive, restless, and insecure.

But behavioral scientists have recently suggested other possibilities. In research using the **Experience Sampling Method**, adolescents were given pagers and beeped from morning to night. Then they filled out self-reports detailing both objective (location, activities, and companions) and subjective data (affect, activation, cognitive efficiency, and motivation). The thousands of self-reports were supplemented by long interviews. This way, changes in moods, the daily ups and downs, could be charted. The researchers, Csikszentmihalyi and Larson, found that adolescents' moods did indeed oscillate between extreme highs and lows, between euphoria and despair.

But these moods did not persist very long. Adolescents experience an extreme mood, then it vanishes, and within 45 minutes they are back to normal. (Not so the adults, whose extreme mood is apt to linger a while. If the adult is elated, this lasts for hours, and the same holds true for sadness.) In other words, youthful highs and lows are more like quick flashes, not persistent moods that might easily lead to seismic upheaval.

Adolescent moods are not related to the individual's pubertal stage (though they may be correlated with hormone levels). Instead, the beeper studies of

Studies indicate that adolescents enjoy spending their time in parks and basements with each other, far from the prying eyes of parents. *(N. Richmond/The Image Works.)*

Csikszentmihalyi and Larson found that much of the variation in moods depends on the social environment: their location, activity, and companions. Youths are much happier when they are in places far removed from adult scrutiny and control: parks and other public places, a friend's home, or the student center. They are unhappy in school classrooms, halls, or library. They are happiest doing art or hobbies, listening to music, resting, or participating in sports. Feelings reach the lowest point when kids are thinking, studying, or doing class work. Most importantly, activities are much more enjoyable when engaged in with friends.

Teenagers go through ups and downs in mood; this occurs as they go from being with friends to being alone, or go from the classroom to a public place, or from hobbies, music, or sports to thinking. When adolescents are in places they like, doing things they enjoy, with companions they prefer, their mood is buoyant. But when in adult-controlled settings, engaging in activities imposed on them, they feel drowsy and down in the dumps. Mental health specialists view these mood swings with alarm. In fact, however, adolescents with wider swings are just as well adjusted as their steadier, nonswing peers.[22]

Parental Reactions to Adolescence

Finally, the psychoanalytic approach to adolescence dwells on conflict with parents. Do teenagers create tension in the home, are they impossible to get along with, do they drive their parents batty? Psychologists have measured how often adolescents and parents clash, over what issues, and why the conflicts arise. How deeply these affect parents, however, has received less scrutiny. As a rule, clinicians, who see adolescents on the analyst's couch, describe them in ominous terms, implying that as adolescence unfolds it inevitably brings rebellion, resistance, and revenge.

But researchers have found that most of the bickering between parents and teens does not involve serious, fundamental issues. Instead, sparring and squabbling revolve around those minor but ancestral hassles familiar to everyone (e.g., cleaning one's bedroom and taking out the garbage). Table 3-1 shows some recent findings on the subject. Most parents report disagreements with their teenager when it comes to helping around the house and family relations; on the other hand, sex and drugs are rarely the source of conflict.

Smetana and Asquith divided parent–adolescent conflict into six types.[24]

Moral Items:
    Taking money from parents without permission
    Hitting brothers and sisters
    Lying to parents
Conventional Items:
    Not doing assigned chores
    Talking back to parents
    Manners
Multifaceted Items:
    Wearing an earring (boy) or heavy makeup (girl)

TABLE 3-1   Parents' Reported Conflict with Adolescents at Least Once a Week[23]

Helping around the house	
White	51%
Black	43%
Hispanic	34%
Family relations	
White	31%
Black	19%
Hispanic	23%
School	
White	25%
Black	16%
Hispanic	14%
Dress	
White	21%
Black	25%
Hispanic	23%
How late youth stays out	
White	13%
Black	16%
Hispanic	11%
Friends	
White	10%
Black	15%
Hispanic	16%
Substance use	
White	4%
Black	2%
Hispanic	4%
Sexual behavior	
White	2%
Black	3%
Hispanic	2%

Not cleaning one's room
Not putting clothes away
Friendship Items:
    Seeing a friend whom parents dislike
    Having a party when parents are away
    Inviting a romantic partner over when parents are away
Personal Items:
    Choosing one's own clothes
    Spending allowance on games
    Listening to obnoxious music
Prudential Items:
    Smoking cigarettes
    Drinking alcohol
    Riding with inexperienced drivers

Nearly all adolescents and parents think parents have a right to set moral rules regarding others' welfare and that these rules are obligatory. Adolescents and parents both see personal issues (acts only involving the self) as lying within the adolescent domain. Adolescents and parents also agree that conventional issues (arbitrary but agreed-upon standards of family or society) are legitimate ones for parents to rule on—it is within their jurisdiction. But on these matters, adolescents seek greater autonomy while parents want greater authority—and that inspires conflict. Adolescents and parents differ to some degree on friendship issues. Adolescents see these as personal, whereas adults worry about friends' leading their kids astray. On prudential issues (acts that may have a negative effect on the individual's health, safety, and comfort), parents generally think they have authority; youngsters disagree.

When conflicts arise, parents often see the issue as one of convention. Adolescents, on the other hand, tend to perceive them as personal. Parents defend themselves by asserting that cultural rules and standards are involved, and breaking these rules could bring embarrassment. Teens tend to reject this line of reasoning and argue that the behaviors in question fall within their personal jurisdiction. As adolescents get older, they expand their definition of what's personal.

Researchers find that adolescents and their parents are not usually separated by a cavernous generation gap. They generally hold similar beliefs and attitudes about the importance of hard work, educational and occupational goals, and the desirability of certain personality traits. In basic values concerning religion, education, and work, adolescents resemble their parents more closely than they resemble their peers. Perhaps this is because socioeconomic status affects these values more than age does (and, by definition, parents and offspring living in the same home have the same socioeconomic status).

Survey research on adolescents and parents finds that about three out of four such families get along pretty well during the adolescent years. The great majority of teens report that they admire their parents, turn to them for advice, and feel appreciated by them. As for the other 25 percent, whose relationship is either strained or rocky, they probably experienced problems with parents before adolescence began. Therefore, in most cases, *reaching the new developmental stage (adolescence) did not cause their difficulties.*[25]

Nevertheless, pop psychology books over the years have suggested that adolescence is a time that parents can only hope they *survive;* the possibility of enjoying such years appears to be out of the question.[26] Is this because the writers have been unduly influenced by the psychoanalytic theories and common stereotypes about youths being reckless, restless, rude, and risk taking? Or is there a grain of truth to the idea—that for those adults whose children are entering adolescence, life takes a sudden, sharp turn for the worse?

When a youngster moves into adolescence, parent–child relations change. They become less close, less affectionate, less involved; and parents are no longer idealized as they were a few years earlier. How do the changes brought on by the child's new status affect parents' psyches? The literature exploring this issue is sparse, so any answer must be regarded as tentative. But one provocative study stands out, and its findings are worth reviewing in some detail.

In *Crossing Paths,* Laurence Steinberg questioned families before and after their first child entered adolescence. Although most youths took the pubertal changes in stride, many parents did not. Over half of the moms and dads underwent alterations in mental health. They conceded that they felt more anxious, depressed, unsure; plus, the dissatisfaction they experienced spread to their work life and their marriage. Many of them complained of headaches and insomnia; they mourned the demise of their sex lives; and they felt aggrieved that their child was having more fun than they were. Their self-esteem dropped—especially the parent who was of the same sex as the oldest child.

Some parents found the child's sudden growth spurt disturbing. They interpreted it as a sign that **they** were getting old. It also signaled a loss of status in the home. Parents no longer towered over the child; they no longer loomed so powerful. Dominance is a comforting feeling to have, but when the child spurts upward in height and weight, that dominance becomes difficult to maintain, leaving parents feeling a bit unsettled. Thus the growth spurt sometimes makes parents feel disheartened, though they may not be able to put their finger on just why that is.

More disturbing than this, however, is that the child takes on a new appearance as a sexually mature being. Parents may find this passage raises ambiguous and troubling emotions. They may have some qualms about their own physical attractiveness and sexual adequacy, their past romantic experiences, and their current marriage. Seeing the child blossom in front of their eyes makes some parents feel uneasy, homely, and yearning for the days when their oldest offspring was still a child. This can cause feelings of envy to bubble to the surface. For a mother whose child is a daughter, feelings of low self-worth and longing for one's youthful days can lead to a midlife crisis.

For fathers, their teenage son's dating seems to inspire anxiety and depression, plus a steep decline in marital satisfaction. No one knows why this happens, and Steinberg (the researcher) was reluctant to confront respondents with a question so ticklish. Therefore, he decided to pose it to some of his friends and colleagues who had adolescent sons. How would they respond to it? Their rueful observations were startling.

> Many of the fathers with whom I have spoken have confessed—albeit with a certain degree of embarrassment—to feeling attracted to their son's girlfriends or to their daughter's female friends [whom some of the fathers described as knockouts].[27]

Early psychiatric exploration had uncovered similar issues faced by the middle-aged fathers. Some came to envy the son, who now enjoyed the prospect of enticing choices in the worlds of work and love.

As children grow older, they deidealize their parents, stop looking up to them with reverence and awe. They get over their childlike admiration and begin to see parents as flawed human beings whose opinions are sometimes quaint, if not patently absurd. Therefore, adolescents may point out these shortcomings to them and on a few occasions express ideas that contradict parental views. This hurts parents, who enjoyed the old days when their kids assumed mom and dad were infallible. They find it hard not to take the new criticism personally. It is hard to brush off, even if they know this is part of the natural process of individuation (i.e., growing up and assuming an identity) that adolescents go through on the way to adulthood.

Another aspect of growing up is detachment: distancing oneself from the parents. This includes seeking more privacy, talking more with friends and less with parents, and avoiding being seen with parents. This transformation, however, leaves many parents saddened. They often feel rejected, abandoned. The mother–daughter relationship is the closest one in many families and severing it can be especially painful for the mother. She may feel empty, lonely, and depressed. For single parents and women with unsatisfactory marriages, the break is especially disturbing.[28]

These findings suggest that parents take their lumps when the oldest child enters adolescence. This stage has been thought of as traumatic for the child going through it, due to the many changes (biological, emotional, cognitive, educational) experienced in a short time span. But, apparently, the transitions are far less devastating for the youth than for mom and dad. For the youngster, growing up means opportunity beckons, one has a future with rights, privileges, freedoms, accomplishments, and individual expression. For parents, though, a new adolescent can be jarring if this is their oldest child and they're unprepared. They visualize for themselves a more ominous future (one that may entail romance dying, sexual powers waning, and occupational life stagnating). Fortunately for the parents, this low point is a temporary blip rather than a continuing state.

Thinking

Biological puberty is an important aspect of adolescence, of course, but there are other aspects as well, including cognitive changes. Swiss psychologist Jean Piaget made a big impact fifty years ago when he divided children's thinking into four stages.[29] He said the first stage, **sensorimotor**, lasts from birth to age two, and during this time infant intelligence is attempting to coordinate sensory experiences with physical movements and actions. From the ages of two to seven, the child can use words and images to represent the world but cannot perform certain mental operations; this is called the preoperational stage. In the stage of concrete operations, children from ages 7 to 11 learn to reason logically about concrete events and classify objects into different sets. Finally, from ages 11 through 15, children move beyond concrete experiences and think in more abstract and logical terms. They may develop thoughts about the ideal parent or hypothesize about why things happen the way they do.

More recent work by David Elkind carries on some aspects of the Piaget tradition and introduces the concepts of the imaginary audience and the personal fable. Both of these are forms of adolescent egocentrism or self-absorption. A teenager who has an imaginary audience is very self-conscious and thinks that all eyes are on him or her. Hence, anything different or out of the ordinary will be noticed: for example, being too tall or too short, wearing the "wrong" clothes, saying the "wrong" thing, or behaving in a way that doesn't fit the mood of the audience.

A **personal fable** is the notion that a person's experience is unique. When a girl goes through a breakup with her boyfriend, she assumes that no one else (including, of course, her mother and father) could possibly understand because (she is certain) they never had to go through such an excruciating ordeal. Another aspect of the personal fable is the sense of invulnerability. The teenager thinks that she cannot get pregnant or get killed or have an accident while driving recklessly—that only happens to *other* people. "I don't have to worry about bad things happening to me. I am invincible." This has an upside in that it enhances self-esteem and confidence.

But its downside means that adolescents may engage in risky behavior because (as in Elkind's model) they think they are indestructible—no serious harm can happen to them. They may believe that they will never die or be disabled or get hurt or otherwise suffer pain because of their risk taking. These ideas of Elkind's are based on anecdotal evidence from an atypical sample—patients who spoke to him in his clinical practice. Despite their dubious research basis, they have been widely cited in the psychological literature and eagerly accepted by the broader public. Furthermore, they resonate with traditional views about youngsters that go back as far as Aristotle.

It is easy to jump from the fact that adolescents engage in risk behaviors (smoking, drinking alcohol, using drugs, driving recklessly, and so on) to the conclusion that they don't grasp the consequences of such acts. It is the simplest explanation that springs to mind: kids don't think, they're imprudent, irrational, and impulsive. When this line of argument was put to a test, however, the results did not support Elkind's claims about adolescent egocentrism and invincibility.

Somewhat surprisingly, most studies of invincibility rely on adult samples instead of adolescents, and most adults think they're unlikely to suffer negative consequences, because they are safer, more proficient, more skillful, and the like. Thus, *adults are biased in their optimistic assessments of themselves;* they see themselves as facing less risk than other people face. Recent studies that compare adolescents with adults in their analysis of risk behavior find very little difference between the two groups. Sometimes, in fact, adults imagine themselves *more* invulnerable than adolescents.[30]

Adolescents are usually aware that their risky behaviors are indeed risky. They recognize the possibility of death, disability, disease, and the pitfalls associated with engaging in certain health-compromising activities. But recent research suggests there may be a rational basis for trying these behaviors. Many activities seen as problematic or risky by society at large are also seen as offering something *positive*. They are viewed by adolescents as pleasurable, producing a rush of adrenaline or an emotional high, providing release from pressure, exploring the unknown, offering novelty, play, and excitement, achieving control, overcoming fear, doing something that is a sign of maturity or adult status, developing interpersonal relationships, increasing group cohesion, achieving independence, and rebelling against authority figures.[31]

The fact that many people are willing to take risks that jeopardize their health and welfare does not mean that they are being irrational. A rational individual

> may find it in his or her interest to take health risks, even with a lethal disease like AIDS, and even if the person understands these risks. . . . We will reduce the rate of a preferred but unsafe sexual behavior only if it leads to a percentage decrease in discounted life expectancy greater than the percentage decline in utility. The argument is that unsafe sex is like unsafe driving. Most of us are willing to reduce our life expectancy by driving a little faster to achieve some other goal, such as arriving on time for an appointment. That is, we are willing to risk a slight increase in our exposure to a deadly risk in return for a small but immediate reward.[32]

Some people are more willing than others to take risks. Gardner and Herman believe adolescents are more nonchalant about risks because they have difficulty seeing far into the future; they are less confident it will turn out well for them. Although they may hope for a lofty career, fabulous penthouse, and magnanimous spouse, some of them *expect* a bleaker future, surrounded by poverty and desperation—in which case they may see no benefit in refraining from high-risk behavior. Their motto becomes, What the hell, what have I got to lose?

This argument by Gardner and Herman contends that despair and hopelessness lead the most impoverished adolescents in urban slums to engage in more high-risk behavior. This perspective resembles the one offered by some of the news commentators discussing slum life in Chapter 1. It runs directly counter to the view expressed by Elkind, however, which says *excessive optimism* propels adolescents into risky activities. It is very unlikely that *both* arguments are valid. Perhaps neither optimism nor pessimism is the engine driving most risky behavior.

Psychologists who discuss cognition are also likely to mention intelligence and IQ scores. There is evidence that kids now are more intelligent than previous generations were at the same age. Nevertheless, people do not always *act* intelligently. Several factors may cause such behavior, such as the following.

1. **Hasty thinking**. Sometimes people act on impulse or reflexively. This usually works fine if the situation is a familiar one. But sometimes the basic situation has an unexpected twist or more complexity than usual. Then the person gets

carried away by first impressions, does not reflect or proceed cautiously, and makes a mistake.

2. **Narrow thinking**. One example of this is "my-side bias," which is to choose one side, to be decisive, even if arbitrarily so, and to act quickly. Some people think this shows leadership. Others think clear-cut, one-sided presentations are more logical or convincing. But in fact, not looking at other options is an easy way to make errors in judgment.

3. **Fuzzy thinking**. This refers to problems of insufficient clarity and precision. People sometimes fail to differentiate between things that on the surface seem the same but on closer inspection prove to be fundamentally different.

4. **Sprawling thinking**. This refers to a failure to concentrate on the essence of an issue. Instead, people's thinking sometimes wanders endlessly in a disorganized manner, jumping helter-skelter from the personalities of the people involved to the causes of a problem to solutions to it.[33]

Adolescent Subculture

Although most scholarship on adolescence has been conducted by psychologists, others, too, have contributed, including sociologist James S. Coleman, who surveyed students in ten northern Illinois high schools during the late 1950s. In *The Adolescent Society,* he claimed that youngsters in industrialized nations, because they cannot be prepared for future skilled occupational roles by parents, are sent to school. Educational institutions take on increasing functions such as extracurricular activities and keep the students for many years; in so doing, they exert a powerful impact on the youths' thinking and behavior.

Cut off from the rest of society, teenagers mingle with each other, and their social life blossoms. They maintain only the slimmest connections with the outside world. Unbeknownst to adults, according to Coleman, youths create a separate subculture, with its own language, symbols, and values that represent a complete break from the culture of adult society. He said that any parent who spoke at length with a teenage son or daughter would quickly discover how disparate the worlds of adolescents and adults are.

Teenagers immerse themselves in a society of peers, whom they associate with in school, in drugstores, cafes, and cars. Thus, the training that parents in olden days gave to their offspring no longer exists. Teens have become segregated in their own society, where their socialization has been taken over by peers. Adolescents now look to their age-mates for approval; their interests are those of other youths and are far removed from adult standards and responsibilities. The most important goal is peer approval or popularity, something they cannot attain by studying or getting good grades. For decades, people have taken Coleman's conclusions to heart.[34]

He described a subculture that valued superficial things such as cars, clothes, sports, and appearance. In it, teens turned to their peers for guidance and sought social success by attending parties and going out on dates. It dismayed Coleman to find that peer culture wielded so much influence and discouraged the kind of thinking and hard work that fostered achievement. Coleman's thesis convinced many sociologists. In part this was because few sociologists carried out research on adolescence, so Coleman had the stage pretty much to himself.

If adolescents in the late 1950s and early 1960s were as academically weak and anti-intellectual as Coleman said, then presumably there would be ample data to confirm it. One of the logical sources of data to consider is SAT scores. In the beginning (1941), few students (about 10,000) took the SAT, and most of them came from high-status families and were destined to attend Ivy League schools.[35] Coleman's book appeared twenty years later, when test takers (nearly all of whom were neither high status nor headed to Harvard) mushroomed to nearly a million; but, surprisingly, scores had changed little.[36] Or consider the Iowa Test of Basic Skills, which *all* students take, not just the college-bound. In the state of Iowa, scores increased dramatically from 1942 to 1964. In addition, more students later continued their education: college enrollment doubled between 1951 and 1961.[37] (This surge was not driven by demography—it occurred *before* baby boomers reached college age.) Such data contradict Coleman's claim that high schoolers in the late 1950s were superficial and nonstudious.

Coleman also insisted that there is a single, homogeneous peer culture. Jere Cohen tested this by reanalyzing the data from one of Coleman's ten schools and found that instead of a single adolescent subculture, there were (1) the academics, who stayed home at night, studied, planned to go to college, rarely dated, and did not smoke or drink; (2) the nonacademics, who did exactly the opposite; and (3) the popular kids, who were regarded as a great date, a desirable friend, and a top athlete.[38] Other researchers also found adolescents to be diverse.

> The teenagers in the ten communities we studied were actually as different from each other as adults are. . . . Teenagers live in poverty or affluence or someplace in between, come from broken or intact families, attend good or bad schools, and encounter very different role models in the communities in which they live. . . . Just as teenagers differ depending on where and how they live, so do the peer groups they form.[39]

Years later, the Columbine tragedy provided a window on modern high school cliques and crowds, showing some of the different directions students may take. As schools grow, *Newsweek* said, they give rise to a bewildering variety of groups:

> athletes and preppies and wannabe gangsters; pot-smoking skaters and sullen punks; gays and nerds and, yes, morbid, chalk-faced Goths. Cliques proclaim their identities with uniforms. . . . Chinos and button-down shirts mark kids as preppies a thousand miles from Andover; baggy jeans signify hip-hop on a Laotian kid in Iowa no less than on a homeboy straight out of Bed-Stuy.[40]

This article may have been a revelation to average American readers, but it rep-not news to scholars specializing in adolescence. Dexter Dunphy and Bradford introduced the distinction between cliques (six to eight close mates, who with each other daily) and crowds (larger groups having the utation) many years ago.[41] Carrying on this work in th

Brown found that some crowds have existed for decades and can be found around the country: jocks, nerds, populars, partyers, alienated youth, and brains. Others are greasers, grungers, and punks. Some changed over the years, of course; for instance, hippies metamorphosed into Valley Girls, and smokers became druggies and head-bangers. A few are strictly local, such as kickers in Texas (their regalia includes cowboy boots and outsized belt buckles).[42]

The clique gives a person a feeling of acceptance and social support. The crowd provides a sense of identity and belonging. These are particularly important when a youth is loosening ties to parents and moving from a small elementary school to a large, impersonal high school. Most early and middle adolescents can't stand being a loner, left to flounder. Rejection is particularly difficult to handle in the midst of adolescent transitions. So youths may gravitate to a particular identity and crowd, even if it's of low status.

Not surprisingly, there's a connection between the crowd one belongs to and the behavior one engages in. There is a good reason some kids are labeled druggies, burnouts, gangbangers, rebels, punks, freaks, brains, jocks, or skaters. *That's the kind of behavior they engage in.* And the relationship is reciprocal: behavior affects reputation (i.e., crowd affiliation) and vice versa. Once you're identified with one particular crowd, change may be difficult. If you're part of the druggie crowd and you decide to give up drugs, other people may refuse to accept your attempt at re-defining yourself. Kids depend on crowd affiliation to serve as stable markers of identity.[43]

Finally, Coleman said, American youngsters have turned against their parents' values. He said his data demonstrated adolescents' isolation from parents and rejection of parental values. The only way to test this is to (1) ask *students* what *their* values are and (2) ask *parents* what *their* values are. Then compare parent and child answers to see how strong the correlations are. This is fundamental procedure, but Coleman did not follow it. He asked students such questions, but failed to survey the parents.[44]

Coleman found that boys in the late 1950s enjoyed sports and cars, whereas girls were more interested in glamour and allure. Both sexes wanted popularity and high status among peers; they wanted to be successful teenagers. Neither sex believed that these goals could be achieved via academic excellence. Parents, however, valued hard work and educational and occupational attainment, not superficial teenage interests—this at least is what Coleman imagined they felt.

Maybe they did. It could be that adults are modern-day Calvinists who endlessly dwell on responsibility while disdaining leisure. But there is reason to doubt it. Considerable evidence exists showing that many adult males care deeply about sports. And more than a handful of adult women are fascinated by beauty, shape, skin, cosmetics, diets, and hair styles—judging by women's magazines and the business (clothing, nail salons, hair salons, exercise centers, and cosmetic As this suggests that teenagers' interests are not so radically different from lescents deriv

r wrote, back in 1963, almost all the values and interests of ado-
their parents. Parents and booster organizations sustain foot-

ball and basketball programs in Illinois high schools as much as students do. And parents care a great deal about prestige and popularity; often they use the same criteria to measure these as their teenage offspring do.

> From Coleman's treatment of the adolescent subculture, one might think that cars and masculine prowess and feminine glamour and social activities and sex and dating and wearing the right clothes . . . were entirely alien to American adults.[45]

How could Coleman imagine that social affairs, sports, and extracurricular activities are elements of an alien adolescent subculture that adults find objectionable? Berger points out that these activities are

> initiated and supported by the schools, sponsored and run by faculty advisors, coaches . . . and considered by grown-ups to be organized training grounds for the assumption of adult responsibilities.[46]

Conclusion

Adolescence has many aspects. Those presented in this chapter are meant to shed some light on three basic areas of adolescent development: the biological, the psychological, and the social. Puberty, cognition, and social relationships are some of the most fundamental issues of adolescence, especially early and middle adolescence. In late adolescence, on the other hand, youngsters begin to prepare for early adulthood, they have matured physically, their brain has developed about as much as it will, and social relationships begin to turn toward more mature male–female dyads instead of cliques and crowds.

It is a common mistake to assume that puberty is a single event or that it sends shock waves through the psyche of everyone going through it. For most youngsters this is not a time of great turmoil, storm and stress, or rebellion. Body image changes. Interest in dating begins to increase slightly. Sexual behavior, too, shows an increase. But each period of life has its own stresses; even the prenatal stage can be difficult (although it is difficult to get first-hand knowledge of that). Puberty is rarely upsetting or tumultuous; most teenagers *want* to have a new, more mature body and to be capable of reproduction.

Puberty may take place during a very trying time for *some youngsters,* but this does not mean that growth spurts and secondary sex characteristics *account for* their difficulties. Maybe they had an equally difficult middle and late childhood. Maybe the switch to middle school was traumatic. Maybe they had to move often, and this meant getting used to new neighbors and new schools, which proved far from easy. Or perhaps they were given a great deal of freedom and little supervision by their parents.

Like rumors of Mark Twain's death, the effects of puberty have been greatly exaggerated; researchers are finding that its effects are less dramatic than is commonly assumed. Most kids go through puberty without becoming depressed or rebellious. There is evidence that puberty is starting earlier than ever before for girls, but even so, most girls and boys are not shocked by the experience. Instead of undergoing storm and stress, most adolescents take the bodily changes in stride. It only becomes a problem if the individual is facing other difficulties at the same time (such as changing schools).

Research shows that for girls, the effects of *early* maturation can be problematic. Those who mature early look more like women, which annoys other girls sometimes but generally makes the male population perk up. This can lead to problems for the early maturers, both psychologically and behaviorally. As for boys, the body of research on pubertal timing among them is limited, though most of the studies that exist find that early maturers are more prone to delinquency. This suggests that when it comes to crime and delinquency, pubertal timing matters more than age does, a fact criminologists seem unaware of.

Some changes take place in the mind as well as the body. Adolescence is a time of increased decision making. Teenagers are able to imagine more options to choose from than children are. This ability continues to increase throughout the adolescent years. Some studies indicate that adolescents are as advanced as adults are when it comes to decision-making skills. Of course, having the ability does not mean it will be used in everyday life, where experience matters considerably in what people decide.

Piaget divided cognition into stages, sensorimotor, preoperational, concrete operational, and formal operational, but later researchers found that individual youngsters did not fit these categories so neatly. And they could be taught more sophisticated ways of thinking—the stages were not nearly as hard-wired as Piaget claimed. David Elkind expanded a different aspect of Piaget's approach when he described the imaginary audience and the personal fable. In the latter, the adolescent feels unique. No one else can understand, because no one else has gone through the same experience and therefore cannot imagine the feelings it engenders—so the youngsters thinks (because of his or her egocentrism).

The personal fable also leads adolescents to think that nothing untoward can happen to them—only other people die in accidents, natural disasters, or severe illnesses. Not me. This in turn fosters adolescent risk-taking, with the individual thinking there is no need to worry, because nothing terrible will happen. This implies that adolescents are by nature hopeful and overly optimistic, and that is why they take chances that put their life and health in jeopardy. But research shows that many adults too take chances that are risky. And adolescents who take risks are usually well aware of the downside. They are not so foolish as to not realize what could happen. They often take risks because they perceive a benefit, usually it's having fun or impressing their friends and associates. Not to participate would risk having these friends call them a wimp. It is also eminently possible that the few daredevils among adolescents are not optimists at all, but believe their future is uncertain, so why not live dangerously.

Having dealt with the biological and psychological elements of adolescence, we next turn to the social side, where one of the arguments is Coleman's claim that adolescents have severed their ties to parents (actually this is an old psychoanalytic belief) and have few connections to other adults. They are segregated by age in public high schools and forced inward toward peers for guidance. Coleman was dismayed by students' wish to be popular, to star in athletics, to have their own car. Academic achievement did not occupy a lofty perch in their value system. Coleman deplored high schoolers' preference for fun over finals, their desire to live for the moment instead of the future. He said they were beyond parents' influence and held in thrall by peers.

Subsequent research has shown that youngsters are not cut off from their families. They take their parents' view into account in making some of the most important decisions of their lives. Peers do indeed matter, especially around ninth grade, when conformity tends to reach its peak. Then crowds and cliques play an important role in the life of the adolescent. And this is especially apparent in the way kids style their hair, choose their clothes, and select their music. But peer influence recedes as adolescents move into their junior and senior years of high school. They continue to mature and begin to prepare for their adult lives.

Several aspects of adolescence impinge on youth crime. Young people inevitably get bigger and stronger during adolescence. Males' testosterone levels rise noticeably. They want more independence and freedom to make their own decisions. They spend more time away from parents and with fun-loving peers. They like to think of themselves as adults and as therefore deserving the same privileges adults have: smoking, drinking, driving, staying out late, having sex, and so on. This desire for adult status can sometimes spill over into drug use, theft, and violence, especially among youths who are alienated from school and family.

When they get bigger and stronger, this creates the impression that they are mature and "grown up" in an emotional sense. This means they are given more opportunities to make their own decisions and choose their own lifestyle. In addition, if they are larger than their mother and there is no father in the family, the mother may give up on trying to control them any longer. She may say: He is beyond my control now, he's a man, I can't do a thing with him now.[47] This makes it easier for youngsters to do whatever they wish, and sometimes what they wish is to engage in deviance.

Key Terms

Adolescence:	the period after childhood and before adulthood
Puberty:	the bodily changes that announce the beginning of adolescence
Menarche:	a girl's first menstruation
Androgens:	steroid hormones that control the development of masculine traits
Internalizing symptoms:	anxiety, shyness, depression, nausea
Externalizing symptoms:	acting out behavior such as fighting and stealing
Deviance hypothesis:	maturing off time, that is, either earlier or later than one's peers, causes problems
Stage termination hypothesis:	maturing early causes problems

Experience Sampling Method:	beeping people at random times throughout the day and having them report what they're doing and feeling at those moments
Sensorimotor:	stage when infant is trying to coordinate sensory experiences with physical movements
Personal fable:	belief that one's experiences are unique; no one else has had them
Hasty thinking:	thinking guided by impulses or first impressions
Narrow thinking:	looking at one side of an issue; bias
Fuzzy thinking:	not looking closely at an issue, not going beyond the surface
Sprawling thinking:	letting the mind wander aimlessly, disorganized thinking

End Notes

[1]Lisa J. Crockett, "Cultural, Historical, and Subcultural Contexts of Adolescence," in John Schulenberg, Jennifer L. Maggs, and Klaus Hurrelmann, eds., *Health Risks and Developmental Transitions During Adolescence* (New York: Cambridge University Press, 1999), pp. 23–53; Frank M. Biro, "Physical Growth and Development," in Stanford B. Friedman, Martin Fisher, S. Kenneth Schonberg, and Elizabeth M. Alderman, eds., *Comprehensive Adolescent Health Care*, 2nd ed. (St. Louis: Mosby-Year Book Medical Publications, 1998), pp. 28–33; Michael Mitterauer, *A History of Youth* (Oxford, England: Basil Blackwell, 1993).

[2]Laurence Steinberg, *Adolescence,* 5th ed. (New York: McGraw-Hill, 1999), p. 4.

[3]Robert M. Malina and Claude Bouchard, *Growth, Maturation, and Physical Activity* (Champaign, IL: Human Kinetics, 1991); J. M. Tanner, *Foetus into Man,* 2nd ed. (Cambridge, MA: Harvard University Press, 1990).

[4]Jeanne Brooks-Gunn and Edward O. Reiter, "The Role of Pubertal Processes," in S. Shirley Feldman and Glen R. Elliott, eds., *At the Threshold* (Cambridge, MA: Harvard University Press, 1993), p. 21.

[5]G. Stanley Hall, *Adolescence,* Volumes one and two (Englewood Cliffs, NJ: Prentice Hall, 1904); Anna Freud, "Adolescence," *Psychoanalytic Study of the Child, 13* (1958), pp. 258–78; Anna Freud, "Adolescence," in Alvin E. Winder and David L. Angus, eds., *Adolescence: Contemporary Studies* (New York: American Book, 1968), pp. 13–24; Anna Freud, "Adolescence as a Developmental Disturbance," in Gerald Caplan and Serge Lebovici, eds., *Adolescence: Psychosocial Perspectives* (New York: Basic, 1969), pp. 5–10; Peter Blos, *On Adolescence* (New York: Free Press, 1962).

[6]Susan Campbell, "Adolescence: A Hellish Mix of Rampaging Emotions," *The Scotsman,* January 13, 1997, p. 13.

[7]Daniel M. Offer, Kimberly A. Schonert-Reichl, and Andrew M. Boxer, "Normal Adolescent Development," in Melvin Lewis, ed., *Child and Adolescent Psychiatry,* 2nd ed. (Baltimore: Williams and Williams, 1996), pp. 278–90. See also Michael Rut-

ter, Philip Graham, Oliver F. Chadwick, and William Yule, "Adolescent Turmoil: Fact or Fiction?" *Journal of Child Psychiatry and Psychology, 17,* no. 1 (January 1976), pp. 35–56; Raymond Montemayor, "Family Variation in Adolescent Storm and Stress," *Journal of Adolescent Research, 1,* no. 1 (Spring 1986), pp. 15–31; Daniel Offer, *The Psychological World of the Teenager* (New York: Basic, 1969); Daniel Offer, Eric Ostrov, and Kenneth Irwin Howard, "The Mental Health Professional's Concept of the Normal Adolescent," *Archives of General Psychiatry, 38,* no. 2 (February 1981), pp. 149–52; Anne C. Petersen, Bruce E. Compas, Jeanne Brooks-Gunn, Mark Stemmeier, Sydney Ey, and Kathryn E. Grant, "Depression in Adolescence," *American Psychologist, 48,* no. 2 (February 1993), pp. 155–68; David Elkind, "Cognitive Development," in Stanford B. Friedman, Martin Fisher, S. Kenneth Schonberg, and Elizabeth M. Alderman, eds., *Comprehensive Adolescent Health Care,* pp. 34–7; Beatrix A. Hamburg, "Psychosocial Development," in Stanford B. Friedman, Martin Fisher, S. Kenneth Schonberg, and Elizabeth M. Alderman, eds. *Comprehensive Adolescent Health Care,* pp. 38–48.

[8]Hester Lacey, "Too Much, Too Young," *The Independent* (London), October 18, 1998, p. 20.

[9]Hakan Stattin and David Magnusson, *Pubertal Maturation in Female Development* (Hillsdale, NJ: Erlbaum, 1990).

[10]Margaret Beale Spencer, Davido Dupree, Dena Phillips Swanson, and Michael Cunningham, "The Influence of Physical Maturation and Hassles on African American Adolescents' Learning Behaviors," *Journal of Comparative Family Studies, 29,* no. 1 (Spring 1998), pp. 189–200.

[11]Kathleen M. Brown, Robert P. McMahon, Frank M. Biro, Pat Crawford, George B. Schreiber, Shari L. Similo, Myron A. Waclawiw, and Ruth Striegel-Moore, "Changes in Self-Esteem in Black and White Girls Between the Ages of 9 and 14 Years," *Journal of Adolescent Health, 22,* no. 2 (February 1998), pp. 7–19; Joan Jacobs Brumberg, *The Body Project* (New York: Random House, 1997); Marcia E. Herman-Giddens and Sandra G. Boodman, "Girls Beginning Puberty Earlier, Study Finds," *Washington Post,* April 22, 1997, p. 7; Jane E. Brody, "Yesterday's Precocious Puberty is Norm Today," *New York Times,* November 30, 1999, p. F8.

[12]Jill M. Cyranowski, Ellen Frank, Elizabeth Young, and M. Katherine Shear, "Adolescent Onset of the Gender Difference in Lifetime Rates of Major Depression," *Archives of General Psychiatry, 57,* no. 1 (January 2000), pp. 21–7.

[13]Susan Harter, *Manual of the Self-Perception Profile for Adolescents* (Denver: University of Denver, 1988).

[14]Jeanne Brooks-Gunn, "Consequences of Maturational Timing Variations in Adolescent Girls," in Richard M. Lerner, Anne C. Petersen, and Jeanne Brooks-Gunn, eds., *Encyclopedia of Adolescence,* Volume two (New York: Garland, 1991), pp. 614–8; Roberta G. Simmons and Dale A. Blyth, *Moving into Adolescence* (New York: Aldine de Gruyter, 1987).

[15]Margaret S. Faust, "Alternative Constructions of Adolescent Growth," in Jeanne Brooks-Gunn and Anne C. Petersen, eds., *Girls at Puberty* (New York: Plenum, 1983), pp. 105–25; Joan Jacobs Brumberg, *The Body Project;* Richard M. Lerner and Cheryl

K. Olson, "'My Body is So Ugly,'" *Parents* (February 1995), pp. 87–8; Michelle Murphy, "I'm Okay!" *Saint Raphael's Better Health* (November-December 1995), pp. 16–20.

[16]Elissa Koff and Jill Rierdan, "Perceptions of Weight and Attitudes Toward Eating in Early Adolescent Girls," *Journal of Adolescent Health, 12,* no. 4 (June 1991), pp. 307–12; Jeanne Brooks-Gunn, "Consequences of Maturational Timing Variations in Adolescent Girls"; Jeanne Brooks-Gunn and Michelle P. Warren, "The Psychological Significance of Secondary Sexual Characteristics in 9- to 11-Year-Old Girls," *Child Development, 59,* no. 4 (August 1988), pp. 1061–9; Roberta G. Simmons and Dale A. Blyth, *Moving Into Adolescence.*

[17]John Dacey and Maureen Kenny, *Adolescent Development* (Boston: McGraw-Hill, 1997).

[18]Michele Ingrassia, "The Body of the Beholder," *Newsweek* (April 24, 1995), pp. 66–7; Richard M. Lerner and Cheryl K. Olson, "My Body is So Ugly"; John Dacey and Maureen Kenny, *Adolescent Development.*

[19]Julia A. Graber, Peter M. Lewinsohn, John R. Seeley, and Jeanne Brooks-Gunn, "Is Psychopathology Associated with the Timing of Pubertal Development?" *Journal of the American Academy of Child and Adolescent Psychiatry, 36,* no. 12 (December 1997), pp. 1768–76; Danielle M. Dick, Richard J. Rose, Richard J. Viken, and Jaakko Kaprio, "Pubertal Timing and Substance Use," *Child Development, 36,* no. 2 (March 2000), pp. 180–9.

[20]Avshalom Caspi, Donald Lynam, Terrie E. Moffitt, and Phil A. Silva, "Unraveling Girls' Delinquency: Biological, Dispositional, and Contextual Contributions to Adolescent Misbehavior," *Developmental Psychology, 29,* no. 1 (January 1993), pp. 19–30. See also Julia A. Graber, Peter M. Lewinsohn, John R. Seeley, and Jeanne Brooks-Gunn, "Is Psychopathology Associated with the Timing of Pubertal Development?"; David Magnusson, *Individual Development from an Interactional Perspective* (Hillsdale, NJ: Erlbaum, 1988); Rainer K. Silbereisen and Baerbel Kracke, "Variation in Maturational Timing and Adjustment in Adolescence," in Sandy Jackson and Hector Rodriguez-Tome, eds., *Adolescence and its Social Worlds* (Hillsdale, NJ: Erlbaum, 1993), pp. 67–94; Roberta G. Simmons and Dale A. Blyth, *Moving Into Adolescence;* Danielle M. Dick, Richard J. Rose, Richard J. Viken, and Jaakko Kaprio, "Pubertal Timing and Substance Use"; Ada Castillo Mezzich, Ralph E. Tarter, Peter R. Giancola, Sandy Y. Lu, Levent Kirisci, and Susan M. Parks, "Substance Use and Risky Sexual Behavior in Female Adolescents," *Drug and Alcohol Dependence, 44,* nos. 2–3 (1997), pp. 157–66; Darrell M. Wilson, Joel D. Killen, Chris Hayward, Thomas N. Robinson, Lawrence D. Hammer, Helena Chmura-Kraemer, Ann Varady, and C. Barr Taylor, "Timing and Rate of Sexual Maturation and the Onset of Cigarette and Alcohol Use Among Teenage Girls," *Archives of Pediatrics and Adolescent Medicine, 148,* no. 8 (August 1994), pp. 789–95.

[21]Joanne M. Williams and Lillian C. Dunlop, "Pubertal Timing and Self-Reported Delinquency Among Male Adolescents," *Journal of Adolescence, 22,* no. 1 (February 1999), pp. 157–71. See also Sonia Cota-Robles, Michelle Neiss, and David C. Rowe, "The Role of Puberty in Violent and Nonviolent Delinquency Among Anglo American, Mexican American, and African American Boys," *Journal of Adolescent Re-*

search, 17, no. 4 (July 2002), pp. 364–76; Julia A. Graber, Peter M. Lewinsohn, John R. Seeley, and Jeanne Brooks-Gunn, "Is Psychopathology Associated with the Timing of Pubertal Development?"; Michael Rutter and David Smith, eds., *Psychosocial Disorders of Young People* (New York: Wiley, 1995); Paula Duke Duncan, Philip L. Ritter, Sanford M. Dornbusch, Ruth T. Gross, and J. Merrill Cartsmith, "The Effects of Pubertal Timing on Body Image, School Behavior, and Deviance," *Journal of Youth and Adolescence, 14,* no. 3 (June 1985), pp. 227–35; Tommy Andersson and David Magnusson, "Biological Maturation in Adolescence and the Development of Drinking Habits and Alcohol Abuse Among Young Males," *Journal of Youth and Adolescence, 19,* no. 1 (February 1990), pp. 33–41; Anne C. Petersen and Lisa J. Crockett, "Pubertal Timing and Grade Effects on Adjustment," *Journal of Youth and Adolescence, 14,* no. 3 (June 1985), pp. 191–206; Harvey Peskin, "Influence of the Developmental Schedule of Puberty on Learning and Ego Functioning," *Journal of Youth and Adolescence, 2,* no. 4 (December 1973), pp. 273–90; Xiaojia Ge, Gene H. Brody, Rand D. Conger, Ronald L. Simons, and Velma McBride Murry, "Contextual Amplification of Pubertal Transition Effects on Deviant Peer Affiliation and Externalizing Behavior Among African American Children," *Developmental Psychology, 38,* no. 1 (January 2002), pp. 42–54; Richard B. Felson and Dana L. Haynie, "Pubertal Development, Social Factors, and Delinquency Among Adolescent Boys," *Criminology, 40,* no. 4 (November 2002), pp. 967–98.

[22]Mihaly Csikszentmihalyi and Reed Larson, *Being Adolescent* (New York: Basic, 1984); Reed Larson and Maryse H. Richards, *Divergent Realities* (New York: Basic, 1994); Elizabeth J. Susman and Anne C. Petersen, "Hormones and Behavior in Adolescence," in Elizabeth R. McAnarney, Richard E. Kreipe, Donald P. Orr, and George D. Comerci, eds., *Textbook of Adolescent Medicine* (Philadelphia: W. B. Saunders, 1992), pp. 125–30.

[23]Brian K. Barber, "Cultural, Family, and Personal Contexts of Parent-Adolescent Conflict," *Journal of Marriage and the Family, 56,* no. 2 (May 1994), pp. 375–86.

[24]Judith G. Smetana and Pamela Asquith, "Adolescents' and Parents' Conceptions of Parental Authority and Personal Autonomy," *Child Development, 65,* no. 4 (August 1994), p. 1151.

[25]Daniel Offer, *The Psychological World of the Teenager;* Daniel Offer, Eric Ostrov, and Kenneth Howard, *The Adolescent: A Psychological Self-Portrait* (New York: Basic, 1981); Michael Rutter, Philip Graham, Oliver F. Chadwick, and William Yule, "Adolescent Turmoil: Fact or Fiction?"; Elizabeth Douvan and Joseph Adelson, *The Adolescent Experience* (New York: Wiley, 1966); Richard M. Lerner, "A Life-Span Perspective for Early Adolescence," in Richard M. Lerner and Terryl T. Foch, eds., *Biological-Psychological Interactions in Early Adolescence* (Hillsdale, NJ: Erlbaum, 1987), pp. 9–34.

[26]Suzie Hayman, *Adolescence: A Survival Guide to the Teenage Years* (New York: Gower, 1986); Paul A. Smyth and Janet Benner, *Parent Survival Training: A Guide for Parents of Teenagers* (Santa Barbara, CA: Joelle, 1987).

[27]Laurence Steinberg, *Crossing Paths* (New York: Simon and Schuster, 1994), p. 179.

[28]*Ibid.*

[29]Barbel Inhelder and Jean Piaget, *The Growth of Logical Thinking From Childhood to Adolescence* (New York: Basic, 1958).

[30]David Elkind, "Egocentrism in Adolescence," *Child Development, 38,* no. 4 (December 1967), pp. 1025–34; Marilyn Jacobs Quadrel, Baruch Fischhoff, and Wendy Davis, "Adolescent (In)vulnerability," *American Psychologist, 48,* no. 2 (February 1993), pp. 102–16; Ruth Beyth-Marom, Laurel Austin, Baruch Fischhoff, Claire Palmgren, and Marilyn Jacobs Quadrel, "Perceived Consequences of Risky Behavior," *Developmental Psychology, 29,* no. 3 (May 1993), pp. 549–63; Baruch Fischhoff and Marilyn Jacobs Quadrel, "Adolescent Alcohol Decisions," in Gayle M. Boyd, Jan Howard, and Robert A. Zucker, eds., *Alcohol Problems Among Adolescents* (Hillsdale, NJ: Erlbaum, 1995), pp. 59–84.

[31]Cynthia Lightfoot, *The Culture of Adolescent Risk-Taking* (New York: Guilford, 1997); Susan Moore and Eleonora Gullone, "Predicting Adolescent Risk Behavior Using a Personalized Cost-Benefit Analysis," *Journal of Youth and Adolescence, 25,* no. 3 (June 1996), pp. 343–59.

[32]William Gardner and Janna Herman, "Adolescent AIDS Risk Taking," in William Gardner, Susan G. Millstein, and Brian L. Wilcox, eds., *Adolescents in the AIDS Epidemic* (San Francisco: Jossey-Bass, 1990), p. 23.

[33]David Perkins, *Outsmarting IQ* (New York: Free Press, 1995).

[34]James S. Coleman, *The Adolescent Society* (New York: Free Press, 1961); LaMar T. Empey, Mark C. Stafford, and Carter H. Hay, *American Delinquency,* 4th ed. (Belmont, CA: Wadsworth, 1999); Talcott Parsons, "Youth in the Context of American Society," in Erik H. Erikson, ed., *The Challenge of Youth* (New York: Doubleday, 1965), pp. 110–41; David Riesman, *The Lonely Crowd* (New Haven, CT: Yale University Press, 1950).

[35]Gerald W. Bracey, "What Happened to America's Public Schools?" *American Heritage, 48,* no. 7 (November 1997), pp. 38–41; David C. Berliner and Laurence Steinberg, "Q: Is the So-Called Educational Crisis a Myth Created by Conservatives?" *Insight on the News, 12,* no. 38 (October 7, 1996), pp. 26–8; David C. Berliner and Bruce J. Biddle, *The Manufactured Crisis* (Reading, MA: Addison-Wesley, 1995).

[36]Willard Wirtz, *On Further Examination* (New York: College Entrance Examination Board, 1977).

[37]Nicholas Lemann, *The Big Test* (New York: Farrar, Straus and Giroux, 1999).

[38]Jere Cohen, "High School Subcultures and the Adult World," *Adolescence, 14,* no. 5 (Fall 1979), pp. 491–502.

[39]Francis A. J. Ianni, *The Search for Structure* (New York: Free Press, 1989), p. 23.

[40]Jerry Adler, John McCormick, Karen Springen, Daniel Pedersen, Nadine Joseph, Ana Figueroa, and Beth Dickey, "The Truth About High School," *Newsweek* (May 10, 1999), p. 56.

[41]Dexter C. Dunphy, *Cliques, Crowds and Gangs* (Melbourne: Cheshire, 1969).

[42]B. Bradford Brown, "Peer Groups and Peer Cultures," in S. Shirley Feldman and Glen R. Elliott, eds., *At the Threshold,* pp. 171–96.

[43]B. Bradford Brown, M. Margaret Dolcini, and Amy Leventhal, "Transformation in Peer Relationships at Adolescence," in John Schulenberg, Jennifer L. Maggs, and Klaus Hurrelman, eds., *Health Risks and Developmental Transitions During Adolescence*, pp. 161–89.

[44]Gary F. Jensen, "Methodological Issues in the Study of Adolescent Society," *University of Washington Journal of Sociology*, 2 (November 1970), pp. 38–46.

[45]Bennett M. Berger, "Adolescence and Beyond," *Social Problems, 10*, no. 4 (Spring 1963), p. 396.

[46]*Ibid.*, pp. 236–7.

[47]Francis A. J. Ianni, *The Search for Structure*, p. 65.

Recommended Readings

Laurence Steinberg, *Adolescence*, 6th ed. (New York: McGraw-Hill, 2002).

Mihaly Csikszentmihalyi and Reed Larson, *Being Adolescent* (New York: Basic, 1984).

Thomas Grisso and Robert G. Schwartz, *Youth on Trial* (Chicago: University of Chicago Press, 2000).

Reed Larson and Maryse H. Richards, *Divergent Realities* (New York: Basic, 1994).

Julia A. Graber, Jeanne Brooks-Gunn, and Anne C. Petersen, *Transitions Through Adolescence* (Mahwah, NJ: Erlbaum, 1996).

Thomas P. Gullotta, Gerald R. Adams, and Carol A. Markstrom, *The Adolescent Experience*, 4th ed. (San Diego: Academic Press, 1999).

CHAPTER 4

Individualistic Theories of Youth Crime

Crime Control Costs

In 1999, according to research conducted for the Bureau of Justice Statistics, America spent $147 billion on police, courts, and prisons, a figure four times the amount spent on criminal justice in 1982. Expenditures rose especially steeply at the federal level, climbing from $4.5 billion in 1982 to $27.4 billion in 1999. One reason: the war on drugs. By 1999, the majority of inmates in federal prisons (60 percent) were locked up because of drug offenses, a percentage far higher than exists in any state prison.[1]

Some of these funds pay for personnel: there are 2.2 million employees in the criminal justice system drawing wages or salaries, including a million police officers and 717,000 prison and jail workers. New buildings and equipment also require an influx of cash. Although criminal justice has lately become one of the nation's growth industries, the boom in expenditures is not divided equally: some parts are basking in resources, but others have been forced to scrimp. Between 1982 and 1999, controlling for inflation, funds spent on the police grew by only 39 percent, while they were soaring for corrections (by 122 percent).[2]

How wisely has this money been spent? Has it made the U.S. crime rate lower than the ones found in other industrialized nations? Comparing crime rates among different countries is complicated because each society has a different reporting system. Plus, populations differ in how willing or reluctant they are to report crime to the authorities. These problems notwithstanding, it is generally conceded that for the last half of the twentieth century the United States had a higher crime rate, a worse crime problem than other Western nations. Back in 1977, for instance, it was pointed out that

There were as many murders in Manhattan each year as in the whole of England and Wales; and Houston is even worse. Detroit, with much the same population as Northern Ireland, has even in these grim days five times the murders.[3]

The same sort of relationship holds among the states. That is, crime rates are high in jurisdictions that spend heavily on criminal justice (District of Columbia, Alaska, and California), and where the justice expenditures are low so are the crime rates (both Dakotas, Maine, Vermont, and West Virginia).[4] Are high crime rates a sign that criminologists have failed, that their theories have proved to be completely futile and unable to control crime? Or are modern criminologists ignored by the officials who set criminal justice policy? An argument could be made that the criminal justice policy of today is actually hundreds of years old, and that it is based on the work of long-dead philosophers—not contemporary criminologists or sociologists.

Early Influences: Religion and Philosophy

Consider the case of Marc-Antoine Calas. When he died of hanging in 1761 in France, his family at first denied, then reluctantly admitted, that it was suicide. Marc-Antoine, at age 28, had threatened many times to kill himself before he actually went ahead and did so. The trial judges, however, for some unknown reason, convicted Marc-Antoine's frail 68-year-old father of murdering his powerfully built son. In those days, punishment was saturated with sadistic elements; it was not for the faint of heart. First, officials subjected Jean Calas to a series of gruesome tortures, but he still refused to admit being guilty. The judges then pronounced the sentence, which directed that he be taken from the prison to the Cathedral. There, kneeling, he was supposed to ask for God, the King, and justice to forgive him. Then the executioner had to take him in a cart to the Place Saint Georges,

> where upon a scaffold his arms, legs, thighs, and loins will be broken and crushed. Finally, the prisoner should be placed upon a wheel, with his face turned to the sky, alive and in pain, and repent for his said crimes and misdeeds, all the while imploring God for his life, thereby to serve as an example and to instill terror in the wicked.[5]

This brutality made a lasting impression on Voltaire, the French philosopher, who had previously paid crime and justice scant attention. The Calas case provoked him to fire off letters and pamphlets of protest and to campaign for a reversal of the legal decision. The campaign eventually succeeded, for the incident received intense publicity, the trial documents were reexamined, Calas was declared not guilty (although too late to save his life), and his family received a special indemnity from the king.

The justice system at the time was based on religion as well as law, accepted torture as a proper technique of information gathering, and assumed that deterrence required punishment so appalling that observers would be stunned. Because crimes incurred the wrath of God, His forgiveness had to be asked for. Crimes were viewed as sins caused by offenders' having made a pact with the devil. The evil had to be physically eradicated from the body. These principles were part of the Catholic dogma of that era. Voltaire, who had no respect for religion before the Calas affair, became even more infuriated with it afterwards. But he did not have the determination to devise an entirely new system of justice based on secular principles.

Shortly thereafter, though, someone else did: Cesare Beccaria, a 26-year-old Italian, who admired not only Voltaire but other Enlightenment thinkers such as Montesquieu, Rousseau, Diderot, Kant, Adam Smith, and Hume. In 1764, Beccaria burst on the intellectual scene with his book *Of Crimes and Punishments.* Previously, he knew practically nothing about criminal law, but he was spurred on by his fellow study group members, especially Pietro Verri. In essence, they assigned him this topic as a term paper. The resulting essay proved to be both controversial and popular. It soon was placed on the Papal Index of forbidden books, a tactic that backfired; the book's influence grew rather than diminishing. By 1800, there were 23 Italian editions printed, an additional 14 in French and 11 in English. In rocketing to worldwide fame, Beccaria attracted all sorts of admirers, from Thomas Jefferson to Russia's Catherine II.[6]

Among his 47 principles, here are a few of the more memorable ones.

1. (3) Laws and legislatures alone can state the punishment for a crime. Judges must not be allowed to add to it.
2. (5) Laws must be written in language people can understand.
3. (6, 7, 8) The punishment should be proportional to the harm caused to society.
4. (12, 16) The purpose of punishment is to prevent the offender from committing further crimes and deter others from doing likewise. Torture and cruelty are not effective.
5. (19) The punishment should be administered as soon as possible after the crime so the human mind will associate these two with each other.
6. (21) Punishment ought to be the same, regardless of the offender's social status.
7. (27) Certainty of mild punishment has more of an impact than an awful punishment that is uncertain.
8. (28) The death penalty is not useful because it teaches men savagery.
9. (41) Since it is better to prevent crimes than punish them, that ought to be the goal of legislation.
10. (47) In sum: Punishment should be public, quick, necessary, lawful, minimal, and proportionate to the crime.[7]

Beccaria had very little to say about prison, but as his ideas caught on, and capital and corporal punishment were forbidden under his proposed system, *something* had to be done with offenders, so prisons eventually became the punishment throughout much of the world. That is Beccaria's practical legacy. The present system of criminal justice does not follow Beccaria in every detail, of course. Speedy trials, for instance, are rare. But in overall design, we are still trying to follow the term paper that friends forced the reluctant 26-year-old to compose two centuries ago.

Lombroso, an Early Biological Criminologist

For years, Beccaria and Jeremy Bentham were classified as the main exemplars of the classical school of criminology. It was said that these two authors believed that humans act based purely on their free will. Hence, crime is something people do voluntarily, because it brings them more pleasure than pain. Actually, that position is now being questioned, for it is not clear that Beccaria believed in free will. It turns out that he was actually a determinist to some degree. Over a hundred years later, he was criticized by *another* famous Italian determinist named Cesare—this one, Cesare Lombroso.

Trained as a physician in nineteenth-century Italy, Lombroso was not a philosopher. He was more accurately described as a scientist, though a rather sloppy one. He rather casually measured various physical parts of prisoners and concluded that they had anomalies that were atavistic or degenerative. *Atavism* means reversion to an earlier stage of evolution—either to a more primitive and savage man or to a subhuman ape or other nonhuman primate. As such, he said, they could not understand or cope with the complex rules of civilized society, and hence they broke them repeatedly.

Lombroso said his theory came to him as a sudden flash of inspiration while he was examining the corpse of the notorious criminal Vilella.

> At the sight of that skull, I seemed to see all of a sudden . . . the nature of the criminal—an atavistic being who reproduces in his person the ferocious instincts of primitive humanity and the inferior animals. Thus were explained anatomically the enormous jaws, high cheek-bones, prominent superciliary arches, solitary lines in the palms, extreme size of the orbits, handle-shaped or sessile ears found in criminals, savages, and apes, insensibility to pain, extremely acute sight, tattooing, excessive idleness, love of orgies, and the irresistible craving for evil for its own sake, the desire not only to extinguish life in the victim, but to mutilate the corpse, tear its flesh, and drink its blood.[8]

After this sudden intuitive insight, Lombroso asserted that physical anomalies or stigmata were signs of defective moral qualities in criminals, who differed from normal persons in kind, not just degree. This idea that criminals were a breed apart was readily accepted a century ago, inspiring, among other literary works, the tale of *Dr. Jekyll and Mr. Hyde.*

This atavistic individual was the *born criminal,* Lombroso said. Later, he added other types: the epileptic criminal, the criminaloid, the occasional criminal, the passionate criminal, and the female criminal, but the focus would continue to be on the atavistic, degenerate, born criminal. Once he had published his book *L'Uomo Delinquente,* founded his journal, and recruited his star pupils Ferri and Garofalo, Lombroso had the ingredients to establish his own school of thought *(the positive school)* and to spread his thinking around the globe. Positivists turned to the world of science to explain criminality, in contrast to the classical school, which was more philosophical and more directed toward policy (improving the criminal justice system).

Although Lombroso still has some diehard supporters today in a few countries, his claims about criminals were undermined long ago by Goring's massive statistical work, *The English Convict*. Goring criticized Lombroso's haphazard methods of investigation and complained that Lombroso distorted the findings to suit his preconceptions. Goring did find some differences between prison inmates and other men (soldiers, undergraduate students, and staff and inmates of hospitals) but they were not the physical anomalies cited by Lombroso. His damning conclusion: the Lombrosian doctrine crumbled when it was put to the test scientifically. There was no physical criminal of the type that Lombroso had described.[9]

Early theory and research by Lombroso and some later "body-type criminologists" (such as Earnest A. Hooton, and William H. Sheldon) argued that constitutional traits were good predictors of crime and delinquency. Their attempt failed completely, however and for this they have been justly ridiculed (Lombroso) or mostly forgotten (Hooton and Sheldon). Partly because of these failures, most mainline researchers avoid considering the connection between biology and crime. Occasionally, however, a journalist may mention such a link, as *New York Times* crime reporter Fox Butterfield did in his study of subway killer Willie Bosket. Willie was not an aberration in the Bosket family; he was just the latest in a long line of murderers (many of whom grew up without their father present). According to Butterfield,

> Science has not advanced far enough to say whether Willie inherited any part of his aggressive tendencies from his father. Willie himself often thought so; he believed he could feel something of his father inside him. But you have to be very careful about drawing such conclusions about biology. The poverty and neglect in which Willie grew up, along with the violence on the streets in his neighborhood, were trouble enough to explain what happened. Still, in later years, researchers would find that some traits of temperament are often heritable.[10]

Evolutionary Psychology

Biology, the study of life, is largely an outgrowth of the work of Charles Darwin, who is best known for two books: *On the Origin of Species by Means of Natural Selection* and *The Descent of Man and Selection in Relation to Sex*.[11] A diligent researcher and brilliant theorist, he created the theory of evolution. Expecting his ideas would produce a storm of outrage, Darwin hesitated. He tried to amass a mountain of data and anticipate every possible criticism. Then Alfred Russel Wallace proposed the same theory in an essay, which forced Darwin to speed up his work on the *Origin of Species.*

Two problems eventually arose. Neither one was Darwin's fault. First, Herbert Spencer coined the term "survival of the fittest" and a new set of sociopolitical ideas appeared, which were called Social Darwinism: If, in the natural world, there was no central authority to protect the weak and feeble, they would be weeded out as all individuals pursued their own ends. Spencer said this process should also be applied to humans. Thus, laissez-faire capitalism, imperialism, colonialism, and disparities in wealth and power were deemed *natural* and worth encouraging.[12] Darwin

Generally recognized as the most eminent scientist of the nineteenth century, Charles Darwin, after reading Malthus's essay on population, was inspired to create the theory of evolution by natural selection. *(Corbis/Bettmann.)*

neither invented nor admired the term "survival of the fittest." Moreover, he was dead set against applying his theory to social and economic affairs. Social Darwinism was not his idea; it probably should have been called Spencerism.

The second embarrassing development came from within Darwin's extended family. Francis Galton, a cousin, worried that Victorian society was too altruistic, that its humanitarianism prevented natural selection from occurring. The sick and needy were cared for and thus allowed to procreate. Eventually, Galton feared, the "less fit" would multiply and outnumber their "betters," which he said would prove to be disastrous. So Galton preached positive **eugenics**, meaning that the so-called genetically superior people should produce more children than they were doing at the time. In the United States, however, the movement took a negative turn and it helped pass laws restricting immigration and sterilizing some of the mentally "unfit." Evolutionary scientists of today deplore and completely reject such policies. To make it clear that they are *not* referring to this political baggage, they call evolutionary thinking "true Darwinism."

True Darwinism includes natural selection, which can be summarized as follows:
In every species, individuals vary greatly in their physical and behavioral traits.
Some of these differences are hereditary.
Some of these traits are suited to the environment: conducive to finding food, avoiding predators, fending off parasites.

Competition is inevitable, because species have many more offspring than can
　　possibly survive. Some individuals will leave fewer offspring than others.
Advantageous traits enable the individuals to live longer and reproduce more.
These advantageous traits will be passed on to the next generation.
The disadvantageous traits that caused other individuals to die early or not re-
　　produce will not be passed on.

In the long run, the advantageous traits will tend to become common in the population. "Survival of the fittest" does not accurately describe this process. Reproduction, not survival, is the key to natural selection. The question that arises next
is what designs in the environment are best suited to reproduction. Such designs
are known as adaptations. Bat sonar, cheetah speed and agility, and the human eye
stand out as some of the more amazing adaptations designed by natural selection
over thousands of generations to solve environmental problems.[13]

Sexual selection is in a sense the opposite of natural selection. The point of sexual selection is to use elaborate ornamentation or display to attract the opposite
sex. The peacock's extravagant tail-feathers are, of course, the standard example.
Having these enables the owner to mate frequently with various peahens, but at the
same time the gaudy feathers constitute an awful burden; because they are so heavy
and cumbersome, and so readily visible to any predators in the area, the peacock
becomes a perfect target for predators. Usually, in the animal kingdom it's the males
who have the more elaborate appearance because they must attract the attention of
the females.

Evolutionary psychology is a recent development within the field of psychology.
(Some experts within this specialization think that psychology should be subsumed
within the field of biology.[14] That is why it is sometimes considered to be a biological approach.) Evolutionary change takes place slowly, requiring thousands of generations. Hence many of the characteristics of today's humans are not well adapted
to their present environment. Instead, they are designed by natural selection for
the environment of evolutionary adaptation (EEA), an environment of the distant
past, the Pleistocene Era (from 1.6 million years ago to 10,000 years ago).

During 99 percent of their existence on earth, people were hunter-gatherers. Some
of their problems were the ones that people still face in the modern world: making
friends, finding a mate, and raising children. Others were different. Because the environment is so different today, some of the traits modern humans have are not
well designed for life in our present-day environment. For instance, it used to be advantageous to have a taste for foods that were sweet, salty, or crammed with fat.
People long ago were in danger of starving or getting insufficient nutrients in their
diet. Now, however, foods with salt, sugar, or fat are readily available, and we consume excessive amounts, resulting in bulging waistlines, high cholesterol, high
blood pressure, and heart attacks.

Evolutionists now tend to believe that natural selection exists for the benefit or
perpetuation, not of species, populations, groups, or individuals but instead of
genes—the units of heredity. Genes (small portions of chromosomes) are replicators.
They make perfect digital copies of themselves. Some have survived millions of

years. Individuals (animals, plants, bacteria, viruses), according to the theory, are machines created by genes to carry the genes for a while (days, years, or decades, depending on the life span of the particular species). Mice and humans are obviously very different kinds of creatures. But, surprisingly, their genes are quite similar. Indeed, even an octopus and an oak tree are not terribly different in the complement of genes they contain.

Genes build organisms to be survival machines. These survival machines, although they differ greatly (for instance, yeast and humans), serve the same purpose, which is to be a temporary vehicle for a short-lived collection of particular genes. The combination may be short lived but the individual genes in some cases will be potentially very long lived. They leap from body to body via sex; egg and sperm combine; and the new combination of chromosomes becomes the genes' bridge to near immortality.

Genes are also ruthlessly selfish. Any gene that was not would have been replaced in the ensuing generations by another gene of the same type (an allele).[15] And they cannot continue their existence unless the individual organism carrying them survives long enough to reach adulthood in pretty good health and reproduces. This means that organisms will tend to be genetically "programmed" to act in ways that ensure they live long enough to attain maturity and try mightily to have offspring that live and thrive. This, of course, can lead to quite selfish behavior. (Is this selfishness moral or desirable? Most people, including most evolutionary psychologists, would say no. They do *not* accept the **naturalistic fallacy:** that *whatever is, is therefore good.*)

One of the areas that evolutionary psychologists like to study is **adaptations:** the inherited characteristics that most members of the species have that arose through natural selection and that helped solve some problem of survival or reproduction during the time of its evolution. A trait that provides only a tiny advantage in reproduction can have enormous consequences in the long run. A trait that provides a 1 percent reproductive advantage will cause the population segment with that advantage to increase from 1 percent of the population to 99 percent in 265 generations (a long time to us, certainly, but not so long in evolutionary thinking).

In the area of long-term mating, women faced the problems of selecting a mate who was (1) *able* to invest time and energy in the relationship, (2) *willing* to invest these, (3) able to protect the entire family, (4) willing to be a good parent, and (5) compatible with the women. Who was likely to fill such a bill? Men who were slightly older, high in status, more ambitious, more dependable, more stable, with a similar personality and similar values to the women.[16]

In primates, generally, females are the main caregivers and therefore a highly desired resource. They carry an egg. They can get pregnant. They carry and nurture a fetus for a long time. They feed the baby their own milk after it is born. This adds up to an exceptionally large investment of time and energy in reproduction. Evolutionary psychology predicts that, because of such a heavy investment, females will be much more selective. They will not be indiscriminant about whom they mate with; instead, they will insist on a man who will provide and protect.[17] Ancestral women who were not so particular, who instead mated with a man who was flighty or philandering, risked being saddled with a completely helpless, dependent child and no protection, no resources, no help for years. In a society in which survival was precarious, food was scarce, predators plentiful, and infant mortality high, the children of such a woman probably would not live to adulthood. Her line and that of other women who chose their mate unwisely would die out. In short, natural selection did not favor such a strategy.

Whereas females produced few and rich DNA packets (eggs or ova), males produced gametes that were numerous and tiny. Indeed, men create twelve million sperm per hour. Although women tend to follow a strategy of seeking one mate of high quality who will invest in the them and their children, evolutionary theory says that men are more drawn to the strategy of greater quantity—to ensure their reproductive **success** they invest less in the offspring and spend more time competing with other men in order to inseminate more women. Men become the *high-variance sex,* for some have intercourse and offspring with many women, and others never have them with anyone. Some men, consequently, reproduce often, others not at all.

Therefore, given the supply and demand, natural selection favors high-risk/high-reward strategists: men who are more competitive, try harder, take more chances, intimidate other men (sometimes with weapons), and willingly court danger if it is going to raise their odds of having sex with women. Women are better off when pursuing a low-risk/low-reward strategy: staying healthy and completing pregnancies, protecting themselves and their children from risk, harm, and danger. Men can take risks in fighting or hunting, in displaying and showing off (in front of women), because this may be amply rewarded. A man may achieve higher wealth or status than his rivals, making him more attractive to women in general or to those women regarded as more desirable.

Among primates, those species in which males are much bigger than the females are the species that are most apt to be **polygynous** (meaning that some males are allowed to have several "wives"). Where the stakes are high, where males compete intensely and violently with each other for mates, size and strength are favored by natural selection. Among humans, males on average are about 20 percent heavier, 50 percent stronger in the upper body, and 100 percent stronger in hand grip than females. Thus it comes as no surprise that anthropological studies of earlier non-Western societies found that 84 percent of them allowed polygyny.[18]

> The only deliverance for a male's genes is through an escape into a female body carrying a fertile egg. Genes can survive in the long term only by jumping ship into offspring. In species that reproduce sexually, the only way to make offspring is to merge one's genes with another individual's. And the only way to do that, for males, is to attract a female of the species through courtship. This is why males of most species evolve to act as if copulation is the whole point of life. For male genes, copulation is the gateway to immortality. This is why males risk their lives for copulation opportunities—and why a male praying mantis continues copulating even after a female has eaten his head.[19]

Next, consider a theory about a particular kind of crime, rape, as formulated by evolutionary psychologists. Although this is an extremely controversial theory, it's presented here because evolutionary psychologists have not developed many other explanations of crime. Most rapes are not committed by teens, but some are. And it is useful to see what an evolutionary psychology explanation looks like. Here we will go over the basic argument. In the coming years, biologists and evolutionary psychologists will decide how valid it is. Here we will merely summarize it.

Thornhill and Palmer

According to Thornhill and Palmer, the evolutionary history of polygyny among humans presented different challenges to reproduction for women than for men, and those who responded successfully to those challenges went on to provide present-day descendents—men and women—with very different psychological adaptations. Women have an enormous investment in parenting, so evolutionary theory predicts that women will be finicky when it comes to mating. It predicts that *males*, because their *minimum* time and energy investment in parenting can be negligible, will be interested in sex with many females.[20] (Indeed, for most primate males, the minimum is the norm.)

In evolutionary terms, success (or fitness) is defined as leaving a large number of children. In evolutionary history, the males with the most reproductive success were those who were willing and able to copulate with many different women, in particular those who were young and highly fertile. Men were more eager to copulate than women were, and this trait promoted seeking out and achieving a larger number of sex partners in evolutionary historical settings. In today's world, there are signs that men continue to be more interested in sex (men are more likely to patronize prostitutes, more likely to watch pornography, and more likely to dream about sex with strangers).

Their greater investment in parenting made females of most species—including humans—selective. They would not want to have offspring by males who had inferior genes, because those same genes would often get passed on to the children. Nor (in the case of humans) would they want to mate with someone unreliable and undependable, who would not help raise, feed, or protect the children. Hence, women in our evolutionary past had to have standards in judging a man. These standards and preferences were then often inherited by later generations (a notion that sociologists find astonishing but evolutionary psychologists say is demonstrated by a great many years of sexual reproduction on this planet).

Standards were beneficial for women, for they prevented disastrous investments in the wrong kind of male. But men (who were not enamored of women's standards) preferred to indulge in sex with a series of women *without* making any long-term *commitment* (which would have involved staying with and helping the eventual mother by providing her and her offspring with resources and protection). Men saw these standards as obstacles they had to hurdle, defenses they needed to overcome.

Under the circumstances, there would have been pressure in ancestral times for selection to favor some traits over others in men. If many men were interested in the same women, this meant conflict, which could take the form of physical feats or violent fights. This kind of struggle favored men who were bigger, stronger, quicker, more violent, more willing to take risks. Inevitably there were some men who got badly hurt or even killed in the battles. Thus the tendency for males to favor a high-risk/high-reward strategy. Men would also be prone to exaggerate their status and lie about their feats, especially in adolescence and early adulthood, when sexual desire reached its peak.[21]

Was coercive mating ever an adaptation in the evolutionary past? Was it designed by natural selection as a way to increase a male's reproductive success? It was in many species, including scorpionflies and waterstriders. The scorpionfly has a clamp on the top of the abdomen that serves this purpose and no other. But in the case of human males, obviously there is no such clamp nor is there anything analogous to it. So the argument with respect to humans is not so easy to make. According to Thornhill and Palmer, if their thinking is valid, then a number of other conditions would also need to be true:

- Men would have evolved to be highly motivated and aroused to perform well in both rape and nonrape contexts.
- Gaining physical superiority over a partner by force would be sexually arousing for them.
- Men's willingness to use this kind of force would change as the men got older.
- The higher the social status of the men, the less likely they would be to force sex on a partner (it would not be necessary).
- Men's willingness to use force would be sensitive to the chance that his actions would be detected.[22]

Their research results tend to provide support for each one of these predictions.

The evolutionary view is able to answer many of the questions that other theories of rape cannot. For example,

1. Why is rape overwhelmingly a male act in all species?
2. Why does rape rarely produce death or serious injury in all species and human societies?
3. Why are so many victims of reproductive age?
4. Why are the victims of reproductive age so much more likely than others to be raped penile-vaginally?
5. Why do victims of this type of rape become more traumatized by it than younger or older women?
6. Why is this type of rape more traumatizing than anal or oral varieties?
7. Why do rapists average about 25 years of age? Why are there so few middle-aged or old-aged rapists?[23]

It is *possible* that a male predisposition for rape arose and spread to others in the following generations. Rape might have increased a man's reproductive success a little bit (compared to men who never had sex or waited for a willing female). In the later generations, there would be more men with this tendency toward sexual aggression if the man could not succeed via normal courting processes. Resorting to rape would be a conditional strategy, employed when the man had little or nothing in the way of status and resources to offer the woman or when the chance of punishment for rape was minimal.

Needless to say, Thornhill and Palmer are not defending rape. They are adamantly against this criminal act. They certainly do *not* say: It is natural, therefore it is a good thing. That would be falling for the naturalistic fallacy. In fact, they devote an entire chapter in their book to detailing the pain and anguish commonly associated with rape. *To try to explain rape is not to condone it,* any more than trying to understand earthquakes, floods, AIDS, murder, or robbery is an attempt to defend those phenomena. The practical value of a good theory of a bad thing is that we may be able to reduce the frequency of such incidents. And that is the ultimate hope of Thornhill and Palmer—to gain an understanding of the phenomenon, then go about reducing it.

But Thornhill and Palmer were subjected to withering blasts from critics even before the book was published. Many of the commentators were not able to understand the authors' arguments, which were often highly technical and couched in language not very clear to readers who have no background in evolutionary psychology. In addition, Thornhill and Palmer were injudicious and undiplomatic when they completely dismissed feminist and social science arguments about rape; this made the commentators in those categories livid.

Behavioral Genetics

People heavily involved in crime often come from criminal families; the most chronic and serious offenders are concentrated in a small subset (5 percent) of families, according to West and Farrington.[24] Their Cambridge Study in Delinquent Development followed more than 400 males in London from childhood until well into adulthood. These boys were contacted every few years, and tabs were kept on a large number of variables. Of the hundreds of measures examined, the best predictor of *antisocial behavior* at age 18 (this included unstable employment, heavy gambling, heavy smoking, drug abuse, drunk driving, sexual promiscuity, and violence) was having a *convicted parent at age 10.*

This meant there was consistency over generations. It could be interpreted as due to genetic factors, environmental factors, or a combination of both. Until the appropriate research is carried out, there is no way to know. If researchers rely on **intact** biological families alone, the results will be impossible to interpret with any confidence. One cannot simply assume that the similarity in criminality between parent and child or between siblings is genetic. Nor can one assume that it's due solely to environment. It is necessary to disentangle the genetic from the environmental sources of resemblance.

This disentangling requires that we turn to quantitative methods used in behavioral genetics. For years, this field of study relied on twin studies of siblings raised together (i.e., in the same family). Identical or **monozygotic** (MZ) twin pairs were compared to same-sex fraternal or **dizygotic** (DZ) twin pairs. MZ twins come from the same fertilized egg **(zygote)**, which splits in two, making almost exact clones or replicates. Fraternal twins come from two separate sperm and two different eggs and have the same degree of genetic similarity as ordinary siblings (which is to say, they share one-half their genes).

If the MZ twins are much more similar to each other than the DZ twins are to each other on the behavior in question (say, antisocial behavior or criminality), then researchers conclude that genetic factors have more impact than environmental ones. But this depends on several unstated assumptions. One of these is that their environments are equal (i.e., parents do not treat MZ twins more alike than they treat DZ twins). Critics hostile toward genetic explanations (and they are legion) find that assumption incredible and therefore they dismiss classic twin studies as largely worthless.

The critics are correct in a sense, for some parents of MZ twins do dress their twins alike, these twins do spend more time together, and so on. That then raises another question: whether these factors have a pronounced effect on the twins' *personality and behavior.* Is this why MZ twins' behavior is more alike than the behavior of DZ twins'? On a superficial level, it seems that the answer must be yes, but this issue cannot be settled by common sense or gut feelings; it needs to be examined empirically, which has been done several times.[25] One of these is the National Merit scholarship twin study conducted by Loehlin and Nichols, who tested the idea by comparing MZ twins treated alike (by parents) with MZ twins treated

Monozygotic twins figure prominently in modern scientists' attempts to disentangle environmental and genetic effects. *(Pat Miller/Stockphoto.com.)*

differently. And then it was noted whether the differences in parental treatment resulted in differences in the twins' personality and behavior. There were 108 correlations in the study, not one of which was strong (the associations ranged from −.08 to +.13).[26] The median correlation was .02, which is most unimpressive. This suggests that when identical twins are treated more alike, such treatment has virtually no impact and can be dismissed as an explanation of MZ twins' similarity in personality or behavior.

Although classic twin studies are the most popular method in quantitative behavioral genetics, they are not the only one. The second most common method is adoption studies. Some children are separated very early from their biological parents and handed over to adoptive parents to rear. The behavior or personality of these children can be compared with that of the (1) biological parents and the (2) adoptive parents. Adoptive parents in these studies have no genetic similarity with the kids they adopt. If the children show much greater resemblance to their biological parents, that is a sign that genetic factors matter. If, on the other hand, the youngsters bear a greater likeness to the adoptive parents in personality and behavior, this indicates that environmental factors exert an important influence. Several American studies employ the adoption design, but most such research has been carried out in Scandinavia, where the existence of national registries allows researchers to draw large samples.

The newest method to appear on the scene is a *combination* of the classic twin design and the adoption design: the twins-raised-apart design. This method was created in response to critics who refused to accept any results produced by classic (raised together) twin studies. The best known work involving twins raised apart has been carried out by Thomas Bouchard and his colleagues at the University of Minnesota. Twins were brought to Minneapolis, where they were put up in a hotel for a week and tested exhaustively for fifty hours. (Exhibit 4-1)

Over the years, the main focus of behavioral genetics research has been on IQ scores, which research shows, have a good deal of heritability. **Heritability,** expressed as a percentage, is how much the genes contribute to individual differences in a particular trait in people. This always refers to the population under study; it does not refer to a particular individual. A simple way to calculate heritability in twin studies is to subtract the correlation among DZ twins from the correlation among MZ twins and multiply by 2. In the case of height, it turns out that this would mean subtracting .45 (45 percent) from .90 (90 percent) and getting .45. Multiply this by 2 and the resulting estimate of heritability for height is .90 (90 percent). Although this is less than the heritability of blood type and eye color, it is still very high; *traits that social scientists study never have a heritability this great.*

Over the years, most investigations of IQ have relied on young people, those who are under the age of 20. When they are studied, it is normally found that the heritability of IQ scores is in the neighborhood of .50. The other 50 percent thus falls under the heading of **environment,** a term which has a very broad meaning in behavioral genetics. In this field of study, environment is a "garbage" category: it includes everything that cannot be attributed to genetics, such as the sounds people hear, the scenes people view, imitation of parents, experiencing certain

EXHIBIT 4-1   The Peculiar Case of the Identical Jims Separated at Birth

The first set of identical twins reared apart that Bouchard studied proved to be especially puzzling. Although separated one month after birth, twins Jim Lewis and Jim Springer had a lot in common. They both loved woodworking and stock-car racing, hated baseball, left love notes around the house, had chest pains and high blood pressure one year before the reunion, had hemorrhoids, underwent vasectomies, had lazy eye in the left eye, suffered migraine headaches, bit their fingernails, took Valium for general nervousness, and put on ten pounds at roughly the same point in life. In school, they were good at math while struggling with English. Furthermore, they had taken family vacations to the same three-block strip of Florida beach (without ever meeting), had worked as sheriff's deputies, drove Chevrolets, chain-smoked Salems, preferred Miller Lite, married a woman named Linda, divorced her, and married a woman named Betty, and then each had a son (one named James Alan and the other James Allen), not to mention a dog named Toy.

This kind of eerie similarity also occurred between some of the other MZ twins raised apart, but the Minnesota team was not interested in amusing coincidences and believe-it-or-not idiosyncrasies. Instead, they were determined to compile an objective statistical record. A large number of MZ and DZ twins were investigated, including those raised together and those separated early and raised apart. They were measured and tested on many different variables such as IQ, personality dimensions, attitudes, and interests.

television programs, reading certain books, eating certain food, living in a particular house and neighborhood *plus any measurement error in the design.*

What would happen if older people were tested instead of kids? Would this make a difference in the heritability estimates for IQ? One might imagine it would. The widespread assumption among those are unfamiliar with quantitative genetics (and that includes just about everyone) is that genes have their greatest impact in the first few years of life, then in later years they wither away and are largely overcome by the impact of the social environment. And that by the time a person reaches middle age, genes no longer exert any influence.

The Minnesota team of researchers, however, found that IQ scores were strongly affected by genetic factors in adulthood; indeed, for adults, about 70 percent of the variation in IQs was attributable to genetics among identical twins raised apart. (One important caveat should be kept in mind. These figures were based on twins who had *not* lived in searing poverty and had not been surrounded by social problems, so the 70 percent figure cannot be extrapolated to the entire population. Environmental disadvantages could very well make a difference in the estimates of heritability. The worse the living conditions are, the greater impact of the environment.)

More relevant to criminology, though, is how much impact environment and genetic factors have on *personality.* There is some degree of consensus in psychology that there are five main personality dimensions, which are

1. *Extraversion:*   Talkative, assertive, active, decisive vs. retiring and withdrawn
2. *Neuroticism:*   Tense, anxious, nervous, moody, worrying vs. quickly gets over upsetting experiences
3. *Conscientiousness:*   Organized, thorough, "planful," responsible vs. irresponsible, frivolous, disorderly, careless
4. *Agreeableness:*   Sympathetic, warm, kind, appreciative vs. hard-hearted, quarrelsome, unfriendly, cold
5. *Openness:*   Wide interests, imaginative, original vs. unreflective, shallow, simple, with narrow interests

Before Bouchard and his colleagues carried out their studies, other researchers had typically attributed about 50 percent of the variation in personality characteristics to genetics. The Minnesota studies produced similar findings. The difference was that the Minnesotans had an ideal sample, one including identical twins reared apart.

In behavioral genetics, variance is divided into two components: genetic factors and environment. As noted earlier, *environment includes everything that is not genetic:* this means shared environment, nonshared environment, and measurement error. **Shared environment** is defined as what the twins have in common, such as the same mother and father, the same home, the same family income and parents' education, the same way of raising children, the same schools, the same place of worship, and so on. **Nonshared environment** refers to idiosyncrasies, that is, environmental factors that might lead the twins to have *different* interests, different levels of intelligence, or different personalities. Elements in the environment that were not shared might be a different fetal position, a special relationship with a parent or teacher, a serious accident or illness, a different college, a different close friend, or a different love interest.

How much does shared environment matter? For many years, most people have been quite sure it was very important. This is a message that, as sociologists, my colleagues and I were taught, readily accepted, and then passed on to tens of thousands of students for the past thirty years. It seemed to be an eternal verity, like the sun rising in the east. Unfortunately, behavioral genetics research indicates that it is not so eternal as we thought. One article after another has demonstrated that shared environment is less influential than people assume.

In most matters of interest to researchers—IQ, personality, attitudes, interests, behavior, illness—shared environment appears to matter very little, according to the data presented in studies such as these: Bouchard (1998); Tellegen et al. (1988), Lykken et al. (1993), Bouchard and McGue (1990), Loehlin et al. (1981), Bouchard (1994), Bouchard et al. (1990), McGue and Bouchard (1998), Loehlin et al. (1997), and Bouchard et al. (1998).[27] David Rowe devoted an entire book to the subject: *The*

Limits of Family Influence.[28] Most of us are astonished to learn that alcoholism, manic depression, autism, schizophrenia, insomnia, smoking, homosexuality, divorce, career choice, job satisfaction, hobbies, happiness, television viewing time, political conservatism, religious beliefs, coffee drinking, contraceptive use, menstrual symptoms, and suicide are affected more by genetics than by shared environment. This is very difficult for most of us to swallow.

If the studies are correct, though, we must ask ourselves several questions: Why do twins raised *apart* resemble each other as much as twins raised *together*? Why do unrelated (i.e., one is adopted) children raised together show virtually *no* similarity in personalities or IQ? Why does being reared in the same home have such a negligible effect? These queries are puzzling and leave us scrambling for answers. But if we cannot answer them, at least we can point out their implications. For one thing, parents receive too much credit when their children turn out to be model citizens and paragons of virtue. Similarly, when kids prove to be the next Charles Manson, parents get more blame than they deserve. Or so it appears, judging from the data.

Does the general finding that genetic factors play an important role in IQ, personality, and behavior also apply to crime and delinquency? Some psychologists who are familiar with the relevant literature assert that there is a strong genetic component to *adult crime* but not for *juvenile delinquency;* they contend that in the case of juvenile delinquency or conduct disorders, shared environment is more important.[29] They do not find that shared environment plays much of a role in any other arena of behavior or personality. But in this one particular realm— *delinquency*—shared environment looms large.

This conclusion, which we will call the received wisdom, has been challenged in an article by Mason and Frick, which supplies a useful meta-analysis of heritability studies of antisocial behavior. It includes only recent studies (those published since 1975) and those with a rigorous methodology. Introducing these criteria reduces the number of studies from 70 to 15 (12 twin studies and 3 adoption studies). On the average, adult samples show higher heritability of crime or antisocial behavior than juvenile samples do, which seems to substantiate the common view of psychologists. But when Mason and Frick analyze the data more closely, they find that studies of adults focus on serious offenses, whereas studies of juveniles include trivial misdeeds. When the trivial offenses are discarded and only serious behaviors are considered, the results are identical for juveniles and adults: (Somers $d = .44$). About 50 percent of the variance in antisocial behavior is thus accounted for by heredity.

Questions have been raised, however, about whether the statistic used by Mason and Frick (Somers d) is appropriate. So we must turn to another, more recent and much more exhaustive meta-analysis by Rhee and Waldman, which examined 95 twin and adoption studies of genetic and environmental influences on antisocial behavior. They found that in these studies, (1) the magnitude of genetic influence was high and it was actually *greater* in childhood and adolescence than in adulthood, (2) shared environment had a considerably weaker influence, and (3) nonshared environment had a strong effect, about equal to that of genetic influence.[30] Thus, the received wisdom looks rather dubious these days.

Next, consider a recent adoption study by Ge et al. on whether adoptees' conduct disorder, antisocial personality disorder, and drug use are related to characteristics of their biological parents or their adoptive parents. This work uncovered some interesting relationships that no one else had explored. The biological parents' problems (such as drugs and alcohol) are fairly strongly related to the child's antisocial behavior. This relationship is not surprising to those who are familiar with the literature on behavioral genetics; high levels of heritability are common for various traits. But biological parents' psychological status was also fairly strongly related to the following measures.

Adoptive fathers' hostility and warmth toward the adoptee
Adoptive fathers' and adoptive mothers' harsh/inconsistent discipline
Adoptive mothers' nurturant/involved discipline

This is striking. How could characteristics of *biological parents* be connected to traits of *adoptive parents*—people they are not related to, never met, and do not know at all? Eventually, Ge et al. came up with an answer, concluding that biological parents' psychological problems led to their children behaving in an antisocial or hostile manner in the adoptive home (a genetic effect). Ge et al. said this was to be expected.

Such findings regarding genetic influences on child antisocial behavior are no longer news and are consistent with recent findings by Cadoret, O'Gorman, Troughton, and Heywood (1985); Cadoret et al. (1986, 1995a, 1995b), Pike et al. (1996) and others. . . .[31]

What was so unexpected was that biological parents' psychological problems were correlated with the way the adoptive parents dealt with the children. Biological parents who were dependent on alcohol or drugs or had antisocial personality disorder were more likely to have a hostile or antisocial child, even though they were separated at the child's birth. The child's antisocial behavior then evoked the adoptive parents' negative reaction (an environmental effect—from child to parent). This kind of gene–environment interaction research takes us far beyond the simple socialization theories and research of past decades. On the other hand, one theory of delinquency (the next one we shall cover) actually anticipates the existence of a biological–environmental interaction.

Moffitt's Theories of Delinquency

Psychologist Terrie Moffitt argues that many people engage in deviant behavior during their adolescent years; for the overwhelming majority of them, such deviance is temporary and situational. There is another group, however, for whom such violations are not temporary, they're stable and persistent. Moffitt therefore formulated two theories of delinquency, one of them sociological and the other biosocial. The biosocial theory focuses on the small group of boys who continue to be far more deviant than most from childhood to middle age. They're called the **Life-Course-Persistent Antisocial Type,** and consistency is their trademark. They engage in biting and hitting at age 4,

> shoplifting and truancy at age 10, selling drugs and stealing cars at age 16, robbery and rape at age 22, and fraud and child abuse at age 30; the underlying disposition remains the same, but its expression changes form as new social opportunities arise. . . . Life-course-persistent antisocial persons lie at home, steal from shops, cheat at school, fight in bars, and embezzle at work.[32]

Moffitt calls this **heterotypic continuity,** which means that the behaviors engaged in, although diverse, all spring from the same underlying antisocial trait.

When people begin deviant careers so early, the causal factors must occur at least as early, that is, around the toddler period or sooner. To learn what these factors are, Moffitt begins by focusing on neural development. Neural development in the fetus may be disrupted by the mother's exposure to lead and other toxic elements; by her use of cigarettes, alcohol, or cocaine; or by poor nutrition; or while pregnant, the mother-to-be may be the victim of violence or abuse. After the baby is born, its neural development may be stunted by a lack of affection, insufficient stimulation, or not enough proper nutrition.

These can translate into neural deficits or disabilities in the infant or young child. Such deficits may be verbal, in which case they affect the child's ability to listen, read, speak, write, and remember. Or they may be executive deficits, which could result in impulsiveness or failure to pay attention. Neural dysfunctions in early childhood are often found among Life-Course Persistents, those who engage in aggressive antisocial behavior from early in life until well into their adult years.

For neural impairments to have an impact this powerful, one would think that they must be quite severe, but Moffitt says they may actually be quite subtle. Even a modest problem is enough to affect the child's temperament and behavior. Such impairments could be dealt with successfully if the children were born to supportive parents who know how to handle offspring with cognitive problems and unpleasant temperaments. But typically, Moffitt says, children with neural deficits are born into families that are disadvantaged.

The parents and children may both have temperaments that are difficult. Vulnerable children generally live with parents who resemble the children and therefore are incapable of effectively coping with them. Because overactive, irritable children may inherit these traits genetically, it's unlikely that they will have understanding but firm parents who know how to control them. More often the parents are impatient, inconsistent, and irritable hotheads themselves. The child therefore does not as a rule get the nurture, special care, and proper stimulation needed to overcome its deficiencies.

When a child (1) is born with minor neural damage, (2) is difficult to raise, and (3) has a family environment that is unfavorable (due to mental illness, poor health, low intelligence, or poverty), this combination poses more than just a stiff challenge; it constitutes an emotional powder keg. Parents are not prepared for the irritating crying, the neediness, the unpleasantness. The difficult infant may grow into the child who proves to be incorrigible. After a while, the mother wears down and gives up the attempt to rein the child in, and so the youngster in effect wins the war of wills.

Once such children are old enough to go to school, they continue the same pattern of behavior. That is, they demonstrate how aggressive and out of control they are, which certainly does not endear them to teachers or students. Quickly they are rejected and fail to associate with pro-social peers; because of this they do not develop social skills. In school, they don't acquire reading or math skills either, thus undermining their chances of later on landing a decent job and having a chance to make a good living. Instead, they give in to their impulsiveness and engage in risky activities such as alcohol drinking, drug use, reckless driving, and dropping out of school.

This is a biosocial theory because Moffitt concentrates on the biological fact of poor neural health caused by heredity or prenatal complications. This manifests itself in a toddler with an unpleasant temperament. Then people in the environment (at first, it's just the parents) react to the child with the difficult temperament. These responses could be ameliorative, but more often they are the exact opposite, which exacerbates the problem. Under the circumstances, the little problem child gets worse instead of better and later on encounters additional difficulties in the neighborhood, school, peer groups, and authority relations. The accumulating problems make it likely that the individual will carry this antisocial style of behavior into the adult years.

Next, consider the second Moffitt theory: **Adolescence-Limited Antisocial Behavior.** She says that this is much more pervasive than the first kind of delinquency: most males in the modern world have a police contact for some act, and most of these contacts occur during adolescence. Because the individuals began this behavior in the teen years, Moffitt says we must turn our attention to the nature of adolescence (not infancy or prenatal conditions) for an explanation. People during their teens become more introspective and self-conscious than they were during the childhood years, more interested in becoming popular with peers, less guided by the attitudes and beliefs of their parents.

Moffitt says kids who turn to delinquency in their teens are imitating the antisocial behaviors of their Life-Course-Persistent peers. They want to copy them, Moffitt says, because the LCP youths tend to get what they want: stylish cars, expensive clothes, drugs, plenty of sex, entrée into adults-only venues, independence from their parents, and a style of life that features risk and danger. To the majority of youngsters entering high school, these desires are out of reach, for they are still financially dependent on their parents and have too little free time or cash on hand to attain them. Biologically, they have already reached adulthood, but socially they are still to some extent treated as, and considered to be, children.

This gap between their biological and social statuses leaves them in a state of frustration. They gaze on the deviant acts of LCP youths with envy because the persisters are getting the benefits of adulthood, the things that other kids long for but are denied. So they start hanging out with the LCPs and occasionally engage in delinquency with them, not for the intimacy of the relationship (which may be minimal) but for the rewards of the illegal or deviant behavior: one looks and feels older if one antagonizes adults, engages in risky behavior, smokes, drinks, has sex, and drives wildly. In Moffitt's words,

> I suggest that every curfew violated, car stolen, drug taken, and baby conceived is a statement of personal independence and thus a reinforcer for delinquent involvement. Ethnographic interviews with delinquents reveal that proving maturity and autonomy are strong personal motives for offending.[33]

According to her, Adolescence-Limited delinquency is normal, of short duration, and does not have a biological basis, unlike Life-Course-Persistent Antisocial behavior, which is abnormal, long lasting, and partly an outgrowth of **prenatal** or **perinatal** factors.

Ideally, Moffitt's Life-Course-Persistent or biosocial theory would be tested longitudinally by measuring **neuropsychological** health in very early childhood and delinquency or antisocial behavior later, throughout childhood and early adulthood. But there are not many data sets that have undertaken this kind of longitudinal measurement, and to begin doing so now would of course take about fifteen or twenty years of research time and require a large financial outlay (hence a hefty grant would be needed).

The research conducted thus far suggests that prenatal and perinatal complications combined with disadvantaged home environments make children more susceptible to early onset delinquency. Mednick and Kandel found that minor physical anomalies such as low-seated ears, furrowed tongue, curved finger, and long third toe (which are reflections of neurological damage) when combined with an unstable family environment predict arrests later on for violent offenses. Brennan and Raine found that delivery complications such as forceps extraction, breech delivery, and umbilical cord **prolapse** combined with an unwanted pregnancy lead to more arrests for assault, rape, or armed robbery.[34]

Gibson et al. found that low verbal IQ at age 7 (an indicator of neuropsychological risk) plus family adversity (low SES or single-parent family) significantly increases the odds of a child becoming an early onset offender. Tibbetts and Piquero found that these same kinds of family adversity when combined with low birth weight also lead to an increased chance of early onset of delinquency among boys. Piquero and Tibbetts studied many kinds of prenatal disturbances, including the presence of venereal disease, pregnancy complications, and a prolapsed cord. These, in conjunction with a weak family structure, increase the likelihood of criminal offending during early adulthood. Gibson and Tibbetts found that maternal smoking during pregnancy and (later on) father absence from the household combine to predict early onset of offending.[35]

Several criminologists have disputed the Moffitt claim that there are two types of offenders. Some argue that there is only one type (e.g., Gottfredson and Hirschi), whereas others contend that there are more than two types.[36] One study, covering London, Philadelphia, and three Racine, Wisconsin, cohorts, found there were usually four or five types (including one labeled nonoffenders). The other types were called low-rate adolescence peaked, high-rate adolescence peaked, low-rate **chronics,** and high-rate chronics.[37]

Most interesting, though, is Moffitt and Caspi's recent study of the Dunedin cohort in New Zealand at the age of 26. They discovered five categories of males.

1. Ten percent followed the life-course persistent path; that is, they met the criteria for extreme antisocial behavior in both childhood and adolescence.
2. Twenty-six percent were adolescence-limited type youths: this means they were extremely antisocial as adolescents but were not so antisocial as children.
3. Eight percent were said by Moffitt to be in recovery. She meant that they were extremely antisocial as children but not as adolescents. (This was an intermediate diagnosis, added years after the original theory was constructed but years before the cohort turned 26.)
4. Five percent were called abstainers because they did not engage in any antisocial behaviors (according to parent-, teacher-, or self-reports) between the ages of 5 and 18.
5. Fifty-one percent of these males did not fit any of the first four categories. Hence they were titled the unclassified group. These tended to be typical, run-of-the mill boys.

What were the long-term experiences of these different groups? We begin with the abstainers, the truly nondelinquent. When they were 18 years old, the future did not look very promising for them. Although they were very good students, they were also timid, overcontrolled, socially awkward, unpopular virgins. By the age of 26, however, their fortunes had taken a turn for the better. By that time they had become optimistic, college-educated, happily married, and established in high-status occupations. They had virtually no mental disorders or psychological adjustment problems.

Although the abstainers seemed to blossom in their early adult years, the recovery group's path proved to be a bit rockier. Moffitt had been optimistic about them when they were 18. Extremely antisocial as children, they seemed to improve markedly during their teen years. She thought they were on the road to success. Unfortunately, by the time they were 26, they were proving that "recovery" was a misnomer. By that point, they resembled the low-level chronics (who had first been identified by Daniel Nagin).[38] Like the life-course persisters, these boys had low IQs and suffered from family adversity during their childhood. As adults, they tended toward depression and anxiety, none of them had married, and they had social phobia and difficulty making friends. As they reached 26, their situation was bleak: they had little education, low-status occupations, financial problems, and little hope for the future.

The life-course persisters did not thrive in adulthood either. As expected, they were the most violent of the five categories, specializing in weapons carrying, robbery, and assault (which was directed more than occasionally at their wives and children). They had problems with substance abuse, conflicts at work, low-status jobs, minimal schooling, and psychiatric difficulties and had an unusually large number of children (a fact bearing on evolutionary theory).

Moffitt originally predicted that the next group (the adolescence limited) would be much better adjusted in adulthood than the life-course persisters. In most respects, this prediction was supported by the data on adult performance. Nevertheless, life at the age of 26 was not smooth sailing for the adolescence limiteds. They had a considerable number of convictions for property crimes and drug offenses and a fair number of psychiatric problems.

Why did the ALs not lead the kind of adult life Moffitt had originally predicted for them? She says the reason for this discrepancy is that the nature of adolescence itself changed during the intervening years. That is, adolescence stretched out longer than it used to, as young men in New Zealand experienced the misery of high unemployment rates and therefore low rates of marriage. This in turn kept them from assuming adult roles, from having the status and privileges that would traditionally have been attained and enjoyed by 26-year-olds.[39]

Self-Control Theory

The next explanation comes from Michael Gottfredson and Travis Hirschi, sociological criminologists whose theory is essentially psychological. They also include an interpretation of the classical school of criminology and in particular Jeremy Bentham. According to the Gottfredson/Hirschi interpretation, all people (whether committing crimes or engaging in other behaviors) are involved in avidly *pursuing their own pleasure and self-interest, while avoiding pain.* From this modest assumption, taken directly from classical criminology, they next make a quantum leap to the following interpretation.

> It tells us that crime presupposes no particular skills or abilities, that it is within the reach of everyone without specialized learning. It tells us that all crimes are alike in that they satisfy ordinary and universal desires. It tells us that people behave rationally when they commit crimes and when they do not. It tells us that people are free to choose their course of conduct, whether it be legal or illegal. And it tells us that people think of and act first for themselves, that they are not naturally inclined to subordinate their interests to the interests of others.[40]

According to the authors, a good way to build a theory of criminal behavior is to work backwards: first determine what the essential elements of crime are and then figure out what personality traits would be compatible with them. With this strategy in mind, they outline six characteristics of crimes:

1. Crimes gratify desires immediately. There is no waiting room, no queue, no cooling off period, no deferral of gratification. "They provide money without work, sex without courtship, revenge without court delays."[41]
2. Crimes are neither difficult nor complex. "In the standard burglary, a young male . . . knocks on a door not far from where he lives. Finding no one home, he tests the door to see if it is open. If it is open . . ., he walks in and looks to

see if the dwelling has anything of interest. . . . In most cases, the items that appeal to these boys are cash, booze, and entertainment equipment."[42]

3. Crimes entail a certain amount of risk, thrills, and excitement. The adrenaline flows, there is a rush, the heart beats faster when there is a risk of getting caught, convicted, and punished.

4. The benefits produced by crimes are few and modest. They pale in comparison to the rewards that come from an ordinary occupation. Plus, the life of crime is incompatible with the routine and responsibility associated with a career or family.

5. Crimes do not normally require very much preparation or proficiency. Those individuals whose hearts are set on becoming muggers need not worry: advanced education and careful training are not prerequisites for this line of work.

6. For crime victims, the pain and suffering may be severe and long-lasting. "Property is lost, bodies are injured, privacy is violated, trust is broken."[43]

Then the authors identify personality traits that criminals are likely to have. These traits when combined with each other constitute what Gottfredson and Hirschi call "low self-control." The authors describe individuals with low self-control in the following way.

1. These people have a disposition to want what they want, and to want them here and now. They are impulsive.

2. They are not willing to persist or work hard to get to the desired goods. A 9-to-5 life is something they couldn't bear.

3. They tend to be doers rather than thinkers, in search of action and adventure. They do not have a demeanor that is cautious or pensive.

4. They tend to have marriages that fall apart, friendships that break up, and jobs they soon quit. They are unable to commit to any of these for the long haul.

5. Their academic and cognitive abilities are far from impressive.

6. They tend to have little or no concern for their fellow man (or woman).

Hence, if someone is hurt or harmed, it does not upset them. In addition, people low in self-control do not specialize in any one type of crime. They dabble in a variety of illegal ventures. Plus, they supplement their force and fraud with other forms of behavior that are "psychologically equivalent," such as smoking tobacco, drinking alcohol, having unwanted pregnancies, getting into automobile accidents, gambling, having illicit sex, and using drugs.

Gottfredson and Hirschi (G & H) insist that low self-control does not result from being explicitly trained or socialized to be this way. Instead, it is among those who are *not well trained or nurtured* that low self-control is most evident. Low self-control is a result of haphazard child rearing. Parents of delinquents are not good at raising kids. They bungle the job by not demonstrating much affection, not disciplining effectively, and not supervising carefully. (Indeed, some of these parents may inadvertently set an example of deviance for their offspring—by getting drunk and perhaps even committing a few crimes.)

In attempting to socialize their children, there are several ways that parents may fail. They may not care about the child; rejection by parents is particularly common in the case of adoption, remarriage, or birth defects. They may be too busy or preoccupied to give the child the needed attention. They may attend to the child enough but fail to realize that the child is misbehaving. Finally, they may realize that the child is doing something forbidden, but they fail to intervene, put a stop to it, or punish the child in any way. Hence, the child keeps on behaving "badly" because family supervision is weak and ineffective.

Hirschi is arguably the most prominent figure in criminology. In addition, he delights in taking extreme positions and dashing cold water on anyone else's theory. Therefore, self-control theory, a real departure from orthodox criminology, was bound to attract a great deal of commentary and reviews by other criminologists. Some of them have been favorable, whereas others have been critical. At first, self-control theory was faulted for relying on circular reasoning: the cause and effect are defined in terms of each other. According to one critic, it is

> tautological to explain the propensity to commit crime by low self control. They are one and the same, and such assertions about them are true by definition. The assertion means low self control causes low self control.[44]

Although at first blush, self-control theory does indeed seem to be tautological, most criminologists who have thought about it for a while have concluded otherwise. G & H set forth what they *believe* are the main characteristics of crime, then use these to *infer* the corresponding personality characteristics of offenders. Finally, researchers can test to see if people who break the law and commit other kinds of deviance are indeed more likely than nonoffenders to have these traits. Certainly it is very possible that (1) most crimes do not neatly fit the description offered by G & H, (2) personality traits may have a relatively modest impact on criminality, and (3) the particular personality traits G & H pinpoint are not the crucial ones leading to criminality. Hence, the theory is not circular. If it were, the correlations found by researchers testing it would be very high. In fact, they are not.

In a recent meta-analysis, Pratt and Cullen brought together numerous studies testing self-control theory. They discovered that on the whole the theory performed quite well. That is, researchers found that low self-control is a consistently good predictor of crime and analogous behaviors such as smoking, drinking to excess, speeding, gambling, and unprotected sex. When given the opportunity, people who are impulsive, insensitive, physical, risk-taking, short-sighted, and nonverbal do commit more than their share of crimes and other imprudent acts.

One question has arisen in measuring self-control. Most researchers believe that it should be measured using attitude scales, but Hirschi and Gottfredson prefer to employ deviant behaviors (a highly dubious tactic). If deviant behavior is correlated with criminal activity, this tells us nothing about causation. It is a correlation anyone would expect to occur, one that has no relevance to any theory. Indeed, it is here that the accusation of tautology seems to an accurate one.

Pratt and Cullen's meta-analysis produced several results worth noting. They found that the relationship between self-control and deviance is stronger

1. Among *community* samples than among samples of offenders
2. Among *female* samples than among male samples
3. Among *adult* samples than among juvenile samples
4. For *analogous* behaviors than for crimes

Self-control theory applies to all groups and all kinds of crime. In this respect, it truly is a general theory of crime. But delinquency theorists are most concerned about *crimes* by *males* and *juveniles*. On these, low self-control proves somewhat less significant.[45]

Conclusion

Psychology and biology are becoming increasingly sophisticated and making discoveries that are worth everyone's attention. And the most sensible approach is to combine the insights and discoveries made in the various fields of study. Criminology can do this because it is by nature a synthetic field not wedded to one single theoretical stance, one particular research design, or one underlying set of assumptions. Some scholars will hasten to don their warrior gear and scream "reductionism" and "biological determinism," knowing that these are fighting words that will rally the troops. A few will resist the temptation to label, however, and ask what those fields have to add to our store of findings and understanding. These few who go out on a limb may some day be rewarded for their efforts. Eventually, there will be new syntheses that other criminologists will take seriously.

Early criminology contained more philosophy than social science. The works of Beccaria and Bentham had more to do with how the criminal justice system ought to operate than what causes crime and delinquency. They wished to bring justice in and to take arbitrary and capricious elements out. They saw the system as subject to abuse by figures who had too much power. This kind of thinking became quite popular around the world and gave rise to many of our present-day criminal justice systems.

Lombroso later introduced the positivist approach by trying to use scientific methods to differentiate between criminals and noncriminals. His notion that some people were criminals because they were born that way (they were throwbacks to an earlier stage of evolution) seems to have grown out of a racist conception of various peoples. In Italy, back then, northerners thought that southerners were inferior, animal-like in both their appearance and their behavior. Needless to say, modern biologists completely disavow this kind of thinking.

Evolutionary psychology deals with natural selection and sexual selection. It does not assume that humans are merely following the rules laid down arbitrarily by their culture. On the contrary, it claims that we are designed by natural selection to thrive in the environment of evolutionary adaptation, that is, from 10,000 to 1.6 million years ago. In that era, could it have been adaptive to be violent, aggressive, and amoral under certain conditions? Obviously, we lack very good evidence, but it is at least plausible to argue that the answer is yes.

Behavioral genetics is another newcomer to the world of academe. Criminologists have generally dismissed genetic arguments as based on flawed methodology. And over the decades they have probably been correct in doing so. But in the past few years, the methodology has improved to the point where detractors need to revisit the issue; they should take notice of the great strides made by behavioral genetics research. Some of this shows that genes do have a role in crime and delinquency; most of this research shows that shared environment has only a modest effect.

Terrie Moffitt has introduced two new types of delinquents: the Life-Course-Persistent Antisocial and the Adolescence-Limited Antisocial. She uses a biosocial theory to explain the first type and a social psychological theory to account for the second one. Some studies seem to indicate support for these theories. On the other hand, it is rare for typological research to discover that delinquents can be neatly pigeonholed into just two types. More commonly, studies identify three, four, or five types.

Gottfredson and Hirschi have introduced a new theory to criminologists, one focusing on personality traits that the authors contend all come together and form a single factor that they call self-control. This is said to be caused by defective childhood socialization and to result in the commission of crimes and analogous acts when there is an opportunity for such behavior. Few researchers have looked at the socialization and opportunity parts of this theory, but Pratt and Cullen indicate considerable support for the part that says low self-control leads to crime.[46]

Key Terms

Eugenics:	a nineteenth-century movement to limit human breeding to the "able," by which was meant the mostly middle and upper classes
Naturalistic fallacy:	the belief that whatever is in nature, is good
Adaptations:	inherited characteristics that solve some problem of survival or reproduction
High-variance sex:	the male sex; members vary a great deal, some having many offspring whereas others have none
Polygynous:	men may have multiple wives
Success (fitness):	producing a large number of offspring
Intact:	not broken; together
Monozygotic:	twin pairs that come from the same zygote (identical)
Dizygotic:	twin pairs that come from two different zygotes (fraternal)
Zygote:	a fertilized egg
Heritability:	extent to which individual differences are traceable to genes
Environment:	(in behavioral genetics) everything that cannot be attributed to genes
Shared environment:	what people in the same family have in common (such as the same home, the same neighbors, the same school)

Nonshared environment:	what people in the same family do not have in common (different age, different best friend, different health condition)
Life-course-persistent antisocial type:	people who are antisocial for many years, beginning in childhood
Adolescent-limited antisocial type:	people whose deviance is limited to a few teenage years
Heterotypic continuity:	the specific behaviors change over the years but all of them spring from the same underlying trait
Prenatal:	occurring before birth
Perinatal:	occurring shortly before birth or shortly afterward
Neuropsychological:	relating to the brain and mental functions such as language, perception, and memory
Prolapse:	an organ (such as the uterus) slipping out of place
Chronic:	lasting, continuing, of long duration

End Notes

[1]Fox Butterfield, "Study Finds Steady Increase at All Levels of Government in Cost of Criminal Justice," *New York Times*, February 11, 2002, p. A14.

[2]*Ibid.*

[3]Sir Leon Radzinowicz and Joan King, *The Growth of Crime* (New York: Basic Books, 1977), p. 6.

[4]Fox Butterfield, "Study Finds Steady Increase at All Levels of Government in Cost of Criminal Justice."

[5]Cited in Piers Beirne, *Inventing Criminology* (Albany: State University of New York Press, 1993), pp. 11–12.

[6]Piers Beirne and James Messerschmidt, *Criminology,* 3rd ed. (Boulder, CO: Westview Press, 2000).

[7]Richard Bellamy, ed., *Beccaria on Crimes and Punishments and Other Writings* (Cambridge, UK: Cambridge University Press, 1995).

[8]Quoted in Gina Lombroso-Ferraro, *Lombroso's Criminal Man* (Montclair, NJ: Patterson Smith, 1972 [1911]), pp. xxiv–v.

[9]Charles Goring, *The English Convict* (Montclair, NJ: Patterson Smith, 1972 [1913]).

[10]Fox Butterfield, *All God's Children* (New York: Avon Books, 1995), p. 141. For those interested in the now dismissed Hooton and Sheldon, see Earnest Albert Hooton, *Crime and the Man* (Cambridge, MA: Harvard University Press, 1939) and William H. Sheldon, *Varieties of Delinquent Youth* (New York: Harper, 1949).

[11]Charles Darwin, *On the Origin of Species by Means of Natural Selection* (London: Murray, 1859); *The Descent of Man and Selection in Relation to Sex* (London: Murray, 1871).

[12]John Cartwright, *Evolution and Human Behavior* (Cambridge, MA: MIT Press, 2000).

[13]Steven J. C. Gaulin and Donald H. McBurney, *Psychology: An Evolutionary Approach* (Upper Saddle River, NJ: Prentice Hall, 2001).

[14]John Tooby and Leda Cosmides, eds., *The Adapted Mind* (New York: Oxford University Press, 1992).

[15]Richard Dawkins, *The Selfish Gene* (New York: Oxford University Press, 1989).

[16]David M. Buss, *Evolutionary Psychology* (Needham Heights, MA: Allyn and Bacon, 1999).

[17]Robert L. Trivers, "Parental Investment and Sexual Selection," in Bernard Grant Campbell, ed., *Sexual Selection and the Descent of Man: 1871–1971* (Chicago: Aldine, 1972), pp. 136–79.

[18]Geoffrey Miller, *The Mating Mind* (New York: Doubleday, 2000); George P. Murdock, *Ethnographic Atlas* (Pittsburgh: University of Pittsburgh Press, 1967).

[19]Geoffrey Miller, *The Mating Mind*, p. 87.

[20]Randy Thornhill and Craig T. Palmer, *A Natural History of Rape* (Cambridge, MA: MIT Press, 2000), p. 39.

[21]*Ibid.*, pp. 53–4.

[22]Joanne Ellison Rodgers, *Sex: A Natural History* (New York: Henry Holt, 2002).

[23]Owen D. Jones, "Sex, Culture, and the Biology of Rape," *California Law Review, 87*, no. 4 (July 1999), pp. 827–941.

[24]Donald J. West and David Farrington, *The Delinquent Way of Life* (London: Heinemann, 1977).

[25]John M. Hettema, Michael C. Neale, Kenneth S. Kendler, "Physical Similarity and the Equal-Environment Assumption in Twin Studies of Psychiatric Disorders," *Behavioral Genetics, 25*, no. 4 (July 1995), pp. 327–35.

[26]John C. Loehlin and Robert C. Nichols, *Heredity, Environment, and Personality* (Austin, TX: University of Texas Press, 1976). For more information on intelligence tests, see Daniel Seligman, *A Question of Intelligence: The IQ Debate in America* (New York: Birch Lane Press, 1992); Ulric Neisser, Gwyneth Boodoo, Thomas J. Bouchard, Jr., A. Wade Boykin, Nathan Brody, Stephen J. Ceci, Diane F. Halpern, John C. Loehlin, Robert Perloff, Robert J. Sternberg, and Susana Urbina, *Intelligence: Knowns and Unknowns* (Washington: American Psychological Association, 1995); Linda Gottfredson, "Intelligence and Social Policy," *Intelligence, 24*, no. 1 (January–February 1997), pp. 1–320; Mark Snyderman and Stanley Rothman, *The IQ Controversy, the Media, and Public Policy* (New Brunswick, NJ: Transaction, 1990).

[27]Thomas Bouchard, "Genetic and Environmental Influences on Adult Intelligence and Special Mental Ability," *Human Biology, 70*, no. 2 (April 1998), pp. 257–79; Auke Tellegen, David T. Lykken, Thomas J. Bouchard, Kimberly J. Wilcox, Nancy L. Segal, and Stephen Rich, "Personality Similarity in Twins Reared Apart and Together," *Journal of Personality and Social Psychology, 54*, no. 6 (June 1988), pp. 1031–9; David T. Lykken, Thomas J. Bouchard, Matthew McGue, and Auke Tellegen, "Heritability of Interests," *Journal of Applied Psychology, 78*, no. 4 (August 1993), pp. 649–61; Thomas J. Bouchard and Matthew McGue, "Genetic and Rearing Environmental

Influences on Adult Personality," *Journal of Personality, 58,* no. 1 (March 1990), pp. 263–92; John C. Loehlin, Joseph M. Horn, and Lee Willerman, "Personality Resemblance in Adoptive Families," *Behavior Genetics, 11,* no. 4 (July 1981), pp. 309–30; Thomas J. Bouchard, "Genes, Environment, and Personality," *Science, 264,* no. 5166 (June 1994), pp. 1700–1; Thomas J. Bouchard, David T. Lykken, Matthew McGue, Nancy L. Segal, and Auke Tellegen, "Sources of Human Psychological Differences," *Science, 250,* no. 4978 (October 1990), pp. 223–8; Matt McGue and Thomas J. Bouchard, Jr., "Genetic and Environmental Influences on Human Behavioral Differences," *Annual Review of Neuroscience, 21* (1998), pp. 1–24; John C. Loehlin, Joseph M. Horn, and Lee Willerman, "Heredity, Environment, and IQ in the Texas Adoption Project," in Robert Sternberg and Elena L. Grigorenko, eds., *Intelligence, Heredity, and Environment* (New York: Cambridge University Press, 1997), pp. 105–25; Thomas J. Bouchard, Jr., Matt McGue, Yoon Mi Hur, and Joseph M. Horn, "A Genetic and Environmental Analysis of the California Psychological Inventory Using Adult Twins Reared Apart and Together," *European Journal of Personality, 12,* no. 5 (September–October 1998), pp. 307–20.

[28]David C. Rowe, *The Limits of Family Influence* (New York: Guilford, 1994).

[29]Michael Rutter, Henri Giller, and Ann Hagell, *Antisocial Behavior by Young People* (New York: Cambridge University Press, 1998), p. 131; C. Robert Cloninger and Irving I. Gottesman, "Genetic and Environmental Factors in Antisocial Behavior Disorders," in Sarnoff A. Mednick, Terrie E. Moffitt, and Susan A. Stack, eds., *The Causes of Crime* (New York: Cambridge University Press, 1987), pp. 92–109; Lisabeth F. DiLalla and Irving I. Gottesman, "Heterogeneity of Causes for Delinquency and Criminality," *Development and Psychopathology, 1,* no. 4 (December 1989), pp. 339–49; Michael J. Lyons, William R. True, Seth A. Eisen, Jack Goldberg, Joanne M. Meyer, Stephen V. Faraone, "Differential Heritability of Adult and Juvenile Antisocial Traits," *Archives of General Psychiatry, 52,* no. 11 (November 1995), pp. 906–15.

[30]Dehryl A. Mason and Paul J. Frick, "The Heritability of Antisocial Behavior," *Journal of Psychopathology, 16,* no. 4 (December 1994), pp. 301–23; Soo Hyun Rhee and Irwin D. Waldman, "Genetic and Environmental Influences on Antisocial Behavior," *Psychological Bulletin, 128,* no. 3 (May 2002), pp. 490–529. For really high estimates of genetic influence on externalizing behavior, see Robert F. Krueger, Brian M. Hicks, Christopher J. Patrick, Scott R. Carlson, William G. Iacono, and Matt McGue, "Etiologic Connections Among Substance Dependence, Antisocial Behavior, and Personality," *Journal of Abnormal Psychology, 111,* no. 3 (August 2002), pp. 411–24 and Susan E. Young, Michael C. Stallings, Robin P. Corley, Kenneth S. Krauter, and John K. Hewitt, "Genetic and Environmental Influences on Behavioral Disinhibition," *American Journal of Medical Genetics, 96,* no. 5 (October 2000), pp. 684–95.

[31]Xiaojia Ge, Rand D. Conger, Remi J. Cadoret, Jenae M. Neiderhiser, William Yates, Ed Troughton, and Mark A. Stewart, "The Developmental Interface Between Nature and Nurture," *Developmental Psychology, 32,* no. 4 (July 1996), p. 586; Remi J. Cadoret, Thomas W. O'Gorman, Ed Troughton, and Ellen Heywood, "Alcoholism and Antisocial Personality," *Archives of General Psychiatry, 42,* no. 2 (February 1985), pp. 161–7; Remi J. Cadoret, Ed Troughton, Thomas W. O'Gorman, and Ellen

Heywood, "An Adoption Study of Genetic and Environmental Factors in Drug Abuse," *Archives of General Psychiatry, 46,* no. 12 (December 1986), pp. 1131–6; Remi J. Cadoret, William R. Yates, Ed Troughton, George Woodworth, and Mark A. Stewart, "Adoption Study Demonstrating Two Genetic Pathways to Drug Abuse," *Archives of General Psychiatry, 52,* no. 1 (January 1995), pp. 42–52; Remi J. Cadoret, William R. Yates, Ed Troughton, George Woodworth, and Mark A. Stewart, "Gene-Environment Interaction in Genesis of Aggressivity and Conduct Disorders," *Archives of General Psychiatry, 52,* no. 11 (November 1995), pp. 916–24; Alison Pike, Shirley McGuire, E. Mavis Hetherington, David Reiss, and Robert Plomin, "Family Environment and Adolescent Depressive Symptoms and Antisocial Behavior," *Developmental Psychology, 32,* no. 4 (July 1996), pp. 590–603.

[32]Terrie E. Moffitt, "Adolescence-Limited and Life-Course-Persistent Antisocial Behavior," *Psychological Review, 100,* no. 4 (October 1993), p. 679.

[33]*Ibid.,* pp. 688–9.

[34]Sarnoff Mednick and Elizabeth Kandel, "Genetic and Perinatal Factors in Violence," in Sarnoff Mednick and Elizabeth Kandel, eds., *Biological Contributions to Crime Causation* (Dordrecht, the Netherlands: Martinus Nijhoff, 1998), pp. 121–34; Patricia A. Brennan and Adrian Raine, "Biosocial Bases of Antisocial Behavior," *Clinical Psychology Review, 17,* no. 6 (September 1997), pp. 589–604.

[35]Chris L. Gibson, Alex R. Piquero, and Stephen G. Tibbetts, "The Contribution of Family Adversity and Verbal IQ to Criminal Behavior," *International Journal of Offender Therapy, 45,* no. 5 (October 2001), pp. 574–92; Stephen G. Tibbetts and Alex R. Piquero, "The Influence of Gender, Low Birth Weight, and Disadvantaged Environment in Predicting Early Onset of Offending," *Criminology, 37,* no. 4 (November 1999), pp. 843–77; Alex Piquero and Stephen Tibbetts, "The Impact of Pre/Perinatal Disturbances and Disadvantaged Familial Environment in Predicting Criminal Offending," *Studies on Crime and Crime Prevention, 8,* no. 1 (March 1999), pp. 52–70; Chris L. Gibson and Stephen G. Tibbetts, "A Biosocial Interaction in Predicting Early Onset of Offending," *Psychological Reports, 86,* no. 2 (April 2000), pp. 509–18.

[36]Daniel S. Nagin, David P. Farrington, and Terrie E. Moffitt, "Life-Course Trajectories of Different Types of Offenders," *Criminology, 33,* no. 1 (February 1995), pp. 111–39; David M. Fergusson and L. John Horwood, "Male and Female Offending Trajectories," *Development and Psychopathology, 14,* no. 1 (March 2002), pp. 159–77; David M. Fergusson, L. John Horwood, and Daniel S. Nagin, "Offending Trajectories in a New Zealand Birth Cohort," *Criminology, 38,* no. 2 (May 2000), pp. 525–51.

[37]Amy V. D'Unger, Kenneth C. Land, Patricia L. McNall, and Daniel S. Nagin, "How Many Latent Classes of Delinquent/Criminal Careers?" *American Journal of Sociology, 103,* no. 6 (May 1998), pp. 1593–630.

[38]Daniel S. Nagin, David P. Farrington, and Terrie E. Moffitt, "Life-Course Trajectories of Different Types of Offenders."

[39]Terrie E. Moffitt, Avshalom Caspi, Honalee Harrington, and Barry J. Milne, "Males on the Life-Course Persistent and Adolescence-Limited Antisocial Pathways," *Development and Psychopathology, 14,* no. 1 (March 2002), pp. 179–207; Terrie E. Moffitt,

Avshalom Caspi, Nigel Dickson, Phil A. Silva, and Warren Stanton, "Childhood-Onset Versus Adolescent-Onset Antisocial Conduct in Males," *Development and Psychopathology, 8,* no. 2 (June 1996), pp. 399–424.

[40]Michael R. Gottfredson and Travis Hirschi, *A General Theory of Crime* (Stanford, CA: Stanford University Press, 1990), p. 5.

[41]*Ibid.,* p. 89.

[42]*Ibid.,* p. 27.

[43]*Ibid.,* p. 89.

[44]Ronald L. Akers, "Self-Control as a General Theory of Crime," *Journal of Quantitative Criminology, 7,* no. 2 (June 1991), p. 203.

[45]Travis C. Pratt and Francis T. Cullen, "Gottfredson and Hirschi's General Theory of Crime," *Criminology, 38,* no. 3 (August 2000), pp. 931–64. See also Joshua D. Miller and Donald Lynam, "Structural Models of Personality and Their Relation to Antisocial Behavior," *Criminology, 39,* no. 4 (November 2001), pp. 765–98.

[46]One who has delved into the socialization issue is Carter Hay in his article, "Parenting, Self-Control, and Delinquency," *Criminology, 39,* no. 3 (August 2001), pp. 707–36.

Recommended Readings

David M. Buss, *Evolutionary Psychology* (Boston: Allyn and Bacon, 1999).

Martin Daly and Margo Wilson, *Homicide* (Hawthorne, NY: Aldine, 1988).

Lee Ellis and Anthony Walsh, *Criminology* (Boston: Allyn and Bacon, 2000).

Anthony Walsh, *Biosocial Criminology* (Cincinnati, OH: Anderson, 2002).

David C. Rowe, *Biology and Crime* (Los Angeles: Roxbury, 2002).

Adrian Raine, *The Psychopathology of Crime* (San Diego, CA: Academic Press, 1993).

Robert Plomin, John C. DeFries, Gerald E. McClearn, and Michael Rutter, *Behavioral Genetics,* 3rd ed. (New York: Freeman, 1997).

Matt Ridley, *Genome* (New York: Harper Collins, 1999).

CHAPTER 5

Chicago School and Strain/ Anomie Theories

Chicago: The Early Years

Explorers originally named it Chicagoua, a Native American word meaning wild onion or skunkweed. Perhaps they were prescient, for years later, living down to its name, the city became notorious for the odor emanating from the Union Stock Yards, poor waste disposal, and factories; the city's coal smoke made the atmosphere blacker than London's. To Max Weber, the city seemed like a human being with the skin removed. Streets contained horse manure and corpses of animals piled high, which quickly attracted millions of rats and bluebottle flies.

> Chicago on the eve of the fair remained one of the most abysmally filthy cities in the industrial world. Most of its streets were unspeakably dirty, the horrible-smelling river remained its sewer, and thick gray smoke . . . discolored its new skyscrapers, stung people's eyes, clogged their lungs, and soiled their clothing.[1]

Despite its modest origins as a stagnant mudhole with only 150 souls, the city grew and by 1871 boasted a population of more than 300,000, more than two million by 1920, and 3.375 million in 1930. When precipitous growth takes place amid conditions this sordid, disease and death are bound to follow. During the early 1850s, each year witnessed an epidemic. One day of heavy rain in 1885 contaminated the water supply, leaving one-eighth of the citizens dead from typhoid fever, dysentery, and cholera.

Such disasters, instead of making Chicagoans sink into despair, had the opposite effect; they galvanized them. With blue-collar jobs continuing to be abundant, migration remained heavy from the 1850s onward. It was migration rather than **natural increase** (the excess of births over deaths) that fueled the city's dynamic growth. By 1857, Chicago had the world's largest railroad network and was its primary grain port; by 1890 it was the second-largest manufacturing center in the United States. City boosters never tired of crowing about its achievements; their big talk and bravado (not the weather) were responsible for the title "the Windy City." Some newcomers became rich almost overnight. They soon won acceptance into high society, although easterners dismissed them as butchers and beer barons from a hog-slaughtering backwater.

Wealth was highly concentrated—in 1850, the richest 1 percent had over half the city's wealth, and the richest 10 percent held 94 percent. The bottom three-fourths of the population were so destitute that, combined, their proportion of the wealth added up to a mere 1 percent. As a result, this "city of millionaires" contained some of the world's most unlivable slums. Along the banks of the Chicago River lived a multitude of vagrants, criminals, drug addicts, and seasonal workers.

Before the Great Fire of 1871, rich and poor lived cheek by jowl. After the city was rebuilt, however, economic segregation in housing became the rule. In general, most cities began a reversal of the historic pattern. For hundreds of years, the poor and disreputable lived on the outskirts of the towns or cities, whereas the center offered magnificent temples, cathedrals, and the great estates of the privileged classes. To live there was a mark of high status. But people began to think differently about the city in the second half of the nineteenth century. This and the rise of the transit system prompted most of the wealthy and powerful to head for the outskirts.

After 1871, almost no one lived in the heart of the city (called the Loop, because that's where the cable cars turned around). Instead, office buildings, hotels, restaurants, theaters, and other businesses dominated this half-mile square. In the area just outside the Loop were the factories and blue-collar workers' homes. Closest to the Loop lived the newly arrived immigrants, packed like sardines, often in the most abject poverty. As families and ethnic groups found their income rising after a few years, they tried to escape by moving farther away from the city center. Their place in the slums was then taken over by the city's newer and even poorer arrivals.

The University of Chicago

Owning Standard Oil made John D. Rockefeller, Sr., the richest man in America. A devout Baptist, he dreamed of funding a small denominational college and chose William Rainey Harper, an Old Testament scholar, as its president and Chicago as its site. But Harper had a more elaborate fantasy—a major university like Harvard or Princeton—and finally cajoled Rockefeller into going along with it. Harper (who never tired of spending other people's money) brought in a star-studded faculty and had ten buildings erected within two years. In the end, 70 million dollars of Rockefeller money (a tidy sum a century ago) were channeled into the project. Other philanthropists declined to contribute their excess wealth because they feared the school would forever be identified in the public mind as a Rockefeller and Standard Oil creation.[2]

Low teaching loads and high salaries lured professors from Eastern universities to this new center for research. No other institution of higher learning had started out at the top with a world-renowned faculty. The University of Chicago also had the luxury of experimenting with new programs—such as the first American graduate department in sociology. Columbia, Kansas, and Michigan soon followed, but they could not match Chicago's exuberance and achievement in this subject. Because the university was entirely new, the more established disciplines could not discredit the new field. Every department started out on an equal footing.

The department reached its zenith from 1915 to 1935, when it dominated sociology in America. Under the dynamic influence of chairman Robert Park, graduate students were encouraged to explore topics that interested them, to gain personal experience by getting inside the subject and living it. He made them use the city as their social laboratory. Park's fascination with city life and urban people grew out of his years as a newspaper reporter and as a secretary to Booker T. Washington, during which time he traipsed around the South, learning about the lives of African Americans.

Sociology students at the University of Chicago ventured out into the populace to observe living conditions and conduct interviews. In the process, many of them wrote theses and dissertations on social problems—for, after all, no American city faced problems more serious than Chicago. Some of these works were published and attained international fame: *The Hobo, The Gold Coast and the Slum, Suicide, The Gang, The Ghetto, Family Disorganization, Mental Disorders in Urban Areas,* and *The Taxi-Dance Hall.*[3] Once they left the University of Chicago, most Ph.D. students who wrote them never again achieved such heights. This is a sign of how stimulating the U. of C. environment was.

Shaw and McKay

To earn a Ph.D. at the University of Chicago, students had to pass the foreign language exam, a task which Clifford Shaw and Henry McKay were not up to. Growing up near a tiny Indiana crossroads, not even a village, Shaw attended school off and on until he was 14, then he was talked into studying for the ministry. McKay was raised on a farm in South Dakota and went to Dakota Wesleyan College for his undergraduate degree. Neither one was at all prepared for foreign languages or for the theories taught by the University of Chicago's German-trained sociologists (George Herbert Mead, William I. Thomas, Albion Small, and Park).

As small-town Midwesterners, Shaw and McKay had no more taste for abstract theory than they had for foreign tongues. Instead, they found their niche in a more practical setting, the Institute for Juvenile Research. Shaw became its director in 1926 and he soon hired McKay, who stayed on until 1972. Their work covered the social psychological (delinquents' autobiographies), the ecological (geographical distribution of delinquents), and prevention (the Chicago Area Project). Shaw, the practitioner, organizer, and charismatic administrator, convinced a number of delinquents to write their life stories and several wealthy industrialists to fund Institute projects. McKay, the isolated scholar, stayed in the background, constructing crime maps and describing research findings.[4]

Medical doctors dominated the literature on criminals until Shaw came along and inspired delinquents to reveal how they got involved in a life of crime. Shaw had access to such youths because he spent the 1920s as a parole officer for the Training School for Boys and a probation officer for the Cook County Juvenile Court. The boys opened up to him because they found him to be a sympathetic listener, a charmer, someone who would remain a close friend for the rest of his life.

Some of the delinquent boys' life stories were published and had a momentous impact, making Shaw and the university world renowned.[5] They opened the eyes of a public that had not had any close contact with delinquents, and they convinced many readers that social influences were powerful. To readers who, in the early years of the twentieth century,

> had been deeply influenced by genetic theories of criminality, he [Shaw] brought the actual voice of the offender presenting his own version of his origins, his growth, and his orientation to the world. A more forceful mode of presenting the force of circumstances in the molding of human lives would have been difficult to devise. The result was a highly compelling insider's view of criminality. . . .[6]

Meanwhile, McKay created maps showing delinquency was concentrated in certain sections of the city: spot maps, rate maps, radial maps, and zone maps, all of them based on decades of data on boys picked up by the police, referred to juvenile court, or sent to training schools. These ecological or mapping data were typical of Chicago research of the 1920s and 1930s, when graduate students based their dissertations on the geographical distribution of mental illness, suicide, or some other social problem (something that public health centers do nowadays).

Ernest Burgess, a Shaw and McKay mentor at the university, was the one who first divided the city into a series of concentric zones around the Loop, the commercial and civic hub. Surrounding this business district was Zone II, known as the zone in transition and composed of an inner ring of factories and an outer ring of neighborhoods in decay, where colonies of immigrants and homeless people existed, where there were gambling dens, brothels, and bootlegging operations. Vice flourished with official indulgence. The residents here eked out a living amid poverty, disease, dilapidated housing, delinquency, and family disintegration. They eagerly awaited the day when they could get out of there; as soon as they had the chance, they fled to greener pastures.

Their destination was Zone III, the zone of working families' homes, generally neighborhoods of second settlement. People there were still close enough to reach their jobs but not so close that they could see and smell the city's worst pollutants. Better residences could be found in Zone IV, where the middle-class businessmen and professionals lived. Finally, Zone V became the commuters' zone, its small incorporated towns housing the well-to-do. (Naturally, this description ignores many details and overstates the case; for example, the black belt and heavy industry along the branches of the Chicago River crossed several zones.)[7]

Immigrants were the focus of early sociological (especially Chicago School) explanations of crime and delinquency. *(Alfred Stieglitz/Getty Images Inc.—Hulton Archive.)*

Shaw and McKay's **ecological studies** of Chicago delinquents appeared in three books, *Delinquency Areas, Social Factors in Juvenile Delinquency,* and *Juvenile Delinquency* and *Urban Areas,*[8] which concluded that

- Juvenile delinquents and recidivists are not randomly dispersed throughout the city. They are instead clustered together in areas close to the central business district and heavy industry.
- Delinquency areas are accompanied by physical deterioration, high rates of people on relief (welfare dependency), high rates of adult crime, and large concentrations of immigrants.
- Delinquency rates decrease the farther outward one goes from the city center. (This has been called various names: the zonal hypothesis, the gradient tendency, or the concentric zone theory.)
- Neighborhoods and communities with high rates of delinquency at one time tend to maintain these high rates over a period of many years.
- Neighborhoods and communities with high rates of delinquency, though consistent in their level of crime and delinquency, experience great change over the years in their ethnic composition.
- As the earlier immigrant groups move out of these areas, the rates of delinquency of their children decrease and fewer of them land in juvenile court.

Other findings were drawn from the books detailing the delinquents' own life stories (these were called **social psychological data**). These biographical reports gave rise to the following conclusions:

- Juvenile delinquency becomes a tradition in certain neighborhoods of the city. Among some of the prominent influences in these areas are highly organized and powerful criminal gangs, fences, and alliances between criminals and corrupt politicians (of which Chicago had an ample supply).
- Juvenile delinquency (particularly, stealing) is nearly always done together, as part of a group. Social groups serve as the means of transmitting delinquency in the areas of high delinquency rates.
- It is in playgroups that the youngest children in the deteriorated areas of the city satisfy their desires for attention, stimulation, and companionship.
- Immigrant parents thwart their sons' desires for fun and games, however, for they expect the boys to go to work for them early on. This alienates the boys, driving them into the arms of companions, as in the following example of Nick, aged 14.

I've had a lot of trouble at home. They all fight me and hate me. They don't want me to play or have any fun with the fellows. They say I ought to work all day and then only play a little at night. . . . They kick me and say they are going to put me out of the house. My father puts pepper in my eyes and hits me with an iron or anything when he gits [sic] mad. They're all against me except the guys on the street. They all like me.[9]

Shaw and McKay said that areas do not become highly delinquent by chance. Instead, this occurs as part of a natural urban process that residents cannot control. The oldest residential homes are built close to industrial and commercial districts. The smoke, soot, noise, and smell render the housing charred, ugly, and undesirable. But because they are the cheapest homes on the market, they attract the newest immigrants, who can't afford to pay for anything better. Then they find themselves stuck there, forced to put up with it, at least for a while.

Many observers at that time (1920 to 1940) would have concluded from these facts that crime and delinquency are caused by race or ethnicity. Shaw and McKay, however, said that the poorest people (migrants from the South and immigrants from Europe) were not at fault; they were forced to settle in the worst slums, and they lacked the skills to overcome (to organize against) the effects of living there. These thus became areas of **social disorganization,** and competing value systems arose: one conventional and one criminal. In areas where there was no social disorganization, in the *low-delinquency areas,* only the conventional value system existed. There, the parents agreed on what was best for their youngsters, and they were backed up by conventional institutions such as the PTA, women's clubs, and churches. In *high-delinquency areas,* the conventional institutions were weaker and had to compete with the criminal value system, which was supported by criminal gangs, rackets, and semilegitimate businesses.[10]

Each day, boys living in the high-delinquency areas saw crime and corruption on display; it became obvious that some people were making a very comfortable living by operating outside the law. Boys often looked up to these criminals and learned to think of them as "big shots." Starting as early as age 5 or 6, children formed playgroups, and initially their offenses, such as stealing apples from the outdoor fruit stands, were modest and based on a desire for fun. But as the years went by and criminal opportunities opened up for them, they defined these acts as childish and moved up to bigger things and more serious crimes, including rape and robbery. Finally, they became professionals, experts, specializing in a particular kind of crime. At least this was what Shaw and McKay thought.

Various empirical studies have tried to test some of the propositions in Shaw and McKay's model. In one of the best of these, Bursik analyzed the relationship between delinquency and sociodemographic indicators, using data that the Institute for Juvenile Research had produced from 1940 to 1970. These sociodemographic indicators of each area of the city were the percentage of the population that was nonwhite, the percentage foreign-born white, the percentage unemployed, the percentage of workers who were professional or technical, the percentage of dwellings that were owner-occupied, the percentage of households with more than one person per room, and the education level (Table 5-1).

This highly informative table has been in the public domain for years, but the findings seem to have gone unnoticed by most criminologists. Shaw and McKay were the prime spokesmen for the view that crime and delinquency are dominated by the lower class. Criminologists believed this before Shaw and McKay's time; after Shaw and McKay's publications, belief became certainty; it was the one statement that virtually all criminologists accepted as fact. In Table 5-1, however, two of the social class measures (education and prestige of occupation) emerge as the weakest predictors of an area's delinquency rate. This finding is all the more remarkable because it comes directly from McKay's own data.

Even more noteworthy is the relationship between delinquency and the percent foreign-born. According to Shaw and McKay, immigrants live in the city's most

TABLE 5-1   Correlations Between Area Delinquency and Other Area Variables[11]

	1940	1950	1960	1970
Nonwhite	.787	.640	.798	.755
Foreign-born	−.402	−.349	−.573	−.451
Unemployed	.676	.766	.786	.706
Professional	−.168	−.373	−.429	−.230
Owner-occup.	−.465	−.527	−.693	−.703
Crowding	.633	.648	.755	.603
Education	−.064	−.156	−.357	.057

dilapidated slums, where they constantly argue with their children, who find it more enjoyable to associate with other youths (who may be delinquents). But the data in Bursik's Table (5-1) show that the areas of Chicago with the most foreign-born actually had *lower* delinquency rates than other areas (the correlations are negative). Although Bursik had little to say about them in his article, these findings raise serious doubts about Shaw and McKay's viewpoint.

Immigration and crime have become hot-button issues in modern politics (even before the terrorist attack on the World Trade Center and the Pentagon), and news stories fuel concern that there is a strong causal link between them. Recent research, however, casts doubt on this assumption. For instance, when Butcher and Piehl compared U.S. cities with each other, they found that the percentage of residents who are recent immigrants seems to have no effect on crime rates. Indeed, controlling for age and gender, immigrants actually have *lower* crime rates. And youths born abroad are significantly less prone to commit crime than native-born youth.[12] Immigrants are much less likely than native-born of the same sex and age to be sent to jails, prisons, or mental hospitals.[13] And despite widespread concern over Mexicans transporting drugs inside the United States, research finds that Hispanics are no more involved in criminal behavior than are other citizens.[14]

Edwin Sutherland

After receiving his bachelor's degree in 1904, Edwin Sutherland spent quite a few years at loose ends, not knowing what to do. He later picked up his Ph.D. in sociology and economics from the University of Chicago. But still did not know what to do, so he did nothing. It was only when E. C. Hayes (who edited the Lippincott series of sociology textbooks) asked him to write a criminology text that Sutherland finally found himself as a criminologist in the 1920s (he was then over 40). Later, he went on to a distinguished career as a sociological criminologist—some say the greatest in history.[15] He made major contributions: nowadays, all discussions of differential association theory, white-collar crime, and professional theft begin by citing his groundbreaking work. The first and last of these three topics are intimately related: the impetus for differential association theory seems to have come from his interviews with the professional thief Broadway Jones. In a 1942 speech Sutherland admitted as much in this epiphany:

> First, I had worked for several years with a professional thief and had been greatly impressed by his statements that a person cannot become a professional thief merely by wanting to be one; he must be trained in personal association with those who are already professional thieves. There I seemed to see in magnified form the process that occurs in all crime.[16]

Sutherland (1) spoke glowingly of professional thieves, calling them organized, efficient, intelligent, well disciplined, and reliable; (2) described their profession as an organization containing statuses, roles, and traditions; and (3) claimed the thieves were drawn from middle- to upper-class backgrounds. He thought Jones, for instance, had been a Harvard student. Later evidence, however, revealed that Broadway had conned Sutherland and did not have such an elite background. Actually, he may have been only a small-time thief, and he certainly was (as Sutherland knew) a drug addict—which common sense would suggest was his *real* motivation for stealing.[17] All of this casts some doubt on Sutherland's subsequent claims about **differential association** theory, which was originally inspired by this one case study.

Differential association theory contains these nine principles:

1. Criminal behavior is learned. Hence no one inherits a tendency or predisposition to engage in crime or thinks about committing a criminal act on his or her own—that is, without having first been trained in the field of crime.

2. Criminal behavior is learned in interaction with other persons in a process of verbal communication (or through gestures, occasionally).

3. The principal part of the learning occurs within intimate personal groups. Thus, family and close friends play the most important roles in inspiring criminality; conversely, mass media such as movies and newspapers have no impact.

4. The learning of crime includes (a) techniques of committing the offense (these are usually very simple) and (b) the specific direction of motives, drives, rationalizations, and attitudes.

5. The attitudes and rationalizations are learned from definitions of the legal codes as favorable or unfavorable. People in America are exposed to both kinds of viewpoints: some of the attitudes they hear expressed state that laws ought to be obeyed; others that they hear argue that breaking the laws would be acceptable. (This is part of Sutherland's conception of differential social organization.)[18]

6. A person becomes delinquent because of an excess of definitions favorable to violation of law over definitions unfavorable to it. Here we see the crux of differential association theory. In effect, Sutherland thinks people are sponges who assimilate the surrounding culture (soaking up the kinds of attitudes they hear more often and behaving in accordance with them). An individual adopts the attitudes he or she hears most often and then acts them out.

7. Differential association may vary in frequency, duration, priority, and intensity. **Priority** means that attitudes one is exposed to early in childhood have the greatest impact; they persist throughout life. **Intensity** refers to the prestige of the people expressing the attitudes or "definitions." The higher the person's status, the more influential his or her views will be with listeners.

8. Learning crime involves the same processes as learning anything else. Sutherland did not say what these were, but he said imitation is not one of them.

9. General needs and values, such as money, status, happiness, or frustration cannot explain crime. Sutherland said these lead to noncriminal behavior as well as criminal acts so they can be forgotten about.[19]

Sutherland went on to become the most widely admired figure in American criminology and still remains so, although he introduced differential association many years ago (1939; two years after *The Professional Thief* was published). His supporters remain numerous and fervent. But in the end a theory must stand or fall based on how well it fits the best available data. How does differential association theory fare when examined in the light of empirical tests? Unfortunately, this is hard to answer, because all the tests have been very indirect. Indeed, the theory is stated in a way that makes direct testing almost impossible.

Why would Sutherland construct a theory that was impervious to direct testing? He admits that he did so because he saw what happened to other theories that were testable: they got destroyed by the data.[20] In addition, though, he misunderstood the basic logic of research methodology. He rejected correlation coefficients, considering them useless. Nothing that is measurable ("concrete conditions"), he argued, could ever be a cause of crime. So he dealt with concepts that no one could measure (such as definitions of the situation one was exposed to over an entire lifetime). Finally, he believed that a theory of crime had to focus on causes that were necessary and sufficient conditions of crime (expressed as a correlation, the relationship had to be a perfect 1.00, something social science never finds in the real world.) Years later, Hirschi and Selvin would identify this as a false criterion of causality.[21]

Sutherland picked up this bit of false logic from his student (and later colleague) Alfred Lindesmith, who called it **analytic induction**, in which a hypothesis is accepted only if it fits every case in the defined universe.[22] This kind of thinking leads to immediate problems. Because correlations between measured variables are never perfect, the researcher who is intent on showing that his or her theory is valid will have to fudge the data somehow to make it seem perfect. And the most convenient way to do that is to employ concepts that do not have any objective indicators or measures.

Normally, researchers attempting to test differential association theory ask a sample of youngsters to answer questions about (1) their own involvement in crime and delinquency and (2) their friends' involvement in delinquency. And such studies always find that these (1 and 2) are associated. But what such a correlation means is unclear, because various interpretations are possible. First of all, as Sutherland suggests, crime and delinquency may be learned from people one associates with intimately, people who have a favorable attitude toward lawbreaking, and who express this attitude orally. One then incorporates this point of view into one's own thinking, and finally one puts these attitudes to work by going out and committing deviant or criminal acts. This model, emphasizing the acquisition of pro-criminal attitudes, is known either as differential association (Sutherland's phrase) or socialization (Kandel's term).[23]

A second point of view contends that learning is not the reason for the correlation between one's own delinquency and that of one's friends. Instead, when one's friends engage in crime or delinquency, one feels the need to go along, to imitate their behavior. One does not want to be singled out as a wimp, sissy, or mama's boy and thereby lose standing as a member of the group. Avoiding ridicule is a powerful motivator for engaging in deviance. This has been described as group pressure but here it will be known as group influence (because it is not necessarily the case that the group actively compels one to take part).[24]

Another perspective says the first two explanations have the causal ordering wrong. According to this third perspective, the individual becomes delinquent *first* and gravitates toward deviant friends *later*. (Hence, there is no social learning, no group pressure, and no group influence. The individual is perfectly capable of becoming delinquent on his or her own.) It is simply a matter of birds of a feather flocking together (the memorable Glueck and Glueck metaphor) or selection (Kandel's word).[25] A youth becomes delinquent first and gradually acquires a set of delinquent friends afterward.

A fourth viewpoint says there are measurement problems with the research: friends' delinquency and one's own delinquency are not related as strongly as studies indicate. Researchers typically rely on *the same person* to report the delinquency of self and that of friends. But the respondent often does not really know how delinquent his or her friends are. Not knowing, the individual hazards a guess, usually based on the assumption that one's friends are as delinquent as oneself. This produces a high (but erroneous) correlation between friends' deviance and one's own.[26] This phenomenon has been called **projection** or attribution.[27]

Sutherland's theory specifically says that it is the friends' attitudes ("definitions") rather than friends' behavior that affects the individual. So Warr and Stafford examined *friends' attitudes* toward deviance, *friends' behavior* (deviant or not deviant), and *one's own attitude* toward deviance to see which would prove to be the best predictor of one's deviance. Why would you commit a series of crimes? What factors would push you in that direction? According to Sutherland, (1) your friends' behavior is irrelevant, and (2) it's your friends' attitudes that directly lead to your becoming delinquent. Warr and Stafford, however, found these were not the case. Instead, they discovered,

1. Friends' attitudes do not matter and one's own attitudes matter only slightly
2. Friends' behavior on the other hand does seem to have an effect; it apparently influences our own behavior.[28]

Hence, the results raise doubts about the validity of differential association theory.

Thus far, we have covered in detail some of the flaws in Sutherland's theory. But recent laboratory research on deviancy by psychologist Thomas Dishion and his colleagues suggests that the theory could have some merit after all. They studied boys aged 13 to 14; each boy was asked to bring to the lab the person with whom he spent the most time. Each pair of friends was asked to participate in the Peer Interaction Task, a discussion of assigned topics. The 25-minute sessions were recorded and videotaped.

The boys were classified by their official record into three types of pairs: both of them delinquent, mixed pairs, and both of them nondelinquent. During the session, the delinquent dyads engaged in twice as much discussion of rule breaking as the mixed dyads and four times as much as the nondelinquent dyads. Also, the delinquent dyads were more likely to reinforce (respond positively to) talk of rule-breaking topics (e.g., stealing, vandalism, drug use, getting into trouble at school, victimization of women or minorities). The researchers found that the amount of time devoted to discussions of deviance were good predictors of future escalation of deviant behavior (two years later), especially if the two boys were not very close friends with each other. (People can spend time with someone but not be very strongly attached.)

Maybe what friends talk about does indeed matter, even though the discussion lasts only a few minutes and takes place in a 25-minute exercise in a psychology lab. This would seem at first blush to suggest that differential association theory does indeed have some validity. Deviant talk plus reinforcement is correlated with an increase in delinquency and drug use when the boys are interviewed two years afterward, at ages 15 or 16. On the other hand, the greatest impact occurs among boys who are not the best of pals, which contradicts Sutherland's assertion that people are most influenced by close, intimate friends. In addition, Dishion and colleagues do not know what other developments influenced delinquency and drug use over the two years; perhaps there were numerous additional factors operating.[29] Thus, Dishion's findings, although suggestive, are not conclusive.

Walter Miller

The final theorist mentioned here under the Chicago School heading, Walter Miller, received his master's degree from the University of Chicago, but in anthropology, not sociology. He later studied delinquent gangs from the perspective of an urban anthropologist, sometimes relying on **unobtrusive observation** (keeping close tabs on what his subjects did and said without giving them any sign that they were being spied on). He would enter a pizza parlor, buy something to eat and sit down in a booth, where he pretended to be completely absorbed in his meal and newspaper reading. In fact, he was listening carefully to the youngsters' conversations and taking extensive notes. From them, he extracted the following conclusions.

- The lower class is defined by its own kind of family structure. Unlike sociologists, who measure class by occupational prestige, education, and income, Miller said that family structure is the decisive element. Specifically, he defined lower-class families as characterized by female-based households and serial monogamy. This means that women (mother, aunt, grandmother) are in charge of the household, they set the rules; men who rotate in and out of their lives neither have much say nor last very long.

- Miller said boys in the lower-class culture grow up with the *belief* that they should not be bossed around by mothers, aunts, or sisters. But that is what they're confronted with. Resenting this, the boys seek escape by congregating on the corner, where they hang out with other guys their age.

- In these all-male peer groups, lower-class culture is preached and passed on. These cultural standards mirror the social experiences of lower-class people in general. Lower-class culture (according to Miller) revolves around six focal concerns: trouble, toughness, smartness, excitement, fate, and autonomy.

Although middle-class people judge each other by achievement and its symbols (such as occupation, car, house, clothes, speaking vocabulary), in the lower class, Miller said, evaluation is more likely to hinge on the amount of trouble a person gets into. He or she is then classified as a "street person" or as "decent" (according to a recent ethnography).[30] **Toughness**, the second lower-class concern, refers to physical strength, bravery, and masculinity (the last of these includes treating women as objects and scorning arts and sentimentality). Miller speculated that the preoccupation with toughness probably reflected the lower-class boys' lack of a father in the home (someone who could define the man's role).

Smartness means the ability to outfox people in situations on the street, to size up victims and take advantage of their weaknesses. Excitement, the next focal concern, entails a search for thrills, excitement, and adventure. This comes after a long week of boredom for most lower-class men. Their excitement (back in the 1950s) often took the form of drinking, gambling, fighting, and trying to pick up women. Fate is another focal concern. Lower-class men assume they cannot control their future by setting goals, so they turn to gambling, where they hope to hit the jackpot, which means they can quit their much disliked job and live in ease and comfort. Finally, there is autonomy. On the overt level, the men express resentment over being controlled by others. But underneath, Miller said, they actually seek out restrictive settings: they associate being bossed around with being loved and cared for by someone (their mother).[31]

Generally speaking, Miller's theory deserves high marks for being original and interesting, but criminologists have greeted it with frosty skepticism. Typically, they have been unimpressed by Miller's argument. More important, though, is what the relevant data show; do they lend credence to Miller's intriguing predictions? When researchers in one study asked delinquents a series of questions about their beliefs, values, opinions, and goals, they did not rate "lower-class concerns" very high nor did they express disdain for "middle-class" goals. But lower-class delinquents did evaluate several lower-class concerns more positively than nondelinquents did. This can be seen in Table 5-2.

Researchers thus found that delinquents gave them different responses than those that Miller overheard in the pizza place. One explanation for the discrepancy is that Miller listened to kids talking to each other when they thought no adults were paying any attention to them. They could exaggerate, brag, pretend to be macho. This was part of an accepted script among kids when they were interacting with each other. They wanted to portray themselves as tough guys, not as children who were well mannered and obedient to their parents.

On the other hand, when middle-class researchers isolate the youths and ask them a series of questions on a questionnaire or in a formal interview setting, the kids know something else is expected of them. So they may decide to play a very different role, that of someone who is respectful of adults and interested in their

TABLE 5-2   Percentage of Youths Who Endorse Lower-class Focal Concerns[32]

	Lower-Class Delinquents	Lower-Class Non-Delinquents	Middle-Class Delinquents	Middle-Class Non-Delinquents
Tough	49%	36%	39%	33%
A fighter	42	22	37	20
Smooth, fast talker	51	43	46	39
Daring	50	38	56	49
Out for kicks	57	22	41	10
Troublemaker	13	4	7	5
Can outwit others	61	38	61	48
Not chicken	89	93	96	87
Not into art & lit	70	57	52	47

approval. Are the kids lying when they give these answers to the middle-class adult researchers? Or were they lying when they were horsing around in front of their peers? Which is their real self? This is a question rarely raised and perhaps impossible to answer. But perhaps the youths have two real selves, or maybe these are merely roles they play.

Strain or Anomie Theory

Shaw and McKay were small-town Midwesterners: as such, they were more practical than philosophical, more empirical than theoretical, drawn more to common people than to armchair intellectualizing. When he was in grad school, Shaw lived in a slum, which may have spurred his interest in such locales. As dyed-in-the-wool empiricists, Shaw and McKay did not find "grand theory" very much to their liking. East Coast sociologists on the other hand followed a different path. They favored the works of European theorists while giving everyday problems of ordinary working stiffs short shrift. The European theorists they pored over included some big names, such as Karl Marx, Max Weber, Georg Simmel, and Emile Durkheim, all of whose works were scrutinized by Talcott Parsons, an instructor at Harvard when Robert Merton arrived as a graduate student. Parsons translated the major European sociologists' works into English and further whetted Merton's already considerable interest in the great masters.

Emile Durkheim

Among the various European theorists, Emile Durkheim wielded particular influence on Parsons and Merton. Merton admired Durkheim most for his ability to plunge into a completely different topic every time he sat down to write a new book. This, to Merton, was what a Renaissance man would do; it was a quality to be emulated. Durkheim has become best known for his four types of suicide: egoistic, altruistic, anomic, and fatalistic. He did not invent the term **"anomie"** (Greeks predating Socrates had used the term)[33] but he breathed new life into it. In ordinary times and circumstances, Durkheim claimed, there is a consensus on what a person of a particular rank and position deserves as compensation for his or her work. Someone who gets paid approximately what's expected will therefore be reasonably satisfied and content. This holds true even though the individual may be living in the most abject poverty, which was the condition in which many people found themselves at the end of the nineteenth century and beginning of the twentieth, when Durkheim was writing.

But when the economy changes and there's an economic boom, the influence of the old standards and expectations built up slowly over many years begins to wane. During economic booms, people's needs and desires escalate. They decide they should be receiving greater and greater rewards; but even when they get what they ask for, they remain unsatisfied. They still feel it is not enough (because others have gotten more). Eventually, they set unattainable goals, fail to reach them, and become disappointed. In a few cases this despair proves overwhelming, and they contemplate suicide. Some not only contemplate it; they actually go through with it. All of this takes place, Durkheim contends, because people's hopes become excessive, and society has not had enough time to adapt, to institute new and more realistic standards for them to learn and embrace as their own.

Durkheim's statements about the dangers of individualism are, of course, theoretical, but they are also moral. He warned his readers that societal regulation disappears in the face of rampant individualism and immoderate ambitions. This cannot bring happiness to the individual; the only result that follows from such circumstances is misery. Sometimes the misery makes the person resort to self-destruction. The solution Durkheim proposed: society must regulate the "passions" better, that is, it must prevent people's ambitions from soaring to inordinate heights.[34] This kind of caution about the dangers of great expectations made sense to Europeans, but would never be heeded in the United States, where high ambitions and dreams of personal success have been central facets of our national culture, from Ben Franklin onward.

Robert Merton

Merton borrowed the term **anomie** from Durkheim. But unlike Durkheim, Merton did *not* use it to mean that society is in flux (due to changing market conditions) and hence cannot regulate the passions and ambitions of individuals, who become prone to serious disappointment. Whereas Durkheim used the term to refer to a type of suicide, Merton used it in reference to crime. Durkheim had in mind the regulating of hopes and passions so that they didn't become excessive. Merton, on the other hand, was concerned with the means people use to achieve such hopes (or goals). And whereas Durkheim had in mind all citizens, Merton dwelt on a particular segment of society, the lower class.

According to Merton, there are **cultural goals** (things widely regarded as worth striving for, especially, wealth) and there are **institutionalized means** or societally approved ways of achieving those goals. The means that Merton had in mind were training and education, getting a normal job, and saving the money that was earned there. (At this point, you may wonder if the average person could realistically become wealthy this way. It would be very difficult, especially during the Depression, which was when Merton first presented his argument.)[35]

Merton noted that everyone in America is strongly encouraged by the culture to be somebody: they're told that, regardless of their class origins, they can become wealthy and successful if they work hard. During the 1930s this viewpoint was bolstered by a series of fictional stories by Horatio Alger in which the hero climbed from the bottom rung of a company to the top through pluck and luck and became a captain of industry (or what we would call a CEO). Nowadays, self-esteem gurus on afternoon talk shows still talk this way, proclaiming that the sky's the limit and that people can become anything they want. And many people believe this to be true, which is one reason why socialism has never caught on in America.

Merton said that although the emphasis on the goals is intense, society is less concerned about which means are used: goals are paramount, but how they are reached is secondary. Emphasizing the goals while caring less about the means creates an imbalance in society, which Merton calls anomie. When society exists in a state of anomie, individuals have several ways they can react, called modes of adaptation. Merton defines these modes in terms of whether the prevailing cultural goals and institutionalized means are accepted or rejected by individuals (Table 5-3). Conformity (Merton says) is the most common mode of adaptation, which means that most people want to become rich, and they follow the culturally prescribed routes for doing so (education, work, saving money). If this were not the most common, then most people would follow the other, more "deviant" modes of adaptation, which would probably result in the society's self-destruction. **Ritualism** entails following the rules but without paying much attention to the goals. Here Merton apparently had in mind bureaucrats and their red tape (i.e., insistence on adhering to countless procedures and filling out endless forms). (Anthropologists fumed at Merton for stealing one of their beloved concepts—ritual—and redefining it in this superficial way.) **Retreatism** involves first trying to achieve success as everyone else does, but then failing, and subsequently giving up, throwing in the towel,

TABLE 5-3   Acceptance of Prevailing Goals

Mode of Adaptation	Goals	Means
Conformity	Accept	Accept
Innovation	Accept	Reject
Ritualism	Reject	Accept
Retreatism	Reject	Reject
Rebellion		Reject and substitute new ones

forgetting all about goals (or means). Merton cited a long and varied list of examples of those he thought fit this description, including psychotics, outcasts, vagrants, vagabonds, and addicts.[36]

For the most part, however, Merton focused his attention on **innovation**: wanting to get rich and resorting to any means available, including quick and dirty ones. In this vein he alluded to the Robber Barons: Rockefeller, Morgan, Carnegie, Vanderbilt, and other industrial and financial magnates who amassed great wealth in the late nineteenth century partly through unethical tactics. They manipulated stocks, gouged customers, hired gangs to beat up workers, built monopolies, and corrupted government from the Senate on down. "The history of the great American fortunes is threaded with strains toward institutionally dubious innovation as is attested by many tributes to the Robber Barons."[37]

After stressing the rough tactics of the Robber Barons and other wealthy tycoons, Merton abruptly changed horses in midstream. Official crime statistics, he said, showed that most crimes are committed by the lower class: this was because "the greatest pressures toward deviation are exerted upon the lower strata."[38] This seems odd, to claim that the way the richest men in America thought and acted could be generalized to the lower class, who were either out of a job or barely able to eke out a subsistence living during the Depression. Nevertheless, that was the thesis Merton developed: the lower class was much like the Robber Barons. They were predatory capitalists without any capital.

He claimed that everyone in America was encouraged to believe he could rise to the top and become a captain of industry. This kind of thinking occupied a central role in American culture, which included tales of rags to riches, of presidents who had grown up in log cabins. Teachers told their students to shoot for the stars, and "'can't' never did nothing." Merton added that this advice was usually heeded by the lower class, who strove mightily to achieve success. But the fact was that they just did not have access to the legitimate means (e.g., high-paying occupations). This meant that they were in a bind, for they were unable to give up on their lofty dreams but also unable to reach them legitimately. Therefore, some people collapsed under the pressure to succeed and turned to illegitimate means, namely, moneymaking crimes.

Merton was a revered figure in sociology, and his theory is one of the most widely cited in the history of social science. It offered a new paradigm, an imaginative way of understanding crime and deviance, but it did not grow out of actual research on criminals or delinquents (Ivy Leaguers in the 1930s rarely got their hands dirty studying the underworld). How valid is this as an explanation of youth crime and delinquency? Are teenage offenders the rational planners that Merton implies? Do they commit crimes purely for financial gain? Do their offenses bring them huge sums of money? Is a life of crime an effective way to attain a high standard of living? Was Al Capone's success in Chicago typical?

One way to test this theory is to examine what kinds of deviant or delinquent acts teenagers engage in most often. When youngsters break the rules, which ones do they break most frequently? A good place to look is an article by Erickson and

Jensen, which lists eighteen activities and the number of times a sample of youths from the Southwest said they engaged in them. These data appear in Table 5-4.

This table shows that most offenses juveniles commit are not very lucrative. The few crimes that are potential moneymakers (auto theft, grand theft, robbery, and armed robbery) fall at the bottom of the list and hence are rarely committed. In fact, instances of drinking outnumber instances of these four offenses combined by 50 to 1. Thus Merton's argument that juveniles pursue crime and deviance in order to attain wealth appears dubious. Drinking, marijuana, smoking tobacco, truancy, and drug use have one thing in common, and it is not moneymaking—instead it is pleasure, which is greatly enhanced by the company of friends. If anything, the data in Table 5-4 (like those in Table 5-2) serve to bolster the sensation-seeking approach, not anomie theory. Youths apparently turn to deviance and delinquency for the kicks these provide, not as a scheme to get rich quick.

What about people a bit older, who turn to moneymaking crime in their early adulthood—do they fit the picture described by Merton? Do they try to build up their assets, amass a small fortune, move up to a middle-class style of life? If we consider the most common of these offenders, robbers and burglars, the answer appears to be no. When they interviewed armed robbers in St. Louis, Wright and

TABLE 5-4   Deviant or Delinquents Acts and How Often They are Committed

Rank	Activity	Frequency[39]
1.	Drinking	45,615
2.	Marijuana	36,872
3.	Smoking	33,802
4.	Drunkenness	28,159
5.	Truancy	13,858
6.	Defying parents	8,774
7.	Drugs	6,113
8.	Shoplifting	2,869
9.	Vandalism	1,532
10.	Petty theft	1,231
11.	Burglary	1,094
12.	Assault	632
13.	Running away	433
14.	Fights	413
15.	Auto theft	304
16.	Grand theft	246
17.	Robbery	232
18.	Armed robbery	137

Decker found that they were not committed to capital accumulation. Instead, they said the idea of robbing only arose when they were strapped for cash. Offenders as a rule simply lurched from one financial crunch to another. Each robbery was committed to satisfy an immediate need. Once they had the cash, they spent it: usually on gambling, drugs, and heavy drinking. Burglars followed the same pattern— many breaking into a building to get more money to keep the party (in their case, crack smoking) going.[40] In *The Protestant Ethic and the Spirit of Capitalism*, Max Weber identified this as a very traditional economic activity, a far cry from the kind of overweening ambition and careful capital accumulation that Merton said were the motives of criminal offenders.[41]

Albert Cohen

Albert Cohen was a prime mover; he got the golden age of delinquency theorizing started. Little progress had been made after Merton and Sutherland wrote their famous theories at the end of the 1930s. No major delinquency theory appeared in the 1940s or early 1950s. Scholars and students were losing interest in the field. When Cohen came along and published *Delinquent Boys* in 1955, he halted the downward spiral and almost single-handedly revived the field. Most scholars were impressed by his theory, and even those who took exception to it felt the need to construct their own theory in response.

Cohen began his explanation by listing the main characteristics of delinquents: he said they tended to be malicious, negativistic, and nonutilitarian. **Malicious** meant they were motivated by spite, anger, hostility, and revenge. They delighted in tormenting well-behaved kids, driving them out of the playgrounds and chasing them home. **Negativistic** meant that they thought their behavior was right precisely because the society at large condemned it as immoral and offensive. **Nonutilitarian** referred to the acts the delinquent youths committed. Contrary to his Harvard mentor Robert Merton, Cohen said that most delinquent acts didn't net any profit. Kids stole things they did not need or use. Theft was not instrumental at all; instead, it was fun, something done just for kicks.

Cohen then added three secondary elements to his description of delinquents: versatility, short-run hedonism, and group autonomy. **Versatility** is the opposite of specialization. Youngsters do not concentrate on one particular form of delinquency and seek to achieve mastery over it like medieval craftsmen. Instead, as dilettantes, they do a little of this, a little of that—for instance, theft, truancy, fighting, smoking, drinking, vandalism. Short-run hedonism meant the boys are impatient and impetuous, out for fun, living for the moment. Hence, they do not take kindly to study, schedules, practice, or planning. Group autonomy was Cohen's term for the closeness the boys feel toward their fellow delinquents and the hostility they harbor toward parents, teachers, and other authorities who criticize the gang. Finally, Cohen said that delinquency is mostly a male, urban, lower-class phenomenon.

How do the youngsters *become* malicious, negativistic, and so on? To explain this, Cohen turned to a discussion of middle-class values. Although other midcentury commentators had often used this term before Cohen, only he spelled out in detail what these values were. He said that there are nine of them, and all children in America are expected to live up to this **middle-class measuring rod**.

- Ambition. This is the determination to get ahead and be somebody, to have high aspirations for achieving difficult goals. According to the middle class, this is a virtue. Is it for the lower class as well? Perhaps not, Cohen said. (On this point he once again parted company with Merton.)
- Individual responsibility. This means looking out for Number One, being resourceful and self-reliant, not sharing with their friends. People who are too generous will find that it interferes with their upward mobility (a race that is best run alone).
- Skills and achievement. Being the best and winning awards and honors are highly prized in middle-class families. The main emphasis is on performance in the classroom, so the indicators of achievement are getting good grades and making the honor roll (a feat that hints at future success in the occupational world).
- Postponing gratification. Middle-class morality emphasizes worldly asceticism, hard work and saving, resisting temptations or self-indulgence, and gearing up to achieve long-range goals.
- Exercising forethought, planning, efficiency, and time management. This means acting rationally, not taking chances or gambling.
- Manners and courtesy. Success in life comes in part from mastering conventional speech and appropriate gestures recognized by polite society. One must be patient and friendly, not surly or tactless. Impulsiveness is apt to antagonize people.
- Control over physical aggression and violence. Although one needs to be able to compete, that does not involve brutality and bloodletting.
- Wholesome recreation. This means play or leisure containing an element of thought, practice, determination, skill, and special knowledge (chess, golf, ballet, and piano or violin playing, perhaps).
- Finally, respect for property. Things belong to their owner. They should be admired and handled carefully, not abused or destroyed.

Cohen did not believe every child was equally adept at living up to these standards. He said that middle-class kids generally were instructed in these norms and values long before they reached school age. Some lower-class youngsters were also up to speed on these, but others were not. The latter had been raised in lower-class homes where the parents did not stress long-range goals or guide their children in that direction. Cohen said the lower-class person appears

to be more dependent upon and "at home" in primary groups and to avoid secondary, segmental and formal relationships more than the middle-class person. He appears to be more spontaneous, emotionally irrepressible, and "anarchic," to give freer and less disguised expression to his aggression. . . . He is less likely to possess, to value, or to cultivate the polish, the sophistication, the fluency, the "good appearance" and the "personality" so useful in "selling oneself" and manipulating others in the middle-class world.[42]

What happens to the children once they enter school? They encounter other children of all social classes, each of whom gets evaluated, Cohen said. The criteria used in judging kids are the nine values cited earlier—the middle-class measuring rod. Kids who fail to live up to the standards find themselves looked down on by teachers and peers alike, then relegated to the bottom of the social status ladder. Apparently, social status distinctions are created early in life, in first grade, according to this analysis.

Kids could take this setback seriously and be heartbroken or they could dismiss it as no big deal. Cohen said the first of these responses is more likely; being consigned to the bottom of the status system leaves the boys in agony. In order to escape their lowly status, they could get together with each other, discuss their problem, and form a group with a delinquent subculture (a set of standards and values quite different from the one generally accepted). These standards would have to be something they're capable of achieving. Cohen said the values chosen for the new subculture are likely to be the exact opposite of the middle-class standards. In the new value system, a boy would win prestige by having low aspirations, by underachieving, by being self-indulgent and living for the moment, and by being rude, aggressive, and destructive. Conceivably, such behavior may earn one respect in the delinquent gang but at the same time it makes one's standing in the rest of society plunge even further.

A number of attempts have been made to test Cohen's theory, but most of them fall short because they do not completely understand the theory. First, it is necessary for the researcher to go back to the beginning of the theory: to determine whether lower-class parents (especially fathers) are indeed more spontaneous, anarchic, and aggressive.[43] Next researchers must determine whether these traits of parents lead their sons to be irresponsible, unskilled, present-oriented, and discourteous. Then it must be shown that these characteristics make the boys unpopular with teachers and other students. After that, it must be shown that this unpopularity leads to status frustration, which prompts the boys to establish a delinquent subculture, where the members are malicious, negativistic, and nonutilitarian.

Some social researchers, if presented with this model of delinquency drawn up by Cohen, would say it is flawed in one respect. Although, on the average, lower-class fathers probably are slightly more emotional and aggressive than other fathers, research does not find them to be anarchic. In fact, quite the contrary. Most lower-class fathers, according to Melvin Kohn, insist on the child being obedient and conformist. Rules matter, because lower-class kids will eventually (i.e., as adults) be taking orders from officials higher in the chain of command in hierarchical organizations. In contrast, middle-class parents teach their children independence, creativity, and "self-actualization," assuming that when these kids grow up they will find work that requires initiative and self-direction.[44] Other research agrees with

Melvin Kohn (not Albert Cohen) that lower-class families (1) place a higher value than other parents on children being obedient, respectful, polite, and courteous and (2) are more inclined to employ child-rearing methods that are strict, harsh, and punitive.[45]

In the racially segregated classrooms of America, Cohen's assertion that schools attract students from all different social classes appears dubious. But many of his other claims appear justified. For example, most youngsters involved in delinquency do commit a variety of acts rather than specializing in just one; this has been demonstrated by many researchers.[46] Plus, most of their deviant acts do not fatten the youngsters' bank accounts; delinquents as a rule do not amass riches during their years of misbehaving. After Cohen made his argument about delinquency being nonutilitarian, Merton cited it in his 1957 book. Although Merton did not come right out and admit he had been wrong when he said juveniles commit offenses to get rich, he at least hinted that he was having second thoughts about it.[47]

Cloward and Ohlin

Once the golden age of delinquency theorizing got under way, Cloward and Ohlin gave it added momentum with their *Delinquency and Opportunity*. A student of Merton's at Columbia University, Cloward carried on his mentor's discussion of strain/anomie. The strain or pressure begins for lower-class boys, Cloward and Ohlin said, when they are taught to want lots of money but face obstacles trying to acquire it via legitimate channels. With their legitimate path to wealth blocked, some lower-class boys turn to illegitimate paths, namely, moneymaking crimes.

Cloward and Ohlin said youths who want to get rich but also want to hold on to their lower-class buddies are the ones most likely to join a delinquent subculture. In the quaint terminology of the 1940s and 1950s, they want big cars, flashy clothes, and swell dames.[48] At some point, the lower-class urban male comes to the realization that he's never going to succeed, never going to make it. This realization forces him to assign blame for such failure, either to himself or society. If he blames society, he will become alienated and regard society's rules as illegitimate, particularly if he considers himself talented and capable. He believes that his failure stems from society discriminating against him. Feeling this way, he then joins other boys in a delinquent subculture; its rules become the ones that he lives by. The boys then become isolated from the rest of society, and more cohesive and dependent on each other.

Cloward and Ohlin are particularly well known for their hypotheses that (1) there are three distinct delinquent subcultures (instead of just one) and (2) the kind of delinquent subculture a youngster joins depends on the kind of neighborhood he lives in. Different areas contain their own kind of subculture. For instance, the criminal subculture arises in organized slums, in neighborhoods that have

1. Successful adult role models, that is, criminals who are able to make a substantial income in their line of work

2. Integration of age levels, which simply means that older criminals teach the younger generation of delinquents how to behave and to succeed financially

3. Cooperation between offenders and semilegitimate figures in the community (e.g., lawyers, politicians, and bail bondsmen)

4. Adult criminals exerting control over the youngsters' behavior so that there is no unnecessary violence, which brings unwanted attention (from the media and the police) to the community.

In this kind of community, it is possible for the teenage males to move up the organizational ladder and some day be on easy street. Here Cloward and Ohlin had in mind those communities run by organized crime, which in New York in 1960 meant the five Mafia families, who were indeed well-off.

But Cloward and Ohlin found that other slums were not so organized in New York in 1960. On the contrary, they appeared to be almost completely disorganized. Young males there did not have a chance to succeed (economically) either legitimately or illegitimately. In their neighborhood, there were no Mafiosi, no successful adult role models to emulate, and therefore no integration of age levels (the adult criminals had no skills or wisdom to pass on to the next generation), no cooperation with lawyers and politicians (who had nothing to gain by dealing with unsuccessful criminals), and no adult control over youths engaging in needless violence. The kids were on their own, and they were frustrated by their lack of opportunity to make big bucks. It was in these neighborhoods where the conflict subculture took root. Young males could not get rich, so they turned to violence, which at least allowed them to vent their frustrations and build a reputation as tough guys.

Unlike the first two, the third subculture did not develop out of any particular neighborhood features. The members of the **retreatist subculture** were not completely the product of their community. They joined this subculture because of their inability to make it in either the legitimate arena or in one of the other delinquent subcultures. Not everyone can be a doctor. Nor can everyone be an accomplished thief or hardened warrior. What happened to those who failed at these? Some, seeing that they were going nowhere, became discouraged and dropped out of the competition. They no longer tried to achieve success, however that was measured. Instead, they drifted into a life of drug use, in particular, heroin (the drug of choice for New York retreatists in 1960, presumably).

With this theory, Cloward and Ohlin established themselves as prominent figures in criminology. In addition, their book attracted the attention of the new administration in Washington. This was the beginning of the 1960s, and the Kennedy people, just recently installed in the White House, were impressed by this bold, new vision set forth by Cloward and Ohlin. The suggestion that delinquency rates would drop if urban male teens had legitimate opportunities appealed to the Kennedys' liberal sensibilities. At first, Cloward and Ohlin got the ball rolling with Mobilization for Youth, a local program designed to provide jobs and organize lower-class communities in a part of lower Manhattan.

When Kennedy was assassinated in 1963, Lyndon Johnson assumed the presidency and rammed a massive pile of legislation through Congress, including the

War on Poverty, which expanded on many Cloward and Ohlin ideas. This series of programs was extremely ambitious, and officials assumed that it would achieve various goals, not the least of which was lowering the crime rate dramatically. That, however, did not happen. Instead, crime rose spectacularly throughout the sixties, making the War on Poverty suspect, especially in the eyes of conservatives.[49]

When the War on Poverty apparently failed, it had the effect of virtually dooming any future attempt to "throw money" at poverty or other social programs to help the poor. No candidate for national office would propose such a policy again. Not in our lifetime or in our children's. Was the failure due to Cloward and Ohlin's theory or to the way the programs were developed? This is difficult to determine with much confidence. Probably both of them were flawed.

It is now clear that the delinquency theory was based on a series of mistaken assumptions. Cloward and Ohlin said that social class is a very powerful predictor of delinquency, that most delinquents are highly talented and motivated, that most crime is aimed at achieving wealth, and that most delinquents specialize in one particular kind of crime, such as theft or violence. All of these have been undermined by later research. But the theory was cleverly written and at the time politically appealing. There was a momentary window of opportunity open for liberal programs, and the Cloward and Ohlin theory captured the liberal imagination.

Politicians, however, do not deal with research and theory testing. They deal with arguments and who can be more convincing to people, manipulating opinion. Truth and fact play only a secondary role. Thus the politicians did not look at questions of whether the theory fit the available data. They just plowed ahead, assuming the theory was valid because it sounded good to them. Blinded by enthusiasm, they committed billions of dollars to the War on Poverty. When it failed, it helped write the epitaph of liberalism and helping the poor. Politicians must bear some of the blame for this. But Cloward and Ohlin, too, must be held accountable. After all, they constructed the theory; they made the errors and miscalculations.

Robert Agnew

The last of the strain theorists is Robert Agnew. He recognized that strain/anomie theories (after dominating the landscape in the 1960s) were reeling from devastating critiques by Hirschi and Kornhauser.[50] But he thought that a revised strain theory could overcome the weaknesses of the previous efforts (by Merton, Cohen, and Cloward and Ohlin). They had been focused narrowly on money problems or status problems faced by lower-class boys in urban areas. Agnew decided to broaden the notion of strain far beyond this.

He conceived of general strain theory as focusing on relationships in which a person is not treated the way he or she wants to be. The second element of general strain theory involves adolescents being pressured into delinquency by negative emotions (including, above all, anger) that often result from the negative relationships just mentioned. Agnew then identified three basic types of strain: failure to achieve the goals one holds dear, loss or threatened removal of things that one values a great deal, and confronting negative life events and experiences.

1. Failure to achieve goals. This comes in several varieties, including those mentioned in the classic strain theories of Merton, Cohen, and Cloward and Ohlin. Lower-class boys aspire to achieve middle-class goals but fail to do so (at least by legitimate means) and feel deeply disappointed by it. Another variety of strain comes from the failure to reach one's expectations, a failure thought to sometimes lead to anger, resentment, and rage. Or the strain may result from putting forth an effort in some enterprise and not receiving a suitable (just and fair) reward for it.

2. Loss of something one values. This could include being dumped or rejected by one's boyfriend or girlfriend, illness or death of a family member or friend, being suspended from school, or moving away from the old neighborhood. All of these can produce anomic feelings.

3. Having to face stressful life experiences. These could be child abuse and neglect, criminal victimization, physical punishment, negative episodes at school or home, violations of one's personal space, suffering verbal insults, living in cramped spaces, putting up with physical pain, and other noxious stimuli.

Agnew contends that experiences such as these tend to lead to anger, which in turn tends to spill over into crime and delinquency, at least under certain conditions. The theory is a relatively new one, and the empirical tests of it have generally been rather favorable. Some observers consider it a marked improvement over the classic strain theories.

But there is one study that does not report much support for it. Interestingly, this study was conducted by Agnew himself. It focused on youngsters and the reasons, motives, or explanations they provided for their own delinquent acts. Here, if Agnew's general strain theory is a very accurate one, most youths should have cited rage or anger as the motive for most of their offenses. In fact, the only offense in which rage or anger figures prominently is vandalism. For other offenses, the most widely noted motive was variously titled fun, pleasure, or having a good time. These motives do not support strain theory. Instead, they underline the importance of sensation seeking as a motive for deviance.[51]

Conclusion

When the Rockefeller fortune built the University of Chicago, it created an ideal opportunity for the scientific study of social problems and deviant behavior, including crime and delinquency. Chicago at the time was sorely afflicted with social problems; vice thrived, with bars, gambling houses, and bordellos in abundance. Its new university had a sociology department whose chairman insisted that graduate students use the city as their laboratory. They did, observing firsthand what it was like to be a hobo, delinquent, or ghetto dweller. The chairman, Robert Park, published little, but he was a charismatic leader who loved new and interesting social facts. "He sparked dozens of students and colleagues, spurring the great ones to distinguished careers and the lesser ones to at least one great work."[52]

Although Shaw and McKay never received their Ph.D.s this didn't hold them back. Together they contributed a good deal to our understanding of delinquency and served as intellectual godfathers for future theorists and researchers. They described delinquency as a natural response to the kind of communities lower-class boys lived in. If they lived in the zone in transition, they experienced extreme poverty, disorganization, and the conflict between conventional and criminal value systems. Boys could see criminal operatives at work, and this allowed them to evaluate crime as a possible future career for themselves.

Sutherland was a close friend of McKay's, but a better theorist than researcher. He, too, saw crime and delinquency as part of a cultural tradition passed along from one generation to the next (instead of being an idea created by the individual or an outgrowth of inherited tendencies). Sutherland made differential association a major theory in 1939, and students of crime and delinquency would read about it for the remainder of the century (though no one was ever able to devise an adequate way to test it).

At this same time Merton fashioned his strain or anomie theory of crime and delinquency. Sutherland had said differential association involved delinquents' learning attitudes in favor of breaking the law, but Merton argued that the crucial lesson people learned was to be ambitious, to strive for success (wealth), and this was impressed on everyone. Unfortunately, not everyone had access to the legitimate means. Those in the lower class had little chance of getting a college education or landing a lucrative job, so they were never going to strike it rich legitimately. Still, they were told by the culture that they could make it and they should try as hard as possible. Under intense pressure to succeed, some resorted to quick and dirty tactics (moneymaking crimes).

Albert Cohen knew Merton and Sutherland in his early days in criminology, so he was able to combine some insights from both of them. He also was creative enough to add his own thoughts to the mix. He began by describing delinquents as malicious, negativistic, and nonutilitarian. Then he went in search of an explanation that could account for these characteristics. He settled on the notion that at school all children were evaluated by their ability to adhere to bourgeois values, which a number of lower-class children were not taught at home and not prepared to live up to at school. After failing to embrace these values, the boys were rejected by others at school. So they got together, formed their own value system, and became terrors at school and elsewhere.

Cloward and Ohlin combined Merton's anomie theory with Cohen's delinquent subculture theory and created a new package, one that had a certain political appeal in the enthusiastic early sixties. The theory was part criminology, part political document, and written in a way that would grab readers. When it finally blossomed into the hugely ambitious War on Poverty, however, its flaws were exposed. The massive program apparently failed (at least as a method of reducing crime) and in the process soured America's elected officials on all future attempts to reduce poverty as a way of dealing with crime.

Walter Miller was never treated with the same reverence as the criminologists mentioned earlier, but he was an original thinker, whose methods and theory resembled those of the Chicago school. He constructed his theory of lower-class culture soon after Cohen's book on delinquent boys appeared. Miller took issue with the idea that lower-class delinquents were reacting against middle-class norms. He believed that the lower class had a long-established culture of its own, and that (if anything) influence flowed from the lower to the middle class. According to Miller, following the tenets of the lower-class culture had the effect of leading a person into trouble with the police and courts.

Key Terms

Natural increase:	the excess of births over deaths
Ecological studies:	Shaw and McKay research that mapped out the location of arrested juveniles
Social psychological data:	Shaw and McKay research that involved delinquent boys' own stories
Social disorganization:	amidst poverty, urban decay, and population turnover, newcomers to the slums have difficulty exercising social control over their offspring, who see crime going on every day
Differential association:	being exposed to verbal expressions of more pro-criminal than anti-criminal attitudes and going on to become criminal oneself because of such exposure
Priority:	being exposed to certain attitudes very early in life; these have more impact on one's thinking than exposure later in life (according to Sutherland)
Intensity:	higher status; their views are more influential to listeners than the views of other people (according to Sutherland)
Analytic induction:	hypotheses must be tested for every case; even if they fail for only one case, they are faulty and must be reformulated or discarded
Projection:	attributing one's own qualities to other people (especially, friends)
Unobtrusive observation:	keeping tabs on people's behavior so secretly that they could not possibly be aware of it
Toughness:	strength, bravery, and masculinity
Smartness:	ability to size up people in a street context and take advantage of their weaknesses
Anomie (Durkheim):	individual desires and expectations become extravagant in economic booms because the old standards break down; finally, their hopes will be dashed and they will be in despair

Anomie (Merton):	cultural goals are greatly overemphasized in the society and institutionalized means underemphasized
Cultural goals:	things widely regarded as worth striving for
Institutionalized means:	socially acceptable ways of attaing the cultural goals
Ritualism:	accepting the means but not the goals
Retreatism (Merton):	rejecting both the goals and means and giving up
Innovation:	accepting the cultural goal of wealth but rejecting the legitimate means of education, hard work, and saving one's earnings
Malicious:	motivated by spite, anger, and revenge
Negativistic:	thinking your behavior is right because the rest of society condemns it as wrong
Nonutilitarian:	not useful; just done for kicks
Versatility:	doing many different things; not specializing in one
Middle-class measuring rod:	middle-class values of ambition, individual responsibility, etc.
Retreatist subculture (Cloward and Ohlin):	double failures who give up trying to succeed and turn to drugs

End Notes

[1]Donald L. Miller, *City of the Century* (New York: Simon and Schuster, 1996), p. 423–4.

[2]Ron Chernow, *Titan* (New York: Random House, 1998).

[3]Nels Anderson, *The Hobo* (Chicago: University of Chicago Press, 1923); Harvey Zorbaugh, *The Gold Coast and the Slum* (Chicago: University of Chicago Press, 1929); Frederic M. Thrasher, *The Gang* (Chicago: University of Chicago Press, 1927); Louis Wirth, *The Ghetto* (Chicago: University of Chicago Press, 1928); Ernst Mowrer, *Family Disorganization* (Chicago: University of Chicago Press, 1927); Robert E. L. Faris and H. Warren Dunham, *Mental Disorders in Urban Areas* (Chicago: University of Chicago Press, 1939); Paul G. Cressey, *The Taxi-Dance Hall* (Chicago: University of Chicago Press, 1932).

[4]Jon Snodgrass, "Clifford R. Shaw and Henry D. McKay: Chicago Criminologists," *British Journal of Criminology, 16,* no. 1 (January 1976), pp. 1–19.

[5]Clifford R. Shaw, *The Jack Roller* (Chicago: University of Chicago Press, 1930); Clifford R. Shaw, Henry D. McKay, and James F. McDonald, *Brothers in Crime* (Chicago: University of Chicago Press, 1938); Clifford R. Shaw, *The Natural History of a Delinquent Career* (Chicago: University of Chicago Press, 1931).

[6]Harold Finestone, *Victims of Change* (Westport, CT: Greenwood, 1976), p. 94.

[7]Ernest W. Burgess, "Urban Areas in Chicago," in Thomas Vernor Smith and Leonard D. White, eds., *Chicago: An Experiment in Social Science Research* (Chicago: University of Chicago Press, 1929), pp. 114–7.

[8]Clifford R. Shaw, Frederick Zorbaugh, Henry D. McKay, and Leonard S. Cottrell, *Delinquency Areas* (Chicago: University of Chicago Press, 1929); Clifford R. Shaw and Henry D. McKay, *Social Factors in Juvenile Delinquency* (Washington: U.S. Government Printing Office, 1931); Clifford R. Shaw and Henry D. McKay, *Juvenile Delinquency and Urban Areas* (Chicago: University of Chicago Press, 1942).

[9]Clifford R. Shaw and Henry D. McKay, *Social Factors in Juvenile Delinquency*, pp. 5–6.

[10]Roy Lotz, Eric D. Poole, and Robert M. Regoli, *Juvenile Delinquency and Juvenile Justice* (New York: Random House, 1985).

[11]Robert J. Bursik, "Urban Dynamics and Ecological Studies of Delinquency, *Social Forces, 63,* no. 2 (December 1984), pp. 399, 411; see also Robert J. Bursik, "Ecological Stability and the Dynamics of Delinquency," in Albert J. Reiss, Jr., and Michael Tonry, eds., *Communities and Crime* (Chicago: University of Chicago Press, 1986), pp. 35–66.

[12]Kristin F. Butcher and Anne Morrison Piehl, "Cross-City Evidence on the Relationship Between Immigration and Crime," *Journal of Policy Analysis and Management, 17,* no. 3 (Summer 1998), pp. 457–93.

[13]Kristin F. Butcher and Anne Morrison Piehl, "Recent Immigrants: Unexpected Implications for Crime and Incarceration," *Industrial and Labor Relations Review, 51,* no. 4 (July 1998), pp. 654–79.

[14]John Hagan and Albert Palloni, "Sociological Criminology and the Mythology of Hispanic Immigration and Crime," *Social Problems, 46,* no. 4 (November 1999), pp. 617–32.

[15]Jeremy Gordon, "Edwin Sutherland and the Theory of Differential Association," http://www.criminology.fsu.edu/crimtheory/sutherland.htm; William Chambliss, "White Collar Crime and Criminology," *Contemporary Sociology, 13,* no. 2 (March 1984), pp. 160–2; Mark S. Gaylord and John F. Galliher, *The Criminology of Edwin Sutherland* (New Brunswick, NJ: Transaction, 1988); Franklin P. Williams, III, "Edwin H. Sutherland," in Marilyn D. McShane and Frank P. Williams, III, eds., *Encyclopedia of Juvenile Justice* (Thousand Oaks, CA: Sage, 2003), pp. 358–61.

[16]Edwin H. Sutherland, *On Analyzing Crime* (Chicago: University of Chicago Press, 1973), p. 17.

[17]Jon Snodgrass, "The Criminologist and His Criminal," *Issues in Criminology, 8,* no. 1 (Spring 1973), pp. 1–17.

[18]See for instance Craig Reinarman and Jeffrey Fagan, "Social Organization and Differential Association," *Crime and Delinquency, 34,* no. 3 (July 1988), pp. 307–27.

[19]Edwin H. Sutherland, Donald R. Cressey, and David F. Luckenbill, *Principles of Criminology,* 11th ed. (Dix Hills, NY: General Hall, 1992), pp. 88–90.

[20]Edwin H. Sutherland, *On Analyzing Crime.*

[21]Travis Hirschi and Hanan C. Selvin, "False Criteria of Causality in Delinquency Research," *Social Problems, 13,* no. 3 (Winter 1966), pp. 254–68; Travis Hirschi and Hanan Selvin, *Delinquency Research* (New York: Free Press, 1967).

[22]Edwin H. Sutherland, *On Analyzing Crime.*

[23]Denise B. Kandel, "Homophily, Selection, and Socialization in Adolescent Friendships," *American Journal of Sociology, 84,* no. 2 (September 1978), pp. 427–36.

[24]Mark D. Reed and Dina R. Rose, "Doing What Simple Simon Says?" *Criminal Justice and Behavior, 25,* no. 2 (June 1998), pp. 240–74; Ruth Beyth-Marom, Laurel Austin, Baruch Fischhoff, Claire Palmgren, and Marilyn Jacobs-Quadrel, "Perceived Consequences of Risky Behaviors," *Developmental Psychology, 29,* no. 3 (May 1993), pp. 549–63; Richard C. Savin-Williams, "An Ethological Study of Dominance Formation and Maintenance in a Group of Human Adolescents," *Child Development, 47,* no. 4 (December 1976), pp. 972–79.

[25]Sheldon Glueck and Eleanor T. Glueck, *Unraveling Juvenile Delinquency* (Cambridge, MA: Harvard University Press, 1950). Originally the phrase came from poet George Wither in 1613.

[26]Lee Jussim and D. Wayne Osgood, "Influence and Similarity Among Friends," *Social Psychology Quarterly, 52,* no. 2 (June 1989), pp. 98–112.

[27]Karl E. Bauman and Susan T. Ennett, "Peer Influence on Adolescent Drug Use," *American Psychologist, 49,* no. 9 (September 1994), pp. 820–22; Gary Marks, John W. Graham, and William B. Hansen, "Social Projection and Social Conformity in Adolescent Alcohol Use," *Personality and Social Psychology Bulletin, 18,* no. 1 (February 1992), pp. 96–101.

[28]Mark Warr and Mark Stafford, "The Influence of Delinquent Peers," *Criminology, 29,* no. 4 (November 1991), pp. 851–66; Mark Warr, *Companions in Crime* (New York: Cambridge University Press, 2002).

[29]Thomas J. Dishion, Kathleen M. Spracklen, David W. Andrews, and Gerald R. Patterson, "Deviancy Training in Male Adolescent Friendships," *Behavior Therapy, 27,* no. 3 (Summer 1996), pp. 373–90; Thomas J. Dishion, Francois Poulin, and Nani Medici Skaggs, "The Ecology of Premature Autonomy in Adolescence," in Kathryn A. Kerns, Josefina M. Contreras, and Angela M. Neal-Barnett, eds., *Family and Peers* (Westport, CT: Praeger, 2000), pp. 27–45; Francois Poulin, Thomas J. Dishion, and Eric Haas, "The Peer Influence Paradox," *Merrill-Palmer Quarterly, 45,* no. 1 (January 1999), pp. 42–61.

[30]Elijah Anderson, *Code of the Street* (New York: W. W. Norton, 1999).

[31]Walter B. Miller, "Lower-Class Culture as a Generating Milieu of Gang Delinquency," *Journal of Social Issues, 14,* no. 3 (Summer 1958), pp. 5–19.

[32]Robert C. Sherwin, Social Class Values and Deviant Behavior. Unpublished Ph.D. dissertation, University of Connecticut, 1968, p. 207; see also James F. Short, Jr., and Fred L. Strodtbeck, *Group Process and Gang Delinquency* (Chicago: University of Chicago Press, 1965).

[33]Marco Orru, *Anomie* (Boston: Allen and Unwin, 1987).

[34]Emile Durkheim, *Suicide* (New York: Free Press, 1951).

[35]Robert K. Merton, "Social Structure and Anomie," *American Sociological Review, 3,* no. 5 (October 1938), pp. 672–82.

[36]Robert K. Merton, *Social Theory and Social Structure* (London: Free Press, 1957), p. 153.

[37]*Ibid.*, p. 141.

[38]*Ibid.*, p. 144.

[39]Maynard L. Erickson and Gary F. Jensen, "Delinquency Is Still Group Behavior!" in Rose Giallombardo, ed., *Juvenile Delinquency* (New York: Wiley, 1982), p. 269.

[40]Richard T. Wright and Scott H. Decker, *Armed Robbers in Action* (Boston: Northeastern University Press, 1997); Richard T. Wright and Scott H. Decker, *Burglars on the Job* (Northeastern University Press, 1994); Neal Shover and David Honaker, "The Criminal Calculus of Persistent Property Offenders," paper presented at the American Society of Criminology meetings, Baltimore, 1990.

[41]Max Weber, *The Protestant Ethic and the Spirit of Capitalism* (New York: Scribner's, 1958).

[42]Albert Cohen, *Delinquent Boys* (New York: Free Press, 1955), p. 97.

[43]One study that has touched on some of these character traits is Lori D'Angelo, Daniel A. Weinberger, and S. Shirley Feldman, "Like Father, Like Son?" *Developmental Psychology, 31,* no. 6 (November 1995), pp. 883–96.

[44]Melvin L. Kohn, "Social Class and Parental Values," *American Journal of Sociology, 64,* no. 4 (January 1959), pp. 337–51; Melvin L. Kohn, "Social Class and the Exercise of Parental Authority," *American Sociological Review, 24,* no. 3 (June 1959), pp. 352–66; Melvin L. Kohn, "Social Class and Parent-Child Relationships," *American Journal of Sociology, 68,* no. 4 (January 1963), pp. 471–80; Melvin L. Kohn, *Class and Conformity,* 2nd ed. (Chicago: University of Chicago Press, 1977).

[45]Milton Rokeach, *The Nature of Human Values* (New York: Free Press, 1973); Rand D. Conger, Katherine L. Conger, Glen H. Elder, Jr., Frederick O. Lorenz, Ronald L. Simons, and Les B. Whitbeck, "A Family Process Model of Economic Hardship and Adjustment of Early Adolescent Boys," *Child Development, 63,* no. 3 (June 1993), pp. 526–54; Michelle L. Kelley, Janis Sanchez-Hucles, and Regina R. Walker, "Correlates of Disciplinary Practices in Working-to-Middle-Class African American Mothers," *Merrill-Palmer Quarterly, 39,* no. 2 (April 1993), pp. 252–64; Katri Raikkonen and Liisa Keltikangas-Jarvinen, "Mothers with Type A Predisposing Child-Rearing Practices," *Journal of Genetic Psychology, 153,* no. 3 (September 1992), pp. 343–54; Laurence Steinberg, Nina Mounts, Susie Lamborn, and Sanford Dornbusch, "Authoritative Parenting and Adolescent Adjustment Across Varied Ecological Niches," *Journal of Research on Adolescence, 1,* no. 1 (1991), pp. 19–36; Andrea A. Sedlak, *National Incidence and Prevalence of Child Abuse and Neglect: 1988* (Washington: Westat, 1991); Andrea A. Sedlak, *Supplementary Analyses of Data on the National Incidence of Child Abuse and Neglect* (Washington: Westat, 1991).

[46]Chester L. Britt, "Versatility," in Travis Hirschi and Michael R. Gottfredson, eds., *The Generality of Deviance* (New Brunswick, NJ: Transaction, 1994), pp. 173–92; David P. Farrington, Howard N. Snyder, and Terrance Finnegan, "Socialization in Juvenile Court Careers," *Criminology, 26,* no. 3 (August 1988), pp. 461–87; Marvin E. Wolfgang, Robert M. Figlio, and Thorsten Sellin, *Delinquency in a Birth Cohort* (Chicago: University of Chicago Press, 1972); Marvin E. Wolfgang, Terrence F. Thornberry, and Robert M. Figlio, *From Boy to Man* (Chicago: University of Chicago Press, 1987).

[47]Robert K. Merton, *Social Theory and Social Structure*, pp. 177–79.

[48]Richard A. Cloward and Lloyd E. Ohlin, *Delinquency and Opportunity* (New York: Free Press, 1960).

[49]Arnold Binder and Susan L. Polan, "The Kennedy-Johnson Years, Social Theory, and Federal Policy in the Control of Juvenile Delinquency," *Crime and Delinquency, 37*, no. 2 (April 1991), pp. 242–61; Frederic N. Cleaveland, *Congress and Urban Problems* (Washington: Brookings Institution, 1969); Peter Marris and Martin Rein, *Dilemmas of Social Reform* (New York: Atherton, 1967); Daniel P. Moynihan, *Maximum Feasible Misunderstanding* (New York: Free Press, 1969).

[50]Travis Hirschi, *Causes of Delinquency* (Berkeley, CA: University of California Press, 1969); Ruth Rosner Kornhauser, *Social Sources of Delinquency* (Chicago: University of Chicago Press, 1978).

[51]Robert Agnew, "Foundation for a General Strain Theory of Crime and Delinquency," *Criminology, 30*, no. 1 (February 1992), pp. 47–87; Robert Agnew and Helene Raskin White, "An Empirical Test of General Strain Theory," *Criminology, 30*, no. 4 (November 1992), pp. 475–99; Robert H. Aseltine, Jr., Susan Gore, and Jennifer Gordon, "Life Stress, Anger and Anxiety, and Delinquency," *Journal of Health and Social Behavior, 41*, no. 1 (March 2000), pp. 256–75; Lisa M. Broidy, "A Test of General Strain Theory," *Criminology, 39,* no. 1 (February 2001), pp. 9–36; Paul Mazerolle and Jeff Maahs, "General Strain and Delinquency," *Justice Quarterly, 17*, no. 4 (December 2000), pp. 753–78; Raymond Paternoster and Paul Mazerolle, "General Strain Theory and Delinquency," *Journal of Research in Crime and Delinquency, 31*, no. 3 (August 1994), pp. 235–63; Robert Agnew, "The Origins of Delinquent Events," *Journal of Research in Crime and Delinquency, 27*, no. 3 (August 1991), pp. 267–94.

[52]Andrew Abbott, *Department and Discipline* (Chicago: University of Chicago Press, 1999), p. 28.

Recommended Readings

Travis Hirschi, *Causes of Delinquency* (Berkeley, CA: University of California Press, 1969).

Ronald Akers, *Criminological Theories*, 3rd ed. (Los Angeles: Roxbury, 2000).

Steven F. Messner and Richard Rosenfeld, *Crime and the American Dream*, 3rd ed. (Belmont, CA: Wadsworth, 2000).

Francis T. Cullen and Robert Agnew, eds., *Criminological Theory*, 2nd ed. (Los Angeles: Roxbury, 2003).

Edwin H. Sutherland, *On Analyzing Crime* (Chicago: University of Chicago Press, 1973).

John H. Laub and Robert J. Sampson, "The Sutherland-Glueck Debate," *American Journal of Sociology, 96*, no. 6 (December 1991), pp. 1402–40.

CHAPTER 6

Social Control, Routine Activities, and Sensation Seeking

Theories are answers to "why" questions, and the question most often posed in criminology and delinquency is, Why do they do it? Over the years, most people have answered this query by zeroing in on deficiencies and defects, that is, what's wrong with the delinquents, the parents, or the neighborhoods where the kids spend their time. A complete list of the deficiencies would require several pages, so let's consider something more manageable—a partial list. Table 6-1 contains several of the more prominent reasons (that criminologists in 1990 cited) for youths turning to delinquency. As you can see, besides the delinquent individuals themselves, several institutions were blamed for failing to keep kids on the straight and narrow.

The Chicago School and strain/anomie theories said conflict, poverty, anger, frustration, class biases, inability to achieve goals, and delinquent subcultures put pressure on youngsters to get involved in delinquency and crime. For the most part, these theories painted delinquents as hapless losers, largely abandoned by middle-class society, pushed around like billiard balls, and consigned to dismal future. In part, this picture resulted from assuming that delinquency is strictly a lower-class subcultural phenomenon.

But nowadays our understanding of social class has changed. We are far less certain about its effects on people, in particular its impact on culture. Perhaps it has only very minor or negligible consequences.[2] Within criminology, self-reports have challenged the old axiom that delinquency is heavily concentrated in the lower class. Therefore, theories that were proposed after self-reports became widespread no longer assumed a strong class–crime connection. Theorists felt free to construct entirely new explanations of delinquency. Soon they did so, beginning with Travis Hirschi in 1969. Other theories would follow; the ones we will mention here are

TABLE 6-1   What Criminologists Identify as the Main Causes of Crime
and Delinquency [1]

	Delinquency	Criminality
Poor supervision in the home or an unstable, uncaring family	50%	30%
An economic system that prevents some from participating	38%	56%
A lack of moral training by the church, family, and school	30%	24%
Peer influences	34%	13%
Individual differences in succeeding in an industrial society	15%	33%
Lack of education or educational opportunity	17%	22%
Biases against the poor in passing and enforcing laws	15%	18%
Availability and use of mind-altering drugs, including alcohol	12%	17%
Labeling and perception by self and others	12%	17%

the routine activities approach and sensation seeking. These conceived of delinquency as normal, enticing things that anyone might do: not just those kids who were angry, frustrated, mired in poverty, or entangled in a delinquent subculture.

For Hirschi, it did not take long to make a name for himself. In his *Causes of Delinquency*, he carried out a scorched earth policy, savaging all of the major theories then reigning in crime and delinquency. At the same time, he introduced his own version of social control theory, which he first set forth in detail, then tested, using new data from the California bay area. Hirschi's combination of ingredients (critique and new theory and empirical testing) was soon acknowledged as a tour de force.

Social Control Theory

When contemplating what to write his dissertation on, Hirschi had the good fortune to acquire a large data set: a just-finished survey of junior and senior high school students from nearby Contra Costa county. Naturally, these data compelled him to work within the limits imposed by self-reports: he had to rely on findings dealing with youths' attitudes, opinions, perceptions, and self-reported behavior. Plus, he needed a theory to test, one focusing on individuals' attitudes and opinions. For this, Hirschi turned to Enlightenment philosophy (Hobbes) and European sociology (Durkheim) in order to cobble together a coherent set of ideas. He called it social control theory.

At its heart lay the *bond to society*, a series of elements that tied some youngsters to the social order and discouraged them from participating heavily in deviance or

Travis Hirschi, iconoclast, critic, original thinker, and creator of social control and self-control theories, has become the dominant criminologist of the modern era. *Courtesy of Travis Hirschi, Steve Agan Photography.*

delinquency. But other youngsters' bond to society was weaker; they were less strongly tied to society, less inhibited: as a result, they had fewer qualms about smoking, drinking, using drugs, vandalizing, fighting, or swiping an SUV. Weak bonds make deviance *possible,* according to Hirschi, but not inevitable. Lacking a strong bond merely frees teens to act as they wish; it does not give them a strong motive for deviance.

Hirschi drew upon the work of several predecessors. For example, in 1957, Jackson Toby combined principles of social disorganization with those from control theory. He said most thefts are committed by kids from deprived neighborhoods, because youth and poverty are accompanied by weak external controls. Adolescents are pulling away from parents but have not attained positions of responsibility yet (they are neither employed nor married). Thus, they are in a stage of life offering the maximum degree of independence. Slum communities exert little control over them, because (Toby said) parents face more urgent concerns such as domestic conflict, physical illness, mental illness, alcoholism, and gambling. Caught up in these troubles, families fail to supervise children adequately.

Toby claimed that education also plays an important part in this drama. People's social class standing can usually be traced back to their academic performance. If they end up on the bottom of the socioeconomic heap, it's largely because of the grades they earned. Low grades could be due in part to parents' failure to exert the proper influence. Parents who pushed their child to keep up with his studies could have prepared him for a career in business or the professions. Those who let him flounder in elementary school cut off this path of ascent. Youngsters who aren't encouraged tend to struggle. Uninterested in school, they annoy teachers and become unruly. Soon, most of them drop out, take up unskilled labor, and (given their lack of discipline) quit that, too.

Out of school and out of work, they begin associating with others in the same predicament. Perhaps everyone has impulses to steal things, but these boys often *act* on their impulses, for they have no **stake in conformity.** That is, they have little to lose if they ever get caught. No high status or honor. No family closeness or respected occupation. If they are stopped by the police and taken to court, they suffer no fall from grace. After all, it's not as though they were on their way to achieving a life of respectability.[3]

Ivan Nye was another Hirschi precursor, but unlike Toby, he did not concentrate on education. In his 1958 book *Family Relationships and Delinquent Behavior,* he (like Piaget) said that in their early years, children don't understand the concepts of right and wrong, so, not knowing any better, they tend to break rules frequently. Later on, they may continue defying them, but then it's on purpose—because delinquency is an easy way to get whatever they want. Hence, Nye viewed *delinquency* as something children do because for them it's *normal and natural.* He argued that it is *conformity* that is *unnatural* and hence must be *taught and trained.* Social control fosters conformity and keeps the child from engaging in delinquency.

Nye divided social control into three types: internal, direct, and indirect. In *internal control,* norms and standards are agreed to and accepted as if the child had created them (without any pressure from adults). The usual way of referring to this phenomenon is to say the child has developed a conscience. In all societies, internal control is the *primary* mechanism of achieving stability and conformity. No one has to follow the child around and monitor every move. Internal control goes everywhere the child goes and costs nothing. But for those youths who have only a modest amount of internal control, additional forms of control are needed.

Direct control is what most people have in mind when they hear the term "control." This refers to supervision, rewards, and punishment, by parents, teachers, police, and others. Some negative sanctions may be subtle and informal, such as a frown, a sigh, a look of disappointment. Others are more obvious—taking away privileges, imposing curfews, piling on extra chores, and slashing allowances. Nye said parents maintain a tighter rein on daughters than sons, and that this accounts for girls' lower rates of delinquency. Direct control has limitations, however: it works only when parents are on the scene. And if it's excessive or overbearing, it makes youths feel stifled and resentful. When this happens, direct control undercuts indirect control.

Indirect control is the individual's affection for parents and conventional figures. Liking them reduces the child's tendency to engage in deviance. The youth does not want to take the chance of getting caught and hence embarrassing, hurting, or disappointing them. Thus, Nye views the family as the most important influence in the life of the child. He does not mean family structure. Instead, he has in mind family members' attitudes and feelings toward each other. Irritable parents who periodically sink into despair or anger, who cannot endure the presence of one another, also make children's lives a headache. Kids may feel they have to escape the conflict and seek out a less contentious environment. Depending on what environment they choose, this can lead to more delinquency. What matters (Nye says) is how youths feel about their parents (not vice versa): Children who reject their parents are much more susceptible to delinquency.[4]

Hirschi's Opus: Causes of Delinquency

During the years when social control theory was barely a blip on the radar screen (the 1970s), the Chicago School and anomie theory dominated crime and delinquency thinking. Labeling theory, too, had its partisans in those days but it was not very theoretical and dealt mostly with other forms of deviance (such as marijuana smoking and mental illness) instead of crime and delinquency. In addition, radical theory made a splash, thanks in part to several books by Richard Quinney,[5] but it dwelt more on adults than teenagers, more on biases in the legal system than on the nature of offenders. Control theory was not a major player yet; no doubt, there were some criminologists who did not know it existed.

This changed in 1969 with the publication of Hirschi's *Causes of Delinquency.* He said (with no small amount of chutzpah) that there were three theories vying for supremacy: strain/anomie, the Chicago school, and control theory (remember: at that moment, 1969, control theory wasn't even on the map). And surprisingly, this bold strategy actually succeeded. Over the years, Hirschi rose from youthful obscurity to become the most widely cited figure in American criminology.[6]

He began his social control theory with the *bond to society,* which included four elements:

1. *Attachment:* Sensitivity to the wishes and opinions of others, caring enough about them to try to avoid hurting them by what you say or do. Some people are more affectionate, caring, and sensitive than others. And those who are will go on to avoid criminal or delinquent acts.

2. *Commitment:* Investment in conventional lines of activity at work, at school, and in the community. The more time and energy devoted to these, the more assets a person has to lose. Everything one has worked for could be ruined if one gets caught robbing a liquor store or assaulting a neighbor. Although attachment reflects the emotional side, commitment deals with the rational, calculating side: costs and benefits, risk and reward.

3. *Involvement:* This means using up all the teenager's free time so that he or she won't have a moment left to engage in deviance or delinquency. (It probably made sense back in the days when nearly everyone lived on a farm, worked the land, and tended herds from sunrise to sunset. Later, urban societies turned to sports, the Boy Scouts, and after-school programs to keep kids involved and out of trouble.)

4. *Belief* in the moral validity of conventional norms. According to this concept, people who believe in the rules will abide by them. Hirschi contends that there

is no other set of rules: no delinquent subculture, no criminal set of values, norms, and beliefs that people accept as valid. Everybody believes in the *conventional* ones. But some believe in them more strongly than others do. Those whose belief is weak or lukewarm are more prone to deviance.[7]

As Nye had earlier, Hirschi argues that deviance and delinquency are not difficult to explain, *they are natural:* (i.e., pleasurable, profitable, and intrinsically attractive). Control theory says *we would all be muggers and check kiters if it weren't for the obstacles in our way* (such as attachment, commitment, involvement, and belief). What is *not natural,* and therefore needs to be *explained,* is *conformity.*

Attachment

Not all the elements of Hirschi's bond to society are equally salient. Much more attention is lavished on attachment. The first question is who or what a youngster may be attached to. Hirschi zeroes in on the big three: parents, school, and peers. The more affection one has for these, he says, the less delinquent one will become. And of these three, the most important one is the parents (not peers, the persons emphasized by other theorists, from Shaw and McKay onward).

Hirschi offers a new theory and an immediate test of it using the data on Contra Costa youngsters. Most criminologists have judged the testing part of the book to be excellent. Nevertheless, a methodologist might quibble with a few of Hirschi's choices of indicators. For instance, to measure attachment to parents, he asks about **virtual supervision:** "Do your parents know where you are and who you're with when you're away from home?" This seems to tap fear of parents more than caring about them. So a better indicator of attachment should be used, one that reflects the affectionate nature of attachment.

One place to search for better indicators is in a national study of teenagers by Sorensen, whose 500 tables cover a variety of adolescent attitudes and behaviors. He has measures tapping affection for parents and respect for their opinions, that is, both aspects of Hirschi's definition of attachment. Sorensen's measure of deviance (sexual experience) is probably not an ideal measure of delinquency now, but it was a satisfactory one when he was doing his research (back in 1973).[8] He divides the sample into **inexperienced** (their sexual activity has not progressed beyond kissing), **beginners** (they have gone beyond kissing but remain virgins), **monogamists** (nonvirgins who prefer to have only one partner), and **adventurers** (nonvirgins who prefer to have experiences with different partners). If control theory is correct, then adventurers should have less love for their parents and less respect for their opinions (Table 6-2).

Table 6-2 shows that for this sample, teenagers with less affection for parents tend to go out and have sex more often. Youths with less respect for parents' opinions are more likely to become adventurers. Those who can't stand to be around their parents, who don't feel affection for them and can't get along with them, tend to become adventurers; very few of them remain inexperienced. But teens who respect their parents' opinions are more apt to remain inexperienced—they don't

TABLE 6-2   Percent of Teens at Each Level Who Agree with Statements About Parents[9]

		Inexperienced	Beginners	Monogamists	Adventurers
I can't stand to be around my parents	True	19%	21%	23%	37%
	False	33%	24%	29%	15%
I don't feel strong affection toward my parents	True	16%	20%	20%	43%
	False	32%	23%	30%	14%
I've given up on getting along with my parents	True	17%	12%	32%	39%
	False	32%	26%	27%	15%
I have much respect for my parents' ideas & opinions	True	32%	25%	27%	15%
	False	15%	17%	30%	37%
I have much respect for my parents' ideas & opinions about sex	True	35%	24%	29%	11%
	False	17%	19%	28%	36%

become adventurers. As social control theory predicts, attachment to parents breeds conformity. (Loeber and Stouthamer-Loeber's meta-analysis of family and delinquency studies found children who rejected their parents were more likely to engage in delinquency.[10] Other studies, too, have found that when attachment is weak, the chances of delinquency increase.)[11]

Next, Hirschi's social control theory takes up the issue of the youth's relationship with school.

> Between the conventional family and the conventional world of work and marriage lies the school, an eminently conventional institution. Insofar as this institution is able to command his attachment, involvement, and commitment, the adolescent is presumably able to move from childhood to adulthood with a minimum of delinquent acts.[21]

But how does a youth become *attached* to school? What is it about the school that would make an adolescent respect, admire, or adore it? For the answer, we have to refer to a 1977 article on IQ.

In it, Hirschi and Hindelang noted that most sociologists think IQ is irrelevant to delinquency, but research indicates otherwise—indeed, IQ scores predict delinquency better than race and social class do. As for why sociologists were so skeptical about the influence of IQ scores on crime and delinquency, there are several reasons. One is that a hundred years ago, a few writers went overboard and made vastly inflated claims about how powerful low IQ was in determining deviant and criminal activity. Eventually, there was a backlash as a groundswell of resistance to all claims of IQ's importance developed. A second factor is that within the field of criminology, Edwin Sutherland wrote scathing reviews of books that tried to link IQ and delinquency. Years later, labeling theorists and delinquency textbooks clung to the view that IQ was essentially irrelevant and, if anything, delinquents were actually smarter than their peers.

Hirschi and Hindelang cited studies by some of the most prominent criminologists of the day—Reiss and Rhodes (1961), Hirschi (1969), Wolfgang, Figlio, and Sellin (1972), and West (1973)—all of which showed strong negative correlations: youths with lower IQ got arrested more often.[22] Other data indicated that this also held true for self-reports (meaning the relationship between IQ and delinquency was not due to low-IQ kids simply being easier for police to detect). In general, delinquents averaged about eight points below others in IQ, which is a substantial difference. The standard objection critics offered is that this is due to the tests' being culturally biased. But that is not a very valid position, Hirschi and Hindelang argue, because the difference (between delinquents' and nondelinquents' IQs) holds up even within the same race and the same social class.

In *Causes of Delinquency,* Hirschi contends that several intervening variables connect IQ with delinquency, and these intervening variables involve the school. This involves a long causal chain that begins with *IQ.* Youngsters who do well on these tests of intelligence usually go on to get better grades in English, math, and history. Of course, there are always some underachievers and overachievers, but generally speaking, course grades are pretty compatible with measured aptitude. (Moreover, IQ tests are just as proficient at predicting grades among blacks as they are among whites.)[23]

Those kids who do well in school, getting good grades on their report cards every six weeks, are more apt to *find school to be enjoyable.* As a rule, people develop a liking for things they excel at, whether these are swimming, spelling, or dancing the salsa; success can be quite invigorating. Those who like school also find it easier to *tolerate classroom rules and school regulations,* rules that ban eating, fighting, tardiness, or talking. Hirschi here assumes that kids like the *academic* part of school, and they prefer to be in a classroom that's run efficiently. (This point of view is open to question.)[24]

Finally, Hirschi contends, students who are willing to put up with the school's authority and rules tend to behave in a conventional manner. In short, they *commit few or no delinquent acts,* or at least fewer than students who find school rules unbearable. This is the causal chain that Hirschi believes links IQ to delinquency. Some of these claims will be tested in the upcoming chapter on school and delinquency.

This brings us to the third form of attachment: the one to peers. Hirschi believes that consistency is a virtue, for he claims that attachment to peers works the same way as attachment to parents. The closer you are to your peers, the less delinquent you will be. According to social control theory, delinquents are not really attached to their peers. Instead, they are poorly socialized and lacking in compassion. Their social skills are deficient, their relationships with others are cold and brittle, which in turn makes them virtually incapable of influencing other people's behavior.

Obviously, this contradicts the subcultural theories. Control theory rejects the notion that gang members develop esprit de corps, that the gang provides

EXHIBIT 6-1   Harry Harlow and the Monkey Experiments

Long ago, children who did not have functioning parents used to be sent to orphanages or foundling homes. They did not thrive there, however, because such institutions proved more adept at providing a home for infection than for children. The death rate was exceptionally high; in many of these homes, all the children died by the age of two.[12] Such disasters prompted the medical establishment at the time to prescribe quarantine. Individuals were to be kept away from each other as much as possible, human contact was to be limited, because it was deemed the ultimate enemy of health.[13]

While medical doctors were warning Americans about the diseases passed through human contact, psychologists were saying that cuddling, comforting, and similar kinds of "mothering" could be dispensed with; infants and little children would become fit without such fussing over them. Indeed, too much cradling and cosseting, they warned, would prove to be destructive. That is, such children would become weak, soft, whiny, fearful, and dependent. This was the position vigorously promoted by John B. Watson, the president of the American Psychological Association.[14]

Mothers in general were then admonished to make sure their small children practiced good hygiene, above all keeping their hands clean. In addition, the experts said it was best to avoid affectionate embraces and other human contact. Hence, infants should not be picked up when they were crying, they should not be held, hugged, or kissed. Instead, the job of the parents was to push children toward full independence as soon as possible, from the very beginning of life. Twentieth-century psychologists were much influenced by behaviorists Pavlov, Watson, and B. F. Skinner,[15] which led them away from considering emotions such as love.

Harry Harlow, who also became a president of the American Psychological Association, thought the behaviorists and mathematical psychologists were wrong. He said there is surely more to life than stimulus and response, more than the operant conditioning of rats and pigeons. He said that feelings and emotions, too, were an important element of motivation in our everyday lives. He argued that among these emotions, love is particularly important. Other psychologists scoffed at the idea, dismissing love as nothing more than silly sentimentality; Harlow said that they showed no interest in its development and seemed unaware it even existed.[16]

The field was so convinced of this that Harlow was a lone voice crying in the wilderness (back in the 1950s). He knew he would have to *demonstrate* that love existed and that it was of critical importance to one's existence. As an experimental psychologist, Harlow could not experiment on human infants (for obvious reasons), nor could he use the standard lab subjects, rats. The latter were too different from humans when it comes to emotions. So he decided to use monkeys, specifically rhesus macaques, who turned out to be an excellent choice for his purposes.

The best-known of these experiments involved the use of two surrogate or substitute mothers.

The first was a cloth mother. She had a smiling face on a round head and a cylindrical body. The cloth mother was made from a block of wood, covered with sponge rubber, and sheathed in tan terrycloth. A light bulb behind her back radiated heat. You could call her an ideal mother, Harry said, "soft, warm and tender, a mother with infinite patience, a mother available twenty-four hours a day, a mother that never scolded her infant and never struck or bit her baby in error."[17] The other mother had a squared, flattish face, two dark holes for eyes, and a frowning mouth. Beneath that scowling visage was another cylindrical body, also warmed by a light bulb, but this time made of wire mesh. It was perfect for climbing, but the wire mother had not a cuddly angle to her. She was metallic all the way through.[18]

The infant monkeys got milk from a bottle in the second one, the wire mom. Up to that time, most psychologists were convinced that infants bonded with their mother only because she reduced their drive for hunger; that is, she fed them. Harlow thought that idea was false; he figured that comfort and contact mattered at least as much as food did. The infant monkeys showed how right he was. They cuddled next to the terrycloth mom for 18 hours a day. When they were taken away from her for a little while, they grew frantic, screeching and crying for her.[19]

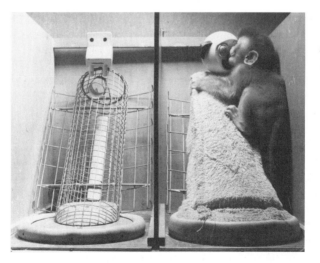

To demonstrate the importance of love, psychologist Harry Harlow designed clever experiments using macaques and two surrogate mothers in his lab at the University of Wisconsin. *(USDA/APHIS/Animal and Plant Health Inspection Service.)*

(*continued*)

EXHIBIT 6-1 (*CONT.*)

Harlow demonstrated to the world that milk was not enough to generate attachment or affection. The wire mom (despite her one important provision—milk) proved deficient as a whole; she was a failure when it came to providing comfort or pleasant contact. And the infants thirsted for precisely that. They had to have someone that they could cling to and be warmed by. It is as if they were born to bond with such a figure. After Harlow's monkey experiments were publicized, it became harder for traditionalists in the psychology establishment to hold on to their old position.

Harlow was the most convincing scholar when it came to proving how important attachment to the mother was. But he was not alone. Konrad Lorenz deserves mention as well. He won a Nobel Prize for his study of **imprinting,** by which he meant the passionate instinctive attachment of baby birds to their mother. Lorenz himself played the mother role with some greylag goslings. He was leaning over their nest when they cracked through their eggshells and began following him wherever he went. This was an unforgettable demonstration, but it was inevitably dismissed by critics, who said that humans are highly flexible and resilient, they're not hardwired like birds or geese.[20]

When Hirschi was preparing his manuscript, he (unlike his predecessors in the history of delinquency theorizing) surely knew of the findings of Harlow and Lorenz. So he was aware of the phenomenon of infant or childhood attachment to the mother (or other caregivers). He also knew that these could be significant. In addition, his theory focused on the positive features of their lives (such as affection for parents) that kept children away from delinquency. Unlike previous theorists, who cited negative conditions pushing youths into crime, Hirschi dwelt on the positive feelings toward parents that fostered conventional behavior.

Nonetheless, Hirschi was not Harry Harlow. Hirschi does not talk about love or addiction to the mother. He uses the term *attachment* instead. This he defines not as love but as caring about the wishes and opinions of others. And in the measurement process, he does not adhere to this definition. Instead, he focuses on whether the child thinks his parents know whom he's with, where he is, and what he's doing when he is out with his associates. This "virtual supervision" may indeed be like a voice of conscience that inhibits delinquency. But it is far removed from the usual meaning applied to attachment.

encouragement and becomes the kid's primary interest, that the gang comes together and thinks of itself as an entity. It dismisses out of hand Albert Cohen's idea that working-class delinquent boys believe in sharing, reciprocity, sticking up for one's fellow gang members. It contradicts Cloward and Ohlin's claim that delinquent boys feel emotionally close to and depend on each other.[25]

TABLE 6-3   Self-Reported Delinquency and Attachment to Peers[26]

	Strong or Moderate Attachment to Deviant Peers	Weak or No Attachment to Deviant Peers	Strong or Moderate Attachment to Conventional Peers	Weak or No Attachment to Conventional Peers
Delinquent	27%	24%	19%	38%
Nondelinquent	73	76	81	62
Total	100%	100%	100%	100%

According to Hirschi, being firmly attached to peers keeps one *out* of trouble. You might respond by saying that this holds true for *some* peers, but not among *delinquent* peers. Hirschi stands firm, though, saying the closer we are to our friends, the less delinquent we'll become, even if these friends are delinquent. One of the best-known tests of this was conducted several years ago by Linden and Hackler, who found that attachment to *conventional friends* makes people less apt to turn to delinquency. But there was a *slight tendency* for closeness to delinquent pals to make a person become *more* delinquent (Table 6-3).

Commitment

Commitment means investment in conventional lines of activity at work, at school, or in the community. When Hirschi talks about work, he means what youths will be doing years later, in their *adult* occupation. We cannot know what that will be because the youngsters studied are still in junior or senior high, when eventual occupations can only be imagined. Therefore, the usual tactic is to ask students what occupations or positions they *aspire to* or what they *expect to attain*. Control theory says high aspirations promote conventional behavior, not delinquency, because delinquent acts sabotage one's chances of reaching a high position.

Strain or anomie theory, on the other hand, says that when someone has high aspirations but expects not to reach them, frustration mounts, then explodes, prompting the individual to resort to crime as a way to make money. The person wants to succeed but does not think that this will happen (because legitimate means, such as college and a steady job, are out of reach). Hirschi says that strain theory's predictions are not borne out, because aspirations and expectations usually coincide; it is rare for someone to have high aspirations but low expectations.

Is there any support for Hirschi's notion that high aspirations make individuals less delinquent? A number of studies, most of them carried out in the 1960s, back up this claim.[27] The reason for this, according to control theory, is that students with high hopes for the future have an investment, a stake in conformity. They do not want their hopes and dreams stopped cold by a youthful indiscretion and an arrest record.

What about the other claim made by control theory—that people keep their aspirations and expectations aligned, so that hardly anyone harbors lofty goals *and* assume they'll never be attained? Strain/anomie theory insists that this combination (high aspirations and low expectations) is very common in the lower class (according to Merton) and among African-American youths (say Cloward and Ohlin). Research by Agnew and Jones found that among people who are deprived, high aspirations are common; and among these objectively deprived individuals with high aspirations, half of them have *inflated* expectations.[28] Hochschild said African Americans who are worst off economically express great confidence that education and hard work will bring them success.[29] Finally, an article by Cernkovich et al. finds that among young adults, blacks are more committed to the American dream than whites are. And (contrary to strain theory) commitment to *economic* goals *does not* lead them to commit moneymaking crimes.[30] High aspirations apparently don't lead to crimes of greed. This research thus supports Hirschi and undermines strain theory.

Involvement and Belief

The third element of the bond to society is involvement. As the age-old saying goes, idle hands are the Devil's workshop. So communities have tried to exhaust adolescents' free time by getting them to take up camping, Cub Scouts, Boy Scouts, Little League, and even midnight basketball. Alas, Hirschi's own data showed that such activities usually fail to reduce delinquency. Why? Because delinquency is not a full-time occupation that requires hours and hours of daily life. Many crimes can be squeezed in between other activities because they take only a few minutes to commit. No parents or adult authorities can possibly use up all of a teenager's time. Here Hirschi's data demolish part of his own theory.

Belief in the moral validity of conventional norms is the final element of the bond to society. Hirschi had in mind the acceptance of laws and police. But other researchers have focused on religious beliefs, which, after all, do condemn sinful behavior, including crime and delinquency. The data have shown (1) that religious beliefs have more deterrent effect in those parts of the country where religious commitment is especially strong and (2) that religiosity has more impact on "victimless crimes" (having to do with underage drinking, smoking, sexual intercourse) than on common law offenses. Religions often identify these as sins to be avoided.

Routine Activities Approach

Ten years after Hirschi's *Causes of Delinquency* was published, Larry Cohen and Marcus Felson came up with the **routine activities** approach, which claimed that there are three requirements for a predatory crime to occur: a motivated offender, a suitable target, and the absence of capable guardians. Then the authors promptly forgot about motivated offenders, never mentioning them again. Their unstated assumption was that under the right circumstances, *anybody* might commit a predatory crime, while under unfavorable circumstances practically *no one* would.

A capable guardian need not be a police officer or a security guard; according to the common complaint, they are almost never around when a person is contemplating a crime (there aren't enough of them to be stationed everywhere). Instead, ordinary citizens going about their daily tasks function as guardians, because they have eyes and ears to notice crimes, identify offenders, and notify the authorities. People staying home at night guard themselves, their family, and their property. Secretaries and receptionists don't sport badges or carry truncheons, but they too are on the lookout for people who could harm the organization. Offenders are hesitant to act when they know they are under observation, even if it's only by a 95-pound secretary.

What makes a target suitable for crime? Thieves prefer to take cars, money, jewelry, electronic gadgets, designer clothes and sneakers, tools, cigarettes, and drugs. They do not make it a policy to carry off grand pianos, full-size freezers, washing machines, king-size beds, or sofas, which are too heavy, too large, too unwieldy, and too easily spotted by onlookers in the vicinity. Potential thieves are enticed by **hot products,** those that are

Concealable
Removable
Available
Valuable
Enjoyable
Disposable

This is known as the CRAVED model. Small things such as money and jewelry can be easily concealed in the offender's pockets or wallet. Objects that are lightweight and not bolted down to the floor pose no removal problems (for instance, designer clothes). Items that are out in the open, not locked up in a vault or safety deposit box, are more accessible to the intruder or burglar. Some merchandise holds greater value for the typical thief (a BMW, therefore, would be preferred to, say, a Hyundai). The products that thieves are most apt to enjoy include alcohol, drugs, cigarettes, and clothes in the latest style. Offenders who want to dispose of stolen goods quickly may opt for cars or jewelry, that is, things that are in high demand and easily marketed.

Routine activities include staying home, going to work, shopping at a mall or supermarket, vacationing on the Greek islands, going out to get your hair or nails done, visiting the city for dinner and a movie, or hanging out on the street with your buddies. Simple and mundane as these appear on the surface, all of them have implications for crime and victimization, and these have been identified by Cohen and Felson. Years ago, the authors noted that crime vaulted to new heights between 1960 and 1975 in spite of declining poverty and unemployment rates and increasing amounts of income and education, trends that should have brought crime down, according to conventional criminological thinking.

But Cohen and Felson said that greater prosperity and education actually encourage crime. According to the routine activities approach,

1. More people were living alone. When they left their home, it was not guarded by anyone else, so burglars could enter without worrying.
2. More people were driving late-model cars. This meant that there were more desirable cars available for thieves to get their hands on.
3. More people were taking vacations. While they were off sunning in Maldives or Mauritius, burglars could take their sweet time ripping off the luxuries left behind at home.
4. More people were going to college. While they were on the way to or from classes, they could be robbed or assaulted, or their apartment could be burgled.
5. More people were going out for dinner and drinks. In bars they were mingling with crowds of strangers. Assaults and robberies could take place in the bar or outside, after someone had too much to drink.
6. More women were entering the labor market. Leaving the home every day made them easier targets and left their homes defenseless.
7. Manufacturers produced a variety of small, lightweight, durable goods. People bought them in great number. Thieves had ample opportunity to steal them.

Prosperity and industrial output combine to make more goods available for the potential thief to snatch. When times are flush, the offender has much more opportunity. These are the ways the routine activities approach accounts for rising crime rates. There is no need to refer to the problems or deficiencies of offenders. Presumably, offenders are normal people who see an advantage and seize it.[31]

Sensation Seeking

Not long ago, D. Wayne Osgood and some of his colleagues at the University of Michigan decided to expand the routine activities approach by moving beyond predatory crime to include other forms of deviant activity. Instead of studying city, state, and national levels of crime, they decided to focus on crime and deviance by individuals. Rather than dwell on targets and guardianship, they elected to concentrate on the people committing the offenses.

In their research, they began by looking into social get-togethers and soon discovered that some people were more involved in socializing than others. In order to measure this activity, the authors asked the following questions:

1. How often do you ride around in a car or motorcycle just for fun?
2. How often do you get together with friends informally?
3. How often do you go to parties or other social affairs?
4. In a typical week, how many evenings do you go out for fun and recreation?

In the sample of young adults surveyed, this kind of socializing was more common among males, D students, 18-year-olds, and individuals with highly educated parents. It was decidedly uncommon among females, A students, 26-year-olds, and those whose parents had little schooling. These were the causes of socializing, according to Osgood. And deviant behavior was one of the important *effects* of such socializing. Those people who socialized a lot tended to engage in more smoking, drinking, marijuana use, vandalism, violence, and theft than those whose social life was lacking.[32]

How might these findings be interpreted? Osgood was trying to fit his ideas into the routine activities framework and therefore did not give a great deal of attention to the individuals' motivations. But when we examine the four indicators of socializing, it is hard to ignore the fact that having fun is at the center of them. Two of the four items mention this term explicitly, and a third item talks about parties, where pleasure seeking presumably occupies a primary role. Thus, Osgood's routine activities research inadvertently provides a segue into the area of sensation seeking.

If a person wants to have a good time (meaning a hedonistic experience), would this encourage him or her to engage in deviant behavior? In answering this, let's begin by discussing some controlled substances. Are these considered pleasurable by the people who are most apt to use them? Marijuana clearly has earned such a reputation; it is widely assumed to induce either a placid dreaminess or euphoric gaiety. As for tobacco, nicotine has the power to induce a buzz in cigarette smokers if they have gone without a smoke for quite a while. In the short run, alcohol has long been known to make drinkers become more cheerful or more boisterous.[33]

This notion—that drugs and alcohol are consumed because of their pleasure-producing effects—is quite well known. Over the years, practically everyone has heard of this, and recently scientists have been delving into the reasons for it (the importance of dopamine and other **neurotransmitters** has been spelled out not only in science reports but nowadays by mass-market magazines available for everyone to read). If this is true of alcohol and drugs, one may ask if it also applies to other forms of deviance, whether they, too, are gratifying indulgences. Several observers have speculated that they might be. According to David Farrington, the noted British criminologist,

> One of the most fundamental motivational ideas is that people (and especially children) are naturally hedonistic and selfish, seeking pleasure and avoiding pain, and, hence, that children need to be trained to behave prosocially rather than antisocially. Another classic idea is that people are motivated to maintain an optimal level of arousal; if their level falls below the optimum, they will try to increase it (e.g., by sensation seeking).[34]

Few research studies have examined these issues; perhaps the best known article is the one by Agnew that asked delinquents why they committed various offenses. Respondents had sixteen choices, two of which reflect hedonism:

1. Pleasure seeking: Did it for fun or enjoyment, liked it, wanted to
2. Thrills: Did it out of curiosity or for thrills or kicks

The most common reason given for most of the offenses (theft, auto theft, fraud, illegal entry, lying about one's age, and hard drug use) was for thrills or pleasure.[35]

What feelings and emotions do crimes evoke in people who commit them—are they mostly positive or negative? This was the sort of question Peter B. Wood et al. had in mind when they surveyed 300 incarcerated male adult felons. You might not expect adults to say they commit crimes for the excitement—*that*, presumably, only motivates deviance by youngsters. Adults, it is generally assumed, commit crime for more practical reasons: they have to make a living, they need the money to get from one day to the next, because they don't have a high-paying legitimate job. This sounds reasonable, but it's not what Wood and his colleagues found. Among the incarcerated men they studied, crime is not just serious work. It is also a way to achieve positive sensations, as Table 6-4 demonstrates.

These results suggest that inmates find crime, especially violence, to be exciting, intrinsically rewarding. Hence, many criminal behaviors are apparently reinforced because of the neurophysiological high they produce. Someone might argue that adult felons in prison are extreme cases (unlike run-of-the-mill delinquents) and that people in the general population would be different, that is, they would *not* find robbery and assault very exciting. Fortunately, Wood et al. asked ordinary college men to imagine how *they* would feel while committing these crimes. Many of the collegians thought committing the offenses would make them feel worried, under stress, afraid, tense, guilty, and sorry. But a substantial portion (from 38 to 56 percent) said that they would feel on a high or rush or they would feel pumped up while engaging in shoplifting, burglary, robbery, or assault.

Although Wood et al. presented these findings about the college men, they did not have much *comment* about them (the collegians served merely as a control group to be contrasted with the adult criminals). Because many college men with no experience with these crimes still imagined they would find them exciting, this suggests the need for further research. Are Americans in the general population attracted to crime by the positive emotions they think it would arouse in them? To explore this question in greater detail, a criminologist at City University (Leona Lee) began surveying a larger sample of collegians, including women as well as men, and from across the country, instead of just one state. She drew on the work of Wood, Osgood, and Zuckerman (who created the idea of sensation seeking).

TABLE 6-4   Sensations Likely to Be Experienced by Inmates Committing Particular Crimes[36]

	Burglary	Robbery	Assault	Rape
On a high or rush	61%	65%	71%	77%
Pumped up	76%	77%	81%	81%
Living on the edge	64%	70%	56%	58%
Happy/excited	50%	59%	44%	73%
Worried	45%	38%	24%	27%
Afraid	45%	40%	26%	23%
Guilty	30%	29%	24%	31%

At the same time I began to think about a hedonistic theory of youth crime. Tentatively, I began toying with the following propositions.

1. From their early years, people develop a personality that is uniquely their own. Because of this kind of personality, people also differ in their emotional responses to the idea of engaging in crime and deviance.

2. The idea of engaging in these acts arouses negative feelings among most individuals: they experience guilt, sadness, anxiety, and so on.

3. But some people react positively to the idea. They find it exciting, it gives them a buzz or rush of adrenaline. Sensation seekers, who have fewer inhibitions and enjoy life in the fast lane, are more likely to find crime exciting, less likely to find it stressful.

4. Those who find the thought of crime exciting are more often than not male and fond of hanging out with peers.

5. Those attracted to the idea of crime find adult-controlled institutions such as the family, school, and church rather boring. They need more excitement than these institutions provide.

6. They tend to avoid marriage and career, finding them too routine, repetitive, and restrictive. They cramp their style and interfere with their adventuresome nature.

7. These people are likely to engage in more sex, drinking, drugs, smoking, and gambling than other individuals. Such acts are known to activate the dopamine synapses of the brain's pleasure center.

8. These people are more likely to engage in acts of violence, too. Violence is sometimes instrumental, but it always has an emotional component. People who have a greater need for excitement usually have a greater tendency to turn to violence.

9. In addition, they commit more moneymaking crimes. Burglary and robbery may be exciting by their very nature. But in addition, the proceeds are often used for pleasure, including, drugs, drinking, sex, and gambling (rather than food or rent).[37]

In the research on college students, Lee asked them questions about sensation seeking, whether they knew people who engaged in various crimes, and how positively and how negatively they themselves felt about the idea of committing various crimes. Table 6-5 shows the correlations between these variables. Here feelings about committing the crime in question are measured by subtracting negative feelings from positive feelings.

These findings reveal that sensation seeking is associated with feeling more positive and fewer negative emotions about committing crime. Feelings about committing crime are in turn related to knowing people who have committed crimes. This theory proposes that sensation seeking (enjoying active, wild, and "crazy" things) inspires people to consider crime as something exciting (rather than frightening). This in turn makes them more likely to meet and get to know people who

TABLE 6-5   Sex, Sensation Seeking, and Knowing Offenders Predict Feelings About Crime

	SSS	Kno Stl	Kno Wk	Kno Van	Kno Drg
Steal Feel	.42	.36	.31	.32	.33
Work Feel	.34	.28	.36	.27	.26
Vand Feel	.38	.27	.26	.34	.29
Robb Feel	.35	.21	.20	.28	.24
Assau Feel	.35	.25	.20	.30	.26
Burgl Feel	.32	.21	.22	.26	.20
Drg Sl Fel	.45	.26	.25	.27	.42

SSS: Sensation-seeking scale

Kno: How well do you know people who. . .

  Stl: Take things from department stores without paying?

  Wk: Take money or valuables from their employer?

  Van: Destroy valuable property belonging to someone they dislike strongly?

  Drg: Sell illegal drugs?

Imagine yourself doing the following (stealing, stealing from work, vandalizing, robbing, assaulting, burglarizing, and selling drugs), how often would you feel

  (Positive) On a high or rush; powerful; pleased with yourself; cool, calm and collected?

  (Negative) Guilty; nervous; worried; sad or depressed?

have committed various crimes. Finally, in a step not studied in our particular research project, knowing people who have committed offenses leads the individual to engage in such behavior as well (perhaps through imitation).

Conclusion

This chapter began with social control theory, then moved on to the routine activities approach, and concluded with the hedonistic point of view. All of them depart from the earlier sociological explanations offered by the Chicago School and anomie theorists. To some degree, the three theories in this chapter reach the conclusions they do because of the research design they employ and the questions they pose. Social control theory relies on self-reports in the form of structured questionnaires. Short and Nye introduced this method to mainstream criminology, and Hirschi's use of it enabled him to bring social control theory to new heights.

The routine activities approach, on the other hand, could not have arisen without victimization surveys. These began with the crime commission appointed by Lyndon Johnson following his defeat of Barry Goldwater. Previously, criminologists concerned themselves with crime, criminals, and punishment, not with the victims. With victimization surveys came new forms of data and later new attempts to understand these data. What did people do that made them more susceptible to victimization? Why were some people singled out by offenders time after time, whereas others went through life untouched by crime? Cohen and Felson took advantage of these findings and theories to fashion their own explanation of rising crime or victimization rates. Thus arose the routine activities approach.

But then Osgood and his colleagues adapted this approach to various deviant behaviors (not just crime) and brought it down to the individual level (instead of crime rates for entire neighborhoods, cities, states, or nations). The routine activities Osgood had in mind were (1) riding around for fun, (2) getting together with friends, (3) going to parties, and (4) spending evenings out for fun. These proved to be excellent predictors of drinking, smoking, drug use, and various types of crime. Osgood said it was because youths were with each other, out of the home, and away from adult authorities' monitoring. But there was more to it than this (as the next approach would note).

The hedonistic approach takes advantage of Osgood's findings plus another kind of data: the youth's own free-flowing commentary rather than answers to a structured questionnaire. Hundreds of youngsters have been asked how they felt committing offenses and what led them to do such acts. Often they comment that it was fun, exciting, thrilling, producing a buzz or rush.[38] This kind of information has been around for a long time, but it received far less attention than the idea that delinquents have social deficiencies.[39]

Key Terms

Bond to society:	a person's acceptance of and connection to the conventional society and culture
Stake in conformity:	investment in conventional institutions such as school or work; respectability that has been achieved
Internal control:	the norms and standards that have been learned and internalized as if they were one's own
Direct control:	norms that are enforced via supervision and sanctions
Indirect control:	obeying the norms so as to maintain a favorable relationship with one's parents
Attachment:	sensitivity to the wishes and opinions of others
Commitment:	investment in conventional lines of activity such as school, sports, work, or marriage
Involvement:	spending time in activities sponsored by mainstream organizations such as the Boy Scouts
Belief:	accepting the moral validity of conventional norms
Virtual supervision:	youths think their parents know where they are and who they're with
Inexperienced:	person whose sexual activity has never exceeded kissing

Beginner:	person who has gone beyond kissing but who remains a virgin
Monogamist:	person who is not a virgin and who prefers to remain in a relationship with one partner at a time
Adventurer:	person who is not a virgin and who seeks to have sexual relations with a number of partners
Imprinting:	instinctive attachment of infants to their mother and following her example
Hot products:	items that are most likely to be stolen
Routine activities:	mundane habits of people that make themselves and their homes more vulnerable or less vulnerable to predatory crime
Neurotransmitters:	chemical substances that transmit nerve impulses across a synapse

End Notes

[1]Lee Ellis and Harry Hoffman, *Crime in Biological, Social, and Moral Contexts* (New York: Praeger, 1990), p. 53.

[2]Felicia R. Lee, "Does Class Count in Today's Land of Opportunity?" *New York Times,* January 18, 2003, pp. B7, B9; Paul W. Kingston, *The Classless Society* (Stanford, CA: Stanford University Press, 2000); David B. Grusky and Kim A. Weeden, "Decomposition Without Death," *Acta Sociologica, 44,* no. 3 (2001), pp. 203–18.

[3]Jackson Toby, "Social Disorganization and Stake in Conformity," *Journal of Criminal Law and Criminology, 48,* no. 1 (May–June 1957), pp. 12–17; Jackson Toby, "Hoodlum or Businessman?" in Marshall Sklare, ed., *The Jews* (New York: Free Press, 1958), pp. 542–50.

[4]F. Ivan Nye, *Family Relationships and Delinquent Behavior* (New York: Wiley, 1958).

[5]Richard Quinney, *The Social Reality of Crime* (Boston: Little, Brown, 1970); Richard Quinney, *Critique of the Legal Order* (Boston: Little, Brown, 1974); Richard Quinney, *Criminal Justice in America* (Boston: Little, Brown, 1974); Richard Quinney, *Criminology* (Boston: Little, Brown, 1974).

[6]Ellen G. Cohn and David P. Farrington, "Changes in the Most-Cited Scholars in Twenty Criminology and Criminal Justice Journals Between 1990 and 1995," *Journal of Criminal Justice, 27,* no. 4 (July 1999), p. 357. This was for the journals *Criminology, Journal of Quantitative Criminology, Journal of Research in Crime and Delinquency, Justice Quarterly, Journal of Criminal Justice, Criminal Justice and Behavior, British Journal of Criminology, Canadian Journal of Criminology,* and *Australian and New Zealand Journal of Criminology.* Lawrence Cohen, too, ranked in the top ten.

[7]Travis Hirschi, *Causes of Delinquency* (Berkeley, CA: University of California Press, 1969), pp. 16–26.

[8]Adolescent sexual intercourse is strongly related to delinquency and drug use, according to the following: Delbert S. Elliott and Barbara J. Morse, "Delinquency and Drug Use as Risk Factors in Teenage Sexual Activity," *Youth and Society, 21,* no. 1

(September 1989), pp. 32–60; Emily Rosenbaum and Denise B. Kandel, "Early Onset of Adolescent Sexual Behavior and Drug Involvement," *Journal of Marriage and the Family, 52,* no. 3 (August 1990), pp. 783–98; David Huizinga, Rolf Loeber, and Terence P. Thornberry, "Longitudinal Study of Delinquency, Drug Use, Sexual Activity, and Pregnancy Among Children and Youth in Three Cities," *Public Health Reports,* 108, supp. 1 (1993), pp. 90–6.

[9]Robert C. Sorensen, *Adolescent Sexuality in Contemporary America* (New York: World, 1973), pp. 381–97.

[10]Rolf Loeber and Magda Stouthamer-Loeber, "Family Factors as Correlates and Predictors of Juvenile Conduct Problems and Delinquency," in Michael Tonry and Norval Morris, eds., *Crime and Justice* (Chicago: University of Chicago Press, 1986), pp. 29–149.

[11]For example, Peggy C. Giordano, Stephen A. Cernkovich, T. Theodore Groat, and M. D. Pugh, "The Quality of Adolescent Friendships," *Journal of Health and Social Behavior, 39,* no. 1 (March 1998), pp. 55–71.

[12]Henry Dwight Chapin, "A Plea for Accurate Statistics in Infants' Institutions," *Transactions of the American Pediatric Society, 27,* (1915), pp. 180–5.

[13]Robert Luther Duffus, and Luther Emmett Holt, Jr., *L. Emmet Holt, Pioneer of a Children's Century* (New York: Appleton-Century, 1940).

[14]Kerrey W. Buckley, *Mechanical Man: John Broadus Watson and the Beginnings of Behaviorism* (New York: Guilford, 1989); James T. Todd and Edward K. Morris, eds., *Modern Perspectives on John B. Watson and Classical Behaviorism* (Westport, CT: Greenwood, 1994).

[15]C. James Goodwin, *A History of Modern Psychology* (New York: Wiley, 1999); Ernest R. Hilgard, *Psychology in America: A Historical Survey* (San Diego: Harcourt, Brace, Jovanovich, 1987).

[16]Harry F. Harlow, "The Nature of Love," *American Psychologist, 13,* no. 12 (December 1958), pp. 673–85.

[17]*Ibid.,* p. 677.

[18]Deborah Blum, *Love at Goon Park* (Cambridge, MA: Perseus, 2002), p. 158.

[19]*Ibid.,* p. 159.

[20]Konrad Lorenz, *Studies in Animal and Human Behavior* (Cambridge, MA: Harvard University Press, 1970).

[21]Travis Hirschi, *Causes of Delinquency,* p. 110.

[22]Travis Hirschi and Michael J. Hindelang, "Intelligence and Delinquency: A Revisionist Review,"*American Sociological Review, 42,* no. 4 (August 1977), pp. 571–87; Albert J. Reiss and Albert L. Rhodes, "The Distribution of Juvenile Delinquency in the Social Class Structure," *American Sociological Review, 26,* no. 5 (October 1961), pp. 720–32; Travis Hirschi, *Causes of Delinquency;* Marvin Wolfgang, Robert M. Figlio, and Thorsten Sellin, *Delinquency in a Birth Cohort* (Chicago: University of Chicago Press, 1972); D. J. West, *Who Becomes Delinquent* (London: Heinemann, 1973).

[23]T. Anne Cleary, "Test Bias," *Journal of Educational Measurement, 5,* no. 2 (Summer 1968), pp. 115–24; Robert Linn, "Ability Testing," in Alexandra K. Wigdor and

Wendell R. Garner, eds., *Ability Testing,* Volume two (Washington: National Academic Press, 1982), pp. 335–88; Julian C. Stanley, "Predicting College Success of Educationally Disadvantaged," *Science, 171,* no. 3972 (February 19, 1971), pp. 640–7; George C. Temp, "Validity of SAT for Blacks and Whites in Thirteen Integrated Institutions," *Journal of Educational Measurement, 8,* no. 4 (Winter 1971), pp. 245–51.

[24]It is not very accurate, according to Samuel G. Friedman, *Small Victories* (New York: Harper and Row, 1990).

[25]Frederic Thrasher, *The Gang;* Albert K Cohen, *Delinquent Boys;* Richard A. Cloward and Lloyd E. Ohlin, *Delinquency and Opportunity* (New York: Free Press, 1960).

[26]Eric Linden and James C. Hackler, "Affective Ties and Delinquency," *Pacific Sociological Review, 16,* no. 1 (January 1973), p. 38.

[27]Delbert S. Elliott, *Delinquency, Opportunity, and Patterns of Orientation.* Unpublished dissertation, University of Washington, 1961; John P. Clark and Eugene P. Wenninger, "Socio-Economic Class and Area as Correlates of Illegal Behavior Among Juveniles," *American Sociological Review, 27,* no. 6 (December 1962), pp. 826–34; Travis Hirschi, *Causes of Delinquency;* Michael J. Hindelang, "Causes of Delinquency," *Social Problems, 20,* no. 4 (Spring 1973), pp. 471–87; James F. Short, Jr., "Gang Delinquency and Anomie," in Marshall B. Clinard, ed., *Anomie and Deviant Behavior* (New York: Free Press, 1964), pp. 98–127; Martin Gold, *Status Forces in Delinquent Boys* (Ann Arbor, MI: Institute for Social Research, 1963); Irving Spergel, "An Exploratory Research in Delinquent Subculture," *Social Service Review, 35,* no. 1 (March 1961), pp. 33–47; also see the more recent work of Tim Wadsworth, "Labor Markets, Delinquency, and Social Control Theory," *Social Forces, 78,* no. 3 (March 2000), pp. 1041–66.

[28]Robert Agnew and Diane H. Jones, "Adapting to Deprivation," *Sociological Quarterly, 29,* no. 2 (Summer 1988), pp. 315–37; see also Gary F. Jensen, "Salvaging Structure Through Strain," in Freda Adler and William S. Laufer, eds., *The Legacy of Anomie Theory* (New Brunswick, NJ: Transaction, 1995), pp. 139–58.

[29]Jennifer Hochschild, *Facing Up to the American Dream* (Princeton, NJ: Princeton University Press, 1995); see also Jay MacLeod, *Ain't No Makin' It* (Boulder, CO: Westview, 1987).

[30]Stephen A. Cernkovich, Peggy C. Giordano, and Jennifer L. Rudolph, "Race, Crime, and the American Dream," *Journal of Research in Crime and Delinquency, 37,* no. 2 (May 2000), pp. 131–70.

[31]Lawrence E. Cohen and Marcus Felson, "Social Change and Crime Rate Trends," *American Sociological Review, 44,* no. 4 (August 1979), pp. 588–608; Marcus Felson, *Crime and Everyday Life,* 3rd ed. (Thousand Oaks, CA: Sage, 2002); Ronald V. Clarke, *Hot Products* (London: British Home Office Research Publications, 1999).

[32]D. Wayne Osgood, Janet K. Wilson, Patrick M. O'Malley, Jerald G. Bachman, and Lloyd D. Johnston, "Routine Activities and Individual Deviant Behavior," *American Sociological Review, 61,* no. 4 (August 1996), pp. 635–55.

[33]William A. McKim, *Drugs and Behavior,* 3rd ed. (Upper Saddle River, NJ: Prentice Hall, 1996).

[34]David P. Farrington, "Motivations for Conduct Disorder and Delinquency," *Development and Psychopathology, 5,* nos. 1–2 (Winter–Spring 1993), p. 228. Marvin Zuckerman is the psychologist responsible for originating the idea of sensation seeking. See any of his many books or articles on the topic. Robert Cloninger developed a similar concept, novelty seeking.

[35]Robert Agnew, "The Origins of Delinquent Events," *Journal of Research in Crime and Delinquency, 27,* no. 3 (August 1990), p. 282.

[36]Peter B. Wood, Walter R. Gove, James A. Wilson, and John K. Cochran, "Nonsocial Reinforcement and Habitual Criminal Conduct," *Criminology, 35,* no. 2 (May 1997), p. 352.

[37]Joan Petersilia, Peter W. Greenwood, and Marvin Lavin, *Criminal Careers of Habitual Felons* (Washington: Department of Justice, 1978); Mike Maguire, *Burglary in a Dwelling* (London: Heinemann, 1982); John J. Gibbs and Peggy L. Shelley, "Life in the Fast Lane," *Journal of Research in Crime and Delinquency, 19,* no. 2 (July 1982), pp. 299–330; Paul F. Cromwell, James N. Olson, and D'Aunn W. Avery, *Breaking and Entering* (Newbury Park, CA: Sage, 1991).

[38]Jack Katz, *The Seductions of Crime* (New York: Basic Books, 1998); Frederic M. Thrasher, *The Gang;* Paul F. Cromwell, "Juvenile Burglary," *Juvenile and Family Court Journal, 45,* no. 2 (1994), pp. 85–91; Walter B. Miller, "Lower-Class Culture as a Generating Milieu of Gang Delinquency"; Mihaly Csikszentmihalyi and Reed Larson, *Being Adolescent* (New York: Simon and Schuster, 1984).

[39]David J. Bordua, "Delinquent Subcultures," *Annals of the American Academy of Political and Social Sciences, 338* (November 1961), pp. 119–36.

Recommended Readings

Marcus Felson, *Crime and Everyday Life,* 3rd ed. (Thousand Oaks, CA: Sage, 2002).

Robert J. Sampson and John H. Laub, *Crime in the Making* (Cambridge, MA: Harvard University Press, 1993).

Scott Briar and Irving Piliavin, "Delinquency, Situational Inducements, and Commitment to Conformity," *Social Problems, 13,* no. 1 (Summer 1965), pp. 35–45.

Allen E. Liska and Mark D. Reed, "Ties to Conventional Institutions and Delinquency," *American Sociological Review, 50,* no. 4 (August 1965), pp. 547–60.

Lawrence Sherman, Patrick Gartin, and Michael Buerger, "Hot Spots of Predatory Crime," *Criminology, 27,* no. 1 (February 1989), pp. 27–55.

Marvin Zuckerman, *Behavioral Expressions and Biosocial Bases of Sensation Seeking* (Cambridge, MA: Cambridge University Press, 1994).

CHAPTER 7

The Family and Youth Crime

The Parsonian Tradition

Where do our ideas about the family come from? You probably could think of a number of sources, perhaps including the Bible, Sigmund Freud, and (if you are not too young) Dr. Benjamin Spock, whose book on baby care was taken as the Bible by many parents during the baby boom. But another, less recognized source is a sociological theory known as structural-functionalism. We encountered two of the main exemplars of this kind of theorizing earlier, Talcott Parsons and Robert Merton. Though Merton evinced little interest in the family, Parsons showed plenty: he considered it the primary institution for socializing children and adolescents.[1]

How do parents exert influence over their sons and daughters? One way is to use their children's feelings of love and caring for them. They have contact with the children for years, during which time they express their views about what is best for them. This way the children come to *want to do* what parents believe the youngsters *ought to do.* Naturally, there are occasions when children misbehave or do things that their parents find objectionable; on such occasions, parents may respond with mild (or not so mild) forms of discipline to make it clear to them that they have violated social rules or expectations.

The socialization that children receive in the family is later buttressed by additional social institutions, such as the churches, schools, and (conceivably) the mass media, each one delivering the same basic message about the norms and expectations that young people and others are supposed to accept and adhere to. When this system of moral education fails to achieve its purpose, when several youths act out, the juvenile or criminal justice system is called on to step in to reinforce the message.[2]

Parsons was writing most of these statements back in the 1950s, when life seemed placid and this kind of well-oiled social system seemed to be in place. But inevitably there were some socialization failures; even the Parsonians were willing to admit that much. These failures were most likely to occur (functionalists contended) when the family structure differed from the form that worked most effectively. The form that worked best, they said, was the two-parent family in which there was a clear division of labor: one parent worked in the paid labor force while the other focused on the domestic front, maintaining the home and family.

Although Parsons and his Harvard colleagues developed their theoretical framework long ago, it has had a potent impact on how criminologists of today think about the family–crime relationship. In particular, some of them still believe that crime and deviance stem from a failure on the part of the parents to properly socialize their children. When people are asked what are the sources of youth crime in America, their first impulse is to heap most of the blame on the parents; thus the public agrees with some of the criminologists.

Specifically, some crime and delinquency researchers started out looking at such elements as the role played by single-parent families, mothers who worked outside the home, fathers who were out of a job, parents who were either lax or erratic in their disciplinary practices, parents who adopted deviant or criminal beliefs or styles of life, and families where affection between parents and children was lacking. All of these factors were derived from the **functionalist** framework that Talcott Parsons and his colleagues developed during the 1950s.[3] Let's look at how valid this framework is.

Competing Theories of Status Attainment

Status **attainment** refers to how successful children become once they reach adulthood—how far they go in terms of education and occupational prestige. This is an important interest within sociology, and several theories have been developed over the years to explain it. In the paragraphs that follow, each of these theories will be presented the way its creators would have you believe: that is, as if the theory were perfectly valid. Of course, most theories have some deficiencies, so do not assume that everything said here is accurate. It is always advisable to take theorists' claims with a grain of salt.

Socialization Theory

Socialization theory draws on Parsons and claims that parents play a determining role in how their children develop. Adults initiate the process, which includes education, training, and imitation; they cannot help but have a powerful impact on the personality and competence of the child, this theory claims. Unfortunately, in most single-parent families, the father is absent almost all the time, and this obviously reduces the time spent with the children (reading, playing, and working together, helping with homework, and having private talks) and decreases the amount of parental control and supervision. When people get divorced, they face economic pressure, work stress, negative life events for the mother (e.g., moving, breaking friendships, having a court case), and these can lead to depression.[4] Such developments may also result in less effective parenting: "Divorced parents made fewer maturity demands, communicated less well, tended to be less affectionate, and showed marked inconsistency in discipline and control of their children in comparison to married parents."[5] Naturally, such parental failings undercut the youngsters' opportunity to develop in ways that are healthy.

Socialization theorists consider the family the primary setting in which children learn how to act, how to relate to others, and how to fit into the society when they become adults. If kids do not have a father present, they will not have a male role model to teach them about finding and keeping a job and achieving in the competitive world of work. The child in a one-parent family is not exposed to a hierarchical model of authority (the single mother and her children are more apt to relate to one another as equals). But in the outside world, there are many hierarchical organizations, and unfamiliarity with this kind of organizational model is a serious handicap.[6] The socialization perspective adds that two parents are optimal for socializing children to grow up and become successful; children from alternative family structures, the theory predicts, typically will not turn out as well.[7]

Economic Theory

Economic theory also draws heavily on Parsons for inspiration. According to economic theory, how successful a person becomes in the social class structure is due in large part to human capital. **Human capital** means improved health and productivity (including standard of living) that results from investments made in individuals. Parents play a pivotal role in their children's acquisition of human capital; they spend time and money in order to develop their children's knowledge, skills, and values. Ideally, according to this theory, there are two parents, and they have a well-established division of labor. The parent with a comparative advantage in the market should concentrate on this line of activity, while the parent with a comparative advantage in household management should concentrate on that.[8]

Economist Gary Becker, who propounded this theory, contends that parents have a powerful effect on their children's future. Two-parent families are based on mothers and fathers providing complementary services and resources: economic resources (father) and household services (mother). Only if children live under this arrangement are they very likely to succeed. Single-parent families suffer not only from greater poverty and economic insecurity but also from the lack of a division of labor. One person cannot provide the children with both economic resources and household services as successfully as two of them could. Children, according to economic theory, should have the highest attainments if they live in a two-parent family, not as high if in a father-only family, and lowest of all if in a mother-only family. This is because of income: single mothers on the average earn only about half the wages or salaries that single fathers make.[9]

The life of a single mother is complicated by many stresses and rarely runs smoothly. *(Mark Richards/PhotoEdit.)*

Evolutionary Psychology

In the view of evolutionary psychologists, biological relationships are extremely significant to people. This view places greater weight on the role of the mother than that of the father. To begin with, mothers invest heavily in their child, providing the most intimate of homes for nine months, then nursing for up to two years after the child is born. All this time it is possible that the father may be contributing nothing at all to the child's welfare. Women have a limited number of children they can raise to adulthood, so they tend to put a high value on each one. On the other hand, a man could impregnate hundreds of women, sire hundreds of children, and never have to deal with pregnancy, childbirth, or nursing.

Evolutionary theory suggests that the optimal family contains two biological parents. The biological father tends to contribute less to the child's well-being than the mother, but if the father knows that the child is biologically his, he contributes more than any other man would. The reason for this is that offspring carries his genes. In contrast to the economic model, the evolutionary perspective assumes that a child will be more likely to thrive living in a mother-only family than in one that is father-only. The evolutionary perspective also takes a rather dim view of families that include a stepparent—because the child does not carry that person's genes and may be seen by the stepparent as competition.[10]

Selection Bias

This perspective says that although family structure is *correlated* with children's attainments, it does not *cause* them. Instead, there is a third variable that causes both family structure and children's attainments—the parents' social or psychological characteristics (traits they had before the marriage, or childbirth, or divorce, or remarriage). It could be that the mothers who never married or who got divorced were already less competent, less intelligent, less motivated, less educated, less committed to the relationship, less interested in children, or less savvy about raising them.

For a number of years, some family sociologists have argued that divorce is not the reason that children from such families do not fare well; instead, it is the conflict and bickering preceding the divorce that have detrimental effects on the children. Children's lower attainments in education and occupation are thus traced back to the discord they were exposed to for years while the mother and father were still married and living in the same household. This line of argument may be considered as a special case of selection bias.

Research Findings

Now let's consider some relevant data to test the various theories we have just sketched. Researchers have looked into the question of how much impact family structure has on the children's attainment and other outcomes, and what theory best explains the relationship between family structure and children's outcomes. But not all the studies reach the same conclusion. This is because they use different data sets, with different measures of family structure and different measures of children's outcomes. They also test different theories and control for different background variables. Under the circumstances, discrepancies in the findings should not come as a great surprise.

Here we will consider one of the best and most recent studies, one that employs four data sets, which are separated by more than thirty years. It also covers all of the theories outlined earlier. This is the 1999 Biblarz and Raftery article on family structure, educational attainment, and socioeconomic success. The authors begin by examining sociological theory, which says that family structure is crucial, and that children from two-parent families should have higher occupational and educational attainment than offspring from any of the single-parent families (divorced, widowed, never married). But Biblarz and Raftery did not find this claim to be valid.[11]

In decades past, most studies simply compared children from two-biological-parent families with kids from all the other types. Hence, they failed to investigate differences among children from the various kinds of families that fall under the heading of "alternative." The four data sets Biblarz and Raftery analyze show that alternative family structures differ from one another—some are more conducive than others to children's educational and occupational attainment: children from single-mother families outperform those from single-father families and stepfamilies (once parental socioeconomic status is controlled for by statistical adjustment).

In the end, Biblarz and Raftery conclude that the only theory supported by their findings (which are more extensive than we can cover in the space here) is the evolutionary approach. Socialization theory fails to account for the fact that children from single-mother families fare better than ones from other alternative family structures. Economic theory mistakenly predicts that children are more apt to prosper if they come from a mother-stepfather family than if they are raised by a single mother. Plus, economic theory assumes (incorrectly) that fathers' higher income will make them more effective parents than mothers are. On the other hand, the evolutionary approach predicts correctly that mothers will invest more in their children than fathers will, and this will pay off in the child's future well-being.

The Biblarz and Raftery study has been presented here for one reason: it shows how hypotheses can be drawn from diverse fields and tested. Unfortunately, it focuses on how family structure affects a child's future (adult) *status attainment. Our* interest lies elsewhere: in how family structure affects the child's *delinquency.* Research on family structure and delinquency is vast, but **atheoretical;** no one has come along to analyze the theories carefully, set forth their implications and predictions precisely, and then test them with extensive data sets as expertly as Biblarz and Raftery did with status attainment.

Still, there is some recent research worth mentioning. Before doing so, we need to review the meta-analyses published back in 1991. You may recall from chapter 1, that most studies showed (1) broken homes were related to status offenses such as running away, smoking, truancy, incorrigibility, and the like but (2) such homes did *not* produce youngsters who committed significantly more violence or property offenses. Lately, several *new* articles have appeared, reexamining the link between family structure and delinquency. We will consider two of these.

In 2002, Rebellon argued that studies of broken homes and delinquency are not grounded in theory and suffer from several methodological deficiencies. One defect is that they tend to lump all families into two types: families are said to be either intact or broken. But as Biblarz and Raftery learned, not all are alike in their effects within these big categories. For instance, there is the question of what to do with families containing one biological parent and one stepparent. Should these be called intact or broken homes? The question is important, because some evidence suggests that these step-families generate more delinquency than other types do.[12]

In 1992 David Farrington found that family type was an important predictor of delinquency; in fact it was as good a predictor as low family income, large family size, poor child rearing, low IQ, and hyperactivity. In 2001 Juby and Farrington reexamined these data from the Cambridge Study and focused on disrupted families. They did not rely on **dichotomies** (the simple comparison of intact vs. broken homes, or one-parent vs. two-parent families). Instead they presented findings on a wealth of factors: how much family conflict there was, whether the father left home, whether the father died, whether the mother left home, whether the mother died, the child's age when the family disruption occurred, and much more.

The three best predictors of delinquency were the mother dying, the mother leaving, and the child living with someone else after the disruption (i.e., not the mother). Consider Figure 7-1, which Juby and Farrington call the postdisruption trajectory. You will notice that self-reported delinquency and juvenile convictions vary a great deal from one family type to another. Clearly, children do much better if left with their mother alone than with relatives, or the father alone, or nonrelatives. This reinforces the status attainment findings of Biblarz and Raftery mentioned previously.

FIGURE 7.1   Convictions and Delinquency for Different Family Structures.[13]

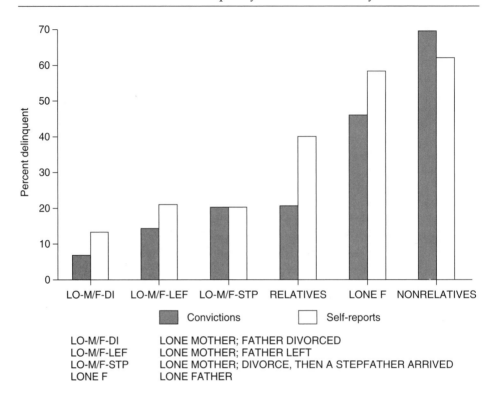

LO-M/F-DI	LONE MOTHER; FATHER DIVORCED
LO-M/F-LEF	LONE MOTHER; FATHER LEFT
LO-M/F-STP	LONE MOTHER; DIVORCE, THEN A STEPFATHER ARRIVED
LONE F	LONE FATHER

Parenting Styles

Many people think that the family has a monumental impact on the child's future. Andrew Cherlin has given this point of view the title THE PARENTS MAKE ALL THE DIFFERENCE. Such a position appears in hundreds of publications. Typical of such writings is Judith Wallerstein's statements about the impact of divorce. She claims that most children are severely harmed by their parents' divorce and that the damage lasts for a quarter century. Unfortunately, Wallerstein had no control group or comparison group (i.e., no kids from nondivorced families) and she neglected to mention that *half the divorced parents she studied had histories of mental illness.* Parents' mental illness, needless to say, is an important background factor, one that researchers need to control when they are analyzing whether family structure has an impact on children's psychological well-being.[14]

Diana Baumrind has identified four styles of parenting commonly found in American families, which she calls authoritative, authoritarian, permissive, and neglecting. *Authoritative* parents (Type 1) are demanding (meaning that they expect and insist upon mature behavior) and they are responsive (i.e., they give the child emotional support, acceptance, and encouragement). *Authoritarian* parents (Type 2) are also demanding but they're not very responsive. *Permissive* parents (Type 3) are the opposite of the authoritarian type, for they are responsive but not demanding. And finally, *indifferent* parents (Type 4) are undemanding and unresponsive.

Authoritative parents (#1) combine warmth and firmness. They take the child's opinion into account when making decisions, they communicate rules clearly, deal with misbehavior directly but not harshly, reward the child for acting appropriately, value effort and achievement, and expect the child to act responsibly. Authoritarian parents (#2) emphasize obedience and conformity. They are the ones in charge, making all the decisions and enforcing the rules. They expect the child to accept them without question or complaint. They do not encourage individual autonomy or independence. Permissive parents (#3) have few rules and expectations, ignore most of the child's inappropriate behavior, and value the child's free expression of wishes and impulses. Indifferent parents (#4) do not know where their child is much of the time or what he or she is doing, and they show little interest in the child's experiences or friends. These parents, immersed in their own interests and needs, put those of the child on the back burner.[15]

Young people raised in authoritative families (#1) generally turn out to be more responsible, more self-assured, more adaptive, more creative, more socially adept, and more successful academically than do youths raised in other families. Adolescents from authoritarian homes (#2) are more dependent, more passive, less curious, less competent socially, and less self-assured. Individuals who grow up in permissive households (#3) are less mature, less responsible, more apt to go along with whatever their peers are doing. Adolescents from homes with indifferent parents (#4) are more likely to engage in sex, drug use, alcohol drinking, and delinquency.[16] This, at least is the point of view endorsed by most psychologists.[17]

Judith Rich Harris

Although there are studies supporting the hypothesis that parenting styles strongly influence children's behavior, not everyone is persuaded. As Cherlin notes, some mavericks break with convention and adopt the view that PARENTS DON'T MAKE ANY DIFFERENCE. In this camp the individual best known is Judith Rich Harris, who has elaborated her ideas in the controversial best seller *The Nurture Assumption.* For years she wrote textbooks in developmental psychology that reflected the opinions of the rest of the field—that nurture is very important and influential. That is, children are socialized first and foremost by the family, whose attitudes and behavior they readily adopt.

But Harris found several problems with the parental socialization thesis. Take, for example, the case of immigrant parents and their little children. Let us say that they come from Russia to the United States to live. The parents probably speak Russian to each other and to their children, simply because it is the only language they know. If they know any English at all, perhaps it is broken and comes with a heavy accent. What happens to their children growing up in the United States? They probably will learn to look and dress like Americans and to speak English like the other people in their neighborhood, with a Boston accent, a Brooklyn accent, a southern accent or whatever accent the kids in the neighborhood speak. They *do not learn* to speak like their parents.

Or, says Harris, consider people who are deaf. Such individuals normally grow up, land a job, and get married, quite frequently to another deaf person. When they have children, some of these children are deaf too, but most of them (90 percent) are not; they can hear and speak without any difficulty. When they coo and babble as babies, or say "mama" and "dada," no one makes a big fuss, because of course the parents cannot hear it. So for years, these children learn nothing of the spoken language from their parents, yet they go on to become fluent speakers of English (or whatever the local tongue may be).[18]

Harris says that what children learn in one context may not pan out when it's tried in another context. A child who cries and acts like a baby may get sympathy from her mom and dad but if she tries this at school, she may be labeled as a pest and a nuisance. Most children carefully distinguish between the home and the outside world. Each environment has its own code of behavior. Even 4-year-olds are quite proficient at switching from one to another. As they get older, they keep their two worlds completely separate: parents aren't told about the problems caused by school bullies, and other children are kept in the dark about any child abuse or spouse battering that may be taking place at home. Thus, socialization by parents really does work, but mostly it works *within the household*. In the outside world, much of it is temporarily forgotten and sloughed off. Children segregate their two lives, keeping them rigidly compartmentalized.

Furthermore, Harris contends, children do not see their parents as being like themselves. Parents are big, hairy, and free to do as they want. Children on the other hand are expected to behave like good little children, not like adults. Imitating adults (by drinking, smoking, swearing, issuing commands, asking personal questions, calling everyone by their first names, or driving cars) is assuredly not acceptable behavior for children. Kids with the audacity to imitate their parents in these ways would be considered impertinent, and would quickly suffer the consequences. Most, however, don't ever try it; they *know* they are children and they *know* how children are supposed to act. And that's how they want it. A child wants to be a successful child, not a successful adult.

Finally, Harris says that middle-class white American parents generally agree that Baumrind is right, and that the authoritative model is indeed the best way to raise children. The only problem is that not all children (even those in the same family) are the same. Some are easy to raise: they sit in the middle of the living room like a contented little Buddha and pose no problem of any kind for their mother and father. Other babies are cranky as can be and out of sorts, hard to please and difficult to control. So the parents who start out by being authoritative may end up becoming either authoritarian or (if they surrender) permissive with the cantankerous little tyke. Parenting style, Harris says, becomes in part *a reaction to the kind of child one has been given* (or saddled with).[19]

Whom should we believe: the socialization theorists like Baumrind or the critics such as Harris? One way to deal with this question is to look at research on the family and antisocial behavior/conduct disorder/delinquency. We can begin with the respected studies conducted by Gerald Patterson and his colleagues at the Oregon Social Learning Center (Exhibit 7-1). These scholars are learning theorists, and their program teaches parents how to become more effective, so we would naturally expect them to endorse the socialization approach.

To Patterson, **coercion** means that **aversive** events are used **contingent on** the behavior of another person. The aversive behaviors of children include criticizing someone's behavior, using a tone of voice that says "don't bother me," shouting, teasing, repeating annoying behavior, attacking someone physically, whining, and

---

EXHIBIT 7-1   Parenting Skills

Many people in our culture assume that just about everybody knows how to bring up a child. But Patterson says that such an assumption is patently false. Over the years, he discovered a great many parents who were blithely unaware of the most basic rules for raising kids:
   (1) Notice what the child is doing.
   (2) Monitor it over long periods.
   (3) Model social skill behavior.
   (4) Clearly state house rules.
   (5) Consistently provide sane punishments for transgressions.
   (6) Provide reinforcement for conformity.
   (7) Negotiate disagreements so that conflicts and crises do not escalate.[20]
Families that go to the Oregon Social Learning Center need professional help because in their homes it is *the children who train the parents.*

   Some of the rules Patterson sets forth need some explanation. What, for instance, are sane punishments? Presumably, these are not insane, that is, they are not beatings, whippings, punches, slaps, and the like. They include taking away things that the child values, such as video games, favorite TV programs, favorite toys, dessert, bicycle, telephone privileges, and visits to friends' homes. They also include adding things that the child does not like, such as making him or her do extra chores around the house.

   Providing reinforcement for conformity also may require an explanation. Some parents insist that conformity is normal behavior, something that is no more than what's expected, and therefore it's not deserving of special praise or a reward of some kind. They take the position that *when the child does something spectacular, then they as parents will stand up and take notice.* But psychologists say that children need to be rewarded for the simple things they do before they will master them and move on to higher levels of accomplishment. Children do not start out as famous research scientists who need only a pat on the back once a year to keep their motivation up.

destroying property. "Contingent" means that these behaviors are more likely to be resorted to if, say, the mother does something unwanted beforehand (for example, she asks the child to take out the garbage or clean up his room).

There are several steps involved in **escape conditioning.** Step 1. A mother tells the child to do something (for instance, his homework). She may do so in a way that indicates she is highly irritated with him. Step 2. The child counterattacks by whining, yelling, claiming that she is picking on him, or saying that the teacher did not assign any homework (a lie). In short, the child *punishes* the mother for her behavior. Step 3. The mother stops scolding the child. So the child wins the war of wills. The long-term outcome of this scenario is that when the mother again demands something, the child will return to coercive behavior to escape the aversive situation. He knows how to defeat her in these confrontations. Step 4. As soon as the mother backs down and gives in, the child stops his counterattack. This immediately rewards the mother for surrendering and makes it more likely she will capitulate in future confrontations.[21] From this description it appears that Patterson identifies the problem children he observes as the products of poor parenting. The parents are unskilled at punishing the child's deviant behavior and inept at **modeling** and **reinforcing prosocial** behavior.

But Patterson does not simply blame the parents. He says that some children are antisocial by nature. Their **abrasiveness** or thievery, for instance, is a personality trait that is stable across time and social contexts. Second, the child often ends up training the parent. Third, antisocial children may be *born* with difficult **temperaments.** For the caretaker, children are prime generators of aversive events. Some children are more difficult to manage than others. These differences in ease of socialization may be constitutional.

> Parents often do not become believers in temperament until after the birth of their second child. Before this time, their child's behavior may be seen as a result of upbringing. With the second child, management strategies that worked well with the first child may no longer be effective. . . . Children differ from each other early in life and these differences have important implications for parent-child interaction. A number of these differences fall under the rubric of child temperament.[22]

Clearly, Patterson does not accept the simple notion that parenting *determines* how the child will behave. Even those who defend the idea that parenting has strong effects, criticize the socialization paradigm: Patterson says that early socialization researchers "relied excessively on deterministic views of parental influence; and failed to attend to the . . . effects of heredity. . . . Unfortunately, the weaknesses of old studies still permeate presentations of socialization research in introductory textbooks."[23] On the other hand, Patterson believes that parenting does play an important role and that inept parents can be retrained to become more effective (he has been doing so for several decades).

As a second test of the extent to which antisocial behavior is due to socialization style, consider the path-breaking multidisciplinary research by Reiss, Neiderheiser, Hetherington, and Plomin. This recent work examines the genetic and social influences on adolescent development. Hoping to find evidence of environmental influence (especially by mothers, fathers, or siblings) on characteristics of adolescents, the authors discovered two characteristics that were influenced by family environment: sociability and autonomy. But they found that other dimensions of adolescent adjustment (especially, antisocial behavior, cognitive agency, and social responsibility) were heavily influenced (in excess of 65 percent) by genetic factors.

Antisocial behavior usually includes disobedience, oppositional behavior, fighting, lying, and stealing *among children;* and *among adolescents* it includes these behaviors plus drug and alcohol consumption and criminality. Cognitive agency includes such measures as the youngster's degree of involvement in schoolwork and scholastic achievement. Although it is not very surprising that scholastic achievement is strongly affected by genetic factors (psychologists have known this for years), most people are astonished by the idea that antisocial behavior is.[24] But the fact is that other researchers, too, have found that there is a genetic component in antisocial behavior by adolescents.[25]

Reiss et al. reported that mother's conflict/negativity (and father's as well) is quite strongly related to antisocial behavior by the adolescent. Conflict/negativity includes her harsh discipline, fighting with the youth, severe criticism, verbal abuse, and punitiveness. These are measured by the mother's report, the child's report, and the research observer's report. In decades past, this relationship was interpreted by social and psychological researchers quite simply: it was taken as evidence of a socialization effect. But now research indicates otherwise. That is, "*the same genetic factors that influence antisocial behavior in adolescents are those that influence the amount of harsh parenting they receive.*"[26]

Ordinarily, there is a strong connection between the child's temperament and the family's response to the child. Knowing the child's temperament is quite helpful in predicting how parents and siblings will react. Aggressive children, for instance, tend to elicit counteraggression from family members. This response then exacerbates the child's aggression. Families interpret signals from the child's behavior and react to the child. When the child's behavior is troublesome, their reactions may serve to make it even worse. There is a considerable research literature showing how the child's temperament is linked to the quality of family relationships.[27]

This does *not* mean that biology is destiny and that human behavior is hardwired. Although many conditions such as autism and obesity have genetic components, behavioral geneticists are quick to point out that genes are *not tyrannical commands.* It is more accurate to describe them as giving people a gentle nudge in one direction or another. There is no single genetic influence on behavior that is all powerful.[28] The relationship between genes and behavior is merely *probabilistic, not deterministic;* and the fact that genes have an influence on something does not mean that it is inevitable or irremediable.[29] *Genes are not influences that parents, friends, teachers, mass media, and other socialization agents in the culture are unable to overcome.* If you have a difficult child, then it just means that you will just have to work harder.

How effective are parents, how committed are they to raising their children well? At a minimum, parenting involves spending time with children. Thus, one of the first and simplest issues a researcher would want to explore is how many hours per week parents devote to their children. This, presumably, will depend on how *old* the child is (parents are of course more attentive to their infants than to their teenagers) and whether the parents are away at work (which reduces time at home, when they could watch over their offspring). When people are *asked* how much time parents spend with their children, they give fairly high estimates. Let's see if the data agree with them.

Csikszentmihalyi and Larson studied high school youths in a Chicago suburb and found that for every 1,000 times the youths were beeped by the researchers, they were alone with their fathers only *ten times,* and *five* of those involved *watching television.* The authors estimated that adolescents spent only five minutes a day alone with the father. Time spent alone with mothers was not very great either, a mere twenty minutes a day.[30] These are brief snatches of time, and probably not much communication goes in during them. Only on vacations do families really get together (and in recent years family vacations are becoming rarer). This is ironic in view of the worries parents express about the malign influences of peers.

Larson and Richards studied a somewhat younger group, fifth graders through ninth graders. They found similar results, however: fathers as a rule (1) are not very warm, sensitive, or close to teenagers; (2) are passive and disengaged; and (3) are alone with their son or daughter an average of 12 minutes a day (and even that is not usually spent interacting with each other). "Dads and teens reported few occasions when talk was their main activity—it accounted for an average of just three minutes a day—and the content of these conversations was restricted in scope. . . . [The] most frequent topic of conversation when adolescents and fathers were alone together was sports."[31] Adolescents spent more time alone with mothers than fathers, but often this time was peripheral. While the two were together, they were not talking to each other or even engaged in the same activity. The mother tended to be immersed in housework while the adolescent was playing a game or watching TV.

Why do parents and adolescents spend so little "quality time" together? In part this is probably because adolescents shut their parents out. *Fifth* graders might be willing to hang out in the kitchen or the living room while their mother's there, but not *eighth* or *ninth* graders, who usually prefer to escape into their bedrooms and close the door. Or join their peers. Parents simply cannot offer the kind of cascading enjoyment adolescents are beginning to discover with peers, nor can they provide the captivating thrill of romantic encounters. Parents are becoming boring. In addition, parents, especially fathers, do not seem to make much of an effort to interact with their teenage sons or daughters. Daughters in particular tend to describe their father as not nurturing or caring; daughters want to talk about people and feelings, but most fathers are neither interested nor experienced in these.[32]

Adoptive Studies

A small number of children who are adopted are genetically at risk for schizophrenia. Does it matter who adopts them? Yes, the adoptive family, too, has an effect (an environmental one). If it is a family with more than its share of troubles and problems, the adopted child is more likely to develop the full-blown syndrome of schizophrenia.[33] There is some evidence that such a pattern also applies to other behaviors or conditions, such as antisocial behavior, substance abuse, and depression. In this vein, consider some of the adoptive research done by Remi Cadoret. Since the late 1970s, Cadoret and his colleagues have studied more than a thousand Iowa families. They looked at children who had been separated from their parents at birth or a few days afterward and adopted by nonrelatives. Some of the biological parents had problems with the police and courts, some had drinking problems, and some didn't get along with others. The issue Cadoret et al. examined was who affected the adopted children more, the biological parents (by contributing their genes) or the adoptive parents (who supplied the environment). They discovered that *both sets of parents* were important, especially in combination with each other.

If the biological parents did not have the kinds of problems cited earlier, the kind of adoptive home environment that child landed in did not matter very much: the problems of adoptive parents did not often lead the adopted children to getting into trouble. In other words, when the children had "good genes" (Cadoret's term), their unfavorable environment was not likely to have a serious negative impact on these youths. But when the youths came from biological parents whose problems were serious, the environment supplied by the adoptive family was crucial.

When the home environment was bad, the children who inherited problem genes were at risk. In these households, the level of childhood and adolescent aggression was dramatically increased. Measures of behavior such as lying, stealing, truancy, and school expulsions were up by as much as 500 percent. Aggressive and antisocial behavior increased dramatically only in children with both "bad genes" and bad homes. This shows that what is being inherited is not bad behavior or aggression, but rather a genetic sensitivity to the environment. The genes don't make them antisocial; the genes make them *vulnerable*.[34] Genetics and environment both have a significant impact on adoptees, but the combination of problematic biological parents and problematic adoptive parents has an especially potent impact.

Child Maltreatment

Child maltreatment primarily includes (1) physical child abuse, (2) child sexual abuse, and (3) child neglect and psychological maltreatment. In the modern era, physical child abuse was "discovered" by C. Henry Kempe and his medical colleagues back in 1962. They published an article in the *Journal of the American Medical Association* that focused on X-rays of children's broken bones and on subdural hematomas. The doctors then coined the term "battered child syndrome" and claimed that the parents who administered the beatings and caused these injuries should be pitied because (the authors assumed) they were suffering from a mental illness.[35]

In subsequent years, media and public interest in the topic exploded. Mushrooming publicity led casual observers to conclude that child abuse was something new or was now taking off and reaching epidemic proportions. In fact, it had been around for many centuries. Before the fourth century, in Rome and Greece, infanticide was legal and socially accepted. Children who were illegitimate, physically defective, or cried a lot were sometimes killed or abandoned. Girls, too, have been especially likely to be infanticide victims. Thus, it is very suspicious that in nineteenth-century China, boys outnumbered girls by four to one in some rural areas that depended on agriculture. According to de Mause, "The history of childhood is a nightmare from which we have only recently begun to awaken. The further back in history one goes, the lower the level of child care, and the more likely children are to be killed, abandoned, beaten, terrorized, and sexually abused."[36] Obviously, these are extreme forms. Most forms of physical child abuse are milder in nature: for instance, there are no broken bones or bad bruises involved. This raises the question of how physical child abuse should be defined.

Coming to a consensus on what constitutes abuse is not easy. Definitions abound but people can't agree on what separates abusive from acceptable behavior. "Slapping, spanking, paddling, and, generally, hitting children for purposes of discipline are accepted, pervasive, adult behaviors in U.S. families. In these instances, although anger, physical attack, and pain are involved between two people of vastly different size, weight, and strength, such behavior is commonly accepted as a proper exercise of adult authority over children."[37] Such behavior is *not accepted* by people who conduct *research* on child maltreatment, however; they regard it as *abusive*.

What effects, if any, does child abuse have on the child's later development? Some researchers identify a series of consequences: medical complications (such as head, chest, and abdominal injuries), cognitive difficulties (decreased intellectual functioning, deficits in memory, perception, problem solving), behavior problems (aggression, fighting, defiance, theft), socioemotional deficits (poor interaction skills, difficulty making friends, stress, low self-esteem, substance use, depression, self-destructive behavior).[38] The victims may be hospitalized, put in special education classes, arrested, or socially avoided.

Physical child abuse (the behavior) has existed for all time but calling it abuse and conducting research on it began only a few decades ago. *(Robert Brenner/PhotoEdit.)*

But the studies linking physical child abuse with behavior problems have some-times been criticized for various methodological flaws: "unrepresentative" sam-ples, lack of comparison samples, retrospective designs, and failure to control for other factors that could affect the relationship between maltreatment and behavior problems. Zingraff and his colleagues tried to avoid these problems in their study and found that the maltreated sample was not much different from the regular sam-ple of school kids once other variables (such as age, gender, race, and family struc-ture) were statistically controlled for. They were not more prone to either property offenses or violent offenses.[39]

Child neglect has not received the same attention as abuse, probably because it is more subtle and less dramatic. It takes several forms, including health care ne-glect (prescriptions not filled, immunizations not obtained), personal hygiene ne-glect (infrequent bathing, poor dental hygiene), nutritional neglect (calories insufficient, food spoiled), neglect of household safety (broken stairs, broken win-dows, fire hazards), neglect of household sanitation (excess garbage, uncontrolled vermin and insects, dirt), inadequate shelter (overcrowding, refusing custody), su-pervisory neglect (children left at home for long periods or allowed to roam the streets at night), and educational neglect (either the children are not enrolled in school or parents let them get away with chronic truancy). In recent years, child neglect has become the most frequently reported type of maltreatment.[40] Not much research has examined the effects of neglect on subsequent development and func-tioning, but there are indications that neglect causes more behavior problems than physical and sexual abuse do.[41]

Lipsey and Derzon Meta-Analysis

Can we predict which children will later become involved in serious crime? To some degree, yes. Mark Lipsey and James Derzon, for instance, provided a meta-analysis of the most often studied predictors of violent or serious offenses (VOSO). The offense behaviors were measured for people aged 15 to 25, whereas the risk fac-tors (predictors) were measured at earlier ages: from 6 to 11, and from 12 to 14 (Table 7-1). Correlations ranged from a low of .04 to a high of .39 and were not the same in childhood as they were in early adolescence. For instance, among children aged 6 to 11, substance use, family SES, and ethnicity are important predictors of future violent or serious offending, but these same variables are very weak predictors among early adolescents aged 12 to 14.

Family factors (denoted by an asterisk in the table) are generally considered by commentators, politicians, and the general public to be the crucial ones leading youngsters into, or keeping them out of, delinquency (as chapter 1 notes). But Table 7-1 casts some doubt on this belief. Among children 6 to 11, family factors are three of the four weakest predictors of future violent or serious offending. Among offspring who are a bit older, family variables make up five of the six weakest pre-dictors. In early adolescence, peer variables appear to have a greater impact than any other predictors (but remember there are measurement problems with peer variables, as mentioned in chapter two).

TABLE 7-1   Ranking of Predictors of Violent or Serious Offending (Correlations)[42]

Predictors at Age 6–11	Predictors at Age 12–14
General offenses (.38)	Social ties (.39)
Substance use (.30)	Antisocial peers (.37)
Male (.26)	General offenses (.26)
Family SES* (.24)	Aggression (.19)
Antisocial parents* (.23)	School attitude/performance (.19)
Aggression (.21)	Psychological condition (.19)
Ethnicity* (.20)	Parent-child relations* (.19)
Psychological condition (.15)	Male (.19)
Parent-child relations* (.15)	Physical violence (.18)
Social ties (.15)	Antisocial parents* (.16)
Problem behavior (.13)	Person crimes (.14)
School attitude/performance (.13)	Problem behavior (.12)
Medical/physical (.13)	IQ (.11)
IQ (.12)	Broken home* (.10)
Other family characteristics* (.12)	Family SES* (.10)
Broken home* (.09)	Abusive parents* (.09)
Abusive parents* (.07)	Other family characteristics* (.08)
Antisocial peers (.04)	Substance use (.06)
	Ethnicity* (.04)

Why would family matter less in early adolescence than in childhood? One reason is that adolescents spend less time at home, less time with parents, more time in public places, more time with peers, whose acceptance they not only seek but crave. Around the age of 13, adolescents are most prone to conformity. This means that they may follow the crowd in tastes and fashion and follow their particular clique in behavior (including smoking, drinking, using drugs, engaging in sex, speeding, shoplifting, and fighting), even when they do not really approve of such behaviors. Morality is sometimes weaker than the desire for acceptance.

James Derzon wrote an unpublished paper focusing specifically on the relationship between family factors and criminal behavior. He was curious to find out if the relationship was as strong as almost everyone seemed to believe it was. What he discovered is that some family variables that are prominently cited by commentators turn out to have very weak associations with criminal activity:

Broken home
Separated from parents
Supervision and involvement
Young parents

Others (not so often cited by commentators) have a stronger relationship:

Parents' education and expectations
Home discord and instability
Child-rearing skills
Family stress[43]

These data indicate that most of the commentators in the media who focus on broken homes and lack of supervision are (1) unfamiliar with the research, (2) pursuing their own agenda, and (3) therefore misleading the public.

If we take the findings in Table 7-1 seriously, we would conclude that what parents do with children aged 6 to 11 matters more than what they do with kids in their early adolescent years. This leads to the question of whether the years *preceding* the age of 6 might be a period when parents have the most influence. Maybe children in early childhood (0 to 5) come under their parents' spell; maybe the way parents raise them in these formative years is particularly important in affecting how the youngsters turn out many years later (such as the ages of 15 to 25).

If that is so, then maybe some parents would benefit from professional help during the years the mother is first pregnant or shortly after her first child is born. This was the thinking behind the nurse home visitation program of David Olds that was first instituted in semirural Elmira, New York, during 1978 to 1980. This program proved to be quite effective in reducing the rate of maternal welfare dependence, child abuse and neglect, closely spaced successive pregnancies, and children's intellectual impairment due to prenatal exposure to tobacco. Researchers then went back years later when the children were 15 years old. They discovered that the children of women visited by nurses (an average of 9 times during pregnancy and 23 times in the two years following birth) were less prone to run away, smoked fewer cigarettes, and drank less alcohol. This suggests that nurse visitation can help unmarried and low-SES mothers raise children more effectively, so that the youngsters are less antisocial or deviant in their midadolescent years.[44]

Conclusion

Until the mid-1970s, the family did not attract very much attention. Politicians, commentators, the general public—none of them got worked up about it. It just wasn't on our agenda; it wasn't a topic that elicited much passion or controversy. In fact, most people regarded it as quite boring. That, however, changed in the ensuing decades, in part because the family itself changed pretty radically, which worried politicians, especially conservatives, who talked about families disintegrating and society falling apart as a result. There was much uneasiness and gnashing of teeth; commentators argued that the family was the glue holding society together, and it seemed to be losing its grip.

If family structure (particularly, broken homes) was important in determining how well children later turned out, then what were the crucial aspects of this structure that had such an impact? This called for theories of how families operate, how they influence youngsters growing up in them. Socialization theory says that parents play a determining role in how their offspring develop. When the father is absent almost all the time, parental supervision, control, and modeling decrease. The result is that children growing up under these circumstances do not learn to behave well or prosper.

Economic theory as set forth by Gary Becker argues that when two parents are around, they spend time and money helping the children develop knowledge, skills, and values. Single-parent households lack the necessary division of labor (necessary meaning father working and mother at home nurturing) and sufficient economic resources. Children turn out worst, according to Becker, when they have to grow up without a father there to help them.

Researchers Biblarz and Raftery recognized the key hypotheses in the various theories (socialization theory, economic theory, etc.) and put them to a test using four data sets. The data indicated that children raised in mother-only families actually turn out quite well, on the average, in terms of adult status attainment. This called into question both the socialization and economic theories but it supported evolutionary theory. Studies of family structure and *delinquency*, though less sophisticated than the Biblarz and Raftery research (on family structure and status attainment) also show that mother-only families are preferable: they give rise to less delinquency than other alternative family structures, such as father-only families.

Studies using data from the 1960s or 1970s had only a small number of father-only families in their sample, so the findings were somewhat tentative. But that's no longer a problem. The number of single-father families is now as large as the number of single-mother families was back in the 1950s. This may not be especially beneficial for the children who live in them, but it is fortunate for family structure/delinquency researchers, who now have sizable samples of single fathers to study.

Diana Baumrind, a prominent socialization theorist, has identified four parenting styles: authoritative (warm but firm), authoritarian (very firm but not warm), permissive (warm but weak-willed), and indifferent. Research has consistently found that children turn out best when they had authoritative parenting, worst if their parents were indifferent. But Judith Rich Harris counters this viewpoint by arguing that parents' style is affected by how the children behave, that children are affected by parenting while they're inside the home but outside it is peers who're the dominant influence.

In keeping with Harris's point of view, the Lipsey-Derzon meta-analysis found that during early adolescence family factors such as broken homes, family SES, and abusive parents have little effect on violent and serious offending by youths years later (15 to 25). Family factors have more impact (on such later offending) when the children are young, between 6 and 11. Perhaps, the parents' biggest influence is exerted when the children are still babies. Indeed, infancy proved to be a time when visiting nurses were able to help mothers change some of their worst habits and become better mothers. The end result was that the children later on grew up to be less deviant.

Key Terms

Functionalism:	a theoretical orientation that treats society as if it were composed of elements working together to maintain and preserve the whole
Human capital	improved health and productivity resulting from (parental) investments in these individuals
Attainment:	accomplishment; how far one goes in education and occupational status
Atheoretical:	not guided by theory; pragmatic
Dichotomy:	a variable with two values (e.g., race divided into white and black)
Authoritarian:	controlling parents who insist on obedience but provide little warmth
Authoritative:	demanding parents who set high standards but are also warm and caring
Permissive:	parends who are indulgent, demanding little but providing warmth
Indifferent:	parents preoccupied with their own lives, not interested in communicating with their children; not demanding or warm
Coercion:	trying to force someone to do something when the person does not want to do it
Aversive:	unwanted; regarded as punishing
Contingent on:	dependent on
Escape conditioning:	getting out of a situation by using coercive tactics
Modeling:	demonstrating how something is done; teaching by example
Reinforcing:	rewarding; making someone likely to use the same behavior again in the future
Prosocial:	acting in a positive manner desired by society; opposite of antisocial
Abrasiveness:	being rough, harsh, bruising, inconsiderate
Temperament:	emotional characteristics that affect a person's actions

End Notes

[1]Greer Litton Fox and Michael L. Benson, "Families, Crime, and Criminal Justice: Charting the Linkages," in Greer Litton Fox and Michael L. Benson, eds., *Families, Crime, and Criminal Justice* (New York: Elsevier, 2000), pp. 1–21.

[2]*Ibid.*

[3]*Ibid.*

[4]Ronald L. Simons and Associates, *Understanding Differences Between Divorced and Intact Families* (Thousand Oaks, CA: Sage, 1996); Diana Baumrind, "Parental Disciplinary Patterns and Social Competence in Children," *Youth and Society, 9,* no. 3 (March 1978), pp. 239–76; Diana Baumrind, "New Directions in Socialization Research," *American Psychologist, 35,* no. 7 (July 1980), pp. 639–52; Elizabeth Thomson, Thomas L. Hanson, and Sara S. McLanahan, "Family Structure and Child Well-Being," *Social Forces, 73,* no. 1 (September 1994), pp. 221–42; Nan Marie Astone and Sara S. McLanahan, "Family Structure, Parental Practices, and High School Completion," *American Sociological Review, 56,* no. 3 (June 1991), pp. 309–20.

[5]E. Mavis Hetherington, Martha Cox, and Roger Cox, "The Aftermath of Divorce," in Joseph H. Stevens and Marilyn Mathews, eds., *Mother-Child Father-Child Relationships* (Washington: National Association for the Education of Young People, 1978), pp. 149–76.

[6]Steven Nock, "The Family and Hierarchy," *Journal of Marriage and the Family, 50,* no. 4 (November 1988), pp. 957–66.

[7]Timothy J. Biblarz and Adrian E. Raftery, "Family Structure, Educational Attainment, and Socioeconomic Success," *American Journal of Sociology, 105,* no. 2 (September 1999), pp. 321–65.

[8]Gary S. Becker, *A Treatise on the Family* (Cambridge, MA: Harvard University Press, 1991), p. 33.

[9]Daniel R. Meyer and Steven Garasky, "Custodial Fathers: Myths, Realities, and Child Support Policies," *Journal of Marriage and the Family, 55,* no. 1 (February 1993), pp. 73–90.

[10]Stephen T. Emlen, "The Evolutionary Study of Human Family Systems," *Social Science Information, 36,* no. 4 (December 1997), pp. 563–89; Martin Daly and Margo I. Wilson, "Violence Against Stepchildren," *Current Directions in Psychological Science, 5,* no. 3 (June 1996), pp. 77–81.

[11]Timothy J. Biblarz and Adrian E. Raftery, "Family Structure, Educational Attainment, and Socioeconomic Success."

[12]Cesar J. Rebellon, "Reconsidering the Broken Homes/Delinquency Relationship and Exploring its Mediating Mechanisms," *Criminology, 40,* no. 1 (February 2002), pp. 103–35; Robert L. Flewelling and Karl E. Bauman, "Family Structure as a Predictor of Initial Substance Use and Sexual Intercourse in Early Adolescence," *Journal of Marriage and the Family, 52,* no. 1 (February 1990), pp. 171–81; Marvin D. Free, Jr., "Clarifying the Relationship Between the Broken Home and Delinquency," *Deviant Behavior, 12,* no. 2 (April 1991), pp. 109–67; L. Edward Wells and Joseph H. Rankin, "Families and Delinquency," *Social Problems, 38,* no. 1 (February 1991), pp. 71–93.

[13]Heather Juby and David P. Farrington, "Disentangling the Link Between Disrupted Families and Delinquency," *British Journal of Criminology, 41,* no. 1 (Winter 2001), pp. 22–40.

[14]Andrew Cherlin, "Going to Extremes: Family Structure, Children's Well-Being, and Social Science, *Demography, 36,* no. 4 (November 1999), pp. 421–8; Judith S. Wallerstein and Sandra Blakeslee, *Second Chances* (New York: Ticknor and Fields, 1989).

[15]Diana Baumrind, "Child Care Practices Anteceding Three Patterns of Preschool Behavior," *Genetic Psychology Monographs, 75,* no. 1 (1967), pp. 43–88; Diana Baumrind, "Current Patterns of Parental Authority," *Developmental Psychology Monograph,* Part 2, *4,* no. 1 (January 1971), pp. 1–103; Eleanor E. Maccoby and J. A. Martin, "Socialization in the Context of the Family," in E. Mavis Hetherington, ed., *Socialization, Personality, and Child Development* (New York: Wiley, 1983), pp. 1–101.

[16]Diana Baumrind, "The Influence of Parenting Style on Adolescent Competence and Substance Use," *Journal of Early Adolescence, 11,* no. 1 (February 1991), pp. 56–95.

[17]Andrew J. Fuligni and Jacquelynne S. Eccles, "Perceived Parent-Child Relationships and Early Adolescents' Orientation Toward Peers," *Developmental Psychology, 29,* no. 4 (July 1993), pp. 622–32; Lawrence A. Kurdek and Mark A. Fine, "Family Acceptance and Family Control as Predictors of Adjustment in Young Adolescents," *Child Development, 65,* no. 4 (August 1994), pp. 1137–46; Susie Lamborn, Nina Mounts, Laurence Steinberg, and Sanford Dornbusch, "Patterns of Competence and Adjustment Among Adolescents from Authoritative, Authoritarian, Indulgent, and Neglectful Families," *Child Development, 62,* no. 5 (October 1991), pp. 1049–65; Laurence Steinberg, Susie D. Lamborn, Nancy Darling, Nina S. Mounts, and Sanford Dornbusch, "Over-Time Changes in Adjustment and Competence Among Adolescents from Authoritative, Authoritarian, Indulgent, and Neglectful Families," *Child Development, 65,* no. 3 (June 1994), pp. 754–70; Diana Baumrind, "Parenting Styles and Adolescent Development," in Richard M. Lerner, Anne C. Petersen, and Jeanne Brooks-Gunn, eds., *Encyclopedia of Adolescence,* Volume two (New York: Garland, 1991), pp. 746–58; Eleanor Maccoby and John Martin, eds., *Handbook of Child Psychology,* Volume four (New York: Wiley, 1983), pp. 1–101.

[18]Judith Rich Harris, *The Nurture Assumption* (New York: Free Press, 1998).

[19]*Ibid.;* see also Sandra Scarr, "Developmental Theories for the 1990s," *Child Development, 63,* no. 1 (February 1992), pp. 1–19.

[20]Gerald R. Patterson, "Children Who Steal," in Travis Hirschi and Michael Gottfredson, eds., *Understanding Crime* (Beverly Hills, CA: Sage, 1980), pp. 73–90.

[21]Gerald R. Patterson, "Coercion as a Basis for Early Age of Onset for Arrest," in Joan McCord, ed., *Coercion and Punishment in Long-Term Perspective* (New York: Cambridge University Press, 1998), pp. 81–105.

[22]Samuel P. Putnam, Ann V. Sanson, and Mary K. Rothbart, "Child Temperament and Parenting," in Marc H. Bornstein, ed., *Handbook of Parenting,* 2nd ed., Volume 1 (Mahwah, NJ: Erlbaum, 2002), p. 255; Gerald R. Patterson, *Coercive Family Process* (Eugene, OR: Castalia, 1982).

[23]W. Andrew Collins, Eleanor E. Maccoby, Laurence Steinberg, E. Mavis Hetherington, and Marc H. Bornstein, "Contemporary Research on Parenting," *American Psychologist, 55,* no. 2 (February 2000), pp. 218–32.

[24]David Reiss, Jenae Neiderhiser, E. Mavis Hetherington, and Robert Plomin, *The Relationship Code* (Cambridge, MA: Harvard University Press, 2000), p. 209.

[25]Even a Marxist criminologist admits this: see David F. Greenberg, Robin Tamarelli, and Margaret S. Kelley, "The Generality of the Self-Control Theory of Crime," in Elin Waring and David Weisburd, eds., *Crime and Social Organization* (New Brunswick,

NJ: Transaction, 2002), p. 58; Philip Graham and Jim Stevenson, "A Twin Study of Genetic Influences on Behavioral Deviance," *Journal of the American Academy of Child and Adolescent Psychiatry, 24,* no. 1 (January 1985), pp. 34–41; Judy L. Silberg, Marilyn T. Erickson, Joanne M. Meyer, Lindon J. Eaves, Michael L. Rutter, and John K. Hewitt, "The Application of Structural Equation Modeling to Maternal Ratings of Twins' Behavioral and Emotional Problems," *Journal of Consulting and Clinical Psychology, 62,* no. 3 (June 1994), pp. 510–21; Jim Stevenson and Philip Graham, "Behavioral Deviance in 13-Year-Old Twins," *Journal of the American Academy of Child and Adolescent Psychiatry, 27,* no. 6 (November 1988), pp. 791–7; William M. Grove, Elke D. Eckert, Leonard Heston, Thomas J. Bouchard, Nancy Segal, and David T. Lykken, "Heritability of Substance Abuse and Antisocial Behavior," *Biological Psychiatry, 27,* no. 12 (June 1990), pp. 1293–1304.

[26]David Reiss, Jenae Neiderhiser, E. Mavis Hetherington, and Robert Plomin, *The Relationship Code,* p. 4

[27]Timothy S. Blackson, Ralph E. Tarter, Christopher S. Martin, and Howard B. Moss, "Temperament Induced Father-Son Family Dysfunction," *American Journal of Orthopsychiatry, 64,* no. 2 (April 1994), pp. 280–92; Gene H. Brody, Zolinda Stoneman, and Michelle Burke, "Child Temperaments, Maternal Differential Behavior, and Sibling Relationships," *Developmental Psychology, 23,* no. 3 (May 1987), pp. 354–62; Mary Gauvain and Beverly Fagot, "Child Temperament as a Mediator of Mother-Toddler Problem Solving, *Social Development, 4,* no. 3 (November 1995), pp. 257–76; Carolyn L. Lee and John E. Bates, "Mother-Child Interaction at Two Years and Perceived Difficult Temperament," *Child Development, 56,* no. 5 (October 1985), pp. 1314–25; Clare Stocker, Judy Dunn, and Robert Plomin, "Sibling Relationships: Links with Child Temperament, Maternal Behavior, and Family Structure," *Child Development, 60,* no. 3 (June 1989), pp. 715–27; Dymphna C. van den Boom, "The Influence of Temperament and Mothering on Attachment and Exploration, *Child Development, 65,* no. 5 (October 1994), pp. 1457–77; Patricia Cohen and Judith S. Brook, "The Reciprocal Influence of Punishment and Child Behavior Disorder," in Joan McCord, ed., *Coercion and Punishment in Long-Term Perspective,* pp. 154–64; Sung Joon Jang and Carolyn A. Smith, "A Test of Reciprocal Causal Relationships among Parental Supervision, Affective Ties, and Delinquency," *Journal of Research in Crime and Delinquency, 34,* no. 3 (August 1997), pp. 307–36.

[28]William Wright, *Born That Way* (New York: Knopf, 1989), p. 14.

[29]Nancy L. Segal, *Entwined Lives* (New York: Dutton, 1999), p. 316; David B. Cohen, *Stranger in the Nest* (New York: Wiley, 1999), p. 13.

[30]Mihaly Csikszentmihalyi and Reed Larson, *Being Adolescent* (New York: Simon and Schuster, 1984), p. 73. Two-thirds of American parents say they would like to devote more time to their children, according to Marilyn Berlin Snell, "The Purge of Nurture," *New Perspectives Quarterly, 7,* no. 1 (Winter 1990), pp. 1–2, but how true this is may be questioned.

[31]Reed Larson and Maryse H. Richards, *Divergent Realities* (New York: Basic, 1994), p. 165.

[32]*Ibid.*

[33]Pekka Tienari, Ilpo Lahti, Anneli Sorri, Mikko Naarala, Juha Moring, Kark-Erik Wahlberg, and Lyman C. Wynne, "The Finnish Adoptive Family Study of Schizophrenia," *Journal of Psychiatric Research, 21,* no. 4 (1987), pp. 437–45; Pekka Tienari, Anneli Sorri, and Ilpo Lahti, "Interaction of Genetic and Psychosocial Factors in Schizophrenia," *Acta Psychiatrica Scandinavica, 71,* Suppl. 319 (1985), pp. 19–30; Pekka Tienari, Lyman C. Wynne, Juha Moring, Ilpo Lahti, Mikko Naarala, Anneli Sorri, Karl-Erik Wahlberg, Outi Saarento, Markku Seitamaa, Merja Kaleva, and Kristian Laksy, "The Finnish Adoption Family Study of Schizophrenia," *British Journal of Psychiatry, 164,* Suppl. 23 (April 1994), pp. 20–6.

[34]Dean Hamer and Peter Copeland, *Living with Our Genes* (New York: Doubleday, 1998), p. 97; Remi J. Cadoret, William R. Yates, Edward Troughton, George Woodworth, and Mark A. Stewart, "Gene-Environment Interaction in the Genesis of Aggressivity and Conduct Disorders," *Archives of General Psychiatry, 52,* no. 11 (November 1995), pp. 916–24; Remi J. Cadoret, Leslie D. Leve, and Eric Devor, "Genetics of Aggressive and Violent Behavior," *Psychiatric Clinics of North America, 20,* no. 2 (June 1997), pp. 301–22; William R. Yates, Remi J. Cadoret, and Edward P. Troughton, "The Iowa Adoption Studies," in Michele C. LaBuda and Elena L. Grigorenko, eds., *On the Way to Individuality* (Commack, NY: Nova Science, 1997), pp. 95–126; Remi J. Cadoret and Colleen Cain, "Environmental and Genetic Factors in Predicting Adolescent Antisocial Behavior in Adoptees," *Psychiatric Journal of the University of Ottawa, 6,* no. 4 (December 1981), pp. 220–5; Remi J. Cadoret, Edward Troughton, Jeffrey Bagford, and George Woodworth, "Genetic and Environmental Factors in Adoptee Antisocial Personality," *European Archives of Psychiatry and Clinical Neuroscience, 239,* no. 4 (February 1990), pp. 231–40.

[35]C. Henry Kempe, Frederic N. Silverman, Brandt F. Steele, William Droegemueller, and Henry K. Silber, "The Battered Child Syndrome," *Journal of the American Medical Association, 181* (July 7, 1962), pp. 17–24.

[36]Lloyd de Mause, *A History of Childhood* (New York: Psychohistory Press, 1974), p. 1; Ping-to Ho, *Studies on the Population of China, 1368–1953* (Cambridge, MA: Harvard University Press, 1959).

[37]Anthony M. Graziano and Karen A. Namaste, "Parental Use of Physical Force in Child Discipline," *Journal of Interpersonal Violence, 5,* no. 4 (December 1990), pp. 449–63.

[38]John W. Fantuzzo, "Behavioral Treatment of the Victims of Child Abuse and Neglect," *Behavior Modification, 14,* no. 3 (July 1990), pp. 316–9; Joan Kaufman and Dante Cicchetti, "The Effects of Maltreatment on School-Aged Children's Socioemotional Development," *Developmental Psychology, 25,* no. 4 (July 1989), pp. 516–24; Cathy Spatz Widom, "Child Abuse, Neglect, and Violent Criminal Behavior," *Criminology, 27,* no. 2 (May 1989), pp. 251–71; Jeffrey M. Williamson, Charles M. Borduin, and Barbara A. Howe, "The Ecology of Adolescent Maltreatment," *Journal of Consulting and Clinical Psychology, 59,* no. 3 (June 1991), pp. 449–57; John S. Wodarski, P. David Kurtz, James M. Gaudin, and Phyllis T. Howing, "Maltreatment and the School-Age Child," *Social Work, 35,* no. 6 (November 1990), pp. 506–13.

[39]Matthew T. Zingraff, Jeffrey Leiter, Kristen A. Myers, and Matthew C. Johnson, "Child Maltreatment and Youthful Problem Behavior," *Criminology, 31,* no. 2 (May 1993), pp. 173–202.

[40]Ching-Tung Wang and Deborah Daro, *Current Trends in Child Abuse Reporting and Fatalities* (Chicago: National Center on Child Abuse Prevention Research, 1998).

[41]Martha F. Erickson and Byron Egeland, "Child Neglect," in John Briere, Lucy Berliner, Josephine A. Bulkley, Carole Jenny, and Theresa Reid, eds., *The APSAC Handbook on Child Maltreatment* (Thousand Oaks, CA: Sage, 1996), pp. 4–20; Philip G. Ney, Tak Fung, and Adele Rose Wickett, "The Worst Combinations of Child Abuse and Neglect," *Child Abuse and Neglect, 18,* no. 9 (September 1994), pp. 705–14; Cynthia A. Rohrbeck and Craig T. Twentyman, "Multimodal Assessment of Impulsive, Neglecting, and Nonmaltreating Mothers and Their Preschool Children," *Journal of Consulting and Clinical Psychology, 54,* no. 2 (April 1986), pp. 231–6; Don Weatherburn and Bronwyn Lind, "Poverty, Parenting, Peers, and Crime-Prone Neighborhoods," *Trends and Issues in Crime and Criminal Justice,* no. 85 (April 1998). This is in keeping with socialization theory, which says that indifferent parenting is the worst kind.

[42]Mark W. Lipsey and James Derzon, "Predictors of Violent or Serious Delinquency in Adolescence and Early Adulthood," in Rolf Loeber and David P. Farrington, eds., *Serious and Violent Offenders* (Thousand Oaks, CA: Sage, 1998), p. 97.

[43]James H. Derzon, "Family Features and Problem, Aggressive, or Violent Behavior," unpublished paper.

[44]David Olds, Charles R. Henderson, Jr., Robert Cole, John Eckenrode, Harriet Kitzman, Dennis Luckey, Lisa Pettitt, Kimberly Sidora, Pamela Morris, and Jane Powers, "Long-Term Effects of Nurse Home Visitation on Children's Antisocial Behavior," *JAMA, The Journal of the American Medical Association, 280,* no. 14 (October 14, 1998), pp. 1238–44.

Recommended Readings

Greer Litton Fox and Michael L. Benson, eds., *Families, Crime, and Criminal Justice* (New York: Elsevier, 2000).

David P. Farrington, "Families and Crime," in James Q. Wilson and Joan Petersilia, eds., *Crime* (Oakland, CA: Institute for Contemporary Studies, 2002), pp. 129–48.

David C. Rowe, *The Limits of Family Influence* (New York: Guilford, 1994).

Bill Henry, Terrie Moffitt, Lee Robins, Felton Earls, and Phil Silva, "Early Family Predictors of Child and Adolescent Behavior: Who Are the Mothers of Delinquents?" *Criminal Behaviour and Mental Health, 3,* no. 2 (1993), pp. 97–118.

Malcolm Potts and Roger Short, *Ever Since Adam and Eve* (New York: Cambridge University Press, 1999).

Glen Elder, Jr., and Rand D. Conger, *Children of the Land* (Chicago: University of Chicago Press, 2000).

Kevin N. Wright and Karen E. Wright, *Family Life, Delinquency, and Crime* (Washington, DC: Office of Juvenile Justice and Delinquency Prevention, 1994).

Vern L. Bengston, Timothy J. Biblarz, and Robert E. L. Roberts, *How Families Still Matter* (New York: Cambridge University Press, 2002).

Gerald R. Patterson, *Coercive Family Process* (Eugene, OR: Castalia, 1982).

Andrew J. Cherlin, *Public and Private Families,* 3rd ed. (New York: McGraw-Hill, 2002).

CHAPTER 8

Schools and Youth Crime

Social Disorder

Historically, Americans extolled the virtues of their schools, visitors came to these shores to find out how we had succeeded in making mass education work, and President Johnson proclaimed education to be the answer to all our problems. Now, however, people are wondering if education itself is the problem. In recent years, a cloud has hovered over the nation's schools, with many Americans concluding that they're failing in the functions they were designed to perform. People fear that teachers are not teaching, students are floundering, standardized test scores are plummeting, and students are becoming more obnoxious. More and more, parents feel the need to pack their sons and daughters off to private school, regardless of the tuition, because they regard big-city public schools as unmitigated disasters. Why does such pessimism abound nowadays? Perhaps some people base it on first-hand knowledge. Others may be reflecting misgivings that periodically appear in reports by the press (like the one from Los Angeles in Exhibit 8-1).

Although Los Angeles schools may have more woes than most, they are not the only ones in a fix. Other school systems, too, suffer from a host of problems; their predicament has in some cases become so worrisome that the state felt compelled to take over. This has occurred in Chicago, Detroit, Boston, Newark, Jersey City, and Washington, D.C. (where the federal government assumed control). Or consider Philadelphia, where 70 percent of the students were below the poverty line, 65,000 were suspended each year, 25 percent were absent on any given day, dropout rates approached 50 percent, and only 13 percent of the juniors could read a

EXHIBIT 8-1   Columnist Jill Stewart's Thoughts on Turning the Tables in L.A. Schools

I've been covering Los Angeles urban affairs. . . long enough to realize that the single most important player in our vast city, the one who can most profoundly affect whether L.A. withers into a Detroit or chugs forward like Manhattan, is the lowly secondary school teacher.

Maybe you think I'm crazy. But teachers at our secondary schools hold the key to determining whether the city's 67,000 **functionally illiterate** kids entering grades 6 through 9 this year will finally learn to read or become part of this year's huge crop of dropouts.

As long as troubled middle schools and high schools churn out kids who can't get past Dick and Jane, vast tracts of L.A. will be bad places to live. This is so because kids who can't learn are filled with cynicism. Many take to the streets, where they become drug dealers, petty criminals, gangbangers, and the like. The schools disaster is why every single real estate agent in Los Angeles tracks one piece of data: How bad are the schools near the home just listed? As the school slides downward, the home values falter and the stable middle-class people move. It's no longer "white flight" these days, but middle-class black and Latino flight. . . .

Nobody seems to know how to teach teens who got screwed by their grade schools. In Los Angeles County, 32 percent of young adults are functionally illiterate. Most of them are products of L.A. Unified, and surprisingly many are native English speakers.

Teenagers hate hearing they need "remedial" anything. You can't use that word around insecure pre-adults. They act out in the teacher's face. They laughingly scream "mother------!" at friends in hopes of being forced by the teacher to stand in the hall—anything to avoid reading aloud and being unmasked as illiterate. . . .

Much of L.A.'s fate now rests upon a new literacy program being launched by Superintendent Roy Romer and the school board, known as "Language!". . .

Doug Lasken, a teacher at Taft High School in the valley taught the new course as a pilot program last year. "It walks kids through the letter-sounds they missed in primary school and has large print that looks simple. But it is brilliantly packaged with a linguistics course that gets harder and harder. . . . The kids understand that while they are finally learning phonics, they are also learning things taught in college, like phonemes."

Taft placed kids in the literacy program based on how well they did on Stanford 9 tests. . . . Lasken found most near the second grade in reading ability. Second grade. After a year of "Language!" most of his kids had improved to about the fourth grade.

The truth is that moving kids up to the fourth grade is a huge victory in high school. . . .

(continued)

Over at Los Angeles High School, history teacher Kevin Glynn says teachers welcome the new effort "because teachers really suffer along with the kids who cannot make any sense of high school texts."

Up to now, Glynn says, high school teachers have tried to impart information without requiring much reading or writing. "So you see a lot of teachers assigning kids to make posters, or many teachers are big on projects that involve no textbooks."

Math teachers are also at a loss at most schools in the district. As of now, the Board of Education requires every ninth-grader to take Algebra 1 instead of the simplistic "Math Investigations" class that low scorers used to take—and generally failed miserably.

While it's nice to see bureaucrats raise math standards, the mystery remains: How do you teach algebra to kids who were not taught to properly add, subtract, multiply, and divide during grade school?[1]

newspaper. In desperation, the state not only took over the schools but it hired a private management firm to turn around those identified as the most troubled.[2]

For a period of years (before the events of September 11, 2001), public attention was riveted on public schools. Television and newspapers described them as violent places, where shootings, stabbings, and aggravated assaults were common occurrences. In central city schools that experienced street gangs, over a third of the students said they were afraid they would be assaulted. Administrators' response to the problem was to institute stricter law enforcement policies ("**zero tolerance**"). Thus, in 1993, when more than 700 school districts around the nation were surveyed, almost 40 percent of them reported using metal detectors, two-thirds of them said they resorted to locker searches, and the same fraction admitted using security officers in their schools. Most property and violent crimes against juveniles take place on school property. No place like that exists for adult victims.[3] On the other hand, less than 1 percent of the homicides and suicides of school-age youths occur while the victim is in school or traveling to or from it.

Are American Adolescents Disengaged from School?

Not long ago, Laurence Steinberg, an expert on adolescence, conducted an extensive research project that surveyed over 20,000 teenagers from nine high schools in Wisconsin and California. These were average schools, not the elite private schools or the most poverty-stricken schools in the most desperate straits. For three years, the researchers surveyed all the students who were enrolled in these nine participating institutions. They relied primarily on questionnaires administered in the classrooms, supplemented with focus groups in order to identify the major crowds (jocks, brains, druggies, etc.) and intensive interviews with students and their parents.

Steinberg focused on the distinction between students who were engaged and those who were **disengaged**. The engaged attend classes, pay attention, are honest when taking tests, participate in class discussions, care about the quality of their performance, concentrate on their work, do the best they can, and hand in their assignments on time. This may seem like nothing more than the normal, minimal expectations for high school students. But Steinberg found that a substantial number of students fail to live up to these standards.

Approximately 40 percent of students are disengaged, just going through the motions. When they are not cutting classes, they put forth little effort inside the classroom. They do not try very hard, they do not pay attention, are easily distracted, have a cavalier attitude toward education, cheat on tests and copy others' homework. They find school boring and irrelevant. They are clearly not interested in academia and willingly admit they are not learning much. They find classes and assignments to be nuisances. The reason they go to school at all is to meet up with friends in order to spend time socializing or goofing off.

The youths who are disengaged do more than just socialize with friends. They are also more likely than other students to use drugs and alcohol, experiment with sex at an early age, experience bouts of depression, and engage in various acts of crime and delinquency. Some psychologists have combined all of these ingredients into a group and referred to them as a syndrome of problem behavior. Lack of interest in school is not an isolated and irrelevant characteristic. It is one part of a much larger picture.

As for the amount of time that high schoolers devote to completing their homework, Steinberg says it's not very much.

> The average American high school student spends about four hours per week on homework outside of school. In other industrialized countries, the average is about four hours per day. Half of all the students in our study reported not doing the homework they are assigned.[4]

If the disengaged do not spend their away-from-school hours immersed in homework assignments, what do they do? Most of their time is devoted to hanging out with friends. What kinds of effects this has depends on the kinds of friends the person has.

> By comparing the academic careers of students who began high school with equivalent grades, but who had different sorts of friends during the school years, we were able to see whether the type of friends that adolescents have actually makes a difference in their school performance.
>
> The answer is that it most certainly does. . . . Youngsters whose friends were more academically oriented. . .did better over the course of high school than students who began school with similar records but who had less academically oriented friends.[5]

Only about one out of five students says that his or her friends think good grades are important. To be sure, adolescents do want to graduate from high school, but they have grave doubts about whether doing well in class or actually learning the material presented in the lectures and textbooks will do them any good in the long run. In addition, when given a choice as to which crowd they would prefer to be associated with, not many (only a tiny fraction of adolescents) choose the brains. More said that they would prefer to lumped in with the druggies and the partyers.

Steinberg found that there were some differences by race and ethnicity. For instance, Asians outpaced all others when it came to attendance, concentration, time spent on homework: they try harder. In part, this is due to their **healthy attributional style**, which assumes that success depends upon on how hard they work at it. Other students are more apt to have an **unhealthy attributional style**, one that assumes failure is due to luck, teacher favoritism, innate ability, test difficulty, and other factors over which the student has no personal control.

Some Asian and Hispanic students in the sample had parents who were born in the United States. Many others had family who were born elsewhere. The advantage you would think ought to lie with those whose families had lived here the longest. But that is not what Steinberg found. Instead, the longer the family lived here, the *worse* the student's school grades and mental health were. The more Americanized youngsters, it appears, are less committed to school, less attentive, less likely to have friends who think doing well academically actually matters.

> Americanized ethnic minority youngsters—Asian and Latino alike—spend significantly more time hanging out with friends, more time partying, more time dating, more time on nonacademic extracurriculars, and more time with peers who value socializing over academics.[6]

Two Longitudinal Studies of Schools and Delinquency

Next, consider two noteworthy longitudinal studies. The first of these was conducted by Hagan and Parker, took place in a suburb of Toronto, Canada, lasted 19 years, and covered two generations: parents and their offspring. The researchers wanted to discover what the earlier generation did (or did not do) that would later affect the chances that their children would engage in delinquent behavior. The first thing you might consider is whether the delinquency of the parents was a good predictor of the delinquency of the kids. Surprisingly, it was not. The correlation was a piddling .06. So Hagan and Parker had to turn elsewhere. They examined a series of other parental characteristics to see if they helped predict the delinquency of their offspring.

1. Detachment of the parent from the grandparents (when the parent was young and not yet a parent)
2. Disengagement of the parent from educational goals (when young)
3. Educational underachievement of the parent (when young)
4. Self-reported police contacts of the parent (when young)
5. Teen parenthood
6. Age of the child

7. Gender of the child
8. Parent dropped out of school
9. Parent unemployed
10. Single parenthood
11. Disengagement of the parent from the child's educational goals
12. Detachment of the parent from the child
13. Parent unemployment × single parenthood (interaction effect)
14. Parent unemployment × teen parenthood (interaction effect)
15. Parent unemployment × school dropout (interaction effect)

Several of these parent characteristics eventually had an effect on the delinquency of the child.

According to Hagan and Parker, the events, conditions, and experiences of the older generation had a cumulative impact on their children. First, some of the parents (while they were still adolescents, single, and childless) disengaged from educational goals. They neither wanted nor expected to get much education. Second, some of these educationally disengaged parents were underachievers in school: their school performance was far below what they could have achieved if they had tried to do their best.

Third, some of the disengaged underachievers went on to have children in their teenage years. Fourth, some of these parents then dropped out of school. Fifth, some of them experienced a double whammy: the combination of unemployment and either teen parenthood or dropout. Sixth, some of them lived for a while as a single parent (probably as a result of divorce). Seventh, their child was detached from (not in close communication with) them. Finally, the child engaged in various acts of delinquency.

Hagan and Parker focus on the academic disengagement of the parents, which includes the first two steps (not wanting an education, and not achieving up to one's abilities) on the long and winding road that eventually leads to their child's delinquent behavior. Each step taken by the parents makes their next step more likely. And when they have taken quite a few of these steps, their options narrow considerably, and the chance that their child will engage in delinquency becomes much greater.

Parents' educational **disinvestment** sets in motion a series of events that years later may push their child toward becoming an offender, although that final step does not take place until approximately twenty years after the parents take their first step. None of this is obvious or inevitable. On the contrary, it is rather hard to believe. But choices are made, difficulties encountered, reactions emerge, and sometimes the results are unfortunate. Disadvantages accumulate, leading to a downward spiral for the parent and the result is a child who gets in trouble early in life. At least that is the picture drawn by the Hagan and Parker findings. Parental disinvestment in education leads to childhood delinquency two decades later.[7]

In this model, therefore, lack of education leads to delinquency years later by the next generation. But could there also be an impact that goes in the opposite direction? That is, consider someone we'll call Rodney. His youthful delinquency undermines his subsequent adult accomplishments, achievements, and life chances. Call this the **Serious Consequences Model**. Perhaps it holds true for many people. But another line of argument says that Rodney commits a few delinquent acts as a callow youth, then grows out of it in a couple of years. He gets serious, settles down, gets married, has a family, and leads a respectable life. Call this the **Passing Phase Model**.

The Passing Phase Model seems very plausible, but how accurate is it when put to the test? In order to investigate this, Tanner, Davies, and O'Grady employed data from the National Longitudinal Survey of Youth. They traced a cohort of individuals from midadolescence to their late twenties. What they wanted to know was whether various kinds of delinquency during the teen years would spoil the outcomes of these individuals in adulthood (that is, a dozen years after the delinquent behavior).

The delinquent behaviors included in the study ranged from very minor (skipping school) to very serious (violent behavior; contact with the criminal justice system, such as arrest, booking, and conviction). Intermediate items included property crimes and using drugs (such as alcohol and marijuana). These youthful behaviors were then used to predict adult educational and occupational outcomes (while controlling for a host of background variables and cognitive skill). Would such offenses make a difference a dozen years later, or would youthful indiscretions prove to be insignificant in the long run?

Tanner et al. found that all five kinds of delinquency affected educational attainment. This held true for males and females, even after controlling for cognitive skill, social class, race, and other variables. Among males, all five varieties of

Sociologists and criminologists are divided on how to think of truancy; some consider it a precursor to delinquency, while others think of it as delinquent itself. *(Michael Newman/PhotoEdit.)*

delinquency also lowered their adult *occupational status* and made them more likely to be *unemployed*. Among females, on the other hand, adolescent flirtations with delinquency did not matter so much occupationally: they did not have much of an impact on later occupational status or unemployment.

Certain types of delinquency proved more influential than others in undermining future attainments. Common sense would suggest that the most serious offenses would have the strongest negative impact on future attainments. But, as often happens, common sense failed to garner much support from the data. Instead, the least serious of the five offenses, skipping school, affected educational attainment more than the others did. (It was not the most powerful of *all* the variables in the study, though; cognitive skill had that honor.) In turn, educational attainment proved to be a key factor in determining an individual's occupational status and chances of being unemployed. In the long run, it turns out that youthful indiscretions did finally catch up to people; they did prove consequential, interfering with success in later life.[8]

School Factors and Delinquent Behavior: Additional Theories

Loss of Teacher Authority

Now consider some older explanations of how schools may be related to youth crime. Paul Copperman presents a complex argument linking several school problems to each another. We will simplify it here and focus on those elements that are related to school delinquency. Figure 8-1 represents his overall argument in diagram form. Teacher authority occupies a central role in this theory and has an important impact on students' academic performance and their school-related delinquency. Teacher authority in turn is affected by the degree of authority wielded by the principal and the amount of support parents offer the school.

Copperman believes that learning suffers if the school principal is weak. Only principals who exercise authority by focusing on curriculum and teaching can create a setting conducive to learning. He thinks that they need to fire teachers who are inept, train those who demonstrate some potential, and support the ones who are performing well. Most principals, however, neglect this function in order to concentrate on a host of other chores. That, Copperman argues, is a misuse of their time.

FIGURE 8.1   Copperman's School Authority Model

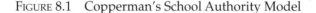

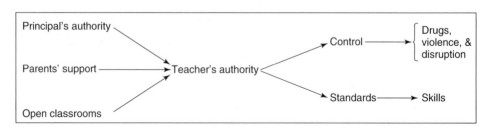

At one time, Copperman says, parental support for school policies and practices was widespread and taken for granted, but now parents tend to rally behind their children and turn against the teachers when there's any disagreement.

> They are not reinforcing the teacher by making sure the children do their school-work everyday. They are not nearly as concerned about their children cutting classes or using drugs. Some parents actively subvert the teacher's authority by denigrating the school or the teacher to their children.[9]

Without parental support for teachers, student respect for teachers falters.

Copperman believes that **open classrooms** also undermine the teachers' authority. The open education movement was influenced in the beginning by A. S. Neill, who ran Summerhill, a private school in England. Americans Charles Silberman, Jonathan Kozol, and John Holt praised his philosophy, and for a while this new approach replaced traditional teaching methods in a number of American schools. Organizationally, open classrooms mean that children are allowed to study whatever they want:

> during their learning activities, children may move freely around the classroom, interacting with other students as they desire; the teacher is to behave in a democratic, nonmanipulative, warm, and respectful way toward his students, providing them with pleasant and enjoyable educational experiences.[10]

In high schools, open education inspired flexible schedules, more electives, and light course loads. Copperman says modern students get to choose both electives and (in required classes) the teacher. This puts teachers on the defensive; to get a sufficient number of students to enroll in their section, they must be likeable, entertaining, and *easy*. This leads to a popularity contest among teachers, and one way to win it is to inflate grades. When one teacher does this, others feel pressure to follow suit. Therefore academic standards are relaxed, leading many students to become slackers and shirkers. They have no incentive to study because they will get good grades anyway. Teacher expectations decrease, students work less, learn less, and suffer declining skills.

With their authority ebbing, teachers no longer have an inhibiting or deterrent effect on student misbehavior in school. Students fear and respect teachers less. With flexible schedules, it is unclear whether any particularly student is legitimately wandering the halls or skipping class. Teachers cannot be sure. If they give students the benefit of the doubt, students will take advantage of the opportunity and cut more classes. This lack of control allows students to get away with more drug use, vandalism, and violence. If free time is plentiful and teachers are reluctant to intervene, deviance and disruption are likely to rise. According to Copperman, they will spin out of control unless school officials take action, that is, suspend or expel the offending students.

Regimentation and Revenge

As you might imagine, most social scientists disagree with the views espoused by the conservative Mr. Copperman, and some of them appear to prefer a theory (like the following, by David Greenberg) that is diametrically opposed to it. According to Greenberg, a New York University sociologist, youth crime takes diverse forms and therefore more than one theory is required to explain it. So he proposes two explanations: one dealing with ordinary theft and another with violence and vandalism. Only the second explanation will be mentioned here, because it is the one that is connected to schooling. He begins by saying that as children get older they are granted increasing freedom by parents. At school, on the other hand, they are denied autonomy and are subjected to public **degradation ceremonies**. The same old rules about smoking, using the bathroom, dress, hair style, and attendance continue to apply year after year; thus, school personnel do not take students' age or level of maturity into account. This policy irritates high school students, who have come to think of themselves as full-fledged adults—not as little children.

Students who perform well in school, attain popularity among their peers, and take part in extracurricular activities may be able to put up with such irritating rules, but those who find themselves in a less favorable situation (low performers, unpopular, nonparticipants) are likely to find the regulations insufferable. They may become hostile toward the school and drift into trouble. In the first half of the twentieth century, they would surely have dropped out, but nowadays more youths remain in school, where (Greenberg says) they are relentlessly rated, evaluated, and graded by the teachers, sometimes even singled out for verbal abuse: he says they may be called lazy or stupid in front of their classmates.

Faced with irksome rules and degrading experiences in the classroom, some youngsters attempt to save face and regain self-esteem. Irritated at being denied autonomy, they may become disengaged and tune out the teacher. They may feel smoldering resentment and show their feelings in their behavior, for instance, by skipping school or breaking the rules.

> Such activities as getting drunk, using drugs, joy-riding, truanting, and adopting eccentric styles of dress . . . can be seen as forms of . . . "conflictual validation of the self." By helping students establish independence from authority. . .these activities contribute to self-regard.[11]

Greenberg contends that school regulations breed frustration among students with low grades and little popularity. This frustration may lead to youth crime, as a way to shore up their battered self-esteem. Such crime could take various forms, from school vandalism to assaulting teachers.

Tracking

Some school observers, particularly labeling theorists, have focused on the evils of tracking. According to one ardent critic of tracking,

> First, students are identified in a rather public way as to their intellectual capabilities and accomplishments and separated into a hierarchical system of groups for in-

struction. Second, these groups are labeled quite openly and characterized in the minds of teachers and others as being of a certain type—high ability, low achieving, slow, average, and so on. Clearly, these groups are not equally valued in the school. . . . Third, individual students in these groups come to be defined by others—both adults and their peers—in terms of these group types. In other words, a student in a high-achieving group is seen as a high-achieving person, bright, smart, quick, and in the eyes of many, good. And those in the low-achieving group come to be called slow, below average . . . dummies, sweathogs, or yahoos. Fourth, on the basis of these sorting decisions . . . teenagers are treated by and experience schools very differently.[12]

Traditional tracking refers to the school administration's grouping of students into college prep, general, vocational, and remedial classes. Students in the college track take a foreign language, the more difficult math courses, and the more advanced science courses.

Opponents of the practice say that students should not be tracked at all. Or they say that if tracking is carried out, the criteria used in selecting students for different tracks should be based entirely on merit. As now practiced, they complain, many students are assigned to the wrong track: some rather low-ability students end up in the college prep track (those teenagers considered by administrators to be serious, well-rounded, and personable, with leadership potential) and some quite capable students do not get put into this track (those from lower-class or minority families, according to the critics).[13]

These track assignments or labels, labeling theorists contend, are important because they may turn out to be irreversible. That is, once assigned to a particular ability group, the individual youngster has little chance of ever being reassigned. Moving up (to college prep from another track) is difficult because students doing so must meet certain requirements. For instance, in some high schools, the rule is that freshman algebra is a prerequisite for sophomore plane geometry, and in the sciences biology must precede chemistry, which must be taken before physics, and so on. According to one estimate, only about 7 percent of students switch into or out of the college prep track.[14]

Critics of tracking say it also has important effects on subsequent careers. It influences whom a student associates with in and out of school, what grades the student gets, what extracurricular activities the student participates in, the student's self-esteem, the student's attendance, attitude toward school, and crime and deviance. According to Polk and Schafer, noncollege-bound youths get worse grades the longer they remain in school, whereas college-bound students' grades improve between their freshman and senior years. Those who decry tracking claim that one's track predicts future grades better than one's social class, IQ, or previous GPA.[15] Another study found that delinquency (being expelled from school, skipping school, engaging in gang fighting, smoking marijuana, and shoplifting, for example) is more strongly related to track position than to sex or social class.[16]

IQ and Delinquency

The relationship between IQ and delinquency has a colorful, some would say sordid, history. A century ago, some commentators made inflated claims that individuals of limited intelligence are led into crime by clever people, and they do not realize that committing crimes in a simpleminded fashion leads to getting caught and punished. Some of this commentary and "research" was remarkably shoddy. And it was often based on overestimates of the IQs of nonoffenders (which were not even measured!). Moreover, in the early days of IQ tests, the results were dubious, due to measurement error of many kinds.

In the early part of the twentieth century, detractors such as Edwin Sutherland wrote harsh reviews of the research in hopes of destroying once and for all the notion that IQ has any effect on crime. These reviews had the effect intended. For many years, criminologists refused to consider IQ seriously. But then Travis Hirschi and Michael Hindelang decided to revisit the issue. In an article in the *American Sociological Review,* they pointed out that there was indeed a relationship between IQ and delinquency: on the average, offenders tended to have an IQ of 8 to 10 points lower than nonoffenders. Although this difference was not as large as the earlier commentators had claimed, it was still very substantial.

Hirschi and Hindelang also looked at the question of spuriousness. Could there be a third variable—such as social class—that causes both IQ and delinquency, as Chambliss and Ryther claimed? Various studies showed that this was not the case: when social class is held constant, youths with lower IQs still have higher rates of delinquency.[17] Another argument is that the IQ-delinquency relationship is real but easily explained by the fact that people with low IQs commit silly crimes and are therefore more easily caught. Although this seems plausible, the question is, What happens when it is put to the test? The best way to test such a notion is to conduct self-report research. In these studies, it does not matter whether the offense is easily detected or whether the offender is easily caught. In self-reports, the issue of detection is removed from consideration. The IQ-delinquency relationship is still as strong among self-report studies as it was in official data research, indicating that ease of getting caught does not explain the relationship between IQ and delinquency.[18]

Hirschi takes the position that IQ's effect on delinquency is mediated by several intervening variables that have to do with school experiences. He contends that IQ tests were originally intended to predict how well a person will do in school. In this regard, such tests are not perfect but they do a respectable job. Students with lower IQs tend not to do well on tests and papers, and generally they get low grades on their report cards. Those who receive such grades tend to become alienated from school. As a rule, people enjoy doing those things they are good at and have little taste for things they perform badly—whether it is school, skiing, skateboarding, or anything else.

Students who find education pointless, Hirschi says, will probably also find the school's many rules and regulations annoying. They hate the prospect of having to knuckle under to the school's authorities. Those who find the rules and authority hard to put up with are likely to break such rules and to become delinquents inside the school and elsewhere. Thus, according to Hirschi, IQ matters only because it leads to unfavorable school experiences: doing poorly on tests, not liking school, finding the rules intolerable, and then breaking the rules.[19]

Research

Copperman believes that if teachers had more authority and could exercise more discipline, students' grades would improve and deviance in the classroom would dwindle. Researchers studying school and delinquency have neither tested nor cited Copperman's work, but inadvertently some supplied data that bear on it. One way they have done so is by comparing private and public high schools. In one study, Catholic school students were found to have higher levels of academic achievement, higher percentages of students going on to college, and lower percentages dropping out. The authors gave two reasons for this difference:

> First, given the same type of student . . . private schools create higher rates of engagement in academic activities. School attendance is better, students do more homework, and students take more rigorous subjects. . . . The indication is that more extensive academic demands are made in the private schools, leading to more advanced courses and thus to greater achievement. . . . Second, student behavior in a school has strong and consistent effects on student achievement. . . . The greatest differences in achievement between private and public schools are accounted for by school-level behavior variables (that is, the incidence of fights, students threatening teachers, and so forth).[20]

Private schools experience fewer behavior problems; indeed, "the *average* public high school is outside the whole range of Catholic schools in the direction of more behavior problems."[21] What is the reason for this disparity? Coleman and his colleagues attribute it to the disciplinary climate. Three-fourths of Catholic-school students say discipline in their school is strict and effective. (This means the schools are well managed. We are not talking about the olden days, when the very mention of Catholic schools conjured up images of sadistic nuns rapping students' knuckles with rulers.) There is a written code of conduct and a list of prohibited behaviors.

The first reaction to the Coleman study was that its results were due to selection bias (i.e., Catholic students were better scholastically and behaved in a more orderly fashion because Catholic schools refuse to admit students with behavior problems or academic weaknesses). And they are quick to expel anybody who fails to measure up to their standards. But, Catholic school administrators point out, about 90 percent of those who apply are admitted and extremely few are ever expelled. Moreover, the students who benefit the most from Catholic schooling are those coming from low-income and minority backgrounds.

Comparing public schools with private schools is not the only way to test the theories. The *Violent Schools—Safe Schools* study examined the relationship between violence and several school characteristics. It found that the schools that made the greatest effort to govern students and enforce rules consistently experienced the least amount of violence. This held true for junior highs, senior highs, rural, urban, and suburban schools. This provides support for Copperman's view and common sense (because most Americans blame school problems on lack of discipline). Considerable evidence also shows that delinquency declines when schools implement firm and fair management programs. Violence against teachers is greater where

According to James Coleman, Catholic school students generally are better behaved and more committed to learning than their peers in public schools. *(Wide World Photos.)*

student misconduct is ignored and students do not perceive rule enforcement to be firm and clear. That is why experts recommend that schools develop disciplinary procedures with clearly specified rules and fair, consistent enforcement.[22]

David Greenberg endorses a view that is the opposite of Copperman's. According to Greenberg, school is a frustrating experience for many students. They have too many rules to follow and too many dictatorial teachers to put up with. These irritate some students and incite them to rebellion, violence, and vandalism against the school. How strong is the evidence in favor of this argument? Not very. The *Violent Schools* report found that rural schools were the most rule oriented and the least responsive to student rights, but they did not experience much violence. Teachers were more likely to be the targets of obscene gestures and comments and violent threats and acts in the urban schools where discipline was lax and inconsistent and teachers were sometimes afraid to enforce rules.

In other nations (Asian, European, Caribbean), teachers tend to have stricter rules than American schools have. Does this lead to rebelling, rioting, robbing students, and attacking teachers? Not as a rule. Generally, those classrooms are models of decorum compared to schools in large American cities. Apparently, most students elsewhere do not mind wearing school uniforms, lining up, studying hard, and obeying a long list of rules. Thus, the Greenberg model, though it appeals to the **libertarian** feelings in many of us, must be regarded with a skeptical eye—it does not seem to fit the data well.

Next, consider the consequences of curriculum tracking. Labeling theorists find this practice appalling; they say it's discriminatory and undemocratic in practice, and disastrous in its consequences. This critique assumes that each student in high school knows which track he or she is in. Research shows, however, that most students are in the dark, unaware of what track they are in or what the tracks are in their school or if indeed there are any.[23] Students in the noncollege tracks are especially likely to misperceive their track and to believe that they are in the college prep category. Far from feeling stigmatized and frustrated, these youths are unrealistically optimistic. Furthermore, the college prep track is becoming less popular among teens. More and more students are choosing the general track, which is neither college prep nor vocational. When asked to choose between vocational and college prep courses, more students say they prefer the vocational. Most of them do not want to be considered a "brain" or "brainiac," which they consider virtually indistinguishable from a nerd.

In fact, the traditional system of tracking was dismantled in most high schools several decades ago (between 1965 and 1975). Since that time, schools have come to resemble shopping malls; students can comparison shop and pick out their own courses, without paying much attention to future consequences. Hence, like a Chinese menu, they choose a few courses from this track and a few from that one, resulting in a great deal of mobility between tracks. A majority of students take courses that are discrepant (i.e., from different tracks); thus, there is little or no socialization effect of tracks any more. Recent studies point to a high incidence of mobility, and none find upward mobility to be rare (Wilson and Rossman, 1993; Hallinan, 1996; Lucas, 1999; Lucas and Good, 2001). As analysts have looked closer, they

> have come to explain this new set of findings by pointing to an unremarked revolution in how schools track students (Lucas, 1999). Evidence suggests that schools no longer formally assign students to overarching tracks that determine their course-taking (Carey, Farris, and Carpenter, 1994; Hayes, 1990). . . . Students make decisions yearly as to which structural path they will follow.[24]

Arum and Beattie carried out some interesting research recently by linking high school experience with the chances of later being imprisoned. They found that some school factors predicted who would later end up behind bars. Labeling theorists have long warned that vocational programs in school have disastrous consequences, most notably, luring students into crime, deviance, and other trouble. Arum and Beattie, however, found that students enrolled in such programs expressed greater satisfaction with school and teachers (than those in the general track). More importantly, students taking at least 15 percent of their coursework in the vocational area were *far less likely than other students to eventually be sent to prison*: 1.4 out of a thousand instead of 6.7 per thousand. "Our results suggest that occupational course work has a role in developing a socially well-adapted and productive citizenry."[25]

As for race and ethnicity, one study found that Asian students were more likely to be assigned to advanced courses than Hispanics with the same test scores, and, surprisingly, several studies found that the assignment process favors African Americans over "nonblacks." The latter finding has been attributed to a modern attempt to "redress the imbalance."[26] Other researchers have found net equality in placement of blacks and Hispanics after controlling for social class and achievement. And several find there is a net advantage for blacks in placement; the traditional form of tracking was dismantled in most schools owing to pressure from civil rights activists.[27]

Finally, the major study of the impact of tracking on delinquency, done years ago, showed that track position was correlated with a large number of variables—but delinquency was not one of them (the associations with delinquency were very weak, none higher than .10). Although students in the college prep track were less delinquent than students in other tracks, the difference was minuscule. Tracking had no significant direct effects or total effects on delinquency, according to this research. Recently, another article found that most track mobility is *upward* and that track location does not predict the delinquency of one's friends.[28]

Next, consider Travis Hirschi's claim that lower IQ leads youngsters to engage in more delinquency (this takes place via a series of mediating variables). To test this notion, we must begin with the very basic question of whether IQ and delinquency are correlated. If they are not, then Hirschi's argument can be dismissed immediately. The evidence suggests we cannot do that, that there really is a connection of some kind between them. Several studies have established this correlation convincingly.[29] So further examination of Hirschi's argument is needed.

Hirschi also claims that students with higher IQs do better in school tests, papers, and report cards. In fact, intelligence tests were originally designed by Binet to do just that: to predict how well children would perform academically. They do reasonably well at this; the correlation between grades and IQ hovers around .50. (Environment does matter, though. Some people do better than their IQ would lead us to expect: surprisingly, this is true even when we compare entire nations with each other. Chinese and Japanese students clearly outperform their American counterparts despite similar IQ scores. Another sign of the environment's role is called the Flynn effect: the fact that IQ scores have been rising for each generation since 1932.)[30]

Hirschi also contends that higher grades lead to more tolerance of school rules, which leads to lower levels of delinquency both in school and outside of it. Researchers have not given much attention to the students' tolerance of rules, but they have examined attachment to school. Some have found that this is related to delinquency in the predicted direction: the more attached they are to schools, the less delinquent they are.[31] Others have looked at commitment to school and found that it too functions as a good predictor of delinquency and youth crime.[32]

Not every piece of research is so supportive of Hirschi's argument linking IQ to school grades to attachment and then to delinquency. Several studies suggest that school grades are *correlated* with delinquency but not *a cause* of it.

> Taken together, these studies suggest that during elementary school, academic performance is best predicted by early problem behavior. Delinquent behavior in early adolescence (e.g., at age 14) is a function of persistent antisocial tendencies more than poor academic performance.[33]

This suggests that Hirschi's theory may have gotten the causal ordering wrong.

Sensation Seeking, School, and Delinquency

American public schools have their problems. Students from the United States rarely do well on international comparisons, whether the subject is math, science, or anything else. Nor are the schools in this country models of decorum. Consider for example Seward Park, on New York's Lower East Side. In classrooms there, the moment the teacher turns her head, students launch so many paper airplanes, the room appears in need of an air traffic controller. Other rooms are filled with

> brigands, "repeaters" who had failed the course from one to three times already. They had bedeviled Jessica [the teacher] daily with fake passes, profane answers, and sundry roughhousing, and they had delighted in their demonism.[34]

New York City is probably not unusual among urban centers in this respect. Consider Berkeley High School in Northern California. In some classes, observers report that students are busy eating a Happy Meal, playing a boom box, and strolling in and out of the room as they please.[35]

School is one of several settings in which adolescents spend a sizable portion of their time; the other major locations are at home and in public. They while away the day with friends, family, classmates, or alone. When teenagers are in an adult-oriented environment such as school, their level of motivation sinks to its lowest ebb. They are least motivated when they are doing what they must do in order to become productive adults. They do not want to be bogged down in tasks that are not of their own choosing—class work, homework, or just plain work. Nor do they relish spending time with people they are forced to be with—their classmates.[36]

In the everyday life of a teenager, the two most important adult-run institutions are the school and the family. Schools take up a third of the youth's waking hours, during which time they feel little enthusiasm. The emotional tone in school is flat, lacking joy and exuberance. Most adolescents are not eager to learn, because much of the material is foreign and difficult, not just languages, but algebra, ancient history, Chaucer, and Shakespeare. While in the classroom, students report feeling bored, sad, constrained, unable to concentrate, and wishing they could be doing something else.

The classroom can't compare with being among friends, who engage in random and crazy acts that offer immediate gratification. Teachers are expected to give negative feedback, quell riotous behavior, and suppress deviance. Lectures rarely appeal to the familiar and interesting. Instead, they dwell on the abstract, complex, and unfamiliar, from statistical formulas to the seven types of ambiguity in the Nun's Priest's Tale. Setting foot in the classroom immediately depresses the mood of many students. Schools are in the business of trying to bend adolescent minds and confront them with challenges, but many students resist, refusing to bend or become engaged. Some do not pay any attention.

The result is that schools tend to create *psychic entropy* in a number of students. This term includes four elements:

1. Instead of happiness and friendliness, the student feels sad, lonely, and irritable.
2. Instead of energetic and competent, the adolescent feels tired, drained, weak, passive, and bored.

3. Rather than feeling involved in pursuing a goal he or she identifies with, the teen experiences a loss of motivation, because the goal is imposed by adults.

4. Rather than being absorbed in and able to think clearly about the activity, the youth cannot concentrate: his or her thoughts wander off.[37]

Psychic entropy has important practical effects. If many students in a classroom feel this way, the odds against the teacher making any intellectual headway with them are overwhelming. In addition, students may be unable to put up with much of this boredom. They may feel it necessary to make up for these long stretches of ennui by doing something that revitalizes their mood and lifts their spirits. Often this entails socializing with friends, away from adults, engaging in wild and crazy activities such as partying, dancing, telling stories, drinking beer, using drugs, having sex, and experimenting with crime and delinquency. These are found by many adolescents to be intrinsically motivating. (1) Feeling active and happy and (2) being amidst friends go together for teenagers and offer a stark contrast to the tedium of the classroom. Some adolescents cannot wait for the bell to ring, for school to end, and for the drinking and pot smoking to begin.[38]

Csikszentmihalyi and Larson show how sociability, school boredom, and hedonism are connected (by citing Greg's typical day).

> Greg's life swings back and forth between slow, tedious times at work and school, when he turns his mind off, and fast, excited times with friends, when he feels truly himself. In school, we often see these two states switching rapidly, as he moves between classes and friends. At work the boredom completely takes over, while during the times he is with other young people excitement and cheer set in.
>
> Greg does not lack **negentropic** experiences, times when he is involved in what he is doing, and enjoying it. He finds challenges in the forbidden activities of drinking and smoking pot, and he looks forward to the unpredictable developments of each crazy night [including brushes with police and general rowdiness].[39]

Students often make up for school boredom by turning to rowdy and deviant acts. The peak period for juvenile arrests is almost immediately after school lets out in midafternoon, when youths blow off steam and act a little crazy.[40]

People feel an attraction to crime, a sensual thrill, which they find so moving that they can recall it in great detail years later. Sensation seeking has proved to be a strong predictor of substance use and criminal activity, better than such old standbys as age, sex, race, social class, and religiosity. When youths are asked what motivated them to engage in larceny, auto theft, fraud, illegal entry, trespassing, alcohol use, marijuana use, and hard drug use, they usually cite pleasure or thrills more than any other reason.[41]

> Many young people use social interaction, sports, rock music, dancing, amusement parks, cars, motorcycles, and other noncriminal activities as their sources of stimulating inputs and sensory reinforcement. But those with few inhibitions may discover the thrills and adventure of juvenile delinquency. . . . As these young people habituate to the novelty and sensory stimulation levels of minor crimes . . . , it becomes increasingly easy for them to explore more serious crimes without major risk of punishment.[42]

Studies find crime and deviance more common among people with low arousal. The usual measures of arousal include heart rate, skin conductance activity, and electroencephalogram (EEG) during rest. Low heart rate and skin conductance and slow-wave EEGs reflect underarousal. Hundreds of investigations of EEGs in criminals and delinquents have been carried out since 1940, and they show EEG abnormalities, especially among recidivists. Violent offenders are two to five times as likely as normals to have EEG abnormalities.[43] As for children and adolescents, a low resting heart rate is the most consistent predictor of antisocial behavior in community samples.

How should low arousal and low heart rate among criminal and antisocial persons be interpreted? There are two principal explanations that have been advanced. One interpretation points to fearlessness among the underaroused. Lack of fear leads people to engage in dangerous and antisocial behavior, such as jumping off buildings or getting in fights. In addition, individuals who have little fear are difficult for parents and teachers to socialize.

Another way of looking at the data claims that low arousal among adolescents is physically uncomfortable and unpleasant. These individuals try to return to a more optimal level of arousal by seeking stimulation, perhaps by committing a burglary or robbery. Which of these explanations has the greater validity? This is hard to say with any confidence. It may be that both explanations are at work. Even children as young as 3 years old have been shown to differ noticeably on both fearlessness and sensation seeking—and each of these proved to be a good predictor of aggressive acts eight years later.[44]

Males and Females and School

Some people find school easy to adjust to, and they thrive in an environment of reading, writing, homework, tests, and papers. Others find school to be a chore and never adjust to it. Does their sex or gender have anything to do with their school performance? Do males perform better than females in the school atmosphere? Or do females outshine the males when it comes to education? Much of the commentary on this issue has been shrouded in ideology. To get a better understanding, we need to look at the relevant data.

Look around your college classroom and count the number of students. Chances are, the women will outnumber the men. The share of college degrees earned by men has been falling for over a century. Between 1970 and 1996, bachelor's degrees earned by women rose by 77 percent, compared to 19 percent among men. Males make up only 44 percent of undergraduate students nowadays, compared to 76 percent in 1950. In 1965 there were 236 all-male colleges; now there are three. (Of the 117 historically black colleges, only one—Morehouse College—has more males than females, and that's because it refuses to accept *any* women.) College admissions offices have had to secretly develop affirmative action programs to admit more men.

In high school, boys are less likely to come to classes prepared, that is, with paper, pen or pencil, and completed homework. Boys are less likely to take foreign language classes, less likely to be involved in extracurricular activities, less committed to school, less competent at reading and writing, less likely to be in an honor society, much more likely to be put in special education classes, much more likely to be diagnosed with attention deficit/hyperactivity disorder, more likely to be suspended, more likely to drop out. From grade school to grad school, females earn higher grades, even in science and math courses.[45] According to Diane Halpern's review of the literature,

> males are over-represented at the low-ability end of many distributions, including the following examples: mental retardation (some types), a majority of attention deficit disorders, delayed speech, dyslexia . . . , stuttering, learning disabilities, and emotional disturbances.[46]

Faced with these problems, it is understandable why boys might be more likely than girls to engage in deviant behavior both in and out of school.

Conclusion

During the nineteenth century, most schools in America were violent, chaotic places. Teachers tried to rein in their unruly and incorrigible charges by resorting to tactics that would strike us as brutality. Horace Mann, for instance, reported seeing over 300 **floggings** in five days he spent at one school.[47] The public in recent years may have thought our modern schools were reverting to the old ways, with violence appearing on school grounds across the nation (but now by the students themselves, not vicious schoolteachers of centuries past). Before September 11, 2001, the public worried enough about schools to say it considered education the nation's top priority.[48]

Laurence Steinberg's three years of research found that about 40 percent of students in high school are disengaged. That is, not trying their best, not paying attention, easily distracted, cheating on tests, and copying each other's homework. They go to school mostly in order to socialize with friends and goof off. He also found that Asians do better in school partly because of their healthy attribution style: they believe that success or failure can be traced back to how much time and effort were devoted to studying. Other students think grades are a function of luck or favoritism on the part of the teacher, so they study less and perform worse on tests and papers.

Hagan and Parker used longitudinal data to compare two generations in Toronto. The experiences of the parent generation had an important impact on the next generation. Academic disinvestment by the parents included (1) not wanting or expecting to get much education and (2) performing at a much lower level than their best in school. This led in some cases to such developments as teenage parenting, dropping out of school, and unemployment. Many years later, when the children of these parents were old enough to do so, they tended to get involved in more delinquency than their age-mates.

Another set of longitudinal data was analyzed by Tanner et al., who traced a cohort from their midadolescent years to their late twenties. They wanted to find out whether youthful delinquency had a negative impact on educational attainment, adult occupational status, and the chance of unemployment. Tanner et al. found that skipping school (though it was the least serious of the various delinquent acts they studied) had the most profound and detrimental impact on future status attainment. Lack of commitment or attachment to school proved costly in the long run. Youthful indiscretions can prove to be harmful later on.

Several theories were considered in this chapter: Copperman's authority model, Greenberg's regimentation and revenge model, Hirschi's IQ and delinquency model, and labeling theory's tracking model. Copperman contends that teacher authority and respect for teachers have been undermined in the modern American culture, where students' rights are expanding. He says this plus the relaxation of academic standards has given students more power and less motivation. They respond predictably enough by working less, caring less, learning less, and trying to get away with more (drug use, violence, and vandalism).

Greenberg takes the opposite point of view by contending that students who are not performing well become irked by the school's many rules and drift into trouble: getting drunk, using drugs, engaging in vandalism, and attacking the teachers who are blamed for calling the students lazy and stupid in front of the entire class and more generally for treating the students like children instead of as fully mature adults. Greenberg's solution to the delinquency problem is to give the students more rights, not subject them to rules or high academic standards.

Tracking, too, has been the subject of theorizing for a number of years. Labeling theorists claim that tracking is unfair to everyone put in the lower tracks by the discriminatory, classist, and racist school administrators. This practice creates a host of problems, they say, including low self-esteem, rampant alienation, and a growing delinquency problem. The students who are placed in one of the lower tracks get the worst teachers and are put in with a group of other kids who are prone to delinquency.

Hirschi's IQ and delinquency model begins with low scores by youngsters on their IQ tests. These substandard scores are reasonably likely to lead to poorer grades on the students' report cards. Low grades in turn make the child more apt to find school is not to his liking. This in turn makes the student fed up with the school rules and regulations. Once the child reaches this point, it is only a short step to delinquent activities. These may take place in school or elsewhere or both.

The Greenberg and labeling theories have considerable appeal on the surface, especially when fleshed out with heartrending examples. These tales appeal to many impressionable readers. But the real test comes from large-scale, objective data, not hand-picked anecdotes. And here neither theory fares very well. Not much delinquency occurs at schools with high standards, where teachers and principals are in control. Where parents are in control and teachers are very democratic, delinquency is high. As for tracking, labeling theory ignores the facts that many students are unaware of the tracks, students choose which courses to take, many prefer the general track, and the vocational track actually seems to make people less apt to commit crimes and land in prison later on. The Copperman and Hirschi arguments enjoy more empirical support, but the latter is open to the criticism that correlations do not always translate into causation: low grades may predict delinquency, but there is reason to believe that they don't cause it.

Sensation seeking has not been explored by most criminologists, but it may be an important factor in delinquency. For instance, Farrington found there were two variables that predicted future delinquency far better than any others: one of these was daring (another term for sensation seeking).[49] In school, many students are not really committing delinquent acts; they are not stealing, fighting, smoking cigarettes, drinking beer, or violating other laws. Instead, they are in search of fun, thrills, a good time, a break from the boredom and routine of ancient history and dry statistics. So they sit in the back row, talk to their neighbors, tell jokes, goof off, eat candy bars, and dream of the excitement they will have once school is out and they can do whatever they want with their friends. They can do deviant things on the way home, sneak over to their friends' homes, go down to the basement, get drunk, smoke pot, have sex, and so on. The classroom experience brings their mood down so far that they feel the need to bring it back up to a high level by engaging in exciting forms of collective deviance.

Males do not perform as well in school as females do. This is not a news flash, of course. But in earlier times the extent of the difference was not recognized. Many people actually thought males were more intelligent than females, that they could do better if they tried, but they would save their energy until they entered the business and professional world, where they would show their true colors. Now we know that males are more often found at the bottom of many distributions. And this may hasten their involvement in delinquency. If they cannot shine in the classroom, they can turn to a more rewarding venue: the streets.

Key Terms

Functionally illiterate:	skills in reading and writing are insufficient for ordinary practical needs
Zero tolerance:	even the most minor violations will be taken seriously and penalized
Disengaged:	not trying hard, not paying attention, easily distracted
Disinvestment:	not wanting an education and not performing up to one's abilities
Healthy attributional style:	thinking that success depends on how hard one works at it
Unhealthy attributional style:	blaming results on luck, favoritism, and other factors that one has no control over
Serious Consequences Model:	youthful delinquency undermines a person's future (adult) achievements and attainment
Passing Phase Model:	youths commit a few delinquent acts as teens but it does not come back to haunt them; they mature, settle down, and lead a conventional adult life
Open classrooms:	school is organized in a way that allows children to concentrate on whatever subject or activity they want
Degradation ceremonies:	being humiliated by the teacher in front of all of one's classmates
Traditional tracking:	school administration sorts students into college prep, general, vocational, and remedial tracks; mobility between tracks is minimal

Libertarian:	believing in freedom of action and thought
Psychic entropy:	sadness, lack of energy, lack of motivation, lack of concentration
Negentropy:	happiness, energy, motivation, concentration
Flogging:	severe beating with a whip

End Notes

[1]Jill Stewart, "Turning the Tables," *New Times Los Angeles* (July 25, 2002), p. 1.

[2]Marjorie Coeyman, "Troubled System, Radical Response," *Christian Science Monitor,* November 13, 2001, p. 12; Michael A. Fletcher, "Philadelphia Schools to be Privately Run Under Pa. Plan," *Washington Post,* November 6, 2001, p. A1.

[3]Wayne N. Welsh, Jack R. Greene, and Patricia H. Jenkins, "School Disorder," *Criminology, 37,* no. 1 (February 1999), pp. 73–115; *Violence in the Schools* (Alexandria, VA: National School Board Association, 1993); Howard N. Snyder and Melissa Sickmund, *Juvenile Offenders and Victims* (Washington, DC: Office of Juvenile Justice and Delinquency Prevention, 1995); Denise G. Gottfredson, *Schools and Delinquency* (New York: Cambridge University Press, 2001).

[4]Laurence Steinberg, *Beyond the Classroom* (New York: Touchstone, 1997), p. 19.

[5]*Ibid.,* pp. 147–8.

[6]*Ibid.,* p. 99.

[7]John Hagan and Patricia Parker, "Rebellion Beyond the Classroom," *Theoretical Criminology, 3,* no. 3 (August 1999), pp. 259–85.

[8]Julian Tanner, Scott Davies, and Bill O'Grady, "Whatever Happened to Yesterday's Rebels?" *Social Problems, 46,* no. 2 (May 1999), pp. 250–74; see also Karl L. Alexander, Doris R. Entwisle, and Carrie S. Horsey, "From First Grade Forward," *Sociology of Education, 70,* no. 2 (April 1997), pp. 87–107.

[9]Paul Copperman, *The Literacy Hoax* (New York: Morrow, 1980), pp. 160–1.

[10]*Ibid.,* p. 66.

[11]David F. Greenberg, "Delinquency and the Age Structure of Society," *Contemporary Crises, 1,* no. 2 (April 1978), pp. 189–223.

[12]Jeannie Oakes, *Keeping Track* (New Haven, CN: Yale University Press, 1985), p. 3.

[13]Aaron V. Cicourel and John I. Kitsuse, *The Educational Decision-Makers* (Indianapolis: Bobbs-Merrill, 1963); Walter Schafer and Carol Olexa, *Tracking and Opportunity* (San Francisco: Chandler, 1971).

[14]Kenneth Polk and Walter Schafer, *Schools and Delinquency* (Englewood Cliffs, NJ: Prentice Hall, 1972).

[15]*Ibid.*

[16]Delos Kelly, "Status Origins, Track Position, and Delinquent Involvement," *Sociological Quarterly, 16,* no. 2 (Spring 1975), pp. 264–71.

[17]Edwin H. Sutherland, "Mental Deficiency and Crime," in Kimball Young, ed., *Social Attitudes* (New York: Henry Holt, 1931), pp. 357–75; Travis Hirschi and

Michael J. Hindelang, "Intelligence and Delinquency," *American Sociological Review, 42,* no. 4 (August 1977), pp. 571–87; William J. Chambliss and Thomas E. Ryther, *Sociology* (New York: McGraw-Hill, 1975); Terrie E. Moffitt, William F. Gabrielli, Sarnoff A. Mednick, and Fini Schulsinger, "Socioeconomic Status, IQ, and Delinquency," *Journal of Abnormal Psychology, 90,* no. 2 (April 1981), pp. 152–6; Donald Lynam, Terrie Moffitt, and Magda Stouthamer-Loeber, "Explaining the Relation Between IQ and Delinquency," *Journal of Abnormal Psychology, 102,* no. 2 (May 1993), pp. 187–96; Marvin E. Wolfgang, Robert M. Figlio, and Thorsten Sellin, *Delinquency in a Birth Cohort* (Chicago: University of Chicago Press, 1972).

[18]Joseph Weis, Delinquency Among the Well-to-Do. Unpublished dissertation, University of California, Berkeley (1973); Donald J. West, *Who Becomes Delinquent?* (London: Heinemann, 1973); Travis Hirschi, *Causes of Delinquency* (Berkeley, CA: University of California Press, 1969).

[19]Travis Hirschi, *Causes of Delinquency.*

[20]James S. Coleman, Thomas Hoffer, and Sally Kilgore, *High School Achievement* (New York: Basic, 1982), p. 178; William M. Evans and Robert M. Schwab, "Finishing High School and Starting College," *Quarterly Journal of Economics, 110,* no. 4 (November 1995), pp. 941–74; Derek Neal, "Measuring Catholic School Performance," *Public Interest* (Spring 1997), pp. 81–7.

[21]James S. Coleman, Thomas Hoffer, and Sally Kilgore, *High School Achievement,* p. 111.

[22]Denise C. Gottfredson, *Schools and Delinquency,* p. 71; Denise C. Gottfredson, David B. Wilson, and Stacy S. Najaka, "The Schools," in James Q. Wilson and Joan Petersilia, eds., *Crime;* Wayne N. Welsh, "The Effects of School Climate on School Disorder," *Annals of the American Academy of Political and Social Sciences, 567* (January 2000), pp. 89–107; A. Troy Adams, "The Status of School Discipline and Violence," *Annals of the American Academy of Political and Social Sciences, 567* (January 2000), pp. 140–56; Jackson Toby, "Getting Serious About School Discipline," *Public Interest* (Fall 1998), pp. 68–83; Richard Lawrence, *School Crime and Juvenile Justice* (New York: Oxford University Press, 1998), p. 22.

[23]James E. Rosenbaum, "Track Misperceptions and Frustrated College Plans," *Sociology of Education, 53,* no. 2 (April 1980), pp. 74–88; Charles F. Manski, "Adolescent Econometricians," in Charles T. Clotfelter and Michael Rothschild, eds., *Studies of Supply and Demand in Higher Education* (Chicago: University of Chicago Press, 1993), pp. 43–60; James E. Rosenbaum, *Making Inequality* (New York: Wiley, 1976).

[24]Samuel R. Lucas, "Effectively Maintained Inequality," *American Journal of Sociology, 106,* no. 6 (May 2001), pp. 1642–90; Bruce L. Wilson and Gretchen B. Rossman, *Mandating Academic Excellence* (New York: Teachers College Press, 1993); Maureen T. Hallinan, "Track Mobility in Secondary School," *Social Forces, 74,* no. 3 (March 1996), pp. 983–1002; Samuel Roundfield Lucas, *Tracking Inequality* (New York: Teachers College Press, 1999); Samuel R. Lucas and Aaron D. Good, "Race, Class, and Tournament Track Mobility," *Sociology of Education, 74,* no. 1 (April 2001), 139–56; Nancy Carey, Elizabeth Farris, and Judi Carpenter, *Curricular Differentiation in Public High Schools* (Rockville, MD: Westat, 1994); Floyd W. Hayes, III, "Race, Urban Politics, and Educational Policy-Making in Washington, D.C.," *Urban Education, 25,* no. 3 (October 1990), pp. 237–57.

[25]Richard Arum and Irenee R. Beattie, "High School Experience and the Risk of Adult Incarceration," *Criminology, 37,* no. 3 (August 1999), p. 533.

[26]Jeannie Oakes, Molly J. Selvin, Lynn Karoly, and Gretchen Guiton, *Educational Matchmaking* (Santa Monica, CA: Rand, 1991); Jeannie Oakes, Adam Gamoran, and Reba N. Page, "Curriculum Differentiation," in Philip W. Jackson, ed., *Handbook of Research in Curriculum* (New York: Macmillan, 1992), pp. 570–608; Sanford M. Dornbusch, Kristan L. Glasgow, and I-Chun Lee, "The Social Structure of Schooling," *Annual Review of Psychology, 47* (1996), pp. 401–29.

[27]Samuel R. Lucas and Adam Gamoran, "Race and Track Assignment," Paper presented at American Sociological Association meetings in Cincinnati, 1991; Adam Gamoran and Robert D. Mare, "Secondary School Tracking and Educational Equality," *American Journal of Sociology, 94,* no. 5 (March 1989), pp. 1146–83; Michael S. Garet and Brian DeLany, "Students, Courses, and Stratification," *Sociology of Education, 61,* no. 2 (April 1988), pp. 61–77; Samuel Roundfield Lucas, *Making Inequality,* p. 140.

[28]Michael Wiatrowski, Stephen Hansell, Charles R. Massey, and David L. Wilson, "Curriculum Tracking and Delinquency," *American Sociological Review, 47,* no. 1 (February 1982), pp. 151–60; Robert Crosnoe, "High School Curriculum Track and Adolescent Association with Delinquent Friends," *Journal of Adolescent Research, 17,* no. 2 (March 2002), pp. 143–67.

[29]Richard Arum and Irenee R. Beattie, "High School Experience and the Risk of Adult Incarceration"; Jennifer White, Terrie E. Moffitt, Avshalom Caspi, Dawn Jeglum Bartusch, Douglas J. Needles, and Magda Stouthamer-Loeber, "Measuring Impulsivity and Examining its Relationship to Delinquency," *Journal of Abnormal Psychology, 103,* no. 2 (May 1994), pp. 192–205; Terrie E. Moffitt and Phil E. Silva, "IQ and Delinquency," *Journal of Abnormal Psychology, 97,* no. 3 (August 1988), pp. 330–3; Donald Lynam, Terrie Moffitt, and Magda Stouthamer-Loeber, "Explaining the Relation Between IQ and Delinquency"; Hakan Stattin and David Magnusson, "Onset of Official Delinquency," *British Journal of Criminology, 35,* no. 3 (Summer 1995), pp. 417–49; David P. Farrington, "The Development of Offending and Antisocial Behavior from Childbood," *Journal of Child Psychology and Psychiatry, 360,* no. 6 (September 1995), pp. 929–64; Marc LeBlanc, Evelyne Vallieres, and Pierre McDuff, "The Prediction of Males' Adolescent and Adult Offending from School Experience," *Canadian Journal of Criminology, 35,* no. 4 (October 1993), pp. 459–78; Marvin D. Krohn and James D. Massey, "Social Control and Delinquent Behavior," *Sociological Quarterly, 21,* no. 4 (Autumn 1980), pp. 529–44.

[30]Ulric Neisser, Gwyneth Boodoo, Thomas J. Bouchard, Jr., A. Wade Boykin, Nathan Brody, Stephen J. Ceci, Diane F. Halpern, John C. Loehlin, Robert Perloff, Robert J. Sternberg, and Susana Urbina, "Intelligence: Knowns and Unknowns," *American Psychologist, 51,* no. 2 (February 1996), pp. 77–102; James R. Flynn, "The Mean IQ of Americans," *Psychological Bulletin, 95,* no. 1 (January 1984), pp. 29–51; James R. Flynn, *Asian-Americans: Achievement Beyond IQ* (Hillsdale, NJ: Erlbaum, 1991).

[31]Wendy L. Lipton and M. Dwayne Smith, "Explaining Delinquent Involvement," *Journal of Research in Crime and Delinquency, 20,* no. 2 (July 1983), pp. 199–213; Michael Wiatrowski and Kristine L. Anderson, "The Dimensionality of the Social Bond,"

Journal of Quantitative Criminology, 3, no. 1 (March 1987), pp. 65–81; Patricia H. Jenkins, "School Delinquency and the School Social Bond," *Journal of Research in Crime and Delinquency, 34,* no. 3 (August 1997), pp. 337–67; Alexander T. Vazsonyi and Daniel J. Flannery, "Early Adolescent Delinquent Behaviors," *Journal of Early Adolescence, 17,* no. 3 (August 1997), pp. 271–93; Carolyn Smith, Alan J. Lizotte, Terence P. Thornberry, and Marvin D. Krohn, "Resilient Youth," in John Hagan, ed., *Current Perspectives on Aging and the Life Cycle* (Greenwich, CT: JAI Press, 1995), pp. 217–47; Minu Mathur and Richard A. Dodder, "Delinquency and the Attachment Bond in Hirschi's Control Theory," *Free Inquiry in Creative Sociology, 13,* no. 1 (May 1985), pp. 99–103.

[32]Stephen A. Cernkovich and Peggy C. Giordano, "School Bonding, Race and Delinquency," *Criminology, 30,* no. 2 (May 1992), pp. 261–91; Patricia H. Jenkins, "School Delinquency and the School Social Bond"; Patricia H. Jenkins, "School Delinquency and School Commitment," *Sociology of Education, 68,* no. 3 (July 1995), pp. 221–39; Carolyn Smith, Alan J. Lizotte, Terence P. Thornberry, and Marvin D. Krohn, "Resilient Youth."

[33]Denise C. Gottfredson, *Schools and Delinquency,* p. 55.

[34]Samuel G. Freedman, *Small Victories* (New York: Harper and Row, 1990), p. 181.

[35]Meredith Maran, *Class Dismissed* (New York: St. Martin's Press, 2000).

[36]Mihaly Csikszentmihalyi and Reed Larson, *Being Adolescent* (New York: Simon and Schuster, 1984).

[37]*Ibid.*

[38]*Ibid.*

[39]*Ibid.,* pp. 113–4.

[40]Howard N. Snyder and Melissa Sickmund, *Juvenile Offenders and Victims: 1999 National Report* (Washington, DC: Office of Juvenile Justice and Delinquency Prevention, 1999), p. 66; Marcus Felson, *Crime and Everyday Life,* 2nd ed. (Thousand Oaks, CA: Pine Forge Press, 1998).

[41]Jack Katz, *The Seductions of Crime* (New York: Basic, 1988); Winsome Rose Gordon and Marie Louise Caltabiano, "Urban-Rural Differences in Adolescent Self-Esteem, Leisure Boredom, and Sensation Seeking as Predictors of Leisure-Time Usage and Satisfaction," *Adolescence, 31,* no. 124 (Winter 1996), pp. 883–901; Helene Raskin White, Erich W. Labouvie, and Marsha E. Bates, "The Relationship Between Sensation Seeking and Delinquency," *Journal of Research in Crime and Delinquency, 22,* no. 3 (August 1985), pp. 197–211; John K. Cochran, Peter B. Wood, and Bruce J. Arneklev, "Is the Religiosity-Delinquency Relationship Spurious?" *Journal of Research in Crime and Delinquency, 31,* no. 1 (February 1994), pp. 92–123; Peter B. Wood, John K. Cochran, and Betty Pfefferbaum, "Sensation Seeking and Delinquent Substance Use," *Journal of Drug Issues, 25,* no. 1 (Winter 1995), pp. 173–93; Robert Agnew, "The Origins of Delinquent Events," *Journal of Research in Crime and Delinquency, 27,* no. 3 (August 1990), pp. 267–94; Roy Lotz and Leona Lee, "Sociability, School Experience, and Delinquency," *Youth and Society, 31,* no. 2 (December 1999), pp. 199–223; David P. Farrington, "Motivations for Conduct Disorder and Delinquency," *Development and Psychopathology, 5,* no. 1 (Winter 1993), pp. 225–41; Paul F. Cromwell, "Juvenile Burglars," *Juvenile and Family Court Journal, 45,* no. 2 (Summer 1994),

pp. 85–91; John C. Coleman and Leo B. Hendry, *The Nature of Adolescence* (London: Routledge, 1989); Joshua D. Miller and Donald Lynam, "Structural Models of Personality and Their Relation to Antisocial Behavior," *Criminology, 39,* no. 4 (November 2001), pp. 765–98.

[42]John D. Baldwin, "The Role of Sensory Stimulation in Criminal Behavior, with Special Attention to the Age Peak in Crime," in Lee Ellis and Harry Hoffman, eds., *Crime in Biological, Social, and Moral Contexts* (New York: Praeger, 1990), p. 208.

[43]Adrian Raine, *The Psychopathology of Crime* (San Diego: Academic Press, 1993).

[44]Adrian Raine, Chandra Reynolds, Peter H. Venables, Sarnoff A. Mednick, and David P. Farrington, "Fearlessness, Stimulation Seeking, and Large Body Size at Age Three Years as Early Predispositions to Childhood Aggression at Age 11 Years," *Archives of General Psychiatry, 55,* no. 8 (August 1998), pp. 745–51.

[45]"Educating Females in U.S. Schools," *Education Digest, 61,* no. 8 (April 1996), pp. 14–18; Daren Fonda, "The Male Minority," *Time* (December 11, 2000), pp. 58–60; Brendan I. Koerner, Viva Hardigg, Deanna Lackaff, James Morrow, Ben Wildavsky, and Mary Lord, "Where the Boys Aren't," *U.S. News and World Report* (February 8, 1999), pp. 46–53; Judith Kleinfeld, "Student Performance: Males Versus Females," *Public Interest* (Winter 1999), pp. 3–20.

[46]Diane Halpern, "Sex Differences in Intelligence," *American Psychologist, 52,* no. 10 (October 1997), pp. 1091–102.

[47]Joan Newman and Graeme Newman, "Crime and Punishment in the Schooling Process," in Keith Baker and Robert J. Rubel, eds., *Violence and Crime in the Schools* (Lexington, MA: Lexington Books, 1980), p. 11; Horace Mann and the Reverend M. H. Smith, *Sequel to the So-Called Correspondence Between the Rev. M. H. Smith and Horace Mann* (Boston: Fowle, 1847).

[48]Jeffrey M. Jones, "Americans Rank Education as Top Priority for the Bush Administration," *Gallup Poll Monthly,* no. 424 (January 2001), pp. 11–13.

[49]David P. Farrington, "Predicting Persistent Young Offenders," in Gary L. McDowell and Jinney S. Smith, eds., *Juvenile Delinquency in the United States and the United Kingdom* (New York: St. Martin's Press, 1999), pp. 3–21.

Recommended Readings

Denise C. Gottfredson, *Schools and Delinquency* (New York: Cambridge University Press, 2001).

Mihaly Csikszentmihalyi and Reed Larson, *Being Adolescent* (New York: Basic, 1984).

Delbert S. Elliott, Beatrix A. Hamburg, and Kirk R. Williams, *Violence in American Schools* (New York: Cambridge University Press, 1998).

Patricia H. Jenkins, "School Delinquency and the School Social Bond," *Journal of Research in Crime and Delinquency, 34,* no. 3 (August 1997), pp. 337–67.

Denise C. Gottfredson, David B. Wilson, and Stacy S. Najaka, "The Schools," in James Q. Wilson and Joan Petersilia, eds., *Crime* (Oakland: Institute for Contemporary Studies, 2002), pp. 149–89.

Richard Lawrence, *School Crime and Juvenile Justice* (New York: Oxford University Press, 1998).

CHAPTER 9

Peers and Youth Crime

As a rule, most criminologists attribute youthful crime and deviance to the social environment and think that misbehavior is fostered by peer relationships and peer influence. Shaw and McKay, central figures in the early Chicago School, seemed to have convincingly established that delinquency is a group behavior. They said childhood groups formed early in life are primarily committed to playing, but it does not take long for them to tire of innocent recreation and move on to more interesting and edgy activity, namely, delinquency.

> The development of relationships with play groups outside of the home represents a significant enlargement of the child's social world. Through them he is subjected to the influence of an increasing number and variety of personalities. . . . Such groupings are usually spontaneous in origin and constitute a form of primary group relationship. [These groups] . . . differ widely in regard to cultural traditions, moral standards, and social activities. In certain areas of the city the practices and social values of many of these groups are chiefly of a delinquent character.[1]

McKay's friend and fellow Chicagoan, Edwin Sutherland, also commented on the social nature of crime. But their views differed in important respects. Shaw and McKay talked about play groups and children committing delinquent acts together for fun. Sutherland focused on adults in a criminal underworld of professionals, who made a living from their craft and learned both the business and pro-criminal attitudes hanging out with other professional criminals. Thus we have a series of contrasts: play versus work, juveniles versus adults, amateurs versus professionals, committing acts together versus learning attitudes from one another, and slum dwellers versus people from loftier class backgrounds.

Play

On most of these issues, Frederic Thrasher, a student of juvenile gangs, agreed with Shaw and McKay. He said the best place to study gang beginnings is in the slums, where children are crowded into a small area. There, spontaneous play groups arise, which provide the boys (there were hardly any girl gangs back in the 1920s, he noted) with thrill, zest, and excitement.

> The most rudimentary form of collective behavior in the gang is interstimulation and response among its own members—motor activity of the playful sort, a talk-fest, the rehearsal of adventure, or a smut session. It may assume the character of a common activity such as gambling, drinking, smoking, or sex. It is this type of behavior that the gang displays and develops at the outset its enthusiasms, its spirit, its esprit de corps.[2]

Thrasher is describing delinquent groups in the slums as they appeared about eighty years ago, when poverty was widespread, especially for those in Chicago's most destitute precincts, where life was precarious. Many residents had a problem: how to take care of large families with low wages. Americans in 1900 were forced to spend 43 percent of the family income on food, which left little for housing, transportation, education, clothing, and entertainment. Only 2 percent of households had electricity and only 10 percent could boast of flush toilets. Life expectancy for those born in 1900 was 46 years for males, 48 for females. Still, it seems, the children were not depressed; they found time for play (since few teenagers were enrolled in school).[3]

That kids like to play is still evident, as shown by Csikszentmihalyi and Larson, who randomly beeped a large sample of students in a modern high school outside Chicago. These teenagers reported enjoying themselves most when they were with friends, being rowdy, loud, crazy, and wild, particularly on Friday and Saturday nights. They were free to party, sing, goof off, get stoned, act crazy, to say and do anything and have friends respond by being even more crazy, creative, and bizarre.

> Teens told of trying to drive an automobile from the back seat and of hanging from railroad trestles while a train passed over. Rowdy activities included driving around yelling, throwing cans on people's yards, and having fights in school. They also included less obnoxious behavior: simply acting silly or "spastic," and other deviations from common, everyday norms. Such a state of uncontrollable glee is the pinnacle of group interactions. . . .[4]

Individually, youths may not be committed to crime, but they may talk each other into an offense and not have the courage to back out of it, for fear the others would consider them sissies. Thrasher gives an example. Three Vanderbilt College students

Peers are of great importance during adolescence. This is a stage of development when American teens enjoy excitement and adventure in the company of their age-mates. *(Doug Menuez/Getty Images, Inc.–Photodisc.)*

were discussing a sack of money left at the post office and how easily it could be stolen. Then the discussion shifted to how easily *they* could do so. They devised a plan, simply as a prank, for they were not really concerned about the money itself. The danger made the prank more delicious. Each expected one of the others to laugh it off. It was merely hypothetical, purely theoretical, not serious. But after a while they began to think about actually carrying out the theft. They momentarily forgot their position in school, their family, and friends and executed the plan. Only later did they appreciate the seriousness of their act.[5]

This means that a group will sometimes act in ways that an individual never would, that a group may lean toward more extreme decisions. Social psychologists refer to this as **risky shift, groupthink,** or the **Abilene Paradox.** Risky shift is the tendency for groups to take greater risks than individuals would. In groupthink, the members sense pressure to maintain unanimity, which discourages critical and independent thinking. In the Abilene Paradox, there is outward acceptance of a group decision, although each person inwardly disagrees with it. Adolescents, who after all want to be popular and accepted, may be more easily influenced by groups than adults are.

The Monitoring the Future studies conducted by the University of Michigan also help explain the role of fun in crime and deviance. These annual studies sample high school seniors, who vary in their level of active sociability (i.e., the number of evenings going out for fun and recreation, frequency of riding around, frequency of getting together with friends informally, and frequency of attending parties). This sociability is correlated with drinking (.43), smoking (.38), property crime (.26), truancy (.26), and violent crime (.25). Just going out, attending parties, and being with friends is often enough to get the ball rolling. Someone makes a suggestion, issues a dare, proposes a new adventure, and the others, wishing to avoid criticism, fail to back out of the proposed plan of action. More likely, they encourage the others and imply that they are just as enthusiastic as anyone.[6] If some of this argument is speculative, the research by Agnew removes all doubt, for it finds that most youths say that most of their burglaries, hard drug use, fraud, thefts, trespassing, alcohol use, marijuana use, and auto thefts are motivated by pleasure or thrills.[7]

Youngsters

Are juveniles the ones who commit their offenses in the company of their peers as opposed to adults, who commit them alone? This would make sense if juveniles have time on their hands, access to peers, and little work or study after school. It is often presumed that adults don't commit crime for fun, because they have to make a living, can't afford to be convicted for something frivolous, and are inclined to settle down due to family, legal occupation, and community.[8] If pleasure and thrills are not the motivating factors for offenses by adults, then peers or cooffenders may not be necessary.

Early studies of delinquency, which relied on official data, found that about 85 percent of delinquent acts were committed as part of a group.[9] Later ones, relying on self-reports, found that too high and settled on a figure close to 65 percent.[10] Finally, Albert Reiss examined data on residential burglary and robbery by juveniles, and he determined that the incidents were evenly divided: 50 percent by lone offenders and 50 percent with two or more offenders. Results differ when the researcher focuses on incidents (the appropriate unit of analysis for our purposes) instead of offenders.[11]

Imagine that there are four burglaries: one committed by Antonio, one committed by Bryant, one committed by Clint, Donte, Emmett, and Grant, and one by Howard, Javon, Kendall, and Luke. If we count incidents, then half are committed by lone offenders, half with cooffenders. But if we ask each participant, "Did you commit the offense alone or with others?" the majority (80 percent) will say it was with others. Asking participants about whether they committed their offenses with others thus leads to results that are quite misleading.

The few studies of adults and their cooffenders indicate that they are less likely to commit their offenses with accomplices. (But much of the data on adults comes from countries other than the United States.) Maybe this is because older men are less sociable than teenagers, or perhaps their crimes aren't meant to show off in front of peers. Maybe they're more profit oriented and they don't want to split the proceeds, or possibly they fear the others will talk too much, get questioned by the police, and reveal the names of their partners.

The fact that adults (more than teens) commit crimes without partners does not mean that such crimes lack excitement or adventure. True, the swaggering and strutting of adolescent risk taking may be absent. But research by Wood and his colleagues shows that prison inmates who contemplate crimes often imagine that they would feel heightened sensations: on a high or rush, pumped up, powerful, living on the edge, intensely alive, and able to do anything. For them, criminal behavior is intrinsically rewarding (even without any cooffenders around to share in the excitement).[12]

Amateurs

Juveniles who commit crimes and other kinds of deviance are normally acting more like amateurs than professionals. This means that they have *not* engaged in weeks or months of careful planning to decide how to commit the crime and which escape route to take. They are *not* trying to maximize the financial payoff, *not* trying to eliminate any chance of being discovered and turned over to the police, in general *not* acting as rational calculators specializing in one particular kind of crime or making it into a lucrative career.

One of the hallmarks of amateurs is their lack of forethought. They commit crimes that bring little or no financial reward, crimes that are sloppy or simpleminded, and ones that lead to getting caught. Examples of these are not hard to find. Take Stanley, the youngster described by Shaw and McKay in *The Jack Roller.* He was instructed in all the techniques of crime by William (his half-brother) and Tony (the local gang leader). Before reaching the age of 10, he had been arrested twenty-three times. But despite his considerable instruction and firsthand experience in crime, Stanley never showed much expertise, never became a professional con man or joined a criminal syndicate. He remained a lowly **jack roller,** and even at that his tactics were laughable. He would strong-arm a drunk or wait for the drunk to pass out in an alley, steal his clothes then wear them the next day in the same area, the victim would see him and alert the cops.[13]

Committing Acts Together

The social nature of delinquency can be interpreted to mean (1) learning techniques at the foot of master criminals (as suggested by Sutherland) or (2) simply committing delinquent acts with one or two of the guys (Shaw and McKay). Both are plausible interpretations of American delinquency in the early part of the twentieth century, especially in Chicago. There, poverty was extreme, population density was high, ethnic segregation pronounced, children numerous (and very few went to high school), and city government and police were known for their corruptibility.

In the beginning, researchers thought they had found support for differential association theory, but in recent years critics have identified a large number of flaws in their measurement of concepts and their interpretation of the results. Finally, scholars, aware of the many problems plaguing those earlier studies, have tried to correct them in modern works. Consider, for instance, publications by Reed and Rose and by Matsueda and Anderson, both of which appeared in 1998.

They note that Sutherland's theory and its competitors cannot adequately be tested unless the study uses longitudinal data to see which comes first: one's delinquent behavior or one's associations with other delinquents. Besides being cross sectional instead of longitudinal, early studies suffered from correlated measurement error. The same respondents were asked about their friends' delinquency as well as their own. They may (out of ignorance) have just assumed or guessed that their friends' level of delinquency was the same as theirs. Therefore, some of the early tests of differential association theory[14] are now regarded as questionable.

Matsueda and Anderson, in their more recent and sophisticated test, find that associating with delinquent peers (i.e., peer influence) does lead to an increase in one's own delinquency later on, but this effect is quite small. They also show that being delinquent leads later on to associating with delinquent peers, and this effect (sometimes called selection or birds of a feather flock together) is considerably stronger.[15] Thus it appears that a youngster who is involved in delinquency will (later on) choose to hang out with other teens who are also into delinquency. This is especially important, because Matsueda is known as a modern-day Donald Cressey, in other words, a staunch defender of differential association theory. Now his findings show something quite different: *that peer influence or socialization is less important than selection.*

The Reed and Rose study cites several other longitudinal studies showing not only that selection is an important factor,[16] but that it is more important than socialization or peer pressure.[17] Moreover, in their own data, they note that adolescents greatly overestimate the attitude similarity between themselves and their friends, that delinquent attitudes have very little effect on delinquent behavior or associations—socialization effects are negligible. The causal relation their data did support is selection: youths who are already delinquent will seek out other delinquents to associate with.[18]

Peers and Youth Crime: Males Versus Females

One point on which all criminologists agree is that males are more likely to engage in crime and delinquency than females are. Gender is the strongest correlate of crime and delinquency in all societies and cultures and all periods of history; it applies to all ages and all racial and ethnic groups.[19] The evidence for these statements comes from official data, self-reports, victimization surveys, and **ethnographic** research. Although the finding that males commit more crime (and more serious crime) is well established, the reasons for it are unclear.

Desperation and trying to escape from family problems inspire delinquency among some youths. Interviews suggest that females are not very committed to crime, that they drift into it after running away from home, where they may have been victims of physical or sexual abuse. Perhaps some of them struggled to live on the streets, which proved difficult and may have forced them to turn to crimes such as prostitution or drug dealing in order to make enough money for food and other necessities.[20] Furthermore, women make up only a small proportion (6 percent) of the prison population. (Even some of *them* are not guilty: They were talked into taking the rap in order to spare their male companions.)

Some criminologists trace the gender gap in criminal offending back to gender roles. According to this line of thinking, offending behavior is completely contrary to the tenets of the traditional female role in society. As long as women and female adolescents subscribe to the traditional role, they will avoid engaging in crime and other deviance. In keeping with this line of reasoning, it is true that more traditional societies have less crime by women than more modern and liberated societies (such as the United States).

But at the individual level, the findings dash cold water on this point of view. There is no strong evidence that women or female adolescents who are more liberated, more committed to women's rights, and less enamored of the traditional role, commit more crime than those with traditional views. Actually, most men and women involved in crime are traditional in their views about gender. This is true for adults and adolescents as well.[21]

What about the role of peers? What kind of impact do they have? Does peer influence explain why females are less drawn to crime and delinquency than males? Some research studies hint that this might be so. University of Michigan survey researchers who conduct the annual Monitoring the Future studies of high school seniors across the country also followed up some of their sample a few years later and (as previously mentioned) found **active sociability** to be a good predictor of crime and deviance. In addition, they discovered that this sociability (riding around in cars, going to parties, etc.) is more common among some seniors and young adults than others. Background variables such as sex, GPA, age, and parents' education exert an important impact on how often these people socialize with peers. Specifically,

> 18-year-old males with D grade-point averages whose parents have graduate or professional degrees typically go riding in a car for fun 110 times per year, visit informally with friends 200 times, go to 40 parties, and spend 170 evenings out for fun. In contrast, 26-year-old females who had A's in high school and whose parents had grade school educations typically go riding in a car for fun 9 times, visit with friends informally 25 times, go to 6 parties, and spend 53 evenings out for fun.[22]

Thus, females are less apt to take part in the kind of sociability that has the potential to lead to crime and deviance.

Another major research project found that peers may affect female deviance, but it depends on certain conditions. Wisconsin psychologists studying a cohort of girls in the Dunedin Multidisciplinary Health and Development project discovered that those who matured early (their menarche arrived earlier than the customary age) were more prone to engage in delinquency at age 13. But this depended on the kind of secondary school they attended. If they went to a coeducational school, early maturation was strongly linked to delinquency. If they went to an all-girls school, however, no such relationship existed. Apparently, blossoming early led them to hang out with older male peers in the coed schools, thus exposing them to deviant influences.[23]

Why should time spent socializing with males increase female involvement in deviant behavior? Some observers suggest that males and females tend to differ in their moral outlooks. They cite Carol Gilligan's comments on the way males and females are raised. In her book on moral development, she said that females are primarily concerned about relationships; they have an overwhelming interest in seeing that others are cared for and not harmed. In contrast, males are more utilitarian: they feel strongly about their rights, and protest any outside interference with them. Males pursue self-interest whereas females dwell on the well-being of others. These gender differences are sometimes said to arise because boys and girls are raised differently by their parents and other socializing agents.[24] According to research by Mears et al., differences in morality do indeed play an important role in the gender gap in crime and delinquency.[25]

But are the differences in morality between the genders entirely due to the way their parents raised them? Are children this malleable and parents this powerful? If culture is the only factor, why are the gender differences found in all the cultures around the world? Just what is it that makes some females more self-interested and less attracted to the ethic of caring for others. Richard Udry asked why some females are more "feminine," whereas others are more "masculine" in their young adult years. Gilligan and others would say that this is due to the parents, who either encouraged more femininity or more masculinity. Udry found this to be true: if mothers encouraged femininity, daughters became more feminine. But it's true only if the daughter (while still a fetus) did *not* receive a higher than average amount of **androgens** in the womb during the second trimester.

If she *did* receive more androgens at that time, she was likely to become more masculine than other females her age in early adulthood. And it did not matter how hard her mother pushed her to be more feminine. Such socialization had little or no impact. This is what we know about females and androgens. Next, Udry speculated about males, who have a much higher concentration of androgens, specifically, about ten times the amount of testosterone. If females with higher than average levels of this are resistant to mothers' encouragement to be more feminine, then males (with far higher levels) should be that much *more resistant.* Purely sociocultural explanations of masculinity/femininity differences (and the ethic of care versus self-interest) may need to be supplemented.[26]

Peer Rejection and Aggression

Sociologists in the field of criminology tend to focus on peers and friends as *negative* influences, drawing youths into various forms of crime and deviance. This point of view has been prominent in sociological circles since early in the twentieth century, when Shaw and McKay said delinquency is a group phenomenon. Developmental psychologists, on the other hand, paint a rosier picture of the impact that friends have on each other. This goes back to Harry Stack Sullivan, who theorized that mutual friendship in childhood and adolescence is necessary, not dangerous; it is vital to a person's social, cognitive, and emotional development. Without it, social skills and competencies will not develop.[27]

Developmental psychologists point out that relationships with peer groups, close friends, and cliques more often lead to prosocial (socially accepted) standards of behavior rather than deviance or antisocial behavior.[28] For instance, research by Clasen and Brown indicates that adolescents feel more pressure to be involved (spend time with friends and go to parties) and to conform (in dress and grooming, for instance) than to engage in drug and alcohol use or minor delinquency. Peer pressures to engage in misconduct are ambivalent, that is, the amount of pressure to engage in it is approximately equal to the amount against engaging in it. On balance, the pressure on the average adolescent to engage in misconduct is weaker than any other peer pressure measured.[29]

Many developmental psychologists focus on children who are sociometrically rejected: that is, those whom many classmates dislike and very few like. (They are not to be confused with the neglected, whom few like or dislike, or the small number of controversial children, who are widely liked and widely disliked.) Study after study has found that there is a strong correlation between (1) being rejected by peers in childhood and (2) engaging in aggressive or disruptive acts. Some research shows that rejected children have other problems as well, such as low self-esteem, inability to cope with stress, and poor performance in school.

The most commonly cited correlate of peer rejection is aggression, whether aggression is measured by peer evaluations, teacher ratings, or observations by researchers. Such findings usually are based on a one-shot cross-sectional survey, which means it is unclear whether rejection causes aggression, aggression causes rejection, or some third variable causes both of them. To establish causation, then, researchers may turn to longitudinal studies (as sociologists sometimes do) or to experiments (a method frequently employed by psychologists).

Two investigations by psychologists in the 1980s combined elements of longitudinal and experimental studies. Coie and Kupersmidt brought together previously unacquainted fourth-grade boys and put them in free-play situations. These boys were previously identified by peers as popular, average, neglected, or rejected. The ten play groups (five containing boys who knew each other and five containing strangers) were composed of one popular, one average, one neglected, and one rejected boy. They met once a week for a month and a half. Videotapes revealed that in both types of groups, the previously rejected boys were more likely to make hostile comments and carry out unprovoked assaults.

Dodge (another psychologist) put second-grade boys together, none of whom knew each other. There were eight boys (not selected for previous sociometric status) in each of the eight groups, and they were observed daily for eight sessions. After the last session, the boys rated each other, giving their positive and negative sociometric choices. Dodge found that those eventually rejected by their peers in the groups had made more hostile comments and hit the other boys. In the early sessions, these rejected boys made frequent approaches but were rebuffed and later became isolated in their play.[30] Both studies found that aggression preceded peer rejection (and was the best predictor of rejection).

Shortly afterward, Bukowski and Newcomb focused on an older group: male and female adolescents who recently started their first year in a middle school. They used a longitudinal design with these youths and found a direct path between aggression in the autumn of that year and being rejected at later measurements. The authors reached the same conclusions as the two previous studies. A longitudinal study by Kupersmidt, Burchinal, and Patterson a decade later produced similar findings.[31] Fergusson et al. examined boys at age 9, then six years later. They found a correlation between rejection at age 9 and hanging out with deviant peers at 15, but this was not a causal connection; instead hanging out with deviant peers at 15 was caused by the individual's own deviance or conduct problems at age 9. This was true for both boys and girls.[32]

According to the research findings of developmental psychologists, adolescents popular with their peers have close friendships and tend to be friendly, humorous, and intelligent, whereas adolescents rejected by peers are more aggressive, irritable, and socially awkward.[33] Generally speaking, about 50 percent of boys identified as rejected prove to be aggressive, impulsive, disruptive, dishonest, and uncooperative. The other 50 percent may be withdrawn, retarded, or physically unattractive. Children's sociometric status is fairly stable over the years, so that popular youths tend to remain popular and rejected ones continue to be rejected. (Neglected children more often move up to become average, later on.)

Thomas Dishion

The Oregon Social Learning Center (located in the medium-sized city of Eugene) has a staff of psychologists who specialize in the study of children, adolescents, and families with behavior problems. One of these psychologists is Thomas Dishion, who, in collaboration with others, has written many papers on deviance and delinquency. We will examine some of their findings and conclusions from the 1990s. They did not discover the relationship between aggression and peer rejection, but they were aware of the literature, because of the articles by Dodge and Coie and others from the early 1980s.

Dishion's work carried this line of inquiry forward, asking what happened next to the youngsters who had been aggressive and who then found themselves disliked by many of their peers and liked by few of them. He found that such boys tended to hang out with other boys who had been aggressive and rejected. In some cases this happened early on, starting as soon as preschool. Normally, though, it took place several years later, when they were in elementary school.

Rejected and aggressive children tended to hang around one another because they did not want to be completely isolated at school, and they did not have much chance of overcoming the resistance built up among the bulk of the other boys. They could hang out with other rejected boys, because these kids were more tolerant of antisocial or aggressive behavior. Indeed, the rejected boys sometimes reinforced such behavior, that is, rewarded it with encouraging comments.

The fact that friendships exist among antisocial boys at ages 9 and 10 does not mean that such relationships are warm and supportive. They are not. More often they are low in quality, last for only a short period, and end on a sour note. Some are marked by a good deal of bossing one another around, and the boys involved often describe the relationships as not very satisfactory. This brings to mind the description found in Travis Hirschi's social control theory: friendship among delinquents is brittle and mostly unpleasant.

Dishion and his colleagues invited 13- and 14-year-old boys into the Oregon Social Learning Center and asked them to bring with them the youngster with

whom they spent the most time. They were then asked to participate in the Peer Interaction Task, in which each boy and his friend spent 25 minutes discussing a
problem-solving task. Each pair of boys (dyad) was videotaped and voice recorded.
After this session, they were interviewed about the nature of their friendship.

The boys in the study were divided into three kinds of dyads: delinquent (both had
an official police record), mixed (one officially delinquent and one nondelinquent),
and nondelinquent (neither had a record). The topics they discussed were coded by
the researchers as either rule breaking or normative. "Rule breaking" included moon-
ing the camera and obscene gestures and discussion of vandalism, stealing, drug
use, and victimizing women. "Normative" was the code given everything else; this
included talking about leisure, school, family, social life, and so on. Reactions were
coded as well. A response was coded "laugh" if the boy laughed or otherwise responded positively to an act or statement. It was coded "pause" if the other boy did
not speak for at least three seconds or otherwise responded negatively.

Dishion and his colleagues call this **deviancy training.** Because the more the
dyads reinforced rule breaking in the laboratory, the more they talked about rule
breaking during the 25 minutes in this setting; and the more they talked about it,
the more they escalated their level of delinquency, violence, and use of controlled
substances over the next two years. Surprisingly, Dishion found that rule-breaking
talk was a better predictor of deviance two years later than it was for the immediate past. Some boys were more apt to escalate over the next two years than others:

1. Those who experienced deviancy training (rule-breaking talk and positive
   responses)
2. Those whose friendship with their partner in the dyad was low in quality.

These have important implications. First of all, they make putting large numbers of
offenders in prison seem foolish. If talking for 25 minutes can lead to crime, imagine what impact living together for months would have.[34]

In addition, the research on deviancy training forces us to rethink differential association theory. The findings suggest Sutherland was right when he said peer discussions that encourage crime and drug use lead to an increase in such behaviors.
On the other hand, contrary to differential association theory, deviancy training
leads to an escalation of deviant behavior when the two boys are not very close,
when their friendship is low in quality. Dishion and his colleagues point out that
delinquents' friendships are far from warm. Instead, they are of short duration and
end acrimoniously. While they last, they are filled with bossiness and coercive
behavior.

Gerald Patterson

Whereas Dishion's work deals with what happens after aggressive boys are rejected
by their peers at school, Gerald Patterson focuses on what precedes the boys' rejection. Patterson, too, works at the Oregon Social Learning Center, where he's stud-

ied many troublesome children interacting with parents (usually the mothers). He contends that training for early-onset delinquency begins in the home, where the instruction is provided mainly by the family members. It starts with disciplinary confrontations in which the child wins and the parents lose.

The child discovers that his aversive behaviors can work wonders; they shut down the aversive behaviors of other family members. The child's aversive acts are many and diverse, including, for instance, arguing, attacking, blaming, bragging, demanding, fighting, irritability, moodiness, screaming, sulking, swearing, throwing tantrums, teasing, and threatening. Having gone through thousands of trials, the antisocial child becomes as skilled as a drill sergeant at coercion.

Imagine, for instance, that a father takes his daughter to Home Depot to buy some house paint. While they're waiting in line, she starts playing with some little items the store is selling, and breaks or destroys them. To prevent further damage, the father takes them away from her and puts them back in their original place. The child then whines and screams at him. Not wanting to make a spectacle, he tries to mollify her by giving them back. In this test of wills, the child defeats the parent and gets reinforced for her aversive behavior. She will use this abrasive interpersonal style to control her parents and, later on, other people she encounters. Although such coercive behaviors seem primitive, they're an effective way to control one's environment.

The child uses aversive behavior contingently (right after someone has used aversive behavior on him, such as turning off the TV, telling him to pick up his toys, or ordering him go to bed). If the parent gives in to the child's aversive behavior (by letting him have what he wants or not forcing him to do what he doesn't want to do), the child will immediately cease this kind of behavior. This cessation by the child is reinforcing for the harried parent, who will be more likely to give in to the child in the future when similar situations arise. In this kind of family, the parent becomes the victim, and the child exercises a good deal of control over the parent.

Although parents of antisocial children make threats and engage in scolding, they seldom follow through. The child soon learns this and responds to the threats and scoldings with aversive behavior of his own, knowing he will not likely be punished. He takes the threats to be mere irritants, not serious signals that he should stop his behavior. Patterson introduces the term **nattering**, by which he means that some parents nag, scold, lecture, or express irritation but do not say "No" or "Stop that behavior right now." They do not back up their threats with actual punishment. Hence the threats are empty.

Why would parents rely on nattering when by all accounts it fails to make the child behave properly? One reason is that parents of antisocial children fear confrontations. They're afraid the child will become more hostile and aggressive, the child will defeat the parent again, and the parent will fail to change the unwanted behavior and be frustrated and humiliated in the attempt by a small youngster. (In the face of constant defeats, some parents avoid confrontation over violations of rules by a most peculiar tactic: they fail to set rules at all. This way they do not have to deal with their adversary.) These sequences of interaction tend to become stable by the time the child has reached five or six years of age.

Parents of antisocial children conclude that punishment won't work with their children, that the only one who could be effective with them is an exorcist. The problem with such parents is that their reactions are not contingent on the child's actions. Instead, the governing factor in their responses is their mood. "They reward and punish on the basis of how they feel. . . . They natter because they are irritated. They physically assault because they are angry. They reward when they are pleased. . . ."[35] They have no idea that they are supposed to train their child by rewarding his good behavior and punishing his bad behavior.

They take good behavior by the child for granted, thinking that this is simply normal behavior, what any child is expected to do. But prosocial behavior is not normal or natural in a child. It has to be taught, trained, encouraged, and rewarded. Parents of antisocial children, instead of praising prosocial acts of all kinds, save their positive comments for the truly extraordinary events, which are bound to be rare among children who have not been given positive feedback for their small improvements.

As for punishment, parents of antisocial children do more of this than parents of "normal" children. But often it's at the end of a long day when their nerves are frayed, and they can't bear the frustration any longer. So they explode and give the child a beating. Naturally, psychologists discourage this approach. Patterson and others instead recommend punishments other than physical abuse, **sane punishments**, such as taking away privileges or requiring additional duties. These might include taking away phone privileges, a favorite toy, TV programs, dessert, or a week's allowance.

Clearly, Patterson sees early-onset antisocial behavior as a product of interaction within the family. Although deviant peers play a role this occurs several years later, and even then the boys go shopping or foraging to find other boys who are already like themselves (abrasive, antisocial, coercive). They do not really have to influence each other or pressure one another into deviant acts. The boys are already willing, because they probably have engaged in hundreds of deviant activities in prior years. (But remember that this is a clinical sample; most boys are not this antisocial, and most delinquents are not early starters. Most do not begin their delinquency until much later, in their adolescent years.)

Deviant Peers or Peers in General?

Ronald Akers, like Donald Cressey and Ross Matsueda, has been a tireless defender of Sutherland's differential association theory and has devoted a lifetime to preserving it, although he has also added bits and pieces to it and retitled it social learning theory. He has provided concepts such as reinforcement, punishment, imitation, and modeling. Under the new theory, individuals are more apt to commit offenses if

1. They associate mostly with people who commit, model, and advocate breaking the norms.
2. Rule breaking is reinforced more than conformity to the norms.

3. They observe more deviant models than conforming ones.
4. They learn to think that committing deviant acts is acceptable behavior.[36]

The gist of this approach is that peers are exceedingly important in luring a young person into breaking the law and that the person being lured is passive, easily seduced.

> Indeed, in some studies, peer association is a stronger predictor of the onset and persistence of delinquency than one's own previous behavior patterns. More frequent and closer association with conventional peers who do not support delinquent behavior is strongly predictive of conformity, while greater association with peers who commit and approve of delinquency is predictive of one's own delinquent behavior.[37]

Two points should be made here: (1) Akers's approach does not agree with Sutherland's on everything and (2) Akers probably overstates the amount of support that exists for his learning theory. Where do Akers and Sutherland not see eye to eye? First of all, Akers began as a behaviorist like his friend at the University of Washington, Robert Burgess; the whole point of behaviorism was to eliminate consideration of mental processes (attitudes, opinions, interpretations, or definitions of the situation) and to focus just on behavior. As a **symbolic interactionist**, however, Sutherland was deeply involved in theorizing about such attitudes and definitions.

Second, Sutherland insisted that imitation is not an element of differential association. He explicitly denied that anyone becomes delinquent or criminal by imitating the behavior of others. Akers, on the other hand, makes imitation a central feature of his theory. In this he is undoubtedly correct. People (including deviants and delinquents) do tend to model their behavior on the acts of others. If that were not true, then the entire field of social psychology would probably have to be overturned. The importance of imitation among humans is difficult to overstate.

Third, reinforcement is crucial to learning theory but never appears in Sutherland's theory of differential association. According to Akers, people who have tried deviance once may or may not continue; to continue, they must get something rewarding from it. The rewards could be prestige, approval, food, money, smiles, laughter, hugs, high fives, and excitement. Most of the research devoted to testing learning theory focuses on mild behaviors such as smoking and drinking rather than criminal acts, but it is clear from the work of Wood et al., that some pretty serious crimes are also seen by offenders as rewarding.[38]

Mark Warr

University of Texas sociologist Mark Warr has published a series of research articles in major journals on a host of topics, including the influence of peers and parents on delinquency. Recently, he produced a book, *Companions in Crime,* that brings all the pertinent research and theorizing together in one volume, to sum up the state of knowledge in this area as of 2002. Generally speaking, Warr does not have an axe to grind or an ideological or theoretical position to defend, which makes his work more objective and thus more credible.

He offers a number of points worth mentioning, beginning with the distinction between peers and parents. Nearly every parent in America has a decidedly negative view about juvenile delinquency and wants his or her children to not engage in it, not get caught doing it, and not bring shame on the family for participating in it. This is true even if the parents are themselves notorious lawbreakers. But Warr says adolescents are a different story, for they view delinquency far more tolerantly (there are some peers who encourage others to take part in it).

In earlier eras, adolescents spent a good deal of time at home with parents (and this is still true in preindustrial societies). Some stayed on the family farm and spent long hours completing their daily chores, slopping the pigs, plowing the fields, bringing in the crops, cleaning the barn, milking the cows, and so on. This onerous schedule left little time to spend with peers. Opportunities for recreation or leisure, excitement or adventure were rare, particularly for those who lived far away on an isolated farm. Nowadays, however, little time is spent with the family. Parents assign few chores, and children are reluctant to do these few. Even eating together as a family is vanishing.[39]

People are guided by the **principle of homophily**. That is, they prefer to spend their time with others who are like themselves; this applies to marriage, friendship, work, neighborhood, advice, support, exchange, and all other relationships.[40] Like themselves in what respects? Warr says teenagers like to be with people who are the same age, race, social class, and (during the early portion of adolescence) the same sex. Nowadays, they are able to spend many hours with their peers, particularly in the United States, where teenagers have more freedom to do as they wish with whomever they choose.[41]

Time itself is important. Time spent with peers increases dramatically as youngsters go from third grade to ninth grade. Also, their desire to conform to peers, to not stick out as "different," reaches a peak around ninth grade (or age 15). They do not want to be seen as too tall, too short, too fat; nor do they want to be viewed as oddballs who act different. They try their hardest to avoid being ridiculed, to avoid being kicked out of the group. Peer status and acceptance are precious assets that early adolescents will do almost anything to retain.

Sometimes a youngster finds his or her status challenged, perhaps called a punk or a bitch or some other adolescent slur. It would not be so bad if the putdown were uttered by an outsider (such as an adult or stranger) but coming from a peer, it's a serious assault on one's reputation. It cannot be ignored, especially if others are around to hear it. The injured party is required to retaliate, to fight for his or her respect. If he or she fails to do so, it may damage the person's social status beyond repair.

Some teenagers are interested in enhancing their standing by engaging in criminal acts. How is this possible? Adolescents tend to have high regard for performances that demonstrate how daring, reckless, tough, and spontaneous one can be. Maybe these traits can be demonstrated via skateboarding, dancing, surfing or some other legal activity. But some individuals think the best way to demonstrate their recklessness is by feats such as vandalism, violence, truancy, or auto theft.

Boys do not act the same way in every situation that they find themselves in; in some contexts they are reluctant to break the law or act wild and crazy. In others they look forward to becoming rowdy and out of control. Their morality has not changed, but their situation has. When they are alone, they usually do not look for trouble (for there is nobody to have fun with). With a bunch of other guys, however, their conscience may recede, their feelings of guilt or shame may evaporate. It's time for them to show off and have a good time.

Does this tendency to conform to one's peers, mean that the individual privately agrees that what they are doing is right? Warr says it does not. Instead, there are two kinds of conformity: one based on acting in accord with one's beliefs and one based on passive compliance—doing what one's pals are doing but not because one thinks it's right. In short, we all do things that (upon reflection) we know were wrong, foolish, and indefensible. This, Warr notes, contradicts Sutherland's differential association theory, which argued that people consistently act in accord with their privately held beliefs and values.

One form of peer phenomenon is delinquent gangs and groups. As Warr points out, gangs make up only a small fraction of all delinquent groups. These two categories have some commonalities, though: they are usually all male, their members about the same age, they lack organization, and their rosters change constantly. When the members commit delinquent acts, it's usually without much planning. Most offenses occur on the spur of the moment. No one gives a thought to committing them until just moments before they're carried out.[42]

Gangs

What is a **gang**? This seems like a simple question, but it has baffled criminologists for decades. Various definitions have been proposed over the years, some more useful than others. In recent years, there has been some modest agreement on a few characteristics. A gang must first of all be a group, usually a rather large one (certainly not the two- or three-person group that Los Angeles law enforcement organizations use in their definition). Second, most gangs have symbols that denote membership, including clothes of a certain type and color (for example, the Bloods and the Crips). This may seem foolish to an outside observer because it makes the gang members more obvious to the police. Third, gangs may have an elaborate system of signs and communication, such as graffiti or hand signals.[43]

The group must not be a temporary, fly-by-night phenomenon; it must last at least a year before it can be taken seriously enough to be called a gang. Some gangs claim to have a particular turf that they protect as their own. It is their territory, their homeland, and they will retaliate against other gangs that invade it. But such territoriality, although commonly found, is not characteristic of all gangs. Finally, gangs commit crime, not all the time and not as an entire gang, but in small groups and more frequently than nongang members do.[44]

How can researchers determine whether a particular individual is actually a gang member? This is less problematic than defining a gang. Different methods have been tried by investigators, but the simplest way turns out to be the best: just ask the person if he or she is. Most of the time, the youngster will answer truthfully, although in a few cases he or she may quibble about whether it should be called a gang or something else, such as a posse or crew. ("Gang" has a negative connotation for many people nowadays, unlike fifty years ago when popular songs had lyrics like "hail, hail, the gang's all here" and "those wedding bells are breaking up that old gang of mine.")

Once a person has been identified as a member of a gang, the next question may be how strongly committed he or she is to it. Some people have been called "wannabes," meaning that they're not core members but exist somewhere out on the fringe. They are not full-time participants who can be counted on to attend meetings, take part in initiations, or engage in drive-by shootings. According to the rapper Ice T, who was once a member of the Crips in South Central Los Angeles, there are three levels of membership in a gang. The hardcore gangster lives the life of the warrior, a wild man always ready to attack the enemy. The member, on the other hand, is more level-headed and enjoys gang life primarily because of the fun and camaraderie. Finally, the affiliate lives in the neighborhood, wears the colors, and adheres to the rules, but shies away from any serious violence.[45]

Gangs are not something new. They have been around for well over a century, although we know little about ones that existed back in the nineteenth century. During the twentieth century, gangs have changed considerably, as Curry and Decker note. The modern gang era (beginning in the 1960s) has several characteristics that made it unlike the previous eras.

> In many ways, [gangs of the 1960s] represented a distinct break with the gangs of the 1890s and the 1920s. For the first time, significant numbers of racial minorities were involved in gang activities. . . . African Americans and Latinos were heavily represented in the gangs of the 1960s, and like their earlier counterparts, these individuals generally were located at the bottom of the social and economic ladders of American society. But . . . these new gangs were more extensively involved in criminal activity, especially violence. The availability of guns and automobiles gave these gangs more firepower and the mobility to interact with and fight gangs in neighborhoods across a city. The more extensive involvement in crime, in turn, led to increased convictions and prison time. As a consequence, the prison became an important site for the growth and perpetuation of gangs. . . . As prison gang members were released and returned to their communities, they brought gang ideology and practices with them. For cities like Los Angeles and Chicago, this helped produce intergenerational gangs. . . . Thus, many neighborhoods found themselves with gang members ("OGs," original gangsters) in their 30s and 40s.[46]

If we know what a gang is, then we should be able to count how many gangs there are. In recent decades, several criminologists have attempted to carry out such counts. What they have found suggests that the number has jumped dramatically over the past 30 years. Walter Miller got the process started in a modest way in 1975, when he polled local informants in a dozen cities across America. He found that six of them reported having a gang problem.[47]

By the mid- to late-1990s, the number of cities studied had expanded exponentially and so had the number of them thought to have a gang problem. Several criminologists had gotten involved in the estimation process by this time. But let's stick with Miller; in 1997 he estimated the number of cities with gang problems had reached 2,100. This is a great leap from his estimate just 22 years earlier. Part of the increase could be traced to the changing method (more cities surveyed), but it is widely assumed that most of the increase is real. Gangs sprouted up all over the place.

Naturally, not all gangs are alike. Because they vary in important dimensions, there have been a number of attempts to divide gangs into various types. Nowadays, one of the more useful typologies describes them as Traditional, Neotraditional, Compressed, Collective, and Specialty. Traditional gangs are the largest in size (they have the most members per gang, averaging around 200), with the longest continuing history, the most Hispanics, the widest range of ages, subgroups such as OGs, Seniors, Juniors, Midgets, and a strong emphasis on territoriality.

The Neotraditional gang has not been around as long, is not as large, but it, too, has subgroups and is territorial. Hence it appears headed toward becoming a Traditional gang a few years from now. Compressed gangs are much smaller (with under 50 members), no subgroups, and not a long history. What they will evolve into remains unclear at this point. They are important, though, because there are more Compressed gangs than any other type in America.

The Collective gang is a bit larger and has been around longer than the Compressed gang, but it still has not spawned any subgroups. It has a higher percentage of African Americans than the other four types. Like the Compressed gang, its future direction is still far from clear. Finally, Specialty gangs are the smallest of all in average size of membership, with no subgroups, a narrow age range, and a short history together. They generally focus on one activity, such as drugs, graffiti, or assault.

Gangs have been described as different from other groups because being part of a gang is a master status, the main criterion by which one defines oneself. Despite this strong identification with the gang, gangs are not very well organized, nor is the leadership well defined. Members typically are versatile, engaging in a series of offenses, including vandalism, theft, truancy, and fighting, rather than developing a specialization in one of these. Once a person becomes a member of a gang, this normally leads to an amplification of his criminal activity.[48]

Conclusion

The more time an adolescent spends socializing with peers, the more acts of crime and deviance he or she is apt to commit. This is the startling conclusion of the Monitoring the Future data produced by the University of Michigan researchers. The authors did not say that the peers the youth were hanging out with were already delinquent. They merely said that these were peers the youngster spends time with, engaging in ordinary teenage activities that in and of themselves were not suggestive of deviance or delinquency. This must be regarded as an important discovery.

As Thrasher noted almost a century ago in his study of juvenile gangs, delinquency often has its origin in small groups of (he said, slum) children at play in their neighborhoods; they are constantly searching for excitement. The same may be said today of youth who are *not* children, those in high school or junior high, whose idea of a good time is participating in rowdy, wild, loud, crazy antics together. They may get carried away, under the group's influence, and escalate to more serious offenses, which, later on, they regret having committed, especially if they get picked up by the police.

Early studies found that about 85 percent of delinquent offenses were committed by groups, usually very small ones, to be sure, with two, three, or four participants. (You may ask if it is reasonable to categorize two people as a group.) Later studies, relying on self-reports, reduced the figure to about 50 percent, when counting incidents instead of offenders. The few studies of adults indicate that their crimes are less likely to be committed with accomplices.

One of the hallmarks of juvenile crime is the lack of forethought and preparation. Youths fail to take the most basic precautions, and commit crimes that net them little in the way of financial reward. Also, they tend to get caught quite easily. Adults presumably are more careful and less foolhardy in planning their schemes. They are less apt to commit crimes purely on some spur-of-the-moment impulse (though of course there are many exceptions, such as alcoholics who rob liquor stores).

Does peer influence help to explain why males are more prone to crime and deviance than females? There is reason to suppose this is so. Boys engage in more of the unsupervised socializing (that sometimes leads to delinquency) than girls do, according to Monitoring the Future. Early maturing girls in coed schools are more delinquent than early maturers in girls' schools. In addition, boys encourage each other to participate in tasks filled with risk and danger so as to impress the girls. They are less likely to exert such pressure on the girls to do this.

Thomas Dishion and his colleagues at the Oregon Social Learning Center conducted an experiment involving delinquent, mixed, and nondelinquent male dyads. Delinquents (i.e., both boys had an official police record) were more likely to "rule break" during the 25-minute session and more likely to reinforce such behavior if their pal did it. Dishion found this kind of "deviancy training" led to an increase in offenses over the next two years. Such an escalation was most evident among the boys who were not close friends (that is, their friendship was of low quality, filled with bossiness and bickering, and apt to end on a sour note).

Dishion's research occurred in the 1990s. Other developmental psychologists in the 1980s had demonstrated that aggressive children, once they start school, will be rejected by their peers. Dishion, however, found that rejected boys can hang out with each other, because they're tolerant of aggression. Patterson meticulously demonstrated how little children were originally trained in their family interactions to become hostile and aggressive in the first place. The picture is thus complete: Patterson shows the original family pattern (becoming aggressive), 1980s psychologists show the reaction of peers at school (rejection), and Dishion shows the reaction of the aggressive boys to their rejection (they band together).

In the modern era, Mark Warr has emerged as the leading investigator of delinquent peers. He notes that parents are adamantly opposed to their children becoming delinquent and getting in trouble (this holds true even when the parents themselves are violators). But fellow adolescents view deviance far more tolerantly. And nowadays little time is spent with the family; even eating dinner together has become a thing of the past. More time is spent with peers in search of recreation. Teens want to be accepted by their peers; status and acceptance are precious assets, which they will go to great lengths to acquire. Sometimes this entails committing crimes to demonstrate heart, daring, and spontaneity. In the rapidly burgeoning world of gangs, this kind of behavior is especially evident.

Key Terms

Risky shift:	the tendency for groups to take greater risks than individuals would
Groupthink:	group members sense pressure to remain united and unanimous, which discourages independent thinking
Abilene Paradox:	there is outward acceptance of a group decision, although each person inwardly disagrees with it
Jack roller:	one who robs drunks
Ethnographic:	anthropological research providing a richly descriptive portrait of a small society or subculture
Active sociability:	going to parties, riding around in cars for fun, etc.
Androgens:	steroid hormones that control the development of masculine traits
Deviancy training:	boys engage in rule breaking, which is reinforced, leading to an escalation of crime and deviance later on
Nattering:	nagging, scolding, not saying "stop," and not backing up threats with actual punishment
Sane punishments:	taking away privileges and increasing chores; not beating
Symbolic interactionism:	social essence of a person lies in a continual process of personal definition and interpersonal negotiation about the social situation
Principle of homophily:	people prefer to spend time with others like themselves
Gang:	long-lasting, crime-committing group with symbols denoting membership and an elaborate system of communication

End Notes

[1]Clifford R. Shaw and Henry D. McKay, *Social Factors in Juvenile Delinquency* (Washington, DC: Government Printing Office, 1931), p. 191.

[2]Frederic M. Thrasher, *The Gang* (Chicago: University of Chicago Press, 1963 [1936]), p. 40.

[3]Roger Simon and Angie Cannon, "An Amazing Journey," *U.S. News and World Report* (August 6, 2001), pp. 10–8.

[4]Mihaly Csikszentmihalyi and Reed Larson, *Being Adolescent* (New York: Simon and Schuster, 1984), p. 168.

[5]Frederic M. Thrasher, *The Gang.*

[6]Roy Lotz and Leona Lee, "Sociability, School Experience, and Delinquency," *Youth and Society, 31,* no. 2 (December 1999), pp. 199–223.

[7]Robert Agnew, "The Origins of Delinquent Events," *Journal of Research in Crime and Delinquency, 27,* no. 3 (August 1990), pp. 267–94.

[8]Robert J. Sampson and John H. Laub, *Crime in the Making* (Cambridge, MA: Harvard University Press, 1993).

[9]William Healy and Augusta Bronner, *Delinquents and Criminals: Their Making and Unmaking* (New York: Macmillan, 1926); Clifford R. Shaw and Henry D. McKay, *Social Factors in Juvenile Delinquency;* Sheldon Glueck and Eleanor T. Glueck, *One Thousand Juvenile Delinquents* (Cambridge, MA: Harvard University Press, 1934); Belle Boone Beard, *Juvenile Probation* (New York: American Book Company, 1934); Norman Fenton, *The Delinquent Boy and the Correctional School* (Claremont, CA: Claremont College Guidance Center, 1935); William C. Kvaraceus, *Juvenile Delinquency and the School* (New York: World Book Company, 1945); Joseph D. Lohman, *Juvenile Delinquency* (Cook County, IL: Office of the Sheriff, 1957); Maynard L. Erickson, "The Group Context of Delinquent Behavior," *Social Problems, 19,* no. 1 (Summer 1971), pp. 114–29.

[10]Maynard L. Erickson, "The Group Context of Delinquent Behavior"; Maynard L. Erickson, "Group Violations and Official Delinquency," *Criminology, 11,* no. 2 (August 1973), pp. 127–60.

[11]Albert J. Reiss, Jr., "Co-Offending and Criminal Careers," in Michael Tonry and Norval Morris, eds., *Crime and Justice* (Chicago: University of Chicago Press, 1988), pp. 117–70.

[12]Peter B. Wood, Walter R. Gove, James A. Wilson, and John K. Cochran, "Nonsocial Reinforcement and Habitual Criminal Conduct," *Criminology, 35,* no. 2 (May 1997), pp. 335–66.

[13]Clifford R. Shaw, *The Jack Roller* (Chicago: University of Chicago Press, 1930).

[14]Early tests included James F. Short, Jr., "Differential Association and Delinquency," *Social Problems, 4,* no. 3 (January 1957), pp. 223–9; James F. Short, Jr., "Differential Association with Delinquent Friends and Delinquent Behavior," *Pacific Sociological Review, 1,* no. 1 (Spring 1958), pp. 20–5; Harwin Voss, "Differential Association and Reported Delinquent Behavior," *Social Problems, 12,* no. 1 (Summer 1964), pp. 78–85. Methodological criticisms may be found in Robert H. Aseltine, Jr., "A Reconsideration of Parental and Peer Influences on Adolescent Deviance," *Journal of Health and Social Behavior, 36,* no. 2 (June 1995), pp. 103–21; Steven Wilcox and J. Richard Udry, "Autism and Accuracy in Adolescent Perceptions of Friends' Sexual Attitudes and Behavior," *Journal of Applied Social Psychology, 16,* no. 4 (1986), pp. 361–74; Terence P. Thornberry and Marvin D. Krohn, "Peers, Drug Use, and Delinquency,"

in David M. Stoff, James Breiling, and Jack D. Maser, eds., *Handbook of Antisocial Behavior* (New York: Wiley, 1997), pp. 218–33; Michael R. Gottfredson and Travis Hirschi, *A General Theory of Crime* (Palo Alto, CA: Stanford University Press, 1990); Susan T. Ennet and Karl E. Bauman, "Peer Group Structure and Adolescent Cigarette Smoking," *Journal of Health and Social Behavior, 34,* no. 3 (September 1993), pp. 226–36; Lynn A. Fisher and Karl E. Bauman, "Influence and Selection in the Friend-Adolescent Relationship," *Journal of Applied Social Psychology, 18,* no. 4 (March 1988), pp. 289–314; Albert D. Farrell and Steven J. Danish, "Peer Drug Associations and Emotional Restraint," *Journal of Consulting and Clinical Psychology, 61,* no. 2 (April 1993), pp. 327–34.

[15]Ross L. Matsueda and Kathleen Anderson, "The Dynamics of Delinquent Peers and Delinquent Behavior," *Criminology, 36,* no. 2 (May 1998), pp. 269–308.

[16]Delbert S. Elliott and Scott Menard, "Delinquent Friends and Delinquent Behavior," in Darnell Hawkins, ed., *Delinquency and Crime* (New York: Cambridge University Press, 1996), pp. 28–67; Mark D. Reed and Pamela Wilcox Rountree, "Peer Pressure and Adolescent Substance Use," *Journal of Quantitative Criminology, 13,* no. 2 (June 1997), pp. 143–80; Terence P. Thornberry, Alan J. Lizotte, Marvin D. Krohn, Margaret Farnworth, and Sung Joon Jang, "Delinquent Peers, Beliefs, and Delinquent Behavior," *Criminology, 32,* no. 1 (February 1994), pp. 47–83.

[17]Mark D. Reed and Pamela Wilcox Rountree, "Peer Pressure and Adolescent Substance Use"; Robert Agnew, "A Longitudinal Test of Social Control Theory and Delinquency," *Journal of Research in Crime and Delinquency, 28,* no. 2 (May 1991), pp. 125–56.

[18]Mark D. Reed and Dina R. Rose, "Doing What Simple Simon Says," *Criminal Justice and Behavior, 25,* no. 2 (June 1998), pp. 240–74.

[19]Darrell Steffensmeier and Emilie Allan, "Looking for Patterns: Gender, Age, and Crime," in Joseph F. Sheley, ed., *Criminology,* 3rd ed. (Belmont, CA: Wadsworth, 2000), pp. 85–127; Scott J. South and Steven F. Messner, "Crime and Demography," *Annual Review of Sociology, 26* (2000), pp. 83–106; Dawn Jeglum Bartusch and Ross L. Matsueda, "Gender, Reflected Appraisals, and Labeling," *Social Forces, 75,* no. 1 (September 1996), pp. 145–76.

[20]Regina A. Arnold, "Processes of Criminalization from Girlhood to Womanhood," in Maxine B. Zinn and Bonnie T. Dill, eds., *Women of Color in American Society* (Philadelphia: Temple University Press, 1989), pp. 88–102; Jean Bottcher, "Gender as Social Control," *Justice Quarterly, 12,* no. 1 (March 1995), pp. 33–57; Eleanor M. Miller, *Street Woman* (Philadelphia: Temple University Press, 1986); Kim English, "Self-Reported Crime Rates of Women Prisoners," *Journal of Quantitative Criminology, 9,* no. 4 (December 1993), pp. 357–82.

[21]Jean Bottcher, "Gender as Social Control"; Meda Chesney-Lind and Randall G. Shelden, *Girls, Delinquency, and Juvenile Justice* (Pacific Grove, CA: Brooks/Cole, 1992); Jocelyn M. Pollock-Byrne, *Women, Prison, and Crime* (Belmont, CA: Wadsworth, 1990); Darrell Steffensmeier and Emilie Allan, "Gender, Age, and Crime," in Joseph F. Sheley, ed., *Criminology,* 2nd ed. (Belmont, CA: Wadsworth, 1995), pp. 83–113.

[22]D. Wayne Osgood, Janet K. Wilson, Patrick M. O'Malley, Jerald G. Bachman, and Lloyd D. Johnston, "Routine Activities and Individual Deviant Behavior," *American Sociological Review, 61,* no. 4 (August 1996), p. 652.

[23]Avshalom Caspi, Donald Lynam, Terrie E. Moffitt, and Phil A. Silva, "Unraveling Girls' Delinquency," *Developmental Psychology, 29,* no. 1 (January 1993), pp. 19–30.

[24]Carol Gilligan, *In a Different Voice* (Cambridge, MA: Harvard University Press, 1982).

[25]Daniel P. Mears, Matthew, Ploeger, and Mark Warr, "Explaining the Gender Gap in Delinquency," *Journal of Research in Crime and Delinquency, 35,* no. 3 (August 1998), pp. 251–66.

[26]J. Richard Udry, "Biological Limits of Gender Construction," *American Sociological Review, 65,* no. 3 (June 2000), pp. 443–57.

[27]Harry Stack Sullivan, *The Interpersonal Theory of Psychiatry* (New York: Norton, 1953).

[28]Frederick S. Foster-Clark and Dale A. Blyth, "Peer Relations and Influences," in Richard M. Lerner, Anne C. Petersen, and Jeanne Brooks-Gunn, eds., *Encyclopedia of Adolescence,* Volume two (New York: Garland, 1991), pp. 767–71; Willard W. Hartup, "Social Relationships and Their Developmental Significance," *American Psychologist, 44,* no. 2 (February 1989), pp. 120–6; James Youniss and Jacqueline Smollar, *Adolescent Relations with Mothers, Fathers, and Friends* (Chicago: University of Chicago Press, 1985).

[29]Donna Rae Clasen and B. Bradford Brown, "The Multidimensionality of Peer Pressure in Adolescence," *Journal of Youth and Adolescence, 14,* no. 6 (December 1985), pp. 451–68.

[30]John D. Coie and Janis B. Kupersmidt, "A Behavioral Analysis of Emerging Social Status in Boys' Groups," *Child Development, 54,* no. 6 (December 1983), pp. 1400–16; Kenneth A. Dodge, "Behavioral Antecedents of Peer Social Status," *Child Development, 54,* no. 6 (December 1983), pp. 1386–99.

[31]William M. Bukowski and Andrew F. Newcomb, "Stability and Determinants of Sociometric Status and Friendship Choice," *Developmental Psychology, 20,* no. 5 (September 1984), pp. 941–52; Janis B. Kupersmidt, Margaret Burchinal, and Charlotte J. Patterson, "Developmental Patterns of Childhood Peer Relations as Predictors of Externalizing Behavior Problems," *Development and Psychopathology, 7,* no. 4 (Fall 1995), pp. 824–43.

[32]David M. Fergusson, Lianne J. Woodward, and L. John Horwood, "Childhood Peer Relationship Problems and Young People's Involvement with Deviant Peers in Adolescence," *Journal of Abnormal Child Psychology, 27,* no. 5 (October 1999), pp. 357–69.

[33]Kathryn R. Wentzel and Cynthia A. Erdley, "Strategies for Making Friends," *Developmental Psychology, 29,* no. 5 (September 1993), pp. 819–26; Alice W. Pole and Karen L. Bierman, "Predicting Adolescent Peer Problems and Antisocial Activities," *Developmental Psychology, 35,* no. 2 (March 1999), pp. 335–46.

[34]Thomas J. Dishion, Francois Poulin, and Nani Medici Skaggs, "The Ecology of Premature Autonomy in Adolescence," in Kathryn A. Kerns, Josefina M. Contreras, and Angela M. Neal-Barnett, eds., *Family and Peers* (Westport, CT: Praeger, 2000), pp. 27–45; Francois Poulin, Thomas J. Dishion, and Eric Haas, "The Peer Influence

Paradox," *Merrill-Palmer Quarterly, 45,* no. 1 (January 1999), pp. 42–61; Thomas J. Dishion, Kathleen M. Spracklen, David W. Andrews, and Gerald R. Patterson, "Deviancy Training in Male Adolescent Friendships," *Behavior Therapy, 27,* no. 3 (Summer 1996), pp. 373–90; Thomas J. Dishion, Deborah Capaldi, Kathleen M. Spracklen, and Fuzhong Li, "Peer Ecology of Male Adolescent Drug Use," *Development and Psychopathology, 7,* no. 4 (Fall 1995), pp. 803–24.

[35]Gerald R. Patterson, *Coercive Family Process* (Eugene, OR: Castalia, 1982), p. 225.

[36]Ronald L. Akers, *Social Learning and Social Structure* (Boston: Northeastern University Press, 1998), p. 51.

[37]*Ibid.,* p. 164.

[38]Peter B. Wood, Walter R. Gove, James A. Wilson, and John K. Cochran, "Nonsocial Reinforcement and Habitual Criminal Conduct."

[39]Robert D. Putnam, *Bowling Alone* (New York: Simon and Schuster, 2000).

[40]Miller McPherson, Lyn Smith-Lovin, and James M. Cook, "Birds of a Feather," *Annual Review of Sociology, 27* (2001), pp. 415–44.

[41]John P. Robinson and Geoffrey Godbey, *Time for Life* (University Park: Pennsylvania State University Press, 1997).

[42]Mark Warr, *Companions in Crime* (New York: Cambridge University Press, 2002); Martin Gold, *Deviant Behavior in an American City* (Belmont, CA: Books/Cole, 1970); Charles A. Kiesler and Sara B. Kiesler, *Conformity* (Reading, MA: Addison-Wesley, 1970); Jerzy Sarnecki, *Delinquent Networks* (Stockholm: National Council for Crime Prevention, 1986).

[43]Ray Hutchison, "Blazon Nouveau: Gang Graffiti in the Barrios of Los Angeles and Chicago," in Scott Cummings and Daniel J. Monti, eds., *Gangs: The Origins and Impact of Contemporary Youth Gangs in the United States* (Albany: State University of New York Press, 1993), pp. 137–71.

[44]G. David Curry and Scott H. Decker, *Confronting Gangs* (Los Angeles: Roxbury, 1998).

[45]Ice T, *The Ice Opinion* (New York: St. Martin's, 1994).

[46]G. David Curry and Scott H. Decker, *Confronting Gangs,* p. 15.

[47]Walter B. Miller, *Violence by Youth Gangs and Youth Groups* (Washington, DC: U.S. Government Printing Office, 1975).

[48]Terence P. Thornberry, Marvin D. Krohn, Alan J. Lizotte, and Deborah Chard-Wierschem, "The Role of Juvenile Gangs in Facilitating Delinquent Behavior," *Journal of Research in Crime and Delinquency, 30,* no. 1 (February 1993), pp. 55–87; Sara B. Battin, Karl G. Hill, Robert D. Abbott, Richard F. Catalano, and J. David Hawkins, "The Contribution of Gang Membership to Delinquency Beyond Delinquent Friends," *Criminology, 36,* no. 1 (February 1998), pp. 93–115; Malcolm W. Klein, Hans-Jurgen Kerner, Cheryl L. Maxson, and Elmar G. M. Weitekamp, *The Eurogang Paradox* (Boston: Kluwer, 2001).

Recommended Readings

Mark Warr, *Companions in Crime* (New York: Cambridge University Press, 2002).
G. David Curry and Scott H. Decker, *Confronting Gangs* (Los Angeles: Roxbury, 1998).

Terence P. Thornberry, *Gangs and Delinquency in Developmental Perspective* (New York: Cambridge University Press, 2003).

Meda Chesney-Lind, *The Female Offender* (Thousand Oaks, CA: Sage, 1997).

Ronald L. Akers, *Social Learning and Social Structure* (Boston: Northeastern University Press, 1998).

Irving Spergel, *The Youth Gang Problem* (New York: Oxford University Press, 1995).

CHAPTER 10

The Police and Youth Crime

Traditional Police

America experimented with police forces in the 1840s and 1850s in several cities, such as New York, Philadelphia, and Boston. Departments were originally created because (1) cities had grown too large to control via night watchmen and constables and (2) they could not deal effectively with riots. Plus, fears of a "dangerous class," supposedly composed mostly of impoverished immigrants, also helped pave the way for the introduction of police. Previously, public fears had *discouraged* governments from forming such organizations (because citizens associated them with tyranny).

The police drew a regular salary, as high as $1,200 in some cities. This may seem trifling to people in today's world, but it was a princely sum back in the 1850s, in fact twice the income of most unskilled workers.[1] Because police forces were large in number and well paid, it didn't take very long for the city machines to realize that they were political plums—and to take advantage of the fact. Police functioned as agents of the political party in power at the time. This meant when that party was voted out of power, many of the police officers it had hired would immediately find themselves booted out of a job.

In addition, officers performed tasks that were for the benefit of the political machine. Machines were decentralized, with a boss running each ward, and that included naming the captain of that precinct (wards and precincts typically had the same boundaries). To secure his rank, the captain had to pay the ward boss a large fee; to maintain it, he had to carry out the boss's orders, which often meant protecting the businesses that the boss wanted left untouched (many of which were illicit). Occasionally, there were investigations and scandals, and the secrets were ex-posed to the entire city.

> Coaxed, prodded, and sometimes bullied . . . the witnesses told a shocking story.
> According to them, the police secured appointments and won promotions through
> political influence and cash payments. In return for regular payoffs, they protected
> gambling, prostitution, and other illicit enterprises. Officers extorted money from
> peddlers, storekeepers, and other legitimate businessmen who were hard pressed
> to abide by municipal ordinances. Detectives allowed con men, pickpockets, and
> thieves to go about their business in return for a share of the proceeds.[2]

In addition, police had many other responsibilities, including cleaning the streets, inspecting boilers, operating ambulances, and providing temporary shelter for the homeless (in the precinct stationhouses). More important, they controlled the way elections were handled, making sure the outcome was in favor of their party.

> Empowered to preserve order at the polls, the patrolman decided whether or not
> to reject repeaters from the lines, protect voters from the thugs, and respond to
> complaints by poll watchers and ballot clerks. If the officers abused their author-
> ity, the citizens had little or no recourse; the local judges were usually in sympa-
> thy with the organization, and by the time the state legislators had received a
> complaint, the election was long over. Whoever dominated the police could as-
> sign to the polls hundreds of tough, well-armed . . . men whose jobs . . . depended
> on the outcome.[3]

Many applicants to the police force were too old, too short, illiterate, seriously ill, or otherwise unfit, but if the ward boss wanted them, they were hired. After all, the people conducting the character checks and the physical testing were them-selves political appointees. Given the lack of oversight, the expectation of corrup-tion, and failure to winnow out the incompetent applicants, police were frequently not committed to their craft. Much of their time on the job was spent loafing. Instead of patrolling the streets, they could be found lounging in saloons, barbershops, bowling alleys, and pool halls, spending their tour eating, drinking, and gossip-ing.[4] This did not earn them much respect from the public.

The fact that some police beat up civilians was not universally regarded as shock-ing; many people (civilians as well as police) saw it as the policeman's job to ad-minister street justice with a few well-aimed blows via the nightstick. Few police were disciplined for excessive use of force. In rare cases, it became part of the offi-cer's identity. "Clubber" Williams was assigned a Broadway beat in 1868, and within two days he

> picked a fight with a pair of local toughs, clubbed them, and pitched them through
> the plate-glass window of a saloon for an encore. When a half dozen of their bud-
> dies emerged, they too were beaten unconscious. For the next four years, he was
> said to have averaged a fight a day.[5]

This kind of notoriety did not prevent Clubber from ascending to the rank of captain.

Police Reform and the Professional Model

Traditional policing entailed walking an assigned beat. The cop was on his own, rarely supervised, able to run his post as he saw fit. He could engage in violence or he could do no work at all. Every ten or twenty years, there would be investigations of police corruption, exposés of scandalous abuses, and calls for reform. Sometimes the exposés led to the election of a new mayor and the appointment of a new police commissioner who was committed to creating a squeaky clean department.

These new commissioners and mayors, although initially popular, often lost favor after a while because sizable proportions of the urban populace longed for the gambling, prostitution, drinking, and other vices that flowed freely under the regimes of the previous mayors. The result was that in a few years, the old-style bosses were returned to city hall, and once they were reinstalled in power, they brought back their police captains, who put the gamblers and pimps back in business again. Departments were as crooked as the tombstones in an old graveyard. One police commissioner, however, had more impact than others (Exhibit 10-1).

Exhibit 10-1   Orlando Wilson and Professional Police Management

In 1921, when he was a student at Berkeley, Orlando W. Wilson needed cash and answered an ad for patrolmen. That was how he met August Vollmer, a giant in the field of police reform and an important influence on young Wilson. From there Orlando moved on to become police chief in Fullerton, California, Wichita, Kansas, then Dean of the School of Criminology at Berkeley, and finally chief of police in Chicago.

Wilson intended to fight crime and suppress vice, and he had no tolerance for officers or supervisors who were incompetent, corrupt, or disloyal. He would brook no interference from the mayor or city council or anyone else. He wrote all the rules for the department, established a rigid chain of command, and made sure the troops out in the field were closely supervised. Wilson supplemented them with the most modern equipment, college-educated personnel, intense training, and advanced communication systems. As chief, he demanded a free hand to sweep out the deadwood.

Upon being hired, Wilson took charge and immediately eliminated most of the foot patrols, which he considered inefficient. He assigned as many officers as possible to one-person patrol cars, then put detectives he could trust in special divisions such as armed robbery, larceny, burglary, auto theft, juvenile crime, and vice. He was constantly replacing veteran officers with younger, more intelligent, more educated personnel.[6]

Later on, Wilson's model of **professional** police would be expanded by other police chiefs to include 911 systems, which enabled a rapid response by cars in the field; they raced to the scene after being alerted by the dispatcher at a central communications center, in hopes of catching the criminal redhanded. Eventually, research in Kansas City found that rapid response resulted in an arrest only in 3 percent of serious crimes.[7] This conclusion was no fluke; replications in other cities led to the same results: less than 3 percent of rapid responses to serious crimes produced an arrest.[8] The police were getting there quickly all right; the problem was that citizens often waited half an hour or so before notifying them. Some victims hesitated because they were in shock and it took a while to regain their bearings. In other cases, the crime was not discovered until hours after it occurred. Following this research, doubts grew in police circles regarding the wisdom of the rapid response strategy.

Furthermore, people began to question why police should be spending all their time riding around in the comfort of an air-conditioned or heated car. Instead of talking with citizens, getting to know them personally, police were isolated, cooped up in their cruisers, cut off from the community they were serving. No relationship of trust could be built this way. Instead, people began to see the police as nameless, faceless intruders, exiting their car, brusquely carrying out their tasks and jumping back in. Such actions were bound to alienate the citizenry.

Community Policing

One of the strongest critics of the professional model was George Kelling. In 1982 he and James Q. Wilson wrote an article for the *Atlantic Monthly* called "Broken Windows."[9] In it, they argued that the professional model was too concerned with serious crime, and it failed to deal with disorder and minor violations. The authors believed that disorder in a community leads to an increase in public fear, a retreat by locals from the stores and streets, leaving these spots to be taken over by more unsavory characters, which leads to a decline in the quality of life and a rise in the rate of crime. The authors recommended a return to the old days of cops walking a beat, getting to know residents.

Some of this argument was compatible with the notion of **community policing,** which is a new philosophy of police and community—cooperating with each other to work on the problems besetting the community. What the police would like to do is to remake the world into a small town like the fictional Mayberry of the *Andy Griffith Show,* where everybody knew the sheriff and the deputy on a friendly, first-name basis, and the problems that inevitably cropped up were quickly identified by the community, reported to the sheriff, and solved cooperatively before they had a chance to get out of hand.[10]

Community policing includes three components: strategic policing, neighborhood policing, and problem-oriented policing. **Strategic policing** identifies problem areas and mobilizes police resources to drive out the drug dealers, prostitutes, or other criminals or causes of disorder so that the community can take over and reestablish order. Who identifies what a problem is? Under community policing, both community and police have their say. The community is represented at the roundtable discussion by local business leaders; someone from the school board or housing association perhaps; people from political, social, and religious associations; and individuals who stand up for the common man or woman of the community. Along with police brass and rank and file, they meet regularly to discuss the problems that concern them.

Police may respond to the problems with aggressive patrol, which includes field stops, traffic stops, plainclothes details, stings, or stakeouts. Or they may rely on saturation patrol. Under this tactic, police from various units and shifts (tactical, traffic, and investigation) put on the uniform and converge on the area as a show of force for about three days. Then they withdraw for a few weeks and assess the response. If the problem resurfaces, the police repeat their tactic.

Neighborhood policing means every police officer tries to maintain a good relationship with the community. Thus every officer (not just those in the juvenile division) must take it upon himself or herself to establish a working relationship with the juveniles on the beat, to draw community support. Under this concept, the neighborhood sets the priorities for the police; it decides which high-crime areas to target. The neighborhood functions like a board of directors, deciding whether to use foot patrols, bike controls, or mini-stations to lower crime, disorder, and fear. The community may also focus on crime prevention through block watch, operation ID, and home security surveys.

Problem-oriented policing grows out of dissatisfaction with earlier forms of policing that were very concerned with management and procedures, very passive (waiting for a phone call from victims to respond), yet reluctant to use the community to help *solve* problems. Problem-oriented policing begins by noticing that one area is suffering from a cluster of similar incidents (say, a gas station has many complaints about robberies, gang members hanging out, and panhandling). Then the community becomes concerned about this and wants something done about it. Finally, the police are called in for talks on how to deal with it. Discussions focus on the impact the problem has on the community, the identification of the most serious threat posed, and the amount of interest the community has in dealing with the problem. The police work with the community members to develop a workable plan of action.

How would these different kinds of police organization affect the way juveniles are handled? This is an important question, because juveniles and police are bound to see a lot of each other. One reason for this frequent contact is that adolescents are not as secretive about their acts of deviance as adult offenders are. They may think they won't get caught or, if caught, won't receive any significant punishment. Also, kids commit some of the more unsophisticated crimes and employ little skill in doing so. Third, they tend to commit their offenses out in the open or as part of a group, which makes them visible to citizens and easier to detect. Finally, many of their misdeeds are spur-of-the-moment, not clever or planned in advance.

In the traditional mode of policing, juveniles would be warned, growled at, and shooed off the corner by the blustery cop walking the beat, occasionally slapped around if the cop had a tendency toward abuse, maybe turned over to the family or the parish priest, but probably would not be arrested. In the olden days, kids were usually considered minor nuisances rather than threats. And if there were a foot race, the old cop was certainly no match for the speedy kids with their broken-field running. When arrests were made, they typically involved police grabbing older men who were easier to catch, particularly those who were drunk and disorderly.

In the professional department, too, arresting juveniles was something the police typically avoided if they could, for juveniles were still considered trivial offenders. Hence the cop seen bringing a youth into the precinct was apt to be ridiculed for wasting his time on insignificant, penny ante activity. Not wanting to face embarrassing comments from his peers, the typical officer steered clear of this kind of case. He preferred to arrest someone who was considered a serious offender by the rest of the department and thus a *real* threat. Best to leave youngsters to the special unit designed for that purpose: the **juvenile bureau**.

What does a juvenile bureau actually do? In large cities that have special bureaus, there may be specialists in vice, investigation, and juveniles. The officers in the juvenile bureau usually have had some college education with a few courses in child development, adolescence, parent-child relations, and so on. The juvenile unit is responsible for investigating any offenses thought to have been committed by minors. Plus, they look into status offenses (such as running away) and cases in which children have been victimized (neglect, abuse, sexual abuse). The juvenile unit is trained to deal with youths by sending them to the appropriate social service agencies in the community or counseling the youths and their parents and developing programs aimed at reducing youth crime.

The professional department replaces cops walking a beat with patrol cars and rapid response to citizen calls for help. But this does not endear the police to the youngsters in the neighborhood. Youths do not know the police personally. Nor do the police know the youths personally. Citizens who call up the police may complain about kids who are merely annoying, not actually committing any crimes. The police are reluctant to intervene; they resent the complainant calling over such a minor incident. But they do intervene, and this antagonizes the youngsters. Critics argue that rapid reaction by impersonal police does not work very well either as crime control or as order maintenance.[11]

In community policing, arrests are sometimes considered a good tactic, sometimes not. The police may arrest a juvenile suspect, but more often they use their **discretion** not to (unless the offense is considered very serious). Ideally, what the officer on the beat would like to do is get to know everyone on the beat, including the at-risk youth and their families, so that when a crime occurs, the officer can go to their home and ask them to help, to tell him what they know about the case, who's involved, where the offender can be found.

This is the kinder, gentler side of community policing. But there is a tougher side to this style of policing too. Citizens consider some situations to be problematic, and they want police to wipe them out with quick strikes at the targets. When police act in that fashion, they are bound to rub some people in the neighborhood the wrong way, including the youngsters rounded up in the sweep or their friends and relatives who soon learn about it. The fact is that any neighborhood has diverse interests: some people want to eliminate drug dealing, prostitution, after-hours clubs, public rowdiness, and gatherings of ominous-looking young males. Others may want these to be left alone, on the grounds that nobody is being hurt and some people actually find these behaviors enjoyable.

We have thus far been assuming that all police are alike in a department, all of them following the lead of the chief. But of course this is not true. In a department there will be considerable variation in working styles from one officer to the next. This variation has been captured by Randolph Grinc, who described members of the Newark, New Jersey, police. He identified five types: the Crime Fighter, the Law Enforcer, the Community-Oriented Welfare Worker, the Professional, and the Ritualist. We will consider the first three of these.

Crime Fighters are often younger than the average officer. More aggressive than most, they thirst for the excitement associated with apprehending dangerous criminals who commit major crimes: homicide, robbery in progress, narcotics, or sexual assault. Because their interest lies in serious cases, crime fighters prefer to ignore minor misdemeanors or service calls, which they view as not real police work. Therefore they consciously avoid family disputes and drunkenness by adults and small amounts of marijuana possession and loitering by juveniles. Crime fighters consider those more appropriate for someone doing social work, a line of work that macho cops disdain.

If youthful offenders are often sensation seekers motivated by a search for thrills, the same thing could be said of crime fighters. Many applicants to the police department are turned down because they have a record of felony arrests; others lack a record but still yearn for life on the edge.

> How does one explain the raw excitement of being a cop? All five senses are involved, especially in dangerous situations. They are stirred in a soup of emotions and adrenaline and provide a rush that surpasses anything felt before. . . . It is an addictive feeling that makes the runner's high in comparison feel like a hangover.[12]

Law Enforcers, too, value crime control more than order maintenance or service, but they do not sneer at nuisance cases such as possessing marijuana. Instead, they contend that arresting people for trivial or "quality of life" offenses prevents future crimes of greater seriousness; it sends a message no crime is going to be tolerated. Law enforcers do not consider themselves guidance counselors, though, so when they make arrests they do not moralize or lecture kids on the error of their ways.

Community-Oriented Welfare Workers (CWWs) are decidedly rare in Newark and perhaps other urban departments too. Instead of being devoted to major crimes or strict enforcement, they focus on helping people solve their problems. These cops make excellent public relations officers and may be involved in activities like the Police Athletic League. Although other police hate working with juveniles, CWWs enjoy this and seek out juveniles in their sector to establish rapport with them. When there is an opportunity to make an arrest, CWWs are more apt to counsel or attempt to reason with the youthful offender. As you might imagine, in the high-testosterone world of policing, CWWs are not admired by their fellow officers; instead, Grinc found, they are usually held up to ridicule.[13]

Attitudes Toward the Police

In the 1960s, the Commission on Law Enforcement and the Administration of Justice investigated the attitudes and opinions the American public held about crime, justice, and various elements of the criminal justice system. The sixties, you will recall, witnessed considerable ferment and unrest, with the civil rights movement, the war in

Vietnam, the assassinations of John Kennedy, Robert Kennedy, and Martin Luther King, Jr., and riots in major cities. Police were often at the center of controversy and in some cases were much criticized for the way they handled incidents.

Researchers took it for granted that the public would hold harsh views of police, would consider them incompetent at crime control and unskilled at dealing with witnesses, victims, suspects, and others encountered on the job. They were surprised to find that as a whole citizens harbored more goodwill than animosity toward the police. In three precincts in Washington, D. C., 85 percent of respondents said police deserve a lot more thanks and respect than they get from the public. "The single most outstanding finding concerning attitudes toward the police was . . . the generally high regard for the police among all groups."[14]

Police in more recent times continue to be regarded in a positive light by most Americans. For instance, the Gallup organization frequently asks the public how much confidence it has in various institutions. From March 1993 to June 2001, the three institutions achieving the highest ratings were always the military, organized religion, and the police. They were rated higher than the presidency and the Supreme Court and much higher than Congress, big business, organized labor, and the criminal justice system. Moreover, police received higher evaluations in the United States and Canada than in other countries. When it comes to solving social problems, Americans have more faith in police than in churches.

But this is not to say there's a blanket endorsement of police by the entire nation. Attitudes and opinions vary from group to group. This was clear in the crime commission studies in the late 1960s (despite the last quote presented) and remains just as evident today. Whites express the most satisfaction with the police, followed by nonblack minorities, and finally by African Americans. Blacks are considerably more likely than whites to express critical views.

1. They are far more dissatisfied than whites with the criminal justice system in America.
2. They are far more likely than whites to regard police protection in black neighborhoods as worse than in white neighborhoods.
3. Few whites say they have been treated unfairly because of their race. In contrast, about 40 percent of blacks say they have been.
4. Is police racism against blacks *very* common? Over 40 percent of blacks think so (a percentage four times higher than among whites).

In a 1997 study of Toronto citizens, Wortly, Hagan, and Macmillan found that black respondents perceived more injustice by police and judges than Chinese or white respondents did. This was true on 10 out of 12 items measuring perceived injustice. Even when the items referred to how police and judges treat Chinese people, black respondents perceived more injustice than the Chinese themselves did. Black respondents who were university-educated and had been stopped by the police during the past two years were the ones most likely to perceive injustice.

Other sources, too, have found black middle and upper classes more critical than lower-class blacks. Better-educated African Americans are more apt than less-educated blacks to disapprove of **racial profiling** and say they've experienced it personally. Compared to poorer blacks, prosperous African Americans are less likely to believe in the American dream, more likely to believe that American society is racist. Successful blacks are more apt than other blacks to say the economic condition of African Americans is much worse than that of whites. They also are more impatient than lower-class African Americans with the pace of progress being made in civil rights.[15]

One article, however, seemed to contradict all of the others. This research found that blacks hold more favorable attitudes toward the police than whites do. How could this be true? Well, a few cities in America have experienced an influx of African Americans in recent decades and an exodus of whites, radically transforming the cities' racial composition. In the most extreme case, Detroit, blacks went from 9 percent of the population in 1940 to 76 percent in 1990. Coleman Young was elected mayor in 1973, and he not only recruited black officers to the force but required that one African American be promoted every time a white officer was and named an African American to be the police chief. Survey research in 1996 showed that blacks in Detroit were more satisfied with the police than whites were, more apt to say police were doing a good job controlling the street sale and use of illegal drugs, and more apt to say police were doing a good job keeping order on the streets and sidewalks.[16]

Although race has usually been a good predictor of support for police and evaluation of police ability to solve crime and treat citizens in a fair and friendly manner, it is not the only variable that predicts opinions about police. Age, too, makes an impact. Several explanations of why this is so have been offered. Older citizens are more fearful, less able to fight off offenders, and thus more dependent on police to intervene. People under the age of fifty are less religious, more moderate politically, and more likely to have attended some college, all of which make people more likely to believe there's police brutality. Younger people place great store by personal freedom and get ticked off when police tell them what to do.[17] But data cited so far are based on the study of adults, so the comparison of older respondents with younger ones is based on a **truncated sampling** of age groups because teenagers are generally excluded. When we turn to studies in which teenagers *are* included in samples, we find that the police are indeed regarded less favorably. This holds true for blacks and whites and continues to exist when respondents' extent of victimization, number of police contacts, social class, and conservatism are controlled for. Young people are more likely to view police as unfair, unfriendly, and unhelpful.[18]

The police are the visible symbol of the entire system, standing out on the front lines. Most juveniles who have any interaction with criminal or juvenile justice officials will have it with the police only, not judges, probation or parole officers, or officials in a jail, prison, or other corrections setting. Juvenile contacts with the police may leave long-lasting impressions, coloring the attitudes of youth toward the police and the rest of the system for years afterward.[19] On the other hand, juvenile attitudes toward the police may reflect other social forces, such as the individual's race, family, or neighborhood.

Normally, studies of juvenile attitudes toward the police are based on samples of high school students. But Leiber, Nalla, and Farnworth (1998) decided it would be more useful to examine delinquents in training schools, detention centers, group homes, and treatment centers because they have much more contact with police than most youths. The authors hypothesized that attitudes toward the police would be affected by three factors: their social environment (minority/majority status, family's economic condition, family structure, and type of neighborhood), delinquent subculture (delinquent attitudes and delinquent behavior), and police–juvenile interactions (warned and released, taken to police station, and wrongly accused). They expected that social environment and delinquent subculture would affect juvenile attitudes toward police both directly and indirectly (through their impact on police contact).

They found some support for this in their data from four counties in Iowa. Delinquent subculture had the strongest effect on all three attitudes toward the police: respect for police, belief in police fairness, and belief in police discrimination. The subculture variables were most effective in predicting respect for police. The kids with the least respect for police were those with delinquent attitudes, those from a high-crime neighborhood, those who had engaged in more delinquent behavior, and those most often taken to the police station. Thus, delinquent subculture plays an important role in determining attitudes toward the police. When the authors analyzed the data separately for black juveniles and white juveniles, they found that for white juveniles frequently being warned and released (hassled?) generated less respect for police, whereas for black juveniles respect for police declined the more often they were taken to the police station (the most severe sanction).[20]

Another major recent investigation of juvenile attitudes toward the police was conducted by Hurst, in Cincinnati high schools, where she found that unlike adults, juveniles don't view police very favorably. Most of them do not like the police, trust the police, or think they're effective at preventing crime. This negative view once again was more pronounced among African-American students than among whites. Most students said they had some contact with the police during the past year; only 12 percent reported no such encounter. Whether it was an arrest or a call for help, adolescents who felt they were not treated well had a jaundiced view of the police. Students who had a dim view of the rest of the criminal justice system also regarded the police negatively; this view of the system was the strongest predictor of attitudes toward the police. And finally, juveniles witnessing or hearing about police misconduct toward someone else (such as rudeness or physical abuse) were usually moved by such vicarious experience to regard police unfavorably.[21]

What about the police? How do they regard their job, their dealings with the public, the law, their relationships with supervisors and management? The early literature on these issues painted an unflattering portrait of cops. Perhaps the best known of these is William Westley's poetic description of them in the late 1940s.

> The duties of the policeman bring him into contact with greatly varied portions of the public. . . . Mostly he meets them in their evil, their sorrow, and their degradation and defeat. . . . He sees this public as a threat. . . . In spite of his ostensible function as protector, he usually meets only those he is protecting them from. . . . The fight in the bar, the driver in a hurry, the bickering mates, the cutters of edges

and finders of angles. . . . To them he is the law, the interfering one, dangerous and a source of fear. He is the disciplinarian, a symbol in brass and blue, irritating, a personal challenge, an imminent defeat and punishment. To him they are the public, an unpleasant job, a threat, the bad ones, unpleasant and whining, self-concerned, uncooperative, and unjust.[22]

Since the 1940s, police departments have become more professional, officers more educated, with higher occupational prestige, and therefore police attitudes and beliefs about the public (one would think) ought to have improved. But there is some evidence that as recently as the late 1970s, police were still an insular group, whose unstated rules still reflected widespread distrust.

Don't give up another cop.

Show balls. In the macho terminology of police, this means don't back down in front of civilians.

Don't trust a new guy until you have checked him out. This is further evidence of the police tendency toward suspicion.

Don't tell anyone more than they have to know. In the Mafia, this would be called omerta; it is one way of avoiding trouble.

Protect your ass. You cannot count on other people in the department to cover for you.

Don't make waves. This means don't do anything that calls attention to you, and don't ask embarrassing questions of the brass.[23]

Reuss-Ianni said the police assigned to the South Bronx in the 1970s encountered a particularly depressing physical and social landscape, which conditioned their views of minorities. Police prejudice has been often noted, and sometimes it has been attributed to their conservative family background. The cops, however, say their hostile attitude toward minorities is learned on the job.[24] Reuss-Ianni also studied officers in a wealthy white area on Manhattan's East Side and found that police still complained about citizens, but in this case it was because the cops were looked down on by people who thought they were better than the police. These citizens could get on the phone to the mayor or the police chief and complain about some officer who did something that displeased them.

Demeanor and Police-Juvenile Encounters

What happens in the field when police and juveniles confront each other? How do juveniles respond when police stop them? How do police respond to the juveniles who are irked at police for interfering with their lives? The literature on these issues began in 1964 with an exploratory article by Piliavin and Briar, who said that juvenile officers had considerable discretion. They were expected to take into account not only the seriousness of the juvenile's offense but also his character, which was inferred from various cues, such as group affiliation, age, race, grooming, clothing, and **demeanor**.

Older juveniles, members of known delinquent gangs, blacks, youths with well-oiled hair, black jackets, and soiled denims or jeans (the presumed uniform of "tough" boys), and boys who in their interactions with officers did not manifest what were considered to be appropriate signs of respect tended to receive the more severe dispositions.[25]

Youths who were contrite and respectful toward the cops were often admonished and released, whereas the stubborn and hot-headed kids were considered punks who deserved the strongest sanction available: arrest. Black juveniles were more often stopped and interrogated than whites, because more of them fit the delinquent stereotype. Most police back then admitted disliking blacks, too; they said it stemmed from black juveniles being less cooperative and less remorseful about the offenses they committed.

So the police management decided that the high-crime areas where black juveniles hung out should be flooded with more cops, which led them to accost more of these youths. This **proactive** position in turn led the juveniles to become either more hostile toward the police or to act nonchalant (to regard the encounters as normal routine). These responses led police to regard such youths as more seriously delinquent, leading to closer surveillance. A vicious circle arose, including more prejudice, more surveillance, more encounters, more hostility, and more distrust.

Not long afterward, in the summer of 1966, Yale scholars Black and Reiss studied police encounters with juveniles in racially homogeneous, high-crime neighborhoods of Chicago, Boston, and Washington, D.C. They discovered that most police encounters with juvenile suspects (72 percent) were citizen initiated (that is, citizens call up the department to report an incident and the dispatcher sends out a patrol car), not police initiated (cops on patrol observe an incident and take some action). Officers were largely **reactive**, dependent on the citizens' moral standards and willingness to get involved.

Once on the scene, patrol officers found that only 5 percent of the incidents involved a felony. The rest were no more serious than youthful rowdiness (what for adults would be classified as disorderly conduct). In addition, most cases did not result in the suspect's arrest; the great majority of youths, 85 percent, were let go, not arrested. But this varied by the race of the suspect, for 21 percent of black suspects were arrested, compared to only 8 percent of white suspects. Only part of this difference was due to black youths committing more serious offenses.

Black and Reiss found that complainants play an important role in the outcome of cases. In these homogeneous neighborhoods, the suspect and complainant were always of the same race. Complainants in a number of cases expressed their opinion about what should be done with the youth (whether he should be arrested or let go). When police were alone (there was no complainant around), they were more likely to arrest a black youth than a white one, but the difference was fairly small: 14 percent versus 10 percent (excluding felonies, traffic cases, and noncriminal disputes). When complainants were around, the police arrested 21 percent of black juveniles but only 8 percent of white kids. Why the difference? In part (Black and Reiss said) it was because black complainants were more likely to be undecided or

Often the interaction between teens and police has an undertone of confrontation to it. In some cases, the police decide to make an arrest. *(Andrew Lichtenstein/ Aurora & Quanta Productions Inc.)*

to prefer an arrest than white complainants, who generally wanted the boy to be released. Police paid attention to the preferences expressed by the complainants. Usually, when complainants wanted the juvenile to be arrested, police complied with their wishes. When complainants lobbied for the suspect to be freed, police *always* complied. Thus, complainants had a potent impact on the police disposition of these cases. This proved costly in the case of black juveniles because they were confronted with a less lenient, less forgiving set of complainants. Therefore, African-American youngsters ended up getting arrested more often.

Studies of more recent vintage find that police grant the complainant's most restrictive request 70 percent of the time. But several factors impinge on the police decision; when the complainant asks for the suspect to be arrested, police hesitate to go along with this request. Also, police are less willing to comply if the suspect and complainant have a close relationship or if the complainant is surly, drunk, or mentally ill. Race, wealth, and the complainant's organizational affiliation do not have a noticeable impact on the police officer's willingness to comply with their request.

What about the role of the juvenile's demeanor—what effect does it have on the police decision to arrest or not? Unlike Piliavin and Briar, Black and Reiss divided demeanor into *three* categories: antagonistic, **civil**, and very deferential. They found that juveniles who were antagonistic or disrespectful toward the police were more likely to be arrested than those who were civil. You may say this is obvious and common sense. But Black and Reiss also discovered something *unexpected:* the very deferential youths also got arrested more than kids who were civil. Why the most respectful youths got arrested more often, no one knows. (We can only speculate: perhaps they were obviously guilty and their being nice was viewed by the officers as a desperate ploy to avoid arrest.) Nearly all of these findings by Black and Reiss were replicated a few years later in another city by Lundman, Sykes, and Clark.[26]

In the Black and Reiss data, 16 percent of the juvenile suspects who were civil toward the police were arrested, as were 22 percent of very deferential juveniles and 22 percent of antagonistic ones. But juveniles were only a small part of the overall study in Boston, Chicago, and Washington. Robert Friedrich reanalyzed the data for the *entire* sample (that is, adults plus juveniles) of encounters with police. He found that 15 percent of suspects who were civil got arrested, compared to 17 percent of the very deferential and 33 percent of the antagonistic. This suggests that demeanor is important for the entire sample, and that antagonism is considerably more likely to result in an arrest than deference or civility.

But there are many additional variables that may affect a suspect's chances of getting arrested. These include the offender's age, sex, race, and social class, the seriousness of the offense, the complainant's preference, the number of citizens on the scene, the number of police there, and so on. When all of these variables are included in a multiple regression, the demeanor of the suspect becomes far less influential. Instead of antagonistic suspects having a *much* greater chance of being arrested than other suspects, the difference withers away to almost *nothing* (4 percent). So, demeanor per se actually has a minimal impact on the decision to arrest. Far more significant than any other factor is how serious the offense is.[27]

Naturally, we would like to be able to cite more recent findings, and fortunately, such data exist in an unpublished paper by Worden and Myers, who studied police on patrol in Indianapolis, Indiana, and St. Petersburg, Florida, during the late 1990s. Like earlier work, they found that most police-juvenile encounters involved relatively minor offenses such as disorderly conduct and shoplifting. But unlike previous research, they discovered a fairly substantial portion of the cases were initiated by the police (especially in Indianapolis, where a curfew was in force).

Table 10-1 shows what police decided to do with the juvenile and adult suspects they encountered. According to these data, adults were more likely to be released (the most lenient option that police had), whereas juveniles were more likely to be subjected to police bluster, threats, and commands (the second most severe option

TABLE 10-1   How Cases are Disposed of in Police Encounters with Juveniles and Adults[28]

Disposition	Juveniles	Adults
Release	18.5%	22.5%
Advise	10.4	9.4
Search/interrogate	25.1	26.5
Command/threaten	33.2	27.5
Arrest	13.1	14.2
Total	100.3%	100.1%

TABLE 10-2   Odds of a Juvenile Being Arrested in an Encounter with Police[29]

	All Encounters	Police Initiated
Male (vs. female)	2.33	7.69*
Minority (vs. white)	1.19	2.09
Crime serious (vs. not)	1.93*	2.59*
Strong evidence (vs. none)	5.82*	12.19*
Disrespect (vs. none)	2.17	1.46

*Means significant at the .05 level of probability.

available). In the present era, it appears, cops no longer treat kids with kid gloves. They get handled as severely as or more severely than adults.

The Worden and Myers study also reveals which factors have the greatest impact on whether police will arrest a juvenile suspect. Table 10-2 gives the odds of arrest when various risk factors are taken into account: the juvenile's gender, the juvenile's race or ethnicity, the seriousness of the offense committed, the strength of the evidence against the suspect, and the juvenile's demeanor toward the police.

When all juvenile encounters with police are included, the most important predictor of arrest is the strength of the evidence. If the case against the youth is strong, then police are six times more likely to make an arrest than if the evidence is flimsy. In police-initiated cases, however, two variables have a very strong effect on the odds of getting arrested: powerful evidence and a suspect who's male. Demeanor and race/ethnicity do not have a statistically significant impact on the odds of being arrested.

Race and Police-Juvenile Encounters

How important is race in the decision to arrest? Friedrich's massive dissertation looked at this issue as well and found the data to be complex and counterintuitive. For instance, arrests were most likely to result if the police officer was black. This held true regardless of the race of the suspect.

Black officer/black suspect   25.4% arrested
White officer/black suspect   21.2%
Black officer/white suspect   17.1%
White officer/white suspect   13.3%

(It should be noted that there weren't many cases of black officers encountering white suspects, however, because most black officers during the 1960s were assigned to largely black parts of the city.)

In the 1960s, white police varied in the amount of prejudice they felt toward African Americans: their attitudes toward blacks ranged from very negative to negative to neutral to positive. But overall, they leaned toward the negative end of the spectrum. Almost none (2.4 percent) of the white officers felt positively about blacks; on the other hand almost one-fourth (23.2 percent) were very negative in their attitudes toward blacks, and the majority of white police were negative (54.2 percent). Another one-fifth were categorized by Friedrich as neutral.

If prejudice was rife in the departments of America's big cities back in the 1960s, how did this translate into behavior in the field? Do racial attitudes of white police affect the chances that they will arrest black suspects? Not surprisingly, Friedrich found the answer was yes. Officers with a *very negative* view of blacks often arrested black suspects (over 27 percent of the time). The likelihood of arrest declined as racial attitudes improved: *negative* white cops arrested 19 percent of black suspects, neutral cops arrested 17 percent.

If the suspect was black and he behaved in a negative manner toward the white cop, there was a 23 percent chance he would be arrested—unless the cop had a positive attitude toward blacks in general. Strangely, if the cop held a positive attitude toward blacks in general, he was *twice* as likely to arrest the suspect. How could this odd finding be explained? According to Friedrich, white police who regard blacks (as a group) favorably have higher expectations of them. Such cops are then especially upset when an individual African-American suspect acts surly toward them. So they are more likely in such cases to make an arrest.[30]

Police Subculture

Over the years, comprehensive analyses of the police in America have consistently invoked the notion of a police subculture. This implies that the police feel that there is a wide gap that separates them from the public they serve. This point of view identifies police as suspicious, distrusting the public, and convinced people don't appreciate the men and women in blue. Because of this, police become **insular**; off the job, they spend a good deal of their time hanging out with their fellow officers, who of course do understand and do appreciate police work (and hence they can carry on a sympathetic discussion of the daily life that officers experience).

Recently, however, Steve Herbert has called these analyses into question and implied that the portrait they present is overdrawn. He contends that police behavior in uniform is often a reflection of other factors, namely, written law, bureaucratic control, adventure (or machismo), safety, competence, and morality. For instance, the law sets forth what police powers and responsibilities are and what techniques can be used (and what cannot). In the field, police face several choices of action; often they rely on their understanding of the law to make the decision, particularly in a department that regards itself as professional. Law legitimizes the entire department, shapes police actions, and is later used to justify them. This also applies to police use of force, which is usually based on legally justified factors, such as resistance by the suspect or safety threats. (On the other hand, police treat males, nonwhites, and young and poor suspects worse, regardless of the suspects' behavior.)

Bureaucratic control involves regulations created by upper management to make cops on the beat behave uniformly (that is, to go by the book) and therefore avoid getting into messy incidents that are played up by the media and give the department a reputation as brutal, corrupt, or incompetent. Failure to live up to departmental guidelines is often met with more severe sanctions than breaking the law or abusing some citizen. Cops who violate departmental guidelines (for instance, if they spend any time outside their own patrol sector) may be swiftly and severely punished.

Police value safety. Therefore, before charging into danger, they want to find out what kind of situation they are getting into and to take the necessary precautions. When knocking on the door of a house or apartment, cops always stand off to the side, just in case the person inside has a gun and decides to shoot through the door. They are told to find out if a car they stop has been stolen or involved in a recent crime.

They distinguish between different areas of the city—the propolice neighborhoods from the ones that are hostile. In the latter areas (which perhaps have gangs), they may roll down the car windows to hear sounds better, release their seat belts, and unlock the shotgun.

Competence is a term that has various meanings. Some departments elect to focus on the number of arrests made, whereas others emphasize community acceptance and satisfaction with police performance. Officers on the beat tend to think of competence as the willingness to pull one's share of the load (rather than sleeping or slacking off) and the ability to handle the tough problems when they crop up, as they do unpredictably on some shifts of duty.

Morality matters to police, though they are thought of as blue-collar workers and not normally described by observers as ethicists or philosophers. They often make references to the struggle between good and evil. The bad guys are called mopes, skells, terrorists, predators, or assholes. This vilifying of the lawbreakers implies that there are two sides and that police are the good guys, protectors of the innocent, and valiant defenders of the good. Accordingly, police tend to see themselves as performing a higher purpose than merely enforcing some arbitrary statutes.

Dwelling on morality gives them a sense that they're cleaning up areas that are polluted, removing toxic agents from the populace. In this cleanup process, some officers volunteer to be sent to the most hazardous neighborhoods, those generally recognized as the territory of violent or notorious gangs. By being sent there, police get to experience the values of morality, adventure, and competence in live action. On the other hand, law, bureaucratic control, and safety sometimes take a back seat in these assignments.[31]

Police and Student Drug Use Prevention

Not all police work involves investigating crimes, taking part in furious car chases, or making arrests. Some officers spend time talking to kids in school, trying to convince them that using illegal drugs is a serious mistake. Project DARE (Drug Abuse Resistance Education) was created in 1983 by the Los Angeles Police Department and the Los Angeles Unified School District (the police chief's son had recently died of drug use), and it quickly spread to schools throughout the United States. In this program a uniformed police officer comes to school and teaches a formal curriculum to fifth and sixth graders. This program is intended to catch them before they begin experimenting with drugs.

The officer tries to build the youngsters' self-esteem and help them develop ways of saying "no." (Los Angeles was home to the Reagans, and at that time Nancy was going public, from the White House, with her "just say no" approach to drug prevention.) The idea was that students who had high self-esteem could better resist the pressure that peers might put on them to try various drugs. The program caught on, and many millions of dollars were spent on it under the assumption that this would indeed cut down on kids' future drug use. Schools had to have *some* drug prevention program, and this is the one most of them chose.

A number of treatment and prevention programs have proved to be successes. Others are considered to be quite promising. A third category of programs is not easily classified: they fall somewhere between success and failure. DARE is in none of these; a number of studies show that it is a failure, a program that neither prevents drug use nor develops negative attitudes toward drugs. Nonetheless, it has a strong nationwide organization and enjoys ample funding from business and government. This combination of ingredients suggests an obvious strategy worth implementing: use the vibrant network that's already in place to implement one of the lesser known, but far more successful programs. Unfortunately, the DARE people are exceedingly resistant to any criticism of their program, so any wholesale changes are highly unlikely.

Police Handling of Gangs

Criminologists say that the number of cities experiencing gang problems has jumped dramatically over the past twenty years. The usual police response to gangs had been to deal with them by relying on the personnel at hand: the officers on patrol, the juvenile bureaus, community relations officers, and investigations (detectives). But in the 1980s, departments began forming a new special group called the police gang unit; by now, more than half of all large departments report having such a unit.

These units are a special branch of the department, separate from the rest of the force, with experts trained to perform specific tasks. Because this is a new unit begun over the past twenty years, it has come into being about the same time as community policing. How compatible are these new developments with each other? Apparently, not very. The gang unit is not filled with generalists who make it a point to hobnob with the public on an everyday basis in order to build up goodwill. Far from it. Indeed, the gang unit is often such an insular group that it barely has ties to the rest of the department.

> Gang unit officers work mostly without any supervision. When officers work the streets, they may go weeks, and perhaps months, without a sergeant observing their work. . . . This often leaves the mission and focus of the gang unit up to individual interests, rather than to a concerted effort on the part of the police organization to develop focused goals and a well-thought-out strategic plan to achieve

those goals. In sum, specialized gang units are not well positioned to facilitate the practice of community-oriented policing, because they are loosely coupled with the larger organization.[32]

One of the emphases of these specialized gang units is **gang suppression**. They respond to street crimes thought to have been committed by gangs. These include serious offenses, such as drive-by shootings, assaults, and drug selling. Police in the gang unit generally believe the best strategy is to reduce gang crime by moving in to catch offenders and seeing to it that they are punished swiftly, surely, and severely. Their model is deterrence, both special and general. Gang units (unlike community policing) do not try to win over the gang members' hearts and minds.

Once upon a time, policy makers held out great hope for milder forms of intervention. Back in the 1960s and 1970s, it was widely argued that gangs grew up in communities that were economically deprived, and that gang members could be turned around, their values and beliefs altered to fit in with mainstream society. In a number of cases, a detached worker was sent in to interact with the gang, to encourage members to get involved in socially acceptable pastimes, such as club activities and sports. Those attempts did not prove particularly successful, however; indeed, some commentators believe that they either (1) made gangs stronger and more cohesive or (2) gave the gangs more respect, a greater reputation. In either case, the result was that the gang became more of a force, more attractive to new members, and more delinquent.

One of the reasons that gang cops prefer to focus on gang suppression is that they have a rather distorted, stereotypical picture of gang members. They tend to believe that all gang members are thugs or thieves committed to a life of crime. Malcolm Klein argues that this is a misinterpretation of the facts. He points out that most gang crime is relatively minor, not more serious than vandalism (such as graffiti), most activity by gang members is not a violation of law, and most gangs are social groups without strong leadership. When gang cops cast all gang members as "violent thugs" who need to be "put away," they are overreacting; they neglect to mention that many youths the cops confront do not belong to gangs or are more peripheral wannabe than actual core member. When police use confrontational tactics with kids who are presumed to be gang members, the effect is to antagonize the youths, make them more likely to join a gang, and to make the gang more cohesive and united.

Conclusion

We have mentioned that police enjoy greater popularity with the American public than the courts do. What we have not done is offer an explanation of this phenomenon. It may seem odd, given that police have a much lower occupational prestige than judges or lawyers have. (Judges and lawyers are white-collar workers who don't get their hands dirty, who have a great deal of education, and who earn higher salaries.) Part of the reason people are unhappy with judges and defense lawyers can be traced to the visibility of "errors." When defense lawyers and judges let defendants go without a trial or severe sentence, the public often finds out about it and gets upset.

When police make an error of lenience (letting an obviously guilty person go on his or her way without being arrested), no one is around to publicize the event. When police arrest someone, the fact may be duly recorded for the public to see on television or read about in the daily news. Where judges are concerned, the public tends to think they are dealing with guilty people all the time, and guilt requires punishment. When a judge lets someone go (perhaps on a "legal technicality"), the public is generally irate. Newspapers and television may complain vigorously. The same response happens when the defendant is found guilty but given a milder sentence than expected.

If police are so popular with the American public, as public opinion polls suggest, then why do they experience so much stress and die at a relatively early age of cancer, heart disease or suicide? The answer seems to lie in the fact that they put their game face on when they meet the public: they show their authority instead of their human compassion. They want to establish one thing above all—that they are in charge. Naturally, this hard-nosed approach does not win them friends among those who are pulled over, picked up, or questioned. The people police interact most with are the deviant, defiant, disgruntled, corrupt, or criminal segments of the population or those who are normally well behaved but who at that moment did something they shouldn't have (and don't want to suffer the consequences).

Police have gone through several stages in their history. America's early police departments were an outgrowth of the London bobbies (named affectionately after their creator, Sir Robert Peel). The British idea was that police should be unarmed, unthreatening, and unfailingly polite, not an occupying military force as earlier versions elsewhere had been. In America, the traditional police were much more beholden to the whims of the urban political machine, which demanded loyalty to its corrupt interests. This was hardly an auspicious beginning for the men in blue. (Women in blue came along a few years later, in some instances to handle children's cases.)

In the reaction against the traditional (political) police style, middle-class citizens and the press proposed a reform city administration, one that would appoint a strong police chief, who would rule with an iron hand and make sure all officers lived up to the rules of professional behavior. Criminals would be pursued immediately, caught, arrested, and sent on to the courts for punishment. Efficiency was the watchword, and high standards among police personnel were thought to be crucial to creating such a force. It took a while, but reformers eventually got their way, in one city after another.

Eventually, problems developed with the impersonal professional officers, so another style of policing was proposed, one that would bring the police closer to the citizens and give the community an active role in decision making. This seemed to promise a new and closer working relationship. Police would no longer sit back in their cars and wait for a serious crime to be phoned in. They would patrol on foot, talk to the people, find out what their needs and expectations were. Under the new system, the old cop standard of us against them would begin to dissolve, or so it was hoped.

But although the philosophy of community policing was on the rise, so was the problem of juvenile gangs. More and more police departments decided they had to create special gang units to deal with the new threat. Some of these units tried to merge their activity with the community policing approach, but in other cities, gang units opted for a much more secretive strategy. They worked alone, not supervised by the brass, not even having much contact with other police department officers. They focused on the most serious crimes thought to involve gang members. The opportunities were there for them to suppress gangs and build up intelligence files. But at the same time, they could (by their sudden strikes) cause dissension in the communities they chose to hit.

Key Terms

Professional:	policing that emphasizes crime control through rapid response by well-trained, well-educated, honest officers
Community policing:	a new philosophy of police and community cooperation in dealing with community problems
Strategic policing:	identifying problem areas and mobilizing police resources to drive out drug dealers, prostitutes, etc.
Neighborhood policing:	every officer tries to maintain a good relationship with the community
Problem-oriented policing:	pinpointing areas in trouble, notifying the public, discussing it with the community, formulating a plan of action
Juvenile bureau:	a police unit responsible for investigating offenses thought to have been committed by minors
Discretion:	usually this means that police have enough evidence to make an arrest but decide not to do so
Crime fighters:	aggressive officers who thirst for homicides and robberies in progress and disdain what they call "social work"
Law enforcers:	police who believe in the power of arrest to deter all kinds of offenses
Community-oriented welfare workers:	police interested in helping people solve their problems
Racial profiling:	originally this meant police were on the lookout for certain traits thought to be common among cars or drivers carrying drugs up the East Coast (race was one of the traits)
Truncated sample:	a sample with one end cut off (e.g., respondents below the age of 18 were never included in the sample)

Demeanor:	how one presents oneself; how one acts or looks
Proactive:	police take the first step; they act on their own and initiate encounters; they actively look for crime
Reactive:	police sit back and wait to be called to a scene
Civil:	normal, that is, neither antagonistic nor very deferential
Insular:	cut off from the rest of society
Gang suppression:	police try to reduce or eliminate gangs via arrests and crackdowns

End Notes

[1]James F. Richardson, *Urban Police in the United States* (Port Washington, NY: Kennikat Press, 1974).

[2]Robert M. Fogelson, *Big City Police* (Cambridge: Harvard University Press, 1977), p. 3.

[3]*Ibid.*, p. 20.

[4]*Ibid.*, p. 31.

[5]James Lardner and Thomas Reppetto, *NYPD* (New York: Henry Holt, 2000), p. 64.

[6]William J. Bopp, *"O.W."* (Port Washington, NY: Kennikat, 1997).

[7]*Response Time Analysis*, Volume II (Kansas City: Kansas City Police Department, 1977).

[8]William Spelman and Dale K. Brown, *Calling the Police: Citizen Reporting of Serious Crime* (Washington, DC: Police Executive Research Forum, 1981).

[9]James Q. Wilson and George L. Kelling, "Broken Windows," *Atlantic* (March 1982), pp. 29–38.

[10]Willard M. Oliver, *Community-Oriented Policing*, 2nd ed. (Upper Saddle River, NJ: Prentice Hall, 2001); Gordon Bazemore and Scott Senjo, "Police Encounters with Juveniles Revisited," *Policing*, 20, no. 1 (1997), pp. 60–82.

[11]Susan Guarino-Ghezzi, "Reintegrative Police Surveillance of Juvenile Offenders," *Crime and Delinquency*, 40, no. 2 (April 1994), pp. 131–53.

[12]Clemens Bartollas and Stuart J. Miller, *Juvenile Justice in America*, 3rd ed. (Upper Saddle River, NJ: Prentice Hall, 2001), p. 64.

[13]Randolph M. Grinc, Policing Juveniles. Unpublished Ph.D. dissertation, New York University, 1990.

[14]Albert D. Biderman, Louise A. Johnson, Jennie McIntyre, and Adrianne W. Weir, *Report on a Pilot Study in the District of Columbia on Victimization and Attitudes Toward Law Enforcement* (Washington, DC: U.S. Government Printing Office, 1967), p. 145; see also Philip H. Ennis, *Criminal Victimization in the United States* (Washington, DC: U.S. Government Printing Office, 1967).

[15]Ronald Weitzer and Steven A. Tuch, "Race, Class, and Perceptions of Discrimination by Police," *Crime and Delinquency*, 45, no. 4 (October 1999), pp. 494–507; Scot

Worley, John Hagan, and Ross Macmillan, "Just Des(s)erts? The Racial Polarization of Criminal Justice," *Law and Society Review, 31,* no. 4 (December 1997), pp. 637–76; Ellis Cose, *Rage of a Privileged Class* (New York: Harper Collins, 1993); Jennifer L. Hoshschild, *Facing Up to the American Dream* (Princeton, NJ: Princeton University Press, 1995); Michael C. Dawson, *Behind the Mule* (Princeton, NJ: Princeton University Press, 1994); Howard Schuman, Charlotte Steeh, Lawrence Bobo, and Maria Krysan, *Racial Attitudes in America* (Cambridge: Harvard University Press, 1997); Frank Newport, "Military Retains Top Position in Americans' Confidence Ratings," *Gallup Poll Monthly,* no. 429 (June 2001), pp. 52–5; Richard Morin, "Nonprofit Faith-Based Groups Near Top of Poll on Solving Social Woes," *Washington Post* (February 1, 2001), p. A1; Ronald Weitzer and Steven A. Tuch, "Perceptions of Racial Profiling," *Criminology, 40,* no. 2 (May 2002), pp. 435–56.

[16]James Frank, Steven G. Brandl, Francis T. Cullen, and Amy Stichman, "Reassessing the Impact of Race on Citizens' Attitudes Toward the Police," *Justice Quarterly, 13,* no. 2 (June 1996), pp. 321–34.

[17]Timothy Flanagan and Michael S. Vaughn, "Public Opinion About Police Abuse of Force," in William A. Geller and Hans Toch, eds., *Police Violence* (New Haven, CT: Yale University Press, 1996), pp. 113–28; Richard G. Zevitz and Robert J. Rettamell, "Elderly Attitudes About Police Service," *American Journal of Police, 9,* no. 2 (1990), pp. 25–39; Larry K. Gaines, Victor E. Keppeler, and Joseph B. Vaughn, *Policing in America,* 2nd ed. (Cincinnati: Anderson, 1997).

[18]Komanduri S. Murty, Julian B. Roebuck, and Joann D. Smith, "The Image of the Police in Black Atlanta Communities," *Journal of Police Science and Administration, 17,* no. 4 (December 1990), pp. 250–7; Tom R. Tyler, *Why People Obey the Law* (New Haven, CT: Yale University Press, 1990); Julian V. Roberts and Loretta J. Stalans, *Public Opinion, Crime, and Criminal Justice* (Boulder, CO: Westview, 2000).

[19]Carl Keane, A. R. Gillis, and John Hagan, "Deterrence and Amplification of Juvenile Delinquency by Police Contact," *British Journal of Criminology, 29,* no. 4 (Autumn 1989), pp. 336–52.

[20]Michael J. Leiber, Mahesh K. Nalla, and Margaret Farnworth, "Explaining Juveniles' Attitudes Toward the Police," *Justice Quarterly, 15,* no. 1 (March 1998), pp. 151–74.

[21]Yolanda G. Hurst, How Kids View Cops. Unpublished Ph.D. dissertation, University of Cincinnati (1997).

[22]William A. Westley, *Violence and the Police* (Cambridge: MIT Press, 1970), p. 49.

[23]Elizabeth Reuss-Ianni, *Two Cultures of Policing* (New Brunswick, NJ: Transaction, 1983), pp. 14–5.

[24]*Ibid.,* p. 38.

[25]Irving Piliavin and Scott Briar, "Police Encounters with Juveniles," *American Journal of Sociology, 70,* no. 2 (September 1964), p. 210.

[26]Stephen D. Mastrofski, Jeffrey B. Snipes, Roger B. Parks, and Christopher D. Maxwell, "The Helping Hand of the Law," *Criminology, 38,* no. 2 (May 2000), pp. 307–42; Donald J. Black and Albert J. Reiss, Jr., "Police Control of Juveniles," *American Sociological Review, 35,* no. 1 (February 1970), pp. 63–77; Richard J. Lund-

man, Richard E. Sykes, and John P. Clark, "Police Control of Juveniles: A Replication," *Journal of Research in Crime and Delinquency, 15,* no. 1 (January 1978), pp. 74–91.

[27]Robert James Friedrich, The Impact of Organizational, Individual, and Situational Factors on Police Behavior. Unpublished Ph.D. dissertation, University of Michigan (1977).

[28]Joan McCord, Cathy Spatz Widom, and Nancy A. Crowell, eds., *Juvenile Crime, Juvenile Justice* (Washington, DC: National Academy Press, 2001), p. 164; Robert E. Wordon and Stephanie M. Myers, "Police Encounters with Juvenile Suspects," unpublished paper, 1999.

[29]Joan McCord, Cathy Spatz Widom, and Nancy A. Crowell, eds., *Juvenile Crime, Juvenile Justice,* p. 245; Robert E. Worden and Stephanie M. Myers, "Police Encounters with Juvenile Suspects."

[30]Robert James Friedrich, The Impact of Organizational, Individual, and Situational Factors on Police Behavior.

[31]Steve Herbert, "Police Subculture Reconsidered," *Criminology, 36,* no. 2 (May 1998), pp. 343–69; Steve Herbert, *Policing Space* (Minneapolis: University of Minnesota Press, 1997); William Terrill and Stephen D. Mastrofski, "Situational and Officer-Based Determinants of Police Coercion," *Justice Quarterly, 19,* no. 2 (June 2002), pp. 215–248.

[32]Vincent J. Webb and Charles M. Katz, "Policing Gangs in an Era of Community Policing," in Scott H. Decker, ed., *Policing Gangs and Youth Violence* (Belmont, CA: Wadsworth, 2003), p. 41.

Recommended Readings

Scott H. Decker, *Policing Gangs and Youth Violence* (Belmont, CA: Wadsworth, 2003).

Irving A. Spergel, *The Youth Gang Problem* (New York: Oxford University Press, 1995).

Lawrence W. Sherman, "American Policing," in Michael Tonry, ed., *The Handbook of Crime and Punishment* (New York: Oxford University Press, 1998), pp. 429–56.

Miriam D. Sealock and Sally S. Simpson, "Unraveling Bias in Arrest Decisions," *Justice Quarterly, 15,* no. 3 (1998), pp. 427–57.

Robert E. Worden and Stephanie M. Myers, Police Encounters with Juvenile Suspects. Unpublished paper, 1999.

Albert J. Reiss, Jr., *The Police and the Public* (New Haven, CT: Yale University Press, 1971).

Jonathan Rubenstein, *City Police* (New York: Farrar, Straus and Giroux, 1973).

Malcolm Klein, *Gang Cop* (Walnut Creek, CA: Altamira, 2004).

CHAPTER 11

Youth and the Juvenile Court

The juvenile court came into being in April 1899, when the Illinois General Assembly passed An Act for the Treatment and Control of Dependent, Neglected, and Delinquent Children. When the law took effect three months later, the first juvenile court opened for business in Chicago, America's second-largest and fastest-growing city. Prime movers in the court's creation included pioneering women, philanthropists, and social workers; Lucy Flower, Julia Lathrop, and Jane Addams spent a decade trying to get their romantic view of children as innocent, immature, and vulnerable enacted into law. To sway the state legislature, they enlisted the American Bar Association, which at the time had much more clout than any women's group and which agreed to present the case to the lawmakers.

The juvenile court movement was composed, in part, of moral crusaders and humanitarians who believed juvenile offenders weren't criminals and didn't deserve punishment. The reformers envisioned a court in which penalties would be meted out only if they promised to bring about positive results—most notably, *rehabilitation.* This court would focus on the child as a person, not on the legal offense committed. It would also arrange for the child to receive some kind of treatment in hopes of curing his or her delinquent tendencies. Finally, rehabilitation meant an emphasis on the individual. Before psychologists or psychiatrists could help the child, they had to diagnose the problem. Special problems required a special cure, one suited to that child alone. The juvenile court philosophy clearly did not have some kind of one-size-fits-all or assembly-line justice in mind.

The juvenile court movement also wished to keep children out of adult (criminal) courts, jails, and prisons. It regarded children as still growing up, still forming their personality. At their stage of growth, hard-line justice would be inappropriate. A

277

more understanding approach better fit their tender years. Subjecting them to the trauma of criminal trials and criminal institutions could propel them into full-blown criminal careers. Emphasis on youths' innocence and immaturity reflected (1) new thinking about adolescence, (2) progressive liberalism, and (3) the nurturing side of the juvenile court advocates. They thought that, as innocents, children needed to be protected from the vices and temptations surrounding them in the big city.

In addition to all of this humanitarianism, some punitive options also existed; serious or intractable youth would be sentenced to institutions as they had since the early part of the nineteenth century.[1] But most youths declared delinquent by the court would be placed on *probation*, a fairly new idea at the turn of the century. They would be assigned a social worker or psychologist, someone they could talk with periodically. Kids would be sent back home, not put away in an institution. The probation officer/social worker would be the right arm of the court and take a hands-on, proactive approach, investigating the child's home and ensuring that improvements were made.

> The child who got into trouble . . . not only brought the state into his or her life, but also opened up the family home to state intervention and extended supervision. Thus, the entire family, not only the child, became the subject for extended case work, which could involve demands to change jobs, find a new residence, become a better housekeeper, prepare different meals, give up alcohol, and abstain from sex.[2]

According to the juvenile court philosophy, many children needed help if they were to become healthy, striving members of modern, urban, industrial society. In rapidly growing places like Chicago, immigrant children needed particular assistance because they were surrounded by vice, and their lower-class immigrant parents failed to provide the needed guidance and control. (Reformers apparently thought that children were better off being protected by the state than the sole property of their fathers. Indeed, neglectful and misguided parents were considered the primary cause of delinquency in the early years of the twentieth century.)[3]

The juvenile court philosophy imagined that the juvenile court staff would provide several kinds of help. Children who seemed headed toward future delinquency would be brought before the court, where a probation officer or psychologist would carry out a detailed analysis to determine what made the child tick. The analyst would not pay much attention to the offense the child had committed (indeed, sometimes there wasn't one). All parties in the court would be united, aiming toward the same goal; that is, they would act in what they thought was in *the child's best interests.*

The new court would *not* feature an **adversary system** in which prosecuting and defense attorneys fought it out to see who could sway the judge or jury. In fact, legal formalities would be dispensed with, to be replaced by informal chats between the juvenile and the judge, who would be seated at a table instead of on high and would wear ordinary clothes instead of a black robe. The judge would speak to the child as a kindly uncle might, not in the manner of a stern Old Testament figure (Exhibit 11-1). The public would be barred from the hearings; and the juvenile's record would be kept private. Both of these rules were put in place because the reformers intended to protect the child's reputation from public scrutiny.

The *juvenile court philosophy* can be summarized as follows.

1. The only justification for legal punishment is that it will bring about *rehabilitation*.
2. Because young people are innocent and immature, they should *not be treated as adult offenders*, lest they become such.
3. Youths who are declared delinquent (or dependent or neglected) should usually receive *probation*, not be sent to a reformatory.
4. Youths should have *a special court*, one that specializes in handling juvenile cases.

This optimistic point of view caught on quickly. Once Illinois passed legislation establishing a juvenile court, other states followed its lead. By 1925, every state except Maine and Wyoming had enacted its own version of such a law. In the decades that followed, juvenile courts spread to every country in the industrialized world.

The ideals we have discussed were expressed by the *juvenile court movement;* but at no time in its history did the actual court consistently live up to them. For

---

EXHIBIT 11-1   The Language of Juvenile Court Versus the Language of Crime

When the reformers created a new court specifically for juveniles, they also invented a new vocabulary intended to distinguish juveniles from adult offenders. Instead of a trial, there is an **adjudication hearing** to see if there is evidence that the allegations are true. Instead of parole, there is **aftercare**. Rather than a crime, there is a *delinquent act*. Rather than being confined in jail, the juvenile is *detained* at a **detention** center. In place of a sentence, a youngster receives a **disposition**. The probation officer is called a *juvenile court officer*. A defendant is known as a *minor*. The prosecutor is called a *petitioner*, and the defense attorney is a **respondent**. The youth is sent not to prison but to long-term secure confinement in an *institution* or **training school**. Juveniles are not indicted; a **petition** is filed against them. They are not subject to arrest; the term for that procedure is *taken into custody*.

Instead of the conventional criminal law terminology (of accusation, proof, guilt, and punishment), the juvenile court opted for social welfare jargon (needs, treatment, protection, and guidance). You may wonder what's the point of such euphemistic language. Is it just an attempt to hide the truth behind a cloud of **obfuscation**? Perhaps it is. But in addition, the juvenile court philosophy wanted to prevent youngsters from being **stigmatized**. The founders of the movement assumed that new terminology would not carry such negative connotations. (In the beginning, they didn't; over the years, however, some of the new terms took on a stigma of their own.)

instance, careful consideration of each juvenile's particular circumstances and what was in the child's best interest—these were generally forgotten because judges had too many cases to handle. Nearly a hundred years ago, Judge Julian Mack alone heard more than *14 thousand cases* during his first three years on the bench. In the early days of the court, anyone could file petitions—family members, school principals, probation officers, child welfare workers—and they did, in droves, overwhelming the court. Probation officers did not adopt the aggressive, proactive stance envisioned by reformers, because they too were swamped with work, saddled with excessive caseloads. Although in theory it was the cornerstone of the juvenile justice system, the probation officer did not even *exist* in most of the juvenile courts in 1920.[4]

The juvenile court did not spring from a vacuum. Instead, it was one of a series of reforms proposed by the Progressives, who had a powerful impact on American politics and thinking from 1880 to 1920. Among other goals, reformers wanted to protect youngsters from premature exposure to the rough-and-tumble world of adults. Besides promoting a separate court for youths, they advocated a child welfare system, child labor laws, school attendance laws, school lunches, vocational education, and kindergartens. They envisioned a wise, caring, **paternalistic** state that would protect children from backbreaking labor in the mines, factories, and sweatshops.

> Many descended into the dark and dangerous coal mines each day, or worked above ground in the coal breakers where harmful clouds of dust were so thick the light could scarcely penetrate even on the brightest days. Others were forced to crouch for hours at a time and face the blinding glare and stifling heat of glass factory furnace rooms. Many children spent their days or nights in the dull, monotonous, noisy spinning rooms of cotton mills, where humid, lint-filled air made it difficult to breathe, and they were kept awake by cold water thrown in their faces.[5]

Child labor laws and school attendance laws were passed in hopes that youngsters would receive enough education to attain a higher position than their parents had been able to reach—the implicit goal was for all to become middle-class Americans.

Different states have different cutoff points for determining adulthood. Connecticut, New York, and North Carolina say that a 16-year-old is an adult and thus automatically sent to criminal court. Georgia, Illinois, Louisiana, Massachusetts, Michigan, Missouri, New Hampshire, South Carolina, Texas, and Wisconsin say that 17 is the age for this adult status. Most, however, have chosen 18 as the age of adulthood or majority for criminal justice purposes. As for drinking, driving, voting, or paying adult fares at the movies, those may be set at a different age. Back in the Middle Ages, 21 was established as the age of adulthood. This was when a man was presumed to be big enough and strong enough to wear armor into battle.

When Illinois legislators established the juvenile court, they had three kinds of children in mind: the dependent, the neglected, and the delinquent. Some experts have distinguished between these categories by defining dependent children as those who were inadequately raised by parents because the parents were mentally or physically incapable, whereas neglected children could have been adequately socialized but the parents chose not to do so. Delinquent children chose to commit delinquent acts more often than other children their age. The juvenile court enthusiasts thought that in all three cases the children were innocent victims of inadequate care by parents. Hence, in the minds of the Progressive reformers, all three conditions (dependent, neglected, and delinquent) reflected parental failure, not the criminality of children. Someone needed to rescue and protect these children, to look after their welfare, because parents were not getting the job done. That someone was the juvenile court.

For decades, the court sailed along; few critics challenged it, and hardly any legal actions were brought against it. When it did finally run into trouble, the criticism came from the liberal left, not, as one might have expected, the conservative right. Liberal expressions of dissatisfaction began in the 1960s; the conservatives' argument against the court did not surface until years later. What faults could liberals find with the court? Generally, they objected to the overreaching power of the judge and juvenile court laws, the absence of procedural law (i.e., due process protections), and the failure to live up to the spirit of the original juvenile court philosophy (which emphasized rehabilitation) (Exhibit 11-2).

Critics said that youths were being taken into custody and sent to court for practically anything: status offenses and peccadilloes such as truancy, running away, smoking, drinking, swearing, incorrigibility, stubbornness, curfew violations, hanging around pool halls, watching adult entertainment, and so on. Indeed, a youngster could be arrested, sent to court, and locked up in an institution for being a *victim* (of neglect or dependency) rather than an *offender*. Critics wondered why the *child* was punished when the ones committing the offenses were the *parents*.

Liberals also charged the juvenile court with failing to adhere to its own philosophy. Sometimes judges were far from being friendly or **avuncular**. Sometimes cases were dealt with like auto parts on an assembly line. Sometimes the court gave no thought to the best interests of the child. Some courts presumed guilt and took it for granted that the child could not be reformed. The juvenile court philosophy turned out to be easier to sustain as theory than to follow in practice. Not surprisingly, the youngsters who were most likely to suffer from the discrepancy were those from lower-class families and neighborhoods. They were the ones most likely to be sent away and locked up in a training school.

Kent v. United States (1966) was the first major juvenile court case in the 1960s to reach the U.S. Supreme Court. This began when a Washington, D.C., judge decided to waive jurisdiction and transfer the defendant to adult court without conducting a transfer hearing. In the criminal trial, Kent was found guilty of housebreaking and robbery and sentenced to thirty to ninety years behind bars. Once the case reached the Supreme Court, Justice Abe Fortas, the Supreme Court appointee who was most knowledgeable about the juvenile court, criticized the juvenile court's procedures. Fortas argued that the juvenile court judge was armed with unlimited power, whereas juveniles were afforded none of the rights that criminal courts give adult defendants. The doctrine of *parens patriae* (in which the state acts as the child's parent or guardian) allowed juvenile courts to follow their own wishes rather

EXHIBIT 11-2   Anthony Platt's Criticism of the Founders of the Juvenile Court

Anthony Platt grabbed the limelight a few decades ago with his book on the juvenile court movement. Entitled *The Child Savers,* this muckraking work skewered the reformers. Platt claimed that they were not benevolent, and they did not humanize the system. Indeed the failure of the juvenile court could be laid at the feet *of the reformers who created it.*

He said that the reformers were middle- and upper-class individuals who were bent on devising new forms of control over the working classes. Platt claimed that the child savers were determined to preserve the existing social class system and its unequal distribution of wealth, not overthrow it: they defended capitalism and rejected socialism. According to Platt, they portrayed the working class as a dangerous class that posed a threat to the civilized society. In his view, the changes they proposed were merely reforms; they did not constitute a fundamental restructuring of society or an alternative to the capitalist system.[6]

Some of these comments were accurate and exceeding obvious. For instance,

1. The reformers were middle and upper class. Lower-class reformers did not exist, and if they had existed they could never have convinced the state legislatures to create a new court designed especially for needy children.
2. The reformers did not lob Molotov cocktails at the establishment; nor did they advocate the forcible overthrow of the government.

But Platt is wrong in claiming that the reformers were essentially punitive in their approach and wished to keep the lower class down permanently. Actually, those reformers who were actively involved with Jane Addams were overwhelmingly benevolent in purpose and wished to rescue children and help them eventually move into the middle class.

than rules of due process. Fortas complained that children in juvenile court found themselves without the protection given adult defendants (due process) and without the solicitous care promised by the juvenile court philosophy. Unfortunately for youths, he said, it combined the worst features of both court systems.

Lawyers, however, could not point to this particular defendant (Morris Kent, Jr.) as an ideal example of innocence or a poster boy for challenging the juvenile justice system. He had committed brutal crimes, rape and robbery, and he did get the chance to defend himself in a criminal court trial. Originally, his lawyers defended him on the grounds that he suffered from a kind of schizophrenia. If crazy, brutal

Kent was not a good choice for challenging the juvenile court, Gerald Francis Gault was, because his crime was trivial and the punishment was disproportionate. In Gila County, Arizona, an insular outpost, Gerald and his friend called up a neighbor, Mrs. Cook, and asked her if her cherries were ripe and she had big bombers. At that time and place, middle-aged women were in no mood for suggestive phone calls, so she called the police, who dragged Gerald off to the detention center. No one informed him of his constitutional rights or told his parents anything—that he had been picked up and taken away, where he had been put, or why. Finally, after scouring the neighborhood and asking everybody, Gerald's mother discovered that he had been arrested and detained. After much prodding, the probation officer grudgingly told her when the first court hearing would take place.

At the hearings in the judge's chambers, the victim, Mrs. Cook, was not asked to attend, let alone testify. On the other hand, Gerald was *forced* to testify, that is, not protected against self-incrimination. He had no lawyer nor was any record kept of the testimony. The judge vaguely recalled an earlier case in which Gerald allegedly stole a baseball glove. Then, too, Gerald was on probation for another minor incident. This plus the phone call (Gerald testified he did not say anything during it) was enough for the judge to declare Gerald habitually immoral and a juvenile delinquent, and send him to the Arizona Industrial School for an indeterminate sentence. Gerald *could* have been kept there until he was 21, a total of six years (though in fact he got out in six months). The Gaults appealed to the Arizona Supreme Court but to no avail.

The Warren Court was the most activist Supreme Court in history, handing down a series of landmark decisions on civil rights and civil liberties in the 1960s. *(Dennis Brack/Black Star.)*

When the case eventually reached the U.S. Supreme Court, the ACLU had taken over the defense, and attorney Norman Dorsen decided to push for a sweeping ruling regarding the juvenile court. He argued that the juvenile court's unlimited discretion led to denial of the right to adequate notice of charges, denial of the right to counsel, denial of the right to confront and cross-examine witnesses, and denial of the privilege against self-incrimination. Gault's original lawyer from Arizona added two more: denial of the right to a transcript of the proceedings and denial of the right to appellate review of the juvenile court's decision.

The case was easy for the activist Warren Court to decide in light of the civil liberties decisions it had already made in criminal cases such as *Mapp, Escobedo,* and *Miranda.* Fortas declared that *parens patriae* was a murky doctrine of dubious relevance when it came to standards juvenile courts should meet. He reiterated his view that the requirements of due process must be satisfied in juvenile proceedings. He added that the Fourteenth Amendment and the Bill of Rights are not for adults only, that the juvenile court's unbridled discretion, although motivated by benevolence, is no substitute for procedure, and the fact that the defendant is a youngster does not justify a kangaroo court. The juvenile court could continue providing a therapeutic method of treatment; that would not be undermined by following due process requirements. The new requirements Fortas insisted on were the same four that Dorsen requested:

1. Right to counsel (court-appointed, if necessary)
2. Right to confront the accuser, who must present testimony under oath
3. Right against self-incrimination
4. Right to timely notice of the charges against him or her

In 1970, the Supreme Court decided the case of *In re Winship.* The New York City juvenile court judge acknowledged that the evidence against 12-year-old Samuel Winship might not establish his guilt beyond a reasonable doubt but that the juvenile court did not require such a high standard of proof; its standard was lower, namely, *a preponderance of the evidence.* The Supreme Court disagreed with that and said from now on, juvenile courts must apply the higher standard of proof in juvenile cases where incarceration might result. This ruling brings the juvenile court more in line with the criminal court.

The juvenile justice system lost some of its luster and legitimacy after the attack in the 1960s. It suffered a more serious blow later when conservatives entered the fray, accusing the court of being soft on youthful criminals, saying that serious crimes ought to bring severe punishments, that age was not a mitigating factor, that juvenile court judges were out of touch—they did not grasp the fact that the crimes committed by today's youth are monstrous and need to be dealt with as such. Several incidents gave the conservative agenda added impetus. The first of these was the Willie Bosket case in New York (Exhibit 11-3).

EXHIBIT 11-3   The Willie Bosket Murders and the Political Response to It

Despite having a very high IQ, cherubic features, and a skinny body, 15-year-old Willie Bosket was as dangerous a career criminal as anyone in New York. No reformatory could handle him. No antipsychotic drugs had an effect on him. He attacked social workers with scissors and set fellow inmates on fire. He had already committed two thousand crimes, which included, by his account, some two hundred armed robberies. His favorite activity was riding the subways in search of winos, who were usually alone, asleep, and easy to rob.

In March of 1978, a few days after Willie bought a gun (at a time when few kids in Harlem had one), he was riding the subway train uptown when he saw a middle-aged man asleep, with sunglasses and a fancy digital watch that glowed. He reminded Willie of a counselor he thoroughly despised at Spofford (New York City's secure detention center). The other passengers got off, leaving Willie and the stranger alone. As Willie started to take the man's watch, he awoke. This was the moment Willie had always imagined: killing someone just for the experience of it. So he shot the man through the sunglasses in the right eye and then again in the temple. That night, he told his sister Cheryl what he had done. They both laughed about it. (She thought he was just running off at the mouth, making it all up.)

Willie soon forgot about it. About a week later, he and his cousin Herman hopped the turnstile and boarded the train again. They found a car with only one passenger, a man in his thirties. Willie asked for his money but he said he had none, so Willie shot him and rifled his pockets, finding a couple of dollar bills.

> The next day, when Herman came over, they sat in the kitchen reading about the murder in the paper. Willie started giggling. He felt like a big-time killer—something he had done had made the front page of the newspaper. He felt no remorse for the killings. The way he had been brought up, and then his life on the street, and all those years in institutions were like a fort that protected him from being sorry for what he did. It was as if he had scored a big victory in the most competitive game of all, violence.[7]

It did not take the police long to finger Willie and Herman as the culprits. Willie, when questioned, proved cagey, and he divulged nothing. Herman, however, was not half so clever; before long, he cracked under the pressure. When Willie went to court, he received the maximum sentence allowable at the time, which meant he would be released when he reached 21 (in five and a half years). New Yorkers following the case were in an uproar over this; they demanded he be given a much stiffer penalty.

(continued)

EXHIBIT 11-3 (*CONT.*)

The *Daily News* revealed that Willie had killed for the fun of it and that shortly before he had been released from Brookwood Center maximum security youth facility, a social worker had warned that he was dangerous and should not be set free. These stories surfaced in the middle of the New York governor's race. The Republican challenger had been campaigning for a new law that would let juveniles be tried as adults for violent crimes. Hugh Carey, the Democratic incumbent, had consistently rejected this approach, calling it too drastic. No other state at the time had adopted such a policy.

But when the news stories broke, Carey felt he was susceptible to accusations of being soft on crime. He blamed the Division of Youth for its failure and called the legislature back for a special session to pass a new law, called the Juvenile Offender Act of 1978.

Under its terms, kids as young as thirteen could now be tried in adult criminal court for murder and would face the same penalties as adults. This was not a small matter. The new law represented a sharp reversal of 150 years of American history, dating to the founding of the New York House of Refuge in 1825. It was the first break with the progressive tradition of treating children separately from adults. . . . The new law also marked a departure from the cherished American ideal of rehabilitation—the notion that kids could be changed and saved. Rehabilitation wasn't working, backers of the new law believed.[8]

Transfers to Criminal Court

In the ensuing years, other states followed New York's example and made it easier to transfer juveniles to adult courts for trial. They lowered the age at which a juvenile could be waived to criminal court, and they expanded the number of crimes for which such a transfer was allowed. States now have several methods of transferring juveniles to adult court for prosecution. *Judicial waiver* is the most common type of transfer on the books, one that nearly every state provides. In it the judge is the main decision maker, although prosecutors are the first to suggest that transfer should be considered. The states usually offer guidelines to the judge as to which factors ought to be considered in making the decision: the age of the juvenile, the seriousness of the offense, the juvenile's history of offenses, and the sophistication of the juvenile. Older, more cunning juveniles who commit more offenses and ones that are more serious have a greater likelihood of being waived to the criminal court.

In some states, the legislatures have passed laws establishing ***presumptive waivers***. Here, the judge still makes the decision, but in certain cases the juvenile must prove that he or she is a good candidate for rehabilitation in the juvenile system. When these statutes are passed, the number of juveniles sent to adult court inevitably increases. For example, after California passed such a law, the number of waiver hearings in Los Angeles increased by 318 percent and actual waivers went up 234 percent.[9]

The vesting of such discretionary power in the hands of one person—the juvenile court judge—may not be a good idea if the judge does not have a very clear understanding of the juvenile in question (and in a great many waiver cases the judge's knowledge may be minimal, biased, or based on dubious information). The judge is particularly unlikely to have sufficient information if the court is located in a big city and the number of cases seen each day is overwhelming. In such instances, the juveniles are hard to remember, as the endless procession of hundreds and thousands of cases becomes so blurred that they are difficult to distinguish from one another.

> Taken as a whole, the ten branches of Los Angeles Juvenile Court, in twenty-eight courtrooms, each a separate fiefdom with different standards, different philosophies, and wildly different outcomes for similar cases, will handle nearly eleven hundred delinquency hearings of one kind or another this day. The most common order issued in Juvenile Court during this tidal flow of hearings is a postponement, putting off action until another day, creating months of delays in a system that is supposed to arrest the downward spiral of young people with the speed and efficiency of a hospital emergency room.[10]

The biggest change in recent years has been the increase in ***statutory exclusion provisions*** enacted by state legislators. Like the Bosket Law in New York, they exclude some youths from having hearings in juvenile court, based on their previous record, the seriousness of the current offense, or a combination of the two. Some states passed such laws in response to the *Kent* decision, whereas others were upset by what they saw as the excessive lenience of juvenile court judges.

The upshot of all this is obvious—more juveniles get sent to criminal court to be tried as adults. For example, consider the result of legislation in Illinois. There, the state passed a law saying that juveniles 15 or older charged with murder, armed robbery, or rape would automatically be transferred to criminal court. When that happened, the number of youths waived to criminal court jumped threefold; from a previous level of 47 per year it rose to 170 (151 of these were because of the automatic transfer provision). One problem with such laws is that they sweep up lesser accomplices who may have merely been along for the ride. And lesser accomplices are particularly common among juveniles.[11] Moreover, the legislation makes no mention of the youth's susceptibility to rehabilitation.

Other states have expanded the role and power of prosecutors at the expense of the juvenile court judge. In the ***direct file system,*** the *prosecutor* has a choice to send the case to a juvenile court or a criminal court. Whatever the prosecutor decides to do, it cannot be appealed. Defenders of this approach cite its convenience and efficiency. Critics say it lends itself to carelessness and abuse. Prosecutors may use transfers to adult court more often in one county than another, more often against blacks than whites. The prosecutor may also give in to political pressures, either from the public or from the legislature.[12]

Juvenile Court Judges

The juvenile court judge was originally imagined to be a person who sat at a table across from the juvenile and talked to him like a kindly uncle. The purpose of this arrangement was to get the youngster to trust the judge, to reveal his innermost thoughts, so that the judge could figure out what made him tick and what kind of treatment would best fit his special needs. Nowadays, however, judges sit up on high, wear a robe, know very little about the youngster, and may let the prosecutor and the defense attorney do all the talking. Paternalistic judges have been replaced by judges whose goal is to keep the case flow moving as rapidly as possible in the face of multiple absences or tardiness of the key players (defendants, witnesses, lawyers, etc.).

Probation Officers

Probation officers were originally supposed to conduct extensive presentence investigations on each youngster (diagnosing the ills and proposing the most appropriate treatment strategy) and to pass along all of this information to the judge. But nowadays most probation officers have a caseload too large for anything but the most cursory investigations. In addition, other problems have surfaced connected with the probation officer's functions, including the following.

In the modern era, juveniles are likely to be tried in court with a lawyer to defend them; some cases are waived to the criminal court for the trial. (*AP/Wide World Photos.*)

Probation reports are routinely late in Juvenile Court, many rife with misspellings and factual errors, sometimes crucial ones. . . . Probation officers are supposed to conduct independent investigations, but this is rarely done. Many simply rely on police arrest reports, even when writing presentence reports . . . at a time when far more recent—and more accurate—trial testimony is available. . . . Once an error is written into a probation report, it can be repeated many times over, since each writer uses the preceding report in a file for background information. . . . Probation officers sometimes fail to check school records, fail to interview crime victims, fail to visit the homes and families of potential probationers.[13]

How are juveniles handled by the court? Once they enter the court to be formally processed for a delinquent offense, how likely are they to be adjudicated *delinquent* ("found guilty" in criminal court language)? Being declared delinquent may happen because the youth admits committing the offense or the court holds a hearing and concludes there is evidence beyond a reasonable doubt that the youngster committed the acts in question. If they are adjudicated delinquent, how likely are youths to be given a residential placement ("sentenced" to a training school, ranch, camp, drug treatment or private placement facility, or group home)? To answer these questions, we can turn to figures supplied by the Office of Juvenile Justice and Delinquency Prevention (Table 11-1).

The low rate of adjudication for homicide contrasts with the high rates for motor vehicle theft and burglary. These may reflect the fact that homicide can be messy, complicated, and hard to prove in a court of law. Perhaps the youth acted

TABLE 11-1   Formally Processed Cases That Are Adjudicated Delinquent; Cases Adjudicated Delinquent That Result in Residential Placement[14]

	Adjud. Delinq.	*Given Residential Placement*
Total delinquency	58%	28%
Criminal homicide	36%	59%
Forcible rape	59%	43%
Robbery	58%	46%
Aggravated assault	57%	31%
Simple assault	51%	26%
Burglary	64%	33%
Larceny-theft	56%	23%
Motor vehicle theft	66%	41%
Vandalism	54%	17%
Drug law violations	58%	24%
Disorderly conduct	45%	16%
Weapons offenses	61%	28%
Liquor law violations	46%	14%

unthinkingly, in the heat of the moment, or was just at the scene and not the one who pulled the trigger. Judges do not want to find a youngster guilty of criminal homicide based on evidence that lends itself to a variety of interpretations. On the other hand, cases of motor vehicle theft or burglary that come before the court are not so complicated, and the facts may be less open to doubt.

In general, Table 11-1 shows that most formally processed cases (58 percent) are declared to be delinquent by the court. This means that despite what the commentators suggest, only a minority of kids are deemed not guilty by the juvenile court judge. Furthermore, a substantial proportion of adolescents declared delinquent by the court (28 percent) do get sent to a residential placement. They don't always "get away with it." They are particularly likely to be sent away if they have been found guilty of homicide, robbery, or rape. This suggests that sentencing is influenced by the seriousness of the offense. Youths declared delinquent for having committed minor offenses such as vandalism, disorderly conduct, or liquor law violations are least likely to be given this severe a sentence.

Defense Attorneys

When Jane Addams and the other Progressive reformers in the movement originally conceived of a juvenile court, they did not have in mind defense attorneys or prosecutors and today's whirlwind of accusations and arraignments, indictments and impeachments, violations and terminations. Nowadays, youth who land in juvenile court find their cases litigated, negotiated, and adjudicated. It is not a child wefare system anymore; it is not a benevolent system in which everyone is concerned with the best interests of the child. The delinquent youth has a fundamental right to counsel. Indigent defendants who face the possibility of incarceration must be provided a lawyer. (In cases of abuse, neglect, or dependency, a guardian ad litem may be appointed by the court to be a child advocate or to help develop a treatment plan.)

Although defense attorneys are not commonly part of the juvenile justice system in some rural locales, they're abundant in urban areas. This, however, does not mean that they are particularly effective. Only 11 percent of defense attorneys in juvenile court spend as many as five hours preparing for a case. Over half the lawyers admit that they have little interest in the substance of juvenile law. Seventy percent have no special screening or experience as co-counsel. Caseloads are so high that they preclude an effective defense. Those for public defenders often exceed 500 per year, with more than 300 of them juvenile cases. In rural areas, caseloads may be much lighter, but attorneys often have to travel long distances to reach the courthouse. With resources scarce, attorneys often fail to file pretrial motions or mount an effective defense; they choose the easy way out, plea bargaining early on. Some judges resent having to deal with defense lawyers in their court and may give harsher sentences because of their presence.[15]

Whether we are talking about defense attorneys, prosecutors, or judges, those who are assigned to the juvenile court are not the cream of the profession. There is a simple reason for this: officials want to succeed and to be recognized by their peers for their accomplishments. But juvenile court personnel are looked down on for handling unimportant cases and not handling them very well. Lawyers complain that people come to juvenile (and especially family court) to resolve their problems, but the court, like some dysfunctional social welfare agency, fails to take the decisive action needed.

Prosecutors

For sixty years, juvenile courts functioned without prosecutors or adversary systems. Nowadays, however, prosecutors have a central role and enjoy broad discretionary powers. In large jurisdictions, a particular prosecutor may handle only juvenile cases; in small jurisdictions, prosecutors tend to handle both adult criminal cases and juvenile court cases. They have the option of dismissing the case, diverting it to another agency, waiving it to the criminal court, or sending it on for juvenile court adjudication. Naturally, they take into account the seriousness of the offense and the youngster's prior record. Because prosecutors prefer to win the case in court, they also pay attention to the strength of the evidence. Weak cases are often dismissed.

Once a decision has been made to send the case on for a hearing in juvenile court, the prosecutor must decide what charges to bring, such as vandalism, burglary, or auto theft. Prosecutors may choose to reduce the original charges or to keep them as they were. In the earlier days (before the *Gault* decision), there were no charges of a specific crime; the juvenile was merely brought before the court on the vague accusation of being *delinquent,* and kids who had committed serious offenses might be treated the same as individuals whose offenses were minor or trivial.

The juvenile court of today does not have time to spare, so judges prefer to keep cases moving. When the docket is clogged (as it usually is), prosecutors are encouraged to settle the cases out of court, that is, via a plea bargain. In this arrangement, the two sides get together and come to an agreement. Usually, the defense pleads guilty and the prosecution settles for reduced charges and a milder punishment.

Intake

Intake occurs after an arrest, and it is the first contact a juvenile has with the juvenile court. Referrals may be made by police, parents, schools, social service agencies, or victims. Nowadays, about 85 percent of delinquency referrals come via the police; the percentage was lower than this in the first half of the twentieth century. About half the cases are for minor offenses such as shoplifting, disorderly conduct, and traffic offenses. An intake officer performs an early informal screening by considering the evidence, the seriousness of the offense, the youngster's past record, age, attitude, demeanor, and so on. Traditionally, the role of intake officer has been handled by a probation officer, and this still holds true in many jurisdictions today. But in other systems, the prosecutor handles the decisions of intake or at least oversees the choices.

Decisions come down to what should be done with the youth. Intake officers have considerable discretion and power; their decisions are neither very visible nor guided by universally accepted standards. In order to gather information, they may conduct interviews with the juvenile, the parents, the victim, and the police. Intake officers can dismiss the case, perhaps with a reprimand, remand the youth to parents' custody, send the youth to counseling, divert the youth to a dispute resolution program, or refer the youth to the prosecutor, who may decide to file a petition.

In the early years of the juvenile court, there was no intake officer. Everyone who wanted to bring a case before the juvenile court judge could do so: police, parents, school personnel, almost anyone. Predictably, this openness led to chaos and overcrowding of the docket, making everyone in the court work overtime and weekends. The court needed someone to act as a quasi-judicial gatekeeper, to direct those cases elsewhere if they did not need to go to a hearing before the judge. Even with an intake officer, there are now 1.8 million delinquency cases a year.

The first decision modern intake officers make is whether the juvenile should be detained. Police officers sometimes request that the youngster be locked up. The screening officer must predict whether the youngster poses a danger to public safety or a flight risk. This calls for a subjective judgment, and where there is much doubt, the officer may err on the side of caution and elect to detain the youth. The screener's worst-case scenario is to let the juvenile go free and then suffer a backlash when the youth subsequently commits a heinous crime that's broadcast to the entire nation.

About one-fifth of delinquency cases are dismissed at intake. Another fourth are processed informally, which often means the youth agrees to probation. More than half the cases are processed formally: an adjudicatory hearing is held or there's a hearing to determine if the minor should be waived to criminal court. Prosecutors have assumed increased influence over intake decision making. That is, the old system (of a probation officer making the decisions under the guidance of the juvenile court judge) may be giving way in some jurisdictions.

The Modern Punitive Trend

If Progressive reformers in years past tried to portray juvenile offenders as innocent children, today's conservatives take a different approach, arguing that such juveniles are no different from adults, who should be held accountable for their crimes. They insist that juvenile offenders are "criminals who happen to be young, not children who happen to be criminal."[16] Their mantra is not *parens patriae,* child saving, or serving the best interests of the child; instead, it is *adult time for adult crime.* Therefore, when get-tough conservative critics of the juvenile justice system use the term *accountability,* they mean deterrence, incapacitation, and retribution.

Liberals who criticized the juvenile court in the 1960s said it had too much power and cast too wide a net, bringing in adolescents who should never have been in the court's jurisdiction. They called for diversion, decriminalization, and deinstitutionalization. Such views were reiterated in the recommendations of the 1967 report of the President's Commission on Law Enforcement and the Administration of Justice and the Second United Nations Congress on the Prevention of Crime and the

Treatment of Offenders (1961). Although some states adopting these recommendations actually widened the net (bringing more kids into the system), there was a tendency to cut back on the number of kids sent to court for status offenses such as

1. Truancy
2. Incorrigibility
3. Running away
4. Loitering and violating curfew
5. Smoking cigarettes
6. Drinking alcoholic beverages
7. Having sexual relations
8. Being wayward or growing up in idleness or crime or hanging out with vicious and immoral persons[17]

Later on, conservatives chipped away at the juvenile court caseload from the other end, that is, the serious cases. This has been called triage. In times of war, medics in the field faced with overwhelming numbers of people who've been injured divide casualties into three groups: those too seriously injured to save, those too mildly injured to worry about now, and those who need help immediately. In the juvenile court, it has been suggested, *both the mildest and worst offenders have been removed, leaving the court with only the intermediate juveniles to handle.* The worst cases were transferred or waived to the criminal court. Originally, transfers were made by the judge, then prosecutorial waivers were allowed in some states, and now legislators have pushed for automatic waiver for juveniles committing certain offenses that are more serious.

What has been the impact of these automatic or legislative transfers from the juvenile to the criminal court? Most of the research on transfers has concentrated on *judicial* waivers, although these make up only 10 percent of the total number of waivers. One study did examine the effect of legislative waiver: David Myers focused on cases in which juveniles were arrested for robbery or aggravated assault and a deadly weapon was involved. Many states have amended their laws to permit automatic transfer in recent years, resulting in more violent juveniles being sent to adult court, where it is assumed that they will receive harsher punishment. Politicians and the public think this will deter. Myers found that

1. Juveniles transferred to adult court were more likely to be released from detention prior to their case being tried.
2. Juveniles transferred to adult court were more likely to be convicted.
3. Of youths convicted, the ones transferred to adult court were more likely to be convicted of the target offense (robbery or aggravated assault) and more likely to be incarcerated.
4. Youths released prior to disposition were more likely to be rearrested before trial if they were transfers to adult court (especially rearrested for violence).

5. After serving their sentence the transfers to adult court were more likely to be rearrested and to be rearrested sooner.[18]

Juveniles waived to adult criminal court received harsher punishment, just as the public and politicians wanted and expected, but on the larger question of whether this had the desired deterrent effect, the results proved disappointing. Despite the assumption that harsh punishment would turn these kids around, it made them *more likely* to get rearrested and to get rearrested *sooner* than the offenders who weren't transferred. In short, transfer had a brutalization effect.

We do not know *why* the transfers to adult court did worse later on. Perhaps adult prisons do not know how to deal with juveniles, who create problems adult prisons aren't accustomed to handling. They do not emphasize treatment, and juveniles who get sent there are more apt to be victimized and to commit suicide. A second argument is that while in prison, juveniles learn from adults—it is a training ground for future criminal activity. A third viewpoint says juveniles transferred to prison are publicly labeled criminals and cannot get a job later on. A fourth argument contends that juveniles sent to prison feel they have been singled out and treated unfairly. This makes them become alienated, which propels them into more criminal activity.[19]

Conclusion

The Progressives dreamed of creating a juvenile court, and they were able to convert this dream into a reality, first in Chicago, later throughout the country. But in practice these courts fell short of the original philosophy or ideal. There were invariably too many cases to be heard and too few judges and probation officers available to do the work on them. Failure to live up to the Progressives' dream was thus virtually preordained.

Libertarians in the 1960s were the first major group to point out the discrepancies between the idealized juvenile court and the courts that existed. Judges, they complained, had excessive power, which they were bound to misuse, whereas juveniles were powerless; they had none of the due process protections that defendants in the criminal court were afforded. The Supreme Court had previously taken a hands-off policy toward juvenile courts, but this policy changed with the ascension of the activist Warren Court. It ruled in the cases of *Kent, Gault,* and *Winship* that the juvenile court should act less arbitrarily and more legalistically (i.e., more like the criminal court).

Later on, conservative critics unleashed a withering attack on juvenile court judges for repeatedly letting offenders off with a slap on the wrist. Emboldened by the continued lack of sanctions, youths would inevitably commit some heinous crime sooner or later, conservatives claimed. This argument won over public opinion and state legislatures, resulting in new laws that sent more juvenile offenders to adult courts for trial, with sometimes disastrous results (recidivism) for the juvenile and the rest of the community. Another case of the old adage: be careful what you wish for, it may come true.

Key Terms

Adversary system: a fight system in the court between the defense side and the prosecution side

Adjudication hearing: a fact-finding hearing in court to determine if the allegations against the youth are correct

Aftercare: juvenile parole; youths are given help in adjusting to life in the community

Detention: being locked up temporarily pending a disposition by the court

Disposition: juvenile sentence; it's supposed to be more rehabilitative than retributive

Petition: document filed in court alleging that the juvenile is a delinquent

Respondent: defense attorney for the juvenile

Training school: basically, a milder version of prison for juveniles

Stigmatized: branded with a bad reputation or label for having engaged in deviant behavior

Obfuscation: jargon used to disguise the true nature of the organization

Paternalistic: protective stance taken by an authority over people assumed to be unable to take care of themselves

Avuncular: like an uncle

Muckraking: digging up dirt and then publicly exposing individuals and organizations for their wrongdoing

Parens patriae: civil court doctrine whereby the state acts as the parent or guardian of the child

Presumptive waiver: unless the judge proves the minor is a good candidate for rehabilitation, state law requires the case be sent to adult court for trial

Statutory exclusion provisions: state law automatically sends certain cases to criminal court

Direct file system: the prosecutor decides which court to send the case to

End Notes

[1]Franklin E. Zimring, "The Punitive Necessity of Waiver," in Jeffrey Fagan and Franklin E. Zimring, *The Changing Borders of Juvenile Justice* (Chicago: University of Chicago Press, 2000), p. 209; Sanford Fox, "Juvenile Justice Reform: A Historical Perspective," *Stanford Law Review,* 22 (June 1970), pp. 1187–1239.

[2]David S. Tanenhaus, "The Evolution of Juvenile Courts in the Early Twentieth Century," in Margaret K. Rosenheim, Franklin E. Zimring, David S. Tanenhaus, and Bernardine Dohrn, eds., *A Century of Juvenile Justice* (Chicago: University of Chicago

Press, 2002), pp. 53–4; Andrew J. Polsky, *The Rise of the Therapeutic State* (Princeton, NJ: Princeton University Press, 1991).

[3]Miriam Van Waters, *Youth in Conflict* (New York: Republic, 1926).

[4]David S. Tanenhaus, "The Evolution of Transfer Out of the Juvenile Court," in Jeffrey Fagan and Franklin E. Zimring, eds., *The Changing Borders of Juvenile Justice*, pp. 18–9; Evelina Belden, *Courts in the United States Hearing Children's Cases* (Washington, DC: United States Children's Bureau, 1920); Steven Schlossman, *Love and the American Delinquent* (Chicago: University of Chicago Press, 1977).

[5]Walter I. Trattner, *Crusade for the Children* (Chicago: Quadrangle, 1970), pp. 41–2.

[6]Anthony M. Platt, *The Child Savers* (Chicago: University of Chicago Press, 1969).

[7]Fox Butterfield, *All God's Children* (New York: Avon, 1996), p. 215.

[8]*Ibid.*, p. 227.

[9]Katherine S. Teilmann and Malcolm Klein, *Summary of Interim Findings of the Assessment of the Impact of California's 1977 Juvenile Justice Legislation* (University of Southern California: Social Research Institute, no date).

[10]Edward Humes, *No Matter How Loud I Shout* (New York: Simon and Schuster, 1996), p. 79.

[11]Robert E. Shepherd, Jr., "The Rush to Waive Children to Court," *Criminal Justice, 10*, no. 2 (Summer 1995), pp. 39–42.

[12]Eric K. Klein, "Dennis the Menace or Billy the Kid: An Analysis of the Role of Transfer to Criminal Court in Juvenile Justice," *American Criminal Law Review, 35*, no. 2 (Winter 1998), pp. 371–410.

[13]Edward Humes, *No Matter How Loud I Shout*, pp. 203–4.

[14]Howard N. Snyder and Melissa Sickmund, *Juvenile Offenders and Victims: 1999 National Report* (Washington, DC: Office of Juvenile Justice and Delinquency Prevention, 1999), pp. 158–9.

[15]Richard A. Lawrence, "The Role of Legal Counsel in Juveniles' Understanding of Their Rights," *Juvenile and Family Court Journal, 34*, no. 4 (Winter 1983–4), pp. 49–58; Jane Knitzer and Merril Sobie, *Law Guardians in New York State: A Study of the Legal Representation of Children* (Executive Committee of the New York State Bar Association, 1984); Patricia Puritz, Sue Burrell, Robert Schwartz, Mark Soler, and Loren Worboys, *A Call for Justice: An Assessment of Access to Counsel and Quality of Representation in Delinquency Proceedings* (Washington, DC: American Bar Association, 1996); Dean J. Champion, *Felony Probation* (Westport, CT: Praeger, 1988).

[16]Alfred S. Regnery, "Getting Away with Murder," *Policy Review*, no. 34 (Fall 1985), p. 65.

[17]Melissa Sickmund, Anne Aughenbaugh, Terrence Finnegan, Howard Snyder, Rowen Poole, and Jeffrey Butts, *Juvenile Justice Statistics, 1995* (Washington, DC: Office of Juvenile Justice and Delinquency Prevention, 1998).

[18]David L. Myers, *Excluding Violent Youths from Juvenile Court* (New York: LFB Scholarly Publishing LLC, 2001), p. 161; Donna Bishop and Charles Frazier,

"Consequences of Transfer," in Jeffrey Fagan and Franklin E. Zimring, eds., *The Changing Borders of Juvenile Justice*, pp. 227–76.

[19]James C. Howell, *Juvenile Justice and Youth Violence* (Thousand Oaks, CA: Sage, 1997); Frances P. Reddington and Allen D. Sapp, "Juveniles in Adult Prisons," *Journal of Crime and Justice, 20*, no. 2 (June 1997), pp. 139–52; Richard B. Freeman, "Crime and the Employment of Disadvantaged Youth," in George E. Peterson and Wayne Vroman, eds., *Urban Labor Markets and Job Opportunity* (Washington, DC: Urban Institute Press, 1992), pp. 201-38; Lawrence W. Sherman, "Defiance, Deterrence, and Irrelevance," *Journal of Research in Crime and Delinquency, 30*, no. 4 (November 1993), pp. 445–73; Raymond Paternoster and LeeAnn Iovanni, "The Labeling Perspective and Delinquency," *Justice Quarterly, 6*, no. 3 (September 1989), pp. 359–94; Donna Bishop and Charles Frazier, "Consequences of Transfer"; Patricia Torbet, Richard Gable, Hunter Hurst IV, Imogene Montgomery, Linda Szymanski, and Douglas Thomas, *State Responses to Serious and Violent Juvenile Crime* (Pittsburgh: National Center for Juvenile Justice, 1996).

Recommended Readings

Margaret K. Rosenheim, Franklin E. Zimring, David S. Tanenhaus, and Bernadine Dohrn, eds., *A Century of Juvenile Justice* (Chicago: University of Chicago Press, 2002).

Barry C. Feld, *Bad Kids: Race and the Transformation of the Juvenile Court* (New York: Oxford University Press, 1999).

Thomas Grisso and Robert G. Schwartz, *Youth on Trial* (Chicago: University of Chicago Press, 2000).

Jeffrey Fagan and Franklin E. Zimring, eds., *The Changing Borders of Juvenile Justice* (Chicago: University of Chicago Press, 2000).

Steven Schlossman, *Love and the American Delinquent* (Chicago: University of Chicago Press, 1977).

CHAPTER 12

Corrections and Prevention

Hope Springs Eternal

Americans have long been known for their pioneering "can-do" spirit. The astute observer of cultures, Luigi Barzini said it's a uniquely American trait to think all problems can be solved with money, Yankee ingenuity, and no help from the rest of the world. In the second half of the twentieth century this kind of **hubris** peaked in two administrations: during the Reagan years and, before that, during Lyndon Johnson's administration (1963–69). Before he got deeply involved in the Vietnam conflict, LBJ declared war on poverty and promised his "fellow Americans" that the great society was just around the corner. That is, not only achievable but imminent.[1]

Confidence also extended to the juvenile justice system, including the correctional or punishment part of the system. Americans have been brimming with optimism at times over the years, as corrections reformers promised new and better methods of rehabilitating offenders. One of the earliest bursts of enthusiasm came in the first part of the 1800s, when New York City devised the House of Refuge (Exhibit 12-1).

The House of Refuge represented a departure from the colonial period in American history, when there were no reformatories. In the colonial era, offenders of a tender age were dealt with by their parents or relatives; on occasion their neighbors or the local clergy might intervene. Moral offenses such as **blasphemy** or **heresy** were considered especially serious in some of the more religious colonies, and in these cases the offenders could be remanded to adult courts.

When the Society for the Reformation of Juvenile Delinquents (composed of prominent, upper-class citizens) began the groundwork for the House of Refuge, it

---

EXHIBIT 12-1   Burrows and Wallace on New York City and the House of Refuge[2]

With only half of the city's children in school and the old apprenticeship system in disarray, it was almost inevitable that thousands of **ragamuffins** would become a fixture of the city scene—lolling along the wharves, begging on the streets, thronging the shipyards, playing cards and spouting profanity. . . . Boys pilfered brass rods, rope, or sheets of copper and sold them to junk dealers. Marauding bands robbed grocery stores and vandalized houses. . . .

The conventional response to errant or merely "vagrant" children was to put them in jail, but chaplain John Stanford began to argue as early as 1815 that incarcerating youthful offenders with adult criminals merely trained a new generation of professional outlaws. Stanford thought that these children should be placed in an "Asylum for Vagrant Youth" where they could be instructed in moral and religious principles and apprenticed to a trade. Stanford's idea languished until the Society for the Prevention of Pauperism fastened on the notion that wayward youths formed the true "core of **pauperism**". . . . Convinced that they could smother pauperism in its cradle, the society's spokesmen lobbied city and state officials to fund the country's first juvenile reformatory.

The New York House of Refuge opened on January 1, 1825, amid farms and orchards on the outskirts of town. The Refuge's charges were children under sixteen, committed by the courts for indefinite terms. Their "**indolent** and worthless" parents, in the Rev. Stanford's phrase, had allowed them to frequent theaters and taverns until ensnared by alcohol, immorality, and crime. Stanford didn't believe they were beyond redemption . . . it was necessary only to put them through "a vigorous course of moral and corporal discipline" to make them "able and obedient". . . .

Day after day they followed the same lockstep routine, parsed by bells. . . . Bells herded them to the washroom, to the chapel, to school, and to breakfast by 7:00 A.M. They worked from 7:30 till noon. . . . Back-to-work bells sounded at 1:00 P.M., wash-and-eat bells at 5:00, work bells again at 5:30, school bells at 8:00. Bells summoned everyone to evening prayers, then for the march back to the cells, where absolute silence was enforced all night.

---

had what seem to us to be mixed motives. On the one hand, it was alarmed by the increasing rates of crime and social disorder it witnessed or heard about, most of which was attributed to young males. On the other hand, members of the Society felt sympathy for the youngsters who were confined in adult institutions, where adult inmates were prone to abuse them physically and psychologically. The Society wanted to separate the youths from the adult correctional facilities and reform them in an institution built specially for them.

Their faith in the House of Refuge was considerable. Therefore it took in not just delinquents but the neglected and dependent as well. Girls were admitted and could be kept there until they turned 18. Boys coming into the institution could be incarcerated longer; they were not eligible for release until 21. The mostly lower-class inmates were supposed to be given moral training, academic education (reading, writing, and arithmetic), and shopwork. The idea was that they would profit from the experience and be ready to assume their place in society as laborers.

The management of the House of Refuge issued annual reports describing how their charges were faring under this new regime. The reports offered glowing descriptions touting the inmates' dramatic improvement. They declared that up to 90 percent of the youths were being rehabilitated, saved from a life of crime. At the time, people reading these reports took them at face value, and child savers from around the nation traveled to New York to find out more about this trumpeted program. By 1876, there were more than fifty juvenile reformatories. Americans assumed that a solution had been found to the problem of incorrigible youth.

The obvious question to be asked is: How justified was this official optimism? The evidence suggests that it was mostly a fiction, a bubble that could burst at any time (when the truth filtered out).

> In many institutions, children were whipped and subjected to severe corporal punishment; in others, they were locked in dungeons, handcuffed, and fed only bread and water. Labor systems did not teach children skills or the habits of industry. Child workers were exploited and abused for profit. . . . Indentured and paroled inmates were, in some instances, abused and exploited by their masters or by community supervisors. Inmate gangs, violence, escapes, sexual encounters, and smuggling disrupted the daily operation of reformatories.[3]

In the *latter* part of the century, New York state again made news in the world of corrections by creating the Elmira Reformatory, a place for offenders who were still quite young, but no longer minors. This occurred several decades after the Civil War, when America became a disorganized society, its rural Protestant values of the village farmers on the wane and cities degenerating into moral cesspools (or so thought many observers at the time). In New York City, rates of crime and deviance increased, and thousands of grog shops, prostitutes, and professional criminals dotted the landscape.[4]

A good deal of the crime was attributed to New York's many and well-known gangs: the Dead Rabbits, Plug Uglies, Forty Thieves, Gas House Gang, and Hell's Kitchen Gang. They were rumored to have huge memberships (as many as 1,500 participants, though such a figure is hard to believe), to be organized along ethnic lines, and to come from the city's slums. These neighborhoods rivaled the gangs when it came to colorful names (e.g., Satan's Circus, Murderers' Alley, and Poverty Lane). The justice system could not corral the youths; neither the city's police nor its courts at the time were effective. Confidence in the penal system, once high, was now broken. The governor reflected the widespread consensus when he said it abounded in evils and errors.[5]

Optimism was restored when Elmira opened in 1876 under the leadership of Zebulon Brockway. From 7:30 a.m. until 4:30 p.m., inmates labored in the iron

Elmira Reformatory did not disappear. Here it is how it appeared earlier in the twentieth century. Not a very inviting place for a youngster. *(Douglas Grundy/ Hulton Archive/Getty Images.)*

foundry, hollow ware works, or the shoe and broom factories. This experience supposedly instilled in them punctuality, order, discipline, and respect for authority. Guest lecturers held forth in the evening, and school classes were taught at night. Sunday, brought mandatory religious services, with lectures on the evils of smoking, drinking, fornication, and laziness, and the value of law, family, work, and God.[6]

Brockway launched a public relations campaign in the 1880s announcing the reforms he had instituted, especially the innovations in academic and vocational education. Reports praised the classes in fine arts such as painting and music plus the mechanical arts of carpentry, bricklaying, stonecutting, plastering, and fresco painting. Wage compensation began in 1889. Youths drawn to recreation could choose from among baseball, basketball, track, and football. A series of reports boasted of Elmira's success in saving nearly all of its graduates.[7]

Because reformatories are usually out in the hinterland hidden from the prying eyes of reporters, the management can usually control the flow of news. Certainly, Brockway accomplished this with uncommon success. But eventually some of the truth about living conditions is likely to filter out, and when that happens, correctional institutions are seen to be far from the model depicted by their spokesmen. Instead, when details seep out, a much grimmer picture emerges. Elmira was no exception to this: the discrepancy between the real and ideal was gaping.

The nation's model correctional institution was overcrowded, understaffed, and grossly mismanaged. Key treatment programs did not fulfill their stated goals and objectives. Violence, escapes, smuggling, theft, homosexuality, revolts, arson, and other forms of resistance were serious problems. Inmates suffered extraordinarily harsh punishments—including severe whippings and months of solitary confinement in dark, cold dungeons—and deliberate psychological torture. Elmira was, quite simply, a brutal prison.[8]

Pessimism and the Move to Shut Down Reformatories

In the 1960s and 1970s, there were more than a few critics who said that juvenile reform schools and training schools were dismal failures, that they made inmates worse upon leaving than they were when they entered. In academic criminology, labeling theorists and conflict theorists were particularly critical of the juvenile justice system. The President's Crime Commission's *Task Force Report: Juvenile Delinquency and Youth Crime* accused the juvenile court judges of being arbitrary and capricious, sending youths to institutions that offered little in the way of rehabilitation. These inflicted the same pains of imprisonment as adult prisons gave adults.[9] Several books in the mid-1970s denounced institutions in even more dramatic fashion.[10]

Ordinarily, such complaints would result in some minor modifications or a few new experimental programs, but nothing truly revolutionary. This time, however, one person in a position to act decisively did so. Jerome G. Miller was appointed the Commissioner of Youth Services for the state of Massachusetts in 1969, and over the next three years he proceeded to release 95 percent of the 1,200 youth locked up in its secure facilities. This was a clear admission that the system was ineffective, and Miller assumed that his innovations would catch on throughout the rest of the nation. And that local communities would provide treatment to the youths who needed it. Actually, neither of these hopes was fulfilled, and state politicians forced him out of office. Nevertheless, Massachusetts remains committed to his original philosophy; it boasts a low rate of juvenile crime and a low rate of juvenile incarceration.[11]

Scared Straight

Some years ago, at Rahway State Prison in New Jersey, a small collection of inmates formed the Lifer's Group. Because they had an excess of free time, they decided to launch a program that would benefit kids in the outside world who seemed headed toward crime. They knew that some of their own children were at risk. This was true, for instance, of the son of the leader of the Lifer's Group, Richard Rowe. He and his fellow inmates wanted to prevent youngsters from making the same mistakes they had.

What could they do? They certainly could not go out into the community and give these future troublemakers counseling or the benefit of their experience with crime and punishment—they were stuck inside for the rest of their lives. Nor could they give money to already established rehabilitation programs. They had very little wealth to give. But they could have some heart-to-heart conversations with the kids if those youths were brought into the prison for firsthand experience with the downside of the criminal life. So that is what Rowe and his associates proposed. Surprisingly, New Jersey criminal justice officials thought it was a good idea and signed off on the program.

In part, officials assumed that (1) deterrence is based on threats and (2) this works best where the threat is credible. Juveniles might not put much stock in threats by ordinary adults, but inmates locked up for life seemed to know what they were talking about; when they talked about the tough life of a prisoner it was eminently believable. Therefore, youngsters were escorted into the prison to get a tantalizing glimpse of what life's like behind bars from the people who had experienced years of it and thus knew it better than anyone else. At the height of the program's popularity at Rahway, there were ten sessions of the Juvenile Awareness Project (its official title) every week, that is, ten different groups of kids coming to the prison.

The youngsters heard the clanging doors of the prison closing behind them, met obnoxious guards, toured the cells, and listened as lifers told vivid stories about deprivation, assault, rape, and murder. These were laced with threats, profanity, intimidation, anger, and bullying. The authoritarian style of presentation was intended to be a shocking confrontation with the emotional terrors facing them if they ever were to land in prison themselves. The kids were expected to recoil in horror at these graphic scenes. Did all the shouting, swearing, and threatening have the desired effect on these youths who listened to it? Program advocates in the New Jersey criminal justice system said it did, that 90 percent of kids experiencing the ranting went on to avoid all further trouble with the law: they cleaned up their act. In short, officials claimed, deterrence worked.

But not everyone was convinced. Rutgers criminologist James Finckenauer was asked to evaluate the program to see if it indeed had the effects its proponents were bragging about. He examined the **experimental group** (kids who had been through the program) and compared them with a **control group** (kids who were similar to the experimental group in many respects but had not been given the tour). He found that kids' attitudes weren't improved by the experience and their behavior did not get any better. Compared to the control group, the experimental group actually got *worse,* becoming *more involved* in crime and deviance. Finckenauer's results did not bring the program to a screeching halt, however, because the policy makers refused to believe them.

One reason they remained unpersuaded was that the program was receiving loads of publicity, mostly flattering. This began with articles in local New Jersey newspapers. Then came an article in the best-selling magazine in America, the *Reader's Digest.* One person who read it decided to make a movie about the program, a television documentary called *Scared Straight!* To everyone's surprise, this turned out to be immensely popular and garnered several awards, including an Oscar and an Emmy. With that kind of publicity, more than thirty states jumped on the bandwagon and created their own program based on New Jersey's internationally famous model.

Given a surplus of Scared Straight programs to evaluate, criminologists carried out studies and published their results not long afterward. Eventually the various investigations became part of a meta-analysis by Mark Lipsey. He found that the general category of treatment they fell into (he called it "deterrence") tended to perform badly; experiments with various kinds of deterrence or fear did not reduce recidivism among the youngsters who had gone though them. In fact, these programs had the opposite effect—offenses increased by as little as 1 percent and as much as 30 percent. Apparently, the programs that officials said were extremely effective were actually doing more harm than good.[12] After the program, kids' behavior worsened.

Did Lipsey's summary of the results curb the enthusiasm of the people in charge of funding these programs? Apparently not. Attempts to dismantle the programs met with fierce resistance. The proponents of the programs had one thing going for them: people believed in simplistic solutions—*panaceas.* And in our society, how people respond to programs generally depends more on their beliefs than on results of careful evaluation studies. And Americans express considerable faith in intimidation and deterrence. Fear works, they believe. So harsh punishment should work even better.

Years later, there were signs that critics were finally making headway, convincing people that scared straight programs were unsuccessful and ought to be scrapped in favor of other programs that have a more positive effect on recidivism. But just about that time, a *new* television project came along. This 1999 program, narrated by Danny Glover, celebrated the 20-year history of scared straight and made another powerful claim—that only 1 percent of the teenagers who had experienced the prison tour had gone on to become career criminals. In the mid- to late-1990s, politicians were grasping at straws; anything tough that promised to curb youth crime grabbed their attention. And the simpler the solution, they more they embraced it. So scared straight programs experienced a revival of popularity.

Boot Camps

Some of the characteristics associated with scared straight programs reappear in boot camps. Both may be classified as corrections fads that caught on among elected politicians as well as the general public. Both were a somewhat punitive response to the urge to get tough with young offenders. Both were carried out in an atmosphere of great excitement and inflated expectations of success. People looked at these programs and said that they were *bound* to succeed—there's no way they could fail.

Obviously, the idea for boot camps in corrections derived from boot camps run by the military (such as the tough Marine Corps program in Parris Island, South Carolina). Movies like *An Officer and a Gentleman* gave audiences the impression that a hard-nosed sergeant or drill instructor could take a **motley** collection of disorganized misfits and whip them into shape, infuse them with responsibility and determination, in just a few weeks. It did not take long for the concept of boot camps for youthful offenders to become the rage in American corrections.

The philosophy behind such a movement was that delinquents and youth criminals needed a healthy dose of structure and discipline in the lives. These they would receive in a correctional boot camp, where they would be part of a platoon of twelve or so youths, their heads would be shaved, they would be subject to

In a correctional boot camp, like a military one, drill sergeants take pleasure in getting up close and personal. *(AP/Wide World Photos.)*

military customs, bullied by bellowing drill instructors, forced to get up at 6 in the morning, to work, march, and drill, and to do physical exercise, until they fell asleep at night. For 90 days they would be immersed in the rigors of military life.

The in-your-face confrontational style of the drill instructors would coincide with strict rules, stern discipline, and regimented living. Boot camp advocates claim that all this sweat, fear, and intimidation instill respect in the troops who previously were **slovenly** and undisciplined. The plan is to first tear down the recruits and humiliate them, then build them up by turning them into a proud, cohesive, and physically fit unit. If it works in the military, why shouldn't it succeed among these kids, ask the defenders of the program.

By the year 2000, there were 70 boot camps operating at the federal, state, and local level in the United States. They served as a short-term **intermediate sanction**: more severe than being put on probation but less severe than being sent to a juvenile training school. Many of the youths sentenced to boot camps had previously failed when given milder sanctions. The boot camps would not accept everyone; they excluded especially violent offenders, sex offenders, and armed robbers.

How successful did these camps prove to be? If recidivism is the criterion, samples of males who went through the program were just as likely to recidivate as comparison groups of boys who didn't go through it. Camps seem to be regarded quite favorably by the boys in them (at least, when they're compared to life inside training school) but the experience has no consistent impact on their propensity to commit crime—which is not affected either positively or negatively. Despite the hype, their effect is negligible.[13]

Institutions

Juvenile institutions are normally divided into short-term versus long-term. Short-term facilities include detention centers, reception and diagnostic centers, shelters, and jails. Long-term placements include ranches, forestry camps, and training schools. Another common division is secure versus nonsecure institutions. **Secure facilities** have locked gates, perimeter walls or fences, motion detectors, sound monitors, and security cameras: most detention centers, reception and diagnostic centers, and training schools fit this description. On the other hand, most shelters, forestry camps, ranches, and farms are nonsecure or open institutions. They don't rely on security hardware to prevent escapes.

In addition, it is customary to distinguish between private and public facilities. There are more private than public institutions, but private ones tend to be smaller, so a majority of the youngsters in juvenile institutions (74 percent) are in public facilities. In these, only 1 percent of males and 9 percent of females are there because of status offenses, whereas in private facilities, the corresponding figures are 11 and 45 percent. Many youths are referred to private institutions by schools or parents; their status offenses are attributed to emotional or psychiatric disorders. In public institutions, females make up less than 12 percent of the population, whereas in private facilities, they constitute more than 18 percent. Ethnicity also figures in; 21 percent of inmates in public institutions are Hispanic compared to 11 percent in private facilities.[14]

When public and private institutions are combined, what offenses are most juveniles in these settings charged with? Not murder, though from TV you might imagine it was, based on the numerous reports about youth gone wild. Only 2 percent are in for that crime. The most common acts that lead to incarceration are (1) **technical violations** and (2) burglary. (Technical violations are violations of the rules of parole or aftercare; these may include drinking, hanging out with other offenders, or failing to report to one's parole officer.) Murder is way down the list, near the bottom.

Black juveniles are overrepresented at all stages of the juvenile justice process. In 1996–97, African Americans made up 15 percent of the general population aged 10 to 17. But they constituted 26 percent of all juveniles arrested, 30 percent of delinquency referrals to the juvenile court, 32 percent of cases adjudicated delinquent, 40 percent of juveniles committed to residential or institutional placements, 46 percent of juveniles transferred to adult court, and 60 percent of juveniles in adult prisons.[15] Why such disproportionate minority confinement exists has been the subject of considerable discussion and dispute.

If black youth commit more offenses or more serious offenses than whites, that could explain part of the disproportion. But there are other explanations that have been offered, including the factor of justice by geography. According to Barry Feld, there are important differences among urban, suburban, and rural locales. Urban counties contain more diverse and less stable populations than rural and suburban counties. This makes their juvenile courts more likely to be formally organized, bureaucratic, and specialized; and more severe in the sentences they hand down.

In Minnesota (where the study took place), urban counties contain many more black citizens than the rural and suburban counties do. Urban crime may foster a "war on crime" mentality, a more repressive response to crime committed by "those people." But in rural and suburban courts, there is not much diversity, not many of "those people," not much call for repression. Administration is more informal, and punitiveness is subordinated to the ethic of care and treatment. The end result, Feld suggests, is that black youths get more severe dispositions throughout the juvenile justice process.[16]

Not everyone who gets arrested as a juvenile will be committed to an institution or residential placement. For example, the number of arrests is about 2.8 million per year. Among juveniles who get arrested, only a small proportion (less than 6 percent) get placed in an institution. Why not lock up most of the youths who are arrested? First of all, there isn't enough room to hold them. Second, there isn't enough staff to handle them. Third, the cost would bankrupt every state that isn't in the red already. Fourth, most people in the juvenile justice system do not think sticking kids in institutions does them much good—it's a last resort.

The usual practice is to put the low-risk youths on probation, the not-so-low-risk youths in a nonsecure placement, and a high-risk youth who commits more serious or more frequent offenses in a secure institution such as a training school. Historically, state training schools were large, housing up to 300, and located far from the cities that supplied the inmates. These resembled adult prisons in some ways, though the training schools were not quite so devoted to punishment, preventing escapes, and stemming the flow of contraband. Maximum-security training schools have high fences or a wall, locked doors, and cells with heavy screens or bars. State training schools are seriously overcrowded in most states. California and Washington, D.C., have the highest proportion of juveniles in institutions.

Originally, policy makers thought that people committed offenses because they were surrounded by too many opportunities for vice and immorality in the big cities. The solution proposed was to exile them to the hinterland, where they would be surrounded by tillers of the soil with high character and the Protestant ethic. Eventually, this kind of reasoning fell by the wayside, and small rural communities began clamoring for institutions for a different reason: they needed the jobs. Some states, however, developed smaller, community-based facilities in the 1970s to give urban juveniles a chance to be closer to their families.

Typically, inmates are incarcerated for about six months and receive treatment such as individual or group counseling, plus education, vocational training, and recreation. Institutions offer transactional analysis, reality therapy, psychotherapy, behavior modification, guided group interaction, and positive peer counseling. Education is certainly needed because most juveniles in institutions are far behind their age-mates in grade level, and many have low IQs and learning disabilities. Inside an institution, teaching is no picnic. Because many of the youths have previously learned to hate schooling and to act up in class, getting them interested in learning is an uphill task.

As for vocational classes, training schools for boys offer various choices, including auto repair, printing, welding, carpentry, woodworking, machine shop and drafting. Training schools for girls also give sex-typed courses, such as cosmetology, sewing, food service, and secretarial skills. Youngsters rarely pursue these lines of work once they are released into society, however, because few employers want to hire them and few unions want them as members.

Recreation in training schools has the enthusiastic support of both the inmates and the staff members. The staff believes that boys will wear themselves out playing basketball, softball, volleyball, flag football, or in some cases boxing, leaving them with no energy to engage in fighting or troublemaking the remainder of the day. In training schools for girls, there is less emphasis on active sports, but also less need, the staff members believe, to wear them out as a device to prevent trouble.

Now let's talk about **detention centers**. These are short-term housing units for juveniles who are awaiting court hearings. About 20 percent of juveniles referred to juvenile court are detained. Most of them are released following a court hearing and given over to the custody of their parents or guardian. Of those not released right away, the average stay is 15 days. At the center they are strip-searched for drugs, weapons, and contraband. Most of the centers offer no treatment programs. Youths are sent to detention for various legal reasons: the juvenile might commit other offenses if released, might harm others, would fail to appear at subsequent court hearings, or has no one to provide supervision or care. Judges sometimes fear that a youth could commit a terrible crime if not detained, and that could ruin the judges' chances of reelection, so they take the easy way out and detain him.

Later on, after they've been found guilty by the courts, youths are sent to a research and diagnostic center, to decide which treatment plan and residential place suits them best. At the center, a psychiatrist evaluates the youngster for mental health problems, a psychologist administers a battery of tests, a social worker does a complete case study and plumbs the youth's background, and an academic specialist assesses the youth's educational strengths and weaknesses.

Once these investigations have been carried out, the staff meets in a case conference to give their reports and make recommendations. On the average, a youth spends one month in the center.

Afterwards, he or she may be sent to a training school or to some other place such as a ranch or forestry camp. In 1992 there were 64 forestry camps, many of them located in Florida and New York, where inmates perform conservation tasks in a state park, cutting grass and weeds, for instance. Ranches, on the other hand, tend to be found mostly in California. Youths sent to such places enjoy the opportunity to be out in the fresh air as opposed to a much more restrictive environment. It is not quite as idyllic as summer camp but it beats being locked up.[17]

Crime Prevention

How can society intervene in people's lives in a way that will bring the crime rate down? There are probably hundreds or thousands of possible options that could be attempted. Among the areas of life in which intervention has been tried are the community, the family, the school, the labor market, hot spots of crime (e.g., bars), police policy, and the system of justice. Some options may entail major overhauls of the area, whereas others amount to little more than tinkering or tweaking. Consider some interventions that have been tried.

At the community level, the most common programs are neighborhood watch groups. At first blush, these might seem promising, because they involve widespread monitoring or surveillance of both persons and property. Witnesses can immediately call the police as soon as they see something suspicious. Unfortunately, these programs have proved easier to launch in low-crime communities than in neighborhoods with high crime rates. In addition, these efforts do not attempt to change either the community itself or the likely offenders.[18] Other programs at the community level that have often been tried are gang prevention, gun buybacks, social workers, and recreation programs (midnight basketball, for instance). The results have not been encouraging; none of these kinds of programs typically produces a noticeable reduction in crime.

Over the past half century or so, the government has pursued several policies that were not *intended* to have an impact on crime but have had the perverse effect of *increasing* it in many neighborhoods. These include urban renewal that ended up destroying friendship networks, massive housing projects that concentrated poor black female-headed households, and the federally funded national highway system that lured low-risk residents out of urban areas to the suburbs. Some city neighborhoods became high-crime areas, prompting an exodus of residents able to leave and (among those who couldn't) a high concentration of the poor and unemployed.[19] In neighborhoods where two-thirds of adults are unemployed, social structure is weak, oppositional culture is prevalent, and rates of drug use, drinking, and gun carrying are high; it's not surprising that violent crime by young people is also a significant problem.[20]

Criminologists raise the obvious question of what government can do about communities marked by hypersegregation, concentrated poverty, family disruption, rampant gang activity, and widespread gun carrying. One thing is certain: it can do far more than the superficial moves it has made so far. For instance, it can pursue policies that discourage slum creation. It can also enact housing policies that disperse the poor, employment policies that stimulate hiring, and education policies that promote better schooling.

Programs That Work

Nurse Home Visitation

We have already mentioned the program in which nurses visit homes of low-income, first-time mothers-to-be and give them pointers on how to improve their health and parenting skills. Nurses visit frequently in the early part of the pregnancy, then visits taper off as the child approaches his or her second birthday. Mr. Olds and his colleagues have been very specific about who should visit and what they should focus on during these visits. Studies show that

1. Women's prenatal health behaviors improve (diet improved and smoking decreased)

2. Complications of pregnancy are reduced

3. Child abuse, neglect, and injuries decline

4. Women space children further apart, reduce their dependence on welfare, and engage in less crime and substance use

5. The children, by the time they turn 15, have fewer arrests and convictions and consume less alcohol.[21]

Sherman argues that other home-visitation programs—not just those involving nurses—also bring about positive outcomes.

> Visitors can be nurses, social workers, preschool teachers, psychologists, or paraprofessionals. They can provide cognitive information, emotional support, or both. They can actively teach parents, with hands on. Or they can passively watch and listen. . . . They can be experienced or novice, enthusiastic or burned out, assertive or hesitant.[22]

He implies that it does not matter who the visitors are or what they do. Although he could be right about this, it seems highly unlikely.

The Incredible Years

While nurse home visitations cover the prenatal period and childhood up to the age of 2, another successful program, the Incredible Years, focuses on children between the ages of 2 and 8. Carolyn Webster-Stratton points out that between 7 and 25 percent of preschool children in America have conduct problems, such as oppositional defiant disorder (ODD) and conduct disorder (CD). Risks for conduct problems are higher when parents are (1) stressed, isolated, mentally ill, poor, and uneducated and (2) critical, inconsistent, hostile, and abusive toward their children.

The Incredible Years program, directed at parents, teachers, and children, focuses on the emotional and behavioral problems of children between the ages of 2 and 8 (Table 12-1). The program begins with BASIC. In this phase, parents are taught acceptable ways of disciplining and parenting by watching hundreds of two-minute video vignettes that exemplify parenting skills. The videos teach interactive play, empathy, and reinforcement, which helps parents develop an understanding of children and their temperaments. The program focuses on nonviolent forms of discipline, such as "time out" and "ignore."

In addition to BASIC, there are other components to the parenting package: EDUCATION to teach reading and school readiness and ADVANCE to overcome family problems such as depression and marital discord. Beyond the parenting package, there are elements devoted to teacher training and child training. Overall, the program tries to cut down on the extent of negative behaviors, noncompliance, and negative emotions; increase the parents' level of competence; and make the child more competent socially. In most evaluations of the program, these objectives have been attained and show staying power of several years.

TABLE 12-1   The Incredible Years Parent, Teacher, and Child Training Program[23]

Intervention	Skills Targeted	Trainee	Setting
BASIC Parent	Play Praise Limit setting Discipline	Parent	Home
ADVANCE Parent	Problem solving Anger management Communication Depression control Support giving & getting	Parent	Home, work, and community
EDUCATION Parent	Academic stimulation Learning routine after school Homework support Reading Limit setting Involvement at school Teacher conferences	Parent	Home–school connection
Teacher Training	Encouragement Incentives Proactive teaching Discipline Positive relationships Social skills training Problem-solving training	Teacher	School
Child Training	Friendship Teamwork Cooperation Communication Anger management Steps to solve problems Quiet hand up Compliance Listening Concentrating	Child	Home and school

Promoting Alternative Thinking Strategies

This program (also known as PATHS) is presented by elementary school teachers in kindergarten through fifth grade as an integral part of the regular yearlong curriculum. It tries to reduce emotional and behavioral problems of children and to increase their social and emotional capability. The founders of the program believe that social–emotional competence has become just as crucial to a young person's successful development as reading, writing, and arithmetic.

There are many different intellectual and theoretical sources that launched this program. One of the more prominent ones is the Affective-Behavioral-Cognitive-Developmental (or ABCD) Model. According to this approach, young children not only feel their emotions but tend to act on them rather than on the basis of a more reasoned and thoughtful interpretation of the situation. They need to learn how to identify their feelings clearly, to understand and regulate such emotions, to control their immediate impulses, and to distinguish between how they feel and how they should react behaviorally to such feelings.

The curriculum's major components are (1) 12 lessons on readiness skills and developing self-control, (2) 56 lessons covering the understanding of emotions, and (3) 33 lessons devoted to interpersonal problem solving. Later on, 30 supplementary lessons provide a kind of reminder or booster shot. Researchers find that the program enhances children's ability to recognize their emotions, understand social problems, think of alternative solutions, and not be so quick to select violence as their mode of response. They learn to develop self-control, to tolerate frustration; furthermore, they become less prone to suffer from bouts of depression and less likely to disrupt classes during school.

Bullying Prevention Program

Bullying includes the outright physical abuse of another via hitting, kicking, punching, and choking, plus more indirect forms such as calling names, **taunting**, malicious teasing, and making obscene gestures. These constitute bullying if carried out over a period of time rather than being just a one-time occurrence. The victim is normally smaller and weaker than the offenders, who often are a small group acting in concert. Bullying makes its youthful victims feel sad, confused, anxious, insecure, and humiliated. Some of them respond by not going to school. The feelings are not always transitory; they may even last into adulthood. Bullies do not usually specialize in this one activity. Instead, they are apt to engage in various offenses and amass a record of several convictions by the time they reach their mid-20s.

As for what causes bullying, various ideas and hypotheses have been floated for consideration over the past thirty years. For example, some commentators blame large school enrollments or the victims' being oddballs who have red hair or some physical anomalies. Dan Olweus did not find any support for these contentions. But he *did* find that personality characteristics are useful in predicting who will become a bully and who will be victimized. He also discovered that the extent of bullying in a school reflects to some degree the attitudes of the teachers who work there.

The Bullying Prevention program tries to reduce the opportunities for bullying and the rewards that flow from it. In this effort, school personnel are assigned the task of administering the program in elementary and junior high schools. The main elements of the program include (1) an anonymous questionnaire to be filled out by all students to determine what forms bullying takes there and how many students are involved as offenders and victims, (2) a committee is formed to create the program plan, (3) teachers explain and enforce the class rules against bullying and meet with parents to enlist their support, and (4) when an episode takes place, the bullies, victim, and parents are brought in for an intervention.

Students receive a strong message that bullying is harmful and won't be tolerated in their community. The program attempts to create an environment in the school and home where

1. Adults demonstrate warmth toward, interest in, and involvement with, their offspring
2. There are clear statements specifying what actions are acceptable in the community and what are offensive
3. Rule violations are consistently followed by negative sanctions (not outbursts of temper or physical beatings)

Evaluations of the program as implemented in Norway have found bullying, vandalism, fighting, theft, and truancy are all reduced substantially, and interpersonal relations in the schools have taken a positive turn.

Big Brothers/Big Sisters of America

Although many of the programs discussed so far are not very well known to the general public, that certainly does not hold true for this organization, which has been around in some form for more than a century. Both Big Brothers and Big Sisters existed as far back as 1902; they trace their origins to New York City. They existed separately until they finally merged in 1977; they adopted an official set of standards and procedures in 1986. These are put into effect by a network of more than 500 local chapters or agencies spread throughout all 50 states.

The original purpose was to reach out to youngsters who needed socialization and guidance from, plus a connection with, an adult role model; they would form a strong one-to-one relationship. Volunteers are screened and trained, then carefully matched with a youngster between the ages of 6 and 18, usually from a single-parent or disadvantaged home. The adult meets at least three times a month with the child for 3 to 5 hours. The males may engage in any number of activities they find interesting, perhaps jogging, fixing cars, or playing basketball. The females may decide on something else, perhaps. The nature of the activity matters less than the fact that they are engaging in it together, establishing a connection.

The program is guided by social workers who set up the match and check with the parent, child, and volunteer frequently to determine how well it's working. The implicit model behind the program is social control theory, which contends that adolescents are most likely to stay out of trouble if they have established a strong positive attachment to an adult figure. Studies indicate that this kind of mentoring program succeeds. Children participating in it are less likely to consume drugs and alcohol, more likely to do well in school, and apt to get along with their parent or parents and their peers better than kids not in the program.

Life Skills Training

Drug use seems to follow two progressions. Frequency increases from nonuse to occasional to frequent use; furthermore, the amount of drug taken at any one time grows. The other progression is from one substance to another, from alcohol and tobacco to marijuana. A subset then continues on to stimulants, opiates, hallucinogens, and so on. Hence, alcohol, tobacco, and marijuana have been called *gateway drugs*: this suggests that they open the gates to possible future use of more serious substances.

Many variables are associated with a higher risk of becoming a drug user. Broadly speaking, these can be classified as background, social, and personal factors. These are listed in more detail in Table 12-2. The Life Skills Training program targets

TABLE 12-2   Integrated Domain Model of Drug Use[24]

Background/Historical	*Social Factors*	*Personal Factors*
Demographic factors	**School factors**	**Cognitive expectancies**
Gender	Academic performance	Adverse drug effects
Age	Academic esteem	Parental drug use
SES/social class	School bonding	Drug prevalence rates
Religion/religiosity	School climate	Attitudes re. drug abuse
Race/ethnicity		Norms re. drug abuse
Biological factors	**Family factors**	**Personal competence**
Sensation seeking	Family structure	Decision making
Temperament	Family management	Anxiety management
	Parental monitoring	Anger management
	Parental drug use	Personal control
	Family attachment	Conflict resolution
Cultural identity	**Media influences**	**Social skills**
Acculturation	Modeling drug use	Communication skills
Ethnic identity	Glamorizing drugs	Assertive skills
	Alcohol/tobacco ads	Complimenting
Environmental	**Peer influences**	**Psychological factors**
Social support	Friends' use of drugs	Self-efficacy
Anomie	Friends' attitudes re. drugs	Self-esteem
Community disintegration		Risk taking
Availability of drugs		Psychological adjustment

Behavior

Cigarettes
Alcohol
Marijuana
Inhalants

youngsters who have not yet developed a drug problem, and who are in their first year of junior high or middle school. It teaches (1) personal self-management skills (such as decision making and problem solving), (2) general social skills (communication, for example), and (3) information and skills directly tied to drug use. The third component covers consequences of drug use, data on actual levels of use, and information on smoking and other drugs' lack of social approval.

Midwestern Prevention Project

This program operates under the assumption that the problem of adolescent drug use cannot be dealt with successfully if only one setting in the environment (e.g., the school) receives attention. Instead, according to the program philosophy, to have an enduring impact and to reach chronic truants and dropouts, there must be a nondrug norm established throughout the entire community. There it contains five components: school, parent education, mass media, community organization, and local government.

The MPP (also known as Project Star) attempts first to reduce adolescents' marijuana use, daily cigarette smoking, and alcohol use, and secondarily these same activities by the parents. The program begins in the school, specifically sixth or seventh grade, when the risk arises for using these gateway drugs. The school part of the program includes classroom sessions run by teachers and facilitated by student peer leaders. These focus on developing skills to counteract pressures to smoke and drink.

The mass media component continues for all five years of the program, offering 31 television, radio, and newspaper announcements, which introduce the school-based component as well as all the other segments of the program to the community as a whole. The parent part of the program swings into action in the second year of the operation and lasts for two years. A committee of parents (supplemented by the school principal and two student peer leaders) implements parent skills training twice a year for all parents, with special emphasis on how to communicate with one's child.

In years three through five, community and government leaders are trained to install drug abuse prevention services. During years four and five, a government subcommittee introduces legislation to reduce supply and limit demand. These may include laws banning cigarette smoking in public places, raising taxes on alcohol, or establishing drug-free zones.

The Midwestern Prevention Program has been instituted in Kansas City and Indianapolis, where it has produced reductions of up to 40 percent in daily cigarette smoking. The decline in marijuana use was nearly as great. These reductions were still holding during the students' senior year in high school. Reductions in alcohol use were somewhat more modest. Parents began to communicate better with their children and to cut back on their own drinking and pot smoking.

Functional Family Therapy

FFT began in 1969 at the University of Utah Family Clinic. Most psychology clinics tend to direct their attention to highly verbal, well-educated, high-income people who take the initiative to get counseling for their problems. FFT took a different direction; it elected to concentrate on individuals who are difficult to reach, treat, and motivate: poor at-risk adolescents aged 11 to 18 and their families. These youngsters did not rush to get help, but instead they often came to the clinics angry, hopeless, and resistant to treatment.

In the beginning sessions, FFT dwells on family members' inner strengths and motivates them to visualize change in their lives. The staff tries to reduce the anger and blaming, to make the family feel comfortable and hopeful that change for the better can indeed occur. The counselor must also be able to win their trust. The program lasts as few as 8 hours or (for more serious cases) as long as 26 hours of direct service, and it may take place in the home, at a clinic, or inside an institution.

In phase two the FFT clinicians move on to the intermediate and long-range behavior changes that are needed. In this part of the treatment, plans are individually tailored to the unique qualities and traits of each family member. The plan includes coping strategies, positive reciprocal behavior, competent parenting, and eliminating the tendency to deal with problems by blaming others.

The third phase of FFT deals with the thorny problem of generalization—applying positive family changes to other problem areas, maintaining change, and preventing relapses. One method FFT employs to achieve this generalization is to connect the family to available community resources. The goal is to improve the family's ability to develop a system of community support and to modify hostile and destructive relationships that previously existed between family members and outsiders (Table 12-3).

FFT deals with a wide range of adolescent problem behaviors: conduct disorders, drug and alcohol abuse, delinquency, and crimes of violence. It attempts to put a stop to such behavior on the part of adolescents who have already entered juvenile justice placements and to prevent their younger siblings from following in the older ones' footsteps.

Multisystemic Therapy

MST is a family-based treatment model for juvenile offenders. It tries to intervene by dealing with the causes of antisocial behavior, which are often located in the family, peers, school, neighborhood, as well as the youth himself or herself. MST contains nine guiding principles.

1. The primary purpose of assessment is to understand the fit between the identified problems and their broader systemic context.
2. Therapeutic contacts emphasize the positive and should use systemic strengths as levers for change.
3. Interventions are designed to promote responsible behavior and decrease irresponsible behavior among family members.
4. Interventions are present focused and action oriented, targeting specified and well-defined problems.
5. Interventions target sequences of behavior within and between multiple systems that maintain the identified problems.

TABLE 12-3 Functional Family Therapy Clinical Model: Intervention Phases Across Time[25]

	Early	Middle	Late
	Engagement and Motivation	**Behavior Change**	**Generalization**
Phase goals	Develop alliances Reduce negativity, resistance Improve communication Minimize hopelessness Reduce dropout potential Develop family focus Increase motivation for change	Develop and implement individualized change plans Change presenting delinquency behavior Build relational skills (e.g., communication and parenting)	Maintain/generalize change Prevent relapses Provide community resources necessary to support change
Risk and protective factors addressed	Negativity and blaming (risk) Hopelessness (risk) Lack of motivation (risk) Credibility (protective) Alliance (protective) Treatment availability (protective)	Poor parenting skills (risk) Negativity and blaming (risk) Poor communication (risk) Positive parenting skills (protective) Supportive communication (protective) Interpersonal needs (depends on context) Parental pathology (depends on context) Developmental level (depends on context)	Poor relationships with school/community (risk) Low level of social support (risk) Positive relationships with school/community (protective)

Assessment

Intervention

(continued)

317

TABLE 12-3 (CONT.)

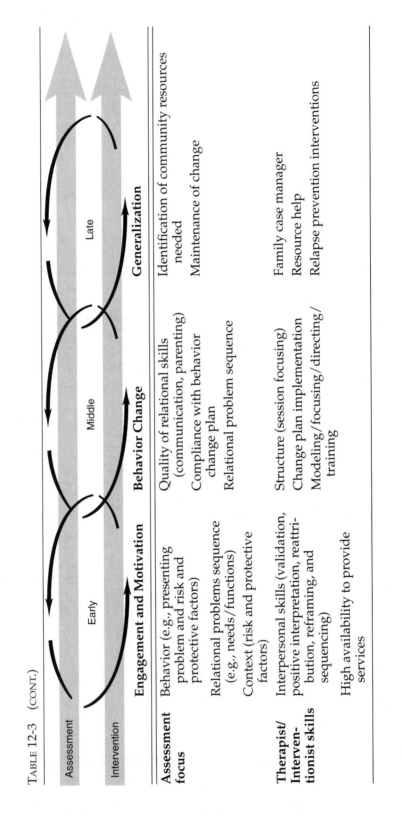

	Engagement and Motivation	Behavior Change	Generalization
	Early	Middle	Late
Assessment focus	Behavior (e.g., presenting problem and risk and protective factors)	Quality of relational skills (communication, parenting)	Identification of community resources needed
	Relational problems sequence (e.g., needs/functions)	Compliance with behavior change plan	Maintenance of change
	Context (risk and protective factors)	Relational problem sequence	
Therapist/ Interventionist skills	Interpersonal skills (validation, positive interpretation, reattribution, reframing, and sequencing)	Structure (session focusing)	Family case manager
		Change plan implementation	Resource help
		Modeling/focusing/directing/training	Relapse prevention interventions
	High availability to provide services		

Assessment

Intervention

6. Interventions are developmentally appropriate and fit the developmental needs of the youth.

7. Interventions are designed to require daily or weekly effort by family members.

8. Intervention effectiveness is evaluated continuously from multiple perspectives.

9. Interventions are designed to promote treatment generalization and long-term maintenance of therapeutic change by empowering caregivers to address family members' needs across multiple systemic contexts.[26]

Because these principles are couched in jargon, perhaps it would be easier to grasp MST by examining a specific case. Take 14-year-old James Hodges, who was referred to MST because of truancy, theft, assault, fighting with peers and teachers, isolation, and failure to take his medicine (Ritalin). His mother established hardly any rules for him, gave in whenever he put up a fuss, and surrendered when he was verbally aggressive. She often felt overwhelmed and hopeless; when depressed, she turned to drinking, which led to oversleeping, missing work, and failure to see if James went to school. James's father, who lived two miles away, had a cocaine habit and before the separation used to beat James. He periodically visited the mother and complained about the way she was raising the child, saying he should beat some sense into the boy. After these visits, the mother drank heavily.

The MST assessed the situation in detail and arrived at a plan featuring five goals:

1. Decrease the mother's depression and alcohol use, because they were related to one another and contributed significantly to her permissive parenting practices, her inability to consistently monitor James's school attendance, and her apprehension about meeting with school officials.

2. Alter the permissive parenting style in order to increase effective discipline and monitoring of school attendance and James's whereabouts at all times.

3. Bolster social support for the mother to decrease depression and alcohol use, change parenting practices, and enable her to assertively manage her estranged husband's disruptive visits.

4. Mend fences between school personnel and the mother so that home–school coordination of interventions for truancy and aggression could be developed.

5. Identify, and increase contact with, prosocial peers for James.[27]

The plan thus calls for strengthening the parent's role in guiding the juvenile, to "empower" her to build an environment suitable for promoting his well-being. MST changes family interaction patterns to inspire responsible behavior and connections with support systems such as school, church, and friends. The goal is to avoid having the juvenile sent to an institution.

Multidimensional Treatment Foster Care

Interestingly, MTDC has much in common with MST. Both rely on parents or parental figures to provide supervision and support while setting limits on behavior. Both take place in the community rather than a clinic. And both carry out interventions in various settings, such as home and school. The main difference concerns the seriousness of the cases: people turn to MTFC when all other options have been tried and have failed (including treatment and institutionalization). MTFC deals only with chronic offenders.

The program involves intervention by a foster parent, not a therapist, social worker, or other treatment professional. These foster parents are carefully selected, trained, and supervised by the MTFC staff. Foster parents closely supervise the youngsters when the kids are at home, at school, or out in the community. When they violate the rules, they are always disciplined.

The MTFC program assumes that the worst strategy for turning a delinquent around is to let him or her associate with fellow delinquents. Perhaps this is merely stating the obvious; maybe everyone knows this to be true. Nevertheless, most programs of group therapy and institutionalization violate this simple rule every day. They throw a group of offenders together to interact with one another and share their opinions on crime and deviance. MTFC strives to do the opposite—to keep the juvenile away from the influence of delinquent peers.

Each person enrolled in MTFC is assigned to a foster home, where he or she gets a clear picture of what's expected throughout the day. Foster parents are trained to set consistent limits, reward progress, maintain a high level of supervision, and monitor peer relationships. There is no free time spent with peers in the absence of adult supervision—at least in the beginning. Later on, when the youth proves to be more trustworthy, the reins may be loosened gradually.

Quantum Opportunities Program

The QOP pilot project was tried out in five cities between 1989 and 1993. This experiment tested whether youths from families receiving food stamps and other forms of public assistance could make a quantum leap in social mobility (that is, up the ladder of opportunity) if they had four years of coordinated services and sustained relationships with a peer group and a caring adult.

The opportunities given to the youngsters included tutoring, computer-based instruction; information about health, alcohol, sex, drugs, family planning, and college planning; and community service to improve conditions in their neighborhood. The students were selected at random from a list of those eligible provided by a local high school. A single QOP coordinator acting as advisor and surrogate parent was responsible for the group of 25 students in each site (city).

The program was designed to

1. Compensate for the lack of opportunities typical of disadvantaged neighborhoods (QOP instills the belief that success is attainable; it helps youths overcome pessimism and set goals and work toward them)
2. Provide contact with people who hold prosocial values and beliefs (the coordinator becomes a surrogate parent, role model, advisor, and disciplinarian)
3. Sharpen skills of the clients and prepare them for success, and
4. Reinforce achievements through positive feedback[28]

At the end of high school, the QOP sample was less likely to have been arrested or convicted of crimes, more likely to have graduated from high school, more likely to go on to further education, and less likely to start having children in their teenage years. The greatest success occurred in Philadelphia, where the staff achieved a strong bond with the students and the group of peers proved most cohesive.

Conclusion

What do people do when they have no real knowledge about something important? They could try to remedy this ignorance by immersing themselves in the technical literature, reading all the latest scientific studies. That's the hard way. Or they could take the easy way out by falling back on the society's store of common sense, myths, and stereotypes. It is safe to say that most people most of the time choose to save themselves a lot of time and work by choosing the latter, while not giving the former a moment's thought.

And so it is with punishment and corrections. Most people think that the best policy is to arrest, prosecute, lock up in an institution to put the offender's criminal career on hold for a while (incapacitation), show the rest of the world what happens when laws are broken (general deterrence), and teach the offender a lesson (special deterrence). Perhaps this makes the public feel better, but does this policy actually produce the benefits it promises?

Individuals held in captivity (a jail, prison, or secure juvenile facility) may stay there six months, a year, or two years, but then they are returned to the community, perhaps in a sour mood. They may think they were mistreated by the justice system and did not deserve to be punished at all or deserved probation. They may emerge from the experience of serving time in an institution convinced that it is a dog-eat-dog world, and that everybody has to take what he can get by any means possible, so the best strategy is to strike first rather than let someone else make you the victim.

Americans have embraced three myths regarding juvenile rehabilitation programs:

1. Nothing works. No one has discovered a way to successfully treat youths who have become caught up in a life of crime and deviance.
2. Serious offenders cannot be dealt with by the juvenile justice system. They should be turned over to the criminal justice system for punishment.
3. Community-based programs do not inspire fear in youthful offenders, which is why they are not as effective as incarceration.

These widely accepted beliefs may be dear to the hearts of politicians and the public, but the publications of Mark Lipsey summarizing the literature on program evaluation undermine all of them.[29]

If society is going to spend many millions of dollars on corrections, it should ask for a report on how well that money is being spent, how much bang it's getting for the buck, what percentage of the offenders in each program have been rehabilitated or at least have reduced their criminal involvement. Apparently, not many politicians call for an investigation of secure facilities. These institutions don't provide figures on recidivism of their ex-inmates. Nor does the general public usually demand such an investigation. Thus institutions may fail miserably in this respect, even though preventing recidivism is presumably their purpose for existing.

What about what are usually called rehabilitation, treatment, or prevention programs? There have been hundreds of them attempted over the years, most of which have had no effect, some of which have actually increased the crime and deviance of the people who have gone through them. In medical language, the latter case is known as an **iatrogenic effect**: the treatment caused the patient to contract a disease, or the therapy made the client's behavior take a turn for the worse.

Other programs, however, have been evaluated carefully by comparing them with a control group (and people were assigned to control group and experimental group randomly) and the experimental group later turned out to be better behaved. These programs that succeed have followed different paths. Some are universal, which means that everyone (in, say, the school's sixth grade or of a certain age in the neighborhood) gets the treatment. These programs are intended to prevent delinquency or drug use from getting started among this particular cohort. A different strategy is to focus instead on a select group of youths who are deemed to be at high risk for deviance because of family problems, poverty, or perhaps their high-crime neighborhood.

Some successful programs emphasize establishing a close personal relationship between the kids and an outside adult figure (for example, Big Brothers/Big Sisters, Quantum Opportunities, and Multidimensional Treatment Foster Care). Others focus on strengthening the child's family, making it more functional and effective (such as Incredible Years and Multisystemic Therapy). Quite a few are organized around a series of lessons presented by regular teachers in elementary, junior high, or senior high school (Bullying Prevention Program, Life Skills Training, Midwestern Prevention Project, and Promoting Alternative Thinking Strategies).

These are based on theories; they involve dealing with the *causes* of delinquency, crime, and drug use. That distinguishes them from the popular programs such as DARE, scared straight, and boot camps, which have no respected sociological theory or psychological theory undergirding them. Instead, they rely on popular slogans and political sound bytes. It is going to be difficult to achieve reform as long as correctional policy is guided by election politics.

Key Terms

Hubris:	overweening pride
Blasphemy:	profane utterance about God or something sacred
Heresy:	controversial doctrine in politics, philosophy, religion, or science
Ragamuffin:	shabbily clothed child
Pauperism:	condition of being extremely poor
Indolent:	habitually lazy or inactive

Experimental group:	the subjects who are given the experimental treatment or stimulus
Control group:	similar group of subjects; they are not given the treatment
Panacea:	a remedy for all ills
Motley:	heterogeneous, incongruous mixture
Slovenly:	untidy in appearance; negligent
Intermediate sanction:	more than probation, less severe than being locked up in an institution
Secure facilities:	those with gates, fences, motion detectors, and other security hardware
Technical violations:	violations of the rules governing behavior while on parole or aftercare
Detention center:	short-term housing unit for juveniles awaiting court hearings
Taunting:	mocking, insulting, jeering
Gateway drugs:	those that open the gates to future use of more serious illicit substances
Iatrogenic effect:	the treatment causes the patient or client to get worse instead of better

End Notes

[1]Luigi Barzini, "The Americans," *Harper's* (December 1981), pp. 29–36, 83–5.

[2]Edwin G. Burrows and Mike Wallace, *Gotham* (New York: Oxford, 1999), pp. 501–2.

[3]Alexander W. Pisciotta, "Reformatories and Reform Schools," in Marilyn D. McShane and Franklin P. Williams, III, eds., *Encyclopedia of Juvenile Justice* (Thousand Oaks, CA: Sage, 2003), p. 319.

[4]Robert H. Wiebe, *The Search for Order, 1877–1920* (New York: Hill and Wang, 1967); Edward Crapsey, *The Nether Side of New York* (Montclair, NJ: Patterson Smith, 1969).

[5]Herbert Asbury, *Gangs of New York* (New York: Knopf, 1928); Charles Z. Lincoln, *State of New York Messages From the Governors* (Albany: Lyon, 1909).

[6]Alexander W. Pisciotta, *Benevolent Repression* (New York: New York University Press, 1994).

[7]*Ibid.*

[8]*Ibid.*, pp. 33–4.

[9]President's Commission on Law Enforcement and Administration of Justice, *Task Force Report: Juvenile Delinquency and Youth Crime* (Washington, DC: U.S. Government Printing Office, 1967).

[10]Joseph H. Sorrentino, *The Concrete Cradle* (Los Angeles: Wollstonecraft, 1975); Kenneth Wooden, *Weeping in the Playtime of Others* (New York: McGraw-Hill, 1976); Thomas J. Cottle, *Children in Jail* (Boston: Beacon, 1977).

[11]Jerome G. Miller, *Last One Over the Wall* (Columbus: Ohio State University Press, 1991).

[12]Mark W. Lipsey, "Juvenile Delinquency Treatment," in Thomas D. Cook, Harris Cooper, David S. Cordray, Heidi Hartmann, Larry V. Hedges, Richard J. Light, Thomas A. Louis, and Frederick Mosteller, eds., *Meta-Analysis for Explanation* (New York: Russell Sage Foundation, 1992), pp. 83–127; Lawrence W. Sherman, Denise Gottfredson, Doris MacKenzie, John Eck, Peter Reuter, and Shawn Bushway, *Preventing Crime* (Washington, DC: National Institute of Justice, 1997); Anthony Petrosino, Carolyn Turpin-Petrosino, and James O. Finckenauer, "Well-Meaning Programs Can Have Harmful Effects!" *Crime and Delinquency, 46,* no. 3 (July 2000), pp. 354–79; James O. Finckenauer and Patricia W. Gavin, *Scared Straight* (Prospect Heights, IL: Waveland, 1999); Richard J. Lundman, *Prevention and Control of Juvenile Delinquency* (New York: Oxford University Press, 2001).

[13]Jeanne B. Stinchcombe and W. Clinton Terry, III, "Predicting the Rate of Rearrest Among Shock Incarceration Graduates," *Crime and Delinquency, 47,* no. 2 (April 2001), pp. 221–42; Doris Layton MacKenzie, David B. Wilson, and Suzanne B. Kider, "Effects of Correctional Boot Camps on Offending," *Annals of the American Academy of Political and Social Sciences, 578* (November 2001), pp. 126–43.

[14]Howard N. Snyder and Melissa Sickmund, *Juvenile Offenders and Victims: 1999 National Report* (Washington: Office of Juvenile Justice and Delinquency Prevention, 1999).

[15]*Ibid.*

[16]Barry C. Feld, "Justice by Geography," *Journal of Criminal Law and Criminology, 82,* no. 1 (Spring 1991), pp. 156–210.

[17]Robert W. Taylor, Eric J. Fritsch, and Tory J. Caeti, *Juvenile Justice* (New York: McGraw-Hill, 2002); G. Larry Mays and L. Thomas Winfree, Jr., *Juvenile Justice* (New York: McGraw-Hill, 2000); Preston Elrod and R. Scott Ryder, *Juvenile Justice* (Gaithersburg, MD: Aspen, 1999).

[18]Wesley Skogan, *Decline and Disorder* (New York: Free Press, 1990).

[19]Wesley Skogan, "Fear of Crime and Neighborhood Change," in Albert J. Reiss, Jr., and Michael Tonry, eds., *Communities and Crime* (Chicago: University of Chicago Press, 1986), pp. 203–29; William Julius Wilson, *The Truly Disadvantaged* (Chicago: University of Chicago Press, 1987); William Julius Wilson, *When Work Disappears* (New York: Knopf, 1996); Leo Schuerman and Solomon Kobrin, "Community Careers in Crime," in Albert J. Reiss, Jr. and Michael Tonry, *Communities and Crime,* pp. 67–100.

[20]Lawrence W. Sherman, Denise Gottfredson, Doris MacKenzie, John Eck, Peter Reuter, and Shawn Bushway, *Preventing Crime.*

[21]*"Blueprints for Violence Prevention,"* www.colorado.edu/cspv/blueprints.

[22]Lawrence W. Sherman, Denise Gottfredson, Doris MacKenzie, John Eck, Peter Reuter, and Shawn Bushway, *Preventing Crime,* Chapter four, p. 8.

[23]Carolyn Webster-Stratton, "The Incredible Years Training Series," *Juvenile Justice Bulletin* (June 2000), p. 3.

[24]Gilbert J. Botvin, "Preventing Adolescent Drug Abuse Through Life Skills Training," in Jonathan Crane, ed., *Social Programs That Work* (New York: Russell Sage, 1998), pp. 230–1.

[25]Thomas L. Sexton and James F. Alexander, "Functional Family Therapy," *Juvenile Justice Bulletin* (December 2000), p. 3.

[26]Sonja K. Schoenwald, Tamara L. Brown, Scott W. Henggeler, "Inside Multisystemic Therapy," *Journal of Emotional and Behavioral Disorders, 8,* no. 2 (Summer 2000), p. 115.

[27]*Ibid.*, p. 117.

[28]"History and Description of the Quantum Opportunities Program," www.colorado.edu/cspv/blueprints, pp. 2–3.

[29]Mark W. Lipsey, "Juvenile Delinquency Treatment," in Thomas D. Cook, Harris Cooper, David S. Cordary, Heidi Hartmann, Larry V. Hedges, Richard J. Light, Thomas A. Louis, Frederick Mosteller, eds., *Meta-Analysis for Explanation;* Mark W. Lipsey, "What Do We Learn From 400 Research Studies on the Effectiveness of Treatment with Juvenile Delinquents?" in James McGuire, ed., *What Works?* (New York: Wiley, 1995), pp. 63–78; Mark W. Lipsey, "Can Intervention Rehabilitate Serious Delinquents?" *Annals of the American Academy of Political and Social Science, 564* (July 1999), pp. 142–66; Mark W. Lipsey and David B. Wilson, "Effective Intervention for Serious Juvenile Offenders," in Rolf Loeber and David P. Farrington, eds., *Serious and Violent Juvenile Offenders* (Thousand Oaks, CA: Sage, 1998), pp. 313–45; James H. Derzon and Mark W. Lipsey, "A Synthesis of the Relationship of Marijuana Use with Delinquent and Problem Behaviors," *School Psychology International, 20,* no. 1 (Fall 1999), pp. 57–68.

Recommended Readings

Robert M. Mennel, *Thorns and Thistles* (Hanover, NH: University Press of New England, 1973).

David J. Rothman, *The Discovery of the Asylum* (Boston: Little, Brown, 1971).

David Garland, *Punishment and Modern Society* (Chicago: University of Chicago Press, 1990).

Jerome G. Miller, *Last One Over the Wall* (Columbus: Ohio State University Press, 1991).

Ira M. Schwartz, *(In)Justice for Juveniles* (Lexington, MA: Lexington, 1989).

Edmund F. McGarrell, *Juvenile Correctional Reform* (Albany: State University of New York Press, 1988).

Index